Music in Vienna
1700, 1800, 1900

Music in Vienna
1700, 1800, 1900

David Wyn Jones

THE BOYDELL PRESS

First published 2016
The Boydell Press, Woodbridge
Paperback edition 2019

ISBN 978 1 78327 107 8 hardback
ISBN 978 1 78327 429 1 paperback

The Boydell Press is an imprint of Boydell & Brewer Ltd
PO Box 9, Woodbridge, Suffolk IP12 3DF, UK
and of Boydell & Brewer Inc.
668 Mt Hope Avenue, Rochester, NY 14620–2731, USA
website: www.boydellandbrewer.com

A catalogue record for this book is available from the British Library

The publisher has no responsibility for the continued existence
or accuracy of URLs for external or third-party internet websites
referred to in this book, and does not guarantee that any content
on such websites is, or will remain, accurate or appropriate

This publication is printed on acid-free paper

Designed and typeset in Garamond Premier Pro and Snell Roundhand
by David Roberts, Pershore, Worcestershire

Printed and bound in Great Britain by
TJ International Ltd, Padstow, Cornwall

In memory of my father,
Dr Arthur Morgan Jones

Contents

1900

Illustrations

For permission to reproduce the following illustrations, thanks are
gratefully given to the British Library (5, 7, 13, 14, 15); Archiv, Bibliothek
und Sammlungen der Gesellschaft der Musikfreunde in Vienna (6, 8,
10, 12); Kunsthistoriches Museum, Vienna, KHM-Museumverband (3);
Theatermuseum, Vienna, KHM-Museumverband (16); and Wien Museum,
Vienna (1).

Preface

ONE of the pleasures of university teaching is to experience the dictum that teachers learn from students as much as students learn from teachers. The content and format of this book have their origins in a postgraduate course I taught for many years at Cardiff University, aimed at students from a wide disciplinary background, history and European studies as well as music. The initial intention was to study the role of music in society in Vienna around 1800, the time of Haydn, Mozart and Beethoven. That soon changed to curiosity about other periods in Viennese musical history, and the idea was born of looking at music in the city a hundred years earlier and a hundred years later as well. From one academic year to the next, successive groups of students responded enthusiastically to this approach, fascinated by the details of musical life in each of the periods, the differences and the continuities. Many also lamented the absence of a book on the subject. In the most basic sense, therefore, my gratitude to these students is fundamental; without them, this volume would never have existed.

A few years elapsed before I was able to turn the idea into reality – a book on music in Vienna that had a broad remit but also engaged with details. I was fortunate enough to be awarded a Major Research Fellowship by the Leverhulme Trust for the period 2013–15 that enabled me to concentrate entirely on the project. I am grateful to the trust for their interest and their implicit view that it fitted in with one of their guiding principles, that funded research should not only reflect the aspiration and curiosity of the individual, but should be accessible and appeal beyond conventional disciplinary boundaries.

Many individuals have helped with the preparation of this book in various capacities, as scholars, librarians, linguists, referees, IT experts and proofreaders, and it is a pleasure to acknowledge their interest as well as their expertise, while absolving them of any responsibility for the misrepresentations and errors that remain. John Deathridge, Simon Keefe and Jan Smaczny were early and willing supporters; several colleagues at Cardiff University with different interests from my own – David Beard, Keith Chapin, Kenneth Hamilton, John O'Connell and Clair Rowden – have, through casual conversation, caused me to pursue, revise and reconsider certain ideas. Richard Chesser and Rupert Ridgewell of the British Library were consistently helpful, informally and formally, as was Peter Linnitt at the library of the Royal College of Music, while staff in the Music Library at Cardiff University were always willing to interpret borrowing conditions in the most enabling way. In Vienna, library staff at the Gesellschaft der Musikfreunde, the Musiksammlung of the Österreichische Nationalbibliothek and the Wien Bibliothek (formerly the Stadt- und Landesbibliothek) were unfailingly cooperative, in particular Otto Biba and Ingrid Fuchs at the Gesellschaft der Musikfreunde. Else Radant Landon and Helen Conway helped with awkward aspects of German translation, Alessandra Palidda with Italian sources, Drew Mabey with recalcitrant technology, and Jessica Kelly admirably fulfilled the role of the interested lay reader with a keen eye for typographical errors. My wife, Ann, and daughter, Yolande, were, as ever, encouragingly supportive during the highs and lows of the project and constantly understanding of my engagement with life in different times and in a different place.

My father died when I started writing this volume. He was not a musical man – in fact, he was comically unmusical – but he was a widely read man, someone who showed real interest in the project and who would have read the book with pleasure and pride. It is with gratitude that I dedicate the book to his memory.

David Wyn Jones
Cardiff, October 2015

The Leverhulme Trust

CHAPTER I

Telling Tales of Music in Vienna

Mozart wrote that it was the best place for his métier; Beethoven called it a cesspit; Schumann described it as the soul of musical Germany; and Mahler said that he became happier the further he got away from it. The image of Vienna as a musical city, one that acted as a mecca for leading composers from Joseph Haydn onwards, and the environment that nurtured many of the most treasured works of the musical canon, from Mozart's *Le nozze di Figaro* and Beethoven's Ninth, to Strauss's Blue Danube waltz and Mahler's Ninth, is a familiar and enduring one. From at least the middle of the nineteenth century it was also one that was consciously nurtured by the city as it embraced composers old and new within its tradition, often glossing over difficulties it had placed in the way of many of them, difficulties that prompted the exasperated comments of Beethoven and Mahler.

Nearly one hundred years ago, at the end of the First World War, Vienna lost its place as the capital city of one of the oldest empires in Europe. While the legacy of Habsburg times is still evident in the city, from the Schönbrunn palace to the popular dessert of *Kaiserschmarrn*, musical history is even more central to its continuing identity. The new baggage hall in Vienna airport greets its arrivals with a large-scale mural of the Blue Danube waltz, more than forty composers and performers are remembered in its street names (from Albrechtsberger to Zemlinsky), the state opera house commands a physical location in the centre of the city, and the Vienna Philharmonic Orchestra, one of the great orchestras of the world, celebrates the New Year with a morning concert of music by the Strauss family that is broadcast to an international audience of millions.

It is an alluring vision, itself part of the history of music in Vienna, but what of its foundations? The city is very frank about its historical base, focussing on music from the Vienna of Mozart in the 1780s to the Vienna of Mahler, Schoenberg, Berg and Webern at the beginning of the twentieth century, and marginalizing musical life from the medieval period to the mid-eighteenth century and from the 1920s to the present day. It is not so frank about the nature of that historical knowledge, overwhelmingly based on biographies of composers who were either born in Vienna or lived there for significant periods of time: Haydn, Mozart, Beethoven, Schubert, Brahms, the Strauss family, Bruckner, Mahler, Wolf and others. Inevitably, in the hands of the biographer, the history of music in Vienna becomes subservient to the history of the individual, a context in which to display the vicissitudes of the creative artist. A consistent biographical trope that emerges is that Vienna often failed its composers – Mozart,

Beethoven, Bruckner and Mahler are familiar examples – a negative trope that is easily turned around to emphasize the ability of that individual to transcend difficulties and write music of lasting appeal. In that way, Vienna surreptitiously claims credit for the difficulties it created or, more fairly, ones that biographers have sometimes exaggerated on behalf of their composers. Even the most ambitious and comprehensive of modern biographies of Viennese composers, such as those of H. C. Robbins Landon on Haydn or Henry-Louis de La Grange on Mahler, both richly informative about musical life in the city, cannot depart from the traditional imperatives of biographical exposition.[1] Understanding the development of music in Vienna through biography is problematic, inevitably prone to the selective and the partial.

Another common perspective is similarly constricting: the long established tradition of teaching musical history through the teaching of style (or style and aesthetic), which naturally privileges the new over the continuing and, especially evident in Viennese musical history from Mozart to Schoenberg, the challenging over the approachable. A more open-minded approach to the history of music in Vienna requires a wider remit, one that is attuned to political and cultural development in general and recognizes that human agency was not the prerogative of composers only, but routinely involved emperors, princes, publishers, institutions, administrators, scholars and others. The nature of these forces, as well as their interaction, changed over time, sometimes subtly, sometimes fundamentally. To write a chronological history of music in Vienna from the Middle Ages to the present day that does justice to these perspectives may well be beyond the capabilities of one author and would, almost certainly, underplay differences from one era to the next. For practical as well as conceptual reasons, therefore, this history takes a different approach, a slice history focussing on three epochs, 1700, 1800 and 1900, a portrait of each period that allows contrasts to emerge and continuities to be articulated. It is not a slice history in the narrowest sense, a chronicle of music in Vienna in each of the three years; that, certainly, would have been possible but would have been unproductively blinkered, events without causes and consequences. Instead, for each epoch, the scope is broadened flexibly either side, from the last siege of Vienna by the Turks in 1683 to the cementing of the Habsburg succession in the 1720s, from the death of Joseph II in 1790 to the Congress of Vienna in 1814–15, and from about 1890 through to the First World War.

Three sequences of determining characteristics represent these periods. The most familiar, especially to music historians, is Baroque, Classical and Modern, a paradigm that is problematic in a number of ways. According to the traditional narratives of music history the Baroque period had its major centres in Italy (Vivaldi), North Germany (Bach), England (Handel) and France (Rameau); Vienna was not home to a composer of equivalent importance. But it was not a musical backwater. On the contrary, music was the favoured recreational and, more important, representational art form of the Habsburg dynasty, key to its identity and, indeed, to its continuing survival. For much of the period the court employed a musical retinue of up to a hundred or more, composers, singers and instrumentalists, to serve its needs, by far the largest in Europe. Since music-making was inextricably linked with Habsburg power, it did not allow the gifted individual to seek a complementary career outside the court, and any notion of freedom of artistic expression was wholly subservient to expression on behalf of the Habsburg family.

For the period around 1800, Classical has always seemed entirely appropriate, especially when joined by the qualifying word Viennese, in terms such as the Viennese Classical Period or the Viennese Classical School. Appropriately enough, these terms were coined by a Viennese, the musicologist Guido Adler, in the first decades of the twentieth century, though they did not become common currency until the 1920s. They reflect the undisputed primacy of three composers – Haydn, Mozart and Beethoven – to which Schubert is sometimes added. This construct, however, did not match outlooks in Vienna around 1800. Haydn was unquestionably the dominant figure, Mozart's posthumous reputation was only beginning to emerge and Beethoven was not to be a commanding figure until the time of the Congress of Vienna. While the idea of a fruitful stylistic interaction between the three composers implied by the term 'school' was a historical reality and their common interest in instrumental genres such as the quartet and the symphony is self-evident, the differences between the composers were even more typical of musical life in Vienna: Haydn was a resourceful composer of oratorio, Mozart a resourceful composer of opera, both genres that proved problematic for Beethoven. There is one other 'Great Composer', however, whose music had a real presence in the musical life of Vienna at the time and never features in the definition of the Classical Period: Handel (habitually spelt Händel), a Baroque composer whose music fascinated Haydn, Mozart and Beethoven, and whose oratorios were regarded by many in Vienna as 'classical' (*klassische*) works that also pointed to a musical future. Only later in the nineteenth century did another combination of composer and genre, Beethoven and the symphony, displace that outlook.

The familiar characteristics of music periodization are equally misleading for the period around 1900. Music in Vienna is routinely described as Modern, the product of a general *fin-de-siècle* aesthetic that is yoked with the decline of the Habsburg empire, an art form that takes its place alongside architecture, literature, painting and psychology in a heightened display of human expression. Carl E. Schorske's brilliant exposition of these themes in his classic book, *Fin-de-siècle Vienna: Politics and Culture*, includes a section on Schoenberg's *Das Buch der hängenden Gärten*, *Erwartung* and *Pierrot lunaire* that creates a powerful image of music working in a shared aesthetic.[2] Similarly, historians of musical style have readily emphasized the cutting edge and the prescient in the works of Mahler, Schoenberg, Berg and Webern. However beguiling, this is an even more exclusive view of music in Vienna than the one associated with the term Classical, one that disregards more traditional features of musical life in the city: the repertoire of the opera houses and the concert halls, and the popularity of operetta. Both these areas have characteristics that are peculiarly Viennese and, since they were also omnipresent, are more fairly representative of musical life in the city.

In a volume that is concerned with the social function of music, a second construct for the three-part division is more helpful: imperial (1700), aristocratic (1800) and bourgeois (1900). These labels point to the principal means of patronage in each epoch, though the last two, in particular, need to be qualified. Around 1700 most music in Vienna was composed and performed at the imperial court, more precisely in the various palaces (up to four) that constituted the annual cycle of visits by the court. This cycle intersected with that of the Catholic liturgical year to create a continuing pattern of operas for name days, birthdays and special occasions, such as weddings, and more than 400 performances of church music every year. It was an essentially exclusive world that was occasionally put on public display in a very choreographed and controlled way. For the average Viennese, the most accessible was the practice of holding services in many of the Catholic churches in Vienna, where the court procession from the Hofburg to the church and its return was witnessed by a loyal and religiously acquiescent public, one that perceived Habsburg power and the Catholic faith as an indivisible whole.

One hundred years later, around 1800, patronage had moved down a social level to the aristocracy, though its nature was more complex than is often assumed. The model of one aristocrat employing a Kapellmeister and a retinue of musicians for his own entertainment and self-promotion – a small-scale version of the earlier imperial patronage – was rapidly becoming a historical memory. Instead, aristocratic patronage was often on a casual basis, commissioning works from composers who were not in their permanent employment or purchasing it independently from music dealers in a flourishing commercial market. It was also socially progressive, showing a willingness to come together in shared patronage of music, particularly opera, oratorio and orchestral music. There was a new sense that the aristocracy could be leaders of public taste, as well as enjoying music in private. Behind the closed doors of their palaces in Vienna, the aristocracy were avid consumers of piano music, songs and string quartets in particular, with women taking a leading role in patronage and performance, another aspect of musical life that has been underplayed. Opera was now a fully public entertainment, presented in two court theatres, the Burgtheater and the Kärntnertortheater, dignified with the description imperial–royal (*kaiserlich–königlich*) but now at one remove from the court, entrusted to the management of others, including, for a while, a consortium of aristocrats.

Alongside the changing nature of aristocratic patronage there was a new force at work around 1800, the emergence of capable and enthusiastic patrons from the professional classes, such as court civil servants, lawyers and bankers, individuals who were prepared to deploy their expertise to serve the common interest in music. One of the earliest was Peter von Braun, an accountant in the court treasury, a successful owner of silk and cotton mills who also established a bank in the city and who was invited to run the court theatres from 1794 to 1807; he was created a baron in 1795.[3] Even more influential was Joseph Sonnleithner, an imperial official who rose through the ranks to become secretary of the court theatres, where he was able to use his literary abilities to fashion librettos for many of the operas that were presented (including Beethoven's *Leonore*) and who later became the first secretary of the Gesellschaft der Musikfreunde.[4] Up to the time of the Congress of Vienna the aristocracy and the emerging bourgeoisie worked productively together on behalf of their favourite pastime. The underlying trend, however, was a gradual waning of aristocratic influence.

By 1900 the levers of musical life were firmly in the hands of the bourgeoisie, typically working for, or on behalf of, institutions such as the Gesellschaft der Musikfreunde, the new suburban theatres, the university, small concert rooms and amateur choral and orchestral societies, to serve a city that had doubled its population in a hundred years, and for which music was a consuming pastime. With the exception of one or two individuals, such as Prince Alfred Montenuovo who represented the court's interests in the management of the new opera house on the Ringstrasse, the aristocracy were no longer a major force in musical life. For its part the imperial court, in particular the popular figure of Emperor Franz Joseph, was able to retain national and international prestige as the funder and ultimate owner of the opera house. During his long reign, from 1848 to 1916, the Habsburg empire had become famously adroit in accommodating political and social change. Likewise in musical life: there was little sense that control had been wrested from either the court or the aristocracy; rather, it had been an evolving process that had produced a cohesive and enthusiastic musical public. As well as cohesion and enthusiasm there were also caution, conservatism and contentment, qualities that play into the more negative connotations of the word bourgeois.

A third overarching construct that can be applied to the tripartite division of this volume relates to the central word Vienna. Musicians in the city in 1900 would readily have accepted the appropriateness of 'Vienna' in any description of its musical character. For the two earlier periods, however, there were other considerations – an emphasis on Habsburg in 1700, and Austrian in 1800 – with little or no sense that what was being represented through music was an image of a city. In 1700 the focus was the imperial and royal dynasty that had ruled for centuries and placed itself at the head of the Counter-Reformation, and the prime function of music at the court was to celebrate and continually reinforce that secular and divine presence. By 1800, as the Habsburgs themselves had depowered the place of Catholicism in favour of religious toleration and were quickly losing political influence on territories in the Holy Roman Empire as a result of the ongoing, increasingly belittling Napoleonic wars, there was a new emphasis on Austria as a fatherland, clearly signalled by the assumption of a new title, Emperor of Austria, and the relinquishing of the old one, Holy Roman Emperor. Since the Burgtheater and the Kärntnertortheater were still court theatres they, too, became Austrian. When the Gesellschaft der Musikfreunde was formally constituted in 1814 it was described as the Society of the Friends of Music of the Austrian Imperial State (Gesellschaft der Musikfreunde des österreichischen Kaiserstaates) not, as much later, the Society of Friends of Music in Vienna (Gesellschaft der Musikfreunde in Wien).

The huge expansion of the city in the nineteenth century, notably the demolition of the old fortress walls in the 1850s and the subsequent building of the Ringstrasse, with its many magnificent, often intimidating buildings, inevitably encouraged a greater emphasis on Vienna. Very self-consciously promoting itself as a *Weltstadt* (a city of the world), it hosted the fifth World Exhibition in 1873, the locus of civic pride as much as of national pride and international ambition. Through their marches, polkas and waltzes the Strauss family projected a Viennese identity rather than an Austrian one, particularly on their many foreign tours. That move from Austria to Vienna was helped by the fact that Czech, Hungarian and, later, Balkan nationalism was making 'Austria' a rather indeterminate, often contested term, one that was best avoided. 'Vienna' did not have that baggage. In its musical life, the city willingly assumed responsibility for continually projecting a historical legacy – *Alt-Wien* (Old Vienna) – that was originally Habsburg or Austrian, a civic identity that was often tinged by a hazy, sentimentalized view of that history. *Musikstadt Wien* became a common utterance, a declaration of an assured personality. It was against this background that the term Viennese Classical School was coined and the Philharmonic orchestra, an outgrowth of the court opera orchestra, formally adopted the title Vienna Philharmonic Orchestra in 1908.

Baroque, Classical, Modern; Imperial, Aristocratic, Bourgeois; and Habsburg, Austria, Vienna: three constructs that invite immediate qualification and reservation. They can only act as a template, a set of complementary thought processes with which to control more than 300 years of musical history. They are about to be probed and tested.

1700

CHAPTER 2

Music at the Imperial and Royal Court

Angelica, vincitrice di Alcina: an opera for the Habsburgs

O N 1 August 1716 the newly appointed British ambassador at the Ottoman court, Sir Edward Wortley Montagu, and his wife, Lady Mary Wortley Montagu, left London on their long journey to Constantinople. Travelling via Rotterdam, The Hague, Nijmwegen, Cologne, Frankfurt, Würzburg, Nuremberg and Regensburg, they arrived in Vienna just over a month later, on 3 September. A particularly challenging aspect of Montagu's new position as ambassador was to act as a diplomatic conduit between the two long-standing adversaries, the Ottoman court in Constantinople and the Habsburg court in Vienna, and he remained in Vienna until mid-November to familiarize himself with the perspective of the Habsburgs. His wife, Lady Mary, was also enquiring and impressionable and had already written several letters back to England about their journey to Vienna, revealing herself as an acute and lively observer of places, customs and personalities. From the imperial capital she wrote seven, often lengthy, letters about the city and the court. Protocol meant that her husband was given highest possible status as the representative of the British King George I at the court of Emperor Karl VI, and Lady Mary was treated accordingly. Her correspondence was a private one and she was able to report on aspects of life at the imperial court that rarely found their way into the diplomatic bag. She was not especially musical, but a clear highlight of the ten-week visit during the autumn of 1716 was her attendance of a performance of a new opera by the court composer, Johann Joseph Fux, to celebrate the birth of an heir to the throne, Archduke Leopold. She wrote to her friend, the poet Alexander Pope:

> Don't fancy, however, that I am infected by the air of these popish Countrys, thô I have so far wander'd from the Discipline of the Church of England to have been last Sunday at the Opera, which was perform'd in the Garden of the Favorita, and I was so much pleas'd with it I have not yet repented my seeing it. Nothing of that kind was ever more Magnificent, and I can easily believe what I am told, that the Decorations and habits cost the Emperour £30,000 Sterling. The Stage was built over a very large Canal, and at the beginning of the 2nd Act divided into 2 parts, discovering the Water, on which there immediately came from different parts 2 fleets of little gilded vessels that gave the representation of a Naval fight. It is not easy to imagine

the beauty of this Scene, which I took particular Notice of, but all the rest were perfectly fine in their kind. The story of the Opera is the Enchantments of Alcina, which gives Opportunity for a great variety of Machines and changes of the Scenes, which are perform'd with a surprising swiftnesse. The Theatre is so large that 'tis hard to carry the Eye to the End of it, and the Habits in the utmost magnificence to the number of 108. No house could hold such large Decorations, but the Ladys all siting in the open air exposes them to great Inconveniencys, for there is but one canopy for the Imperial Family, and the first night it was represented, a shower of rain happening, the Opera was broke off and the company crouded away in such confusion, I was almost squeezed to Death.[1]

This was quite a different experience from attending the opera in the King's Theatre in the Haymarket in London. As Lady Mary suggests, the subject matter, the evil magic powers of Alcina that are overcome by the love of Angelica and Medoro, was a familiar one, in painting and music as well as in literature, and the opera was in Italian, the international language of the genre. But almost everything else about the occasion was a new experience. There was a sizeable audience but it was not a public occasion. For the Habsburg court it was a demonstration of dynastic prestige and power appropriate for the celebration of the birth of a son and heir. The entire administrative and musical resources of the court had spent five months developing the project. The court poet, Pietro Pariati, wrote the libretto; the court Kapellmeister, Johann Joseph Fux, wrote most of the music, assisted in some of the ballets by Nicola Matteis; the father and son team of Ferdinando and Giuseppe Galli-Bibiena looked after the staging; two of the court dancers, Simon Pietro Levassori and Alexander Philebois, were responsible for the choreography; and two fencing masters, Guerrevi and Karl Skizzenbach, looked after the three battle scenes.[2] The vocal music is distributed between seven characters and consisted of twenty-five arias, four choruses, three duets and two quintets; there were, in total, twenty-seven changes of scene. The orchestral sonority too was compelling, especially at the beginning and the end of the opera when Fux divided his forces into two orchestras, each consisting of four trumpets, timpani and strings.

For Lady Mary, however, it was the open-air presentation that stayed in her memory. Located a couple of miles outside the city walls to the south-east, the Favorita was the preferred country residence of Karl VI who typically spent much of the autumn there. Although the palace had a small theatre the landscaped gardens were much more frequently used for large-scale operas. A specially prepared arena was reached through a grotto and the audience viewed a stage area built above a waterway, which provided a broad view of armadas, processions and battles. To aid their understanding of the unfolding entertainment guests were given a choice of having the libretto in the original Italian or in German translation, both printed by the imperial printer Johann Peter van Ghelen. In the case of *Alcina* it was a substantial item of fifty-one pages, with six pull-out engravings of some of the more spectacular scenes.[3]

The malign magical world of *Angelica, vincitrice di Alcina* precluded sustained appreciation of the work as an allegory of imperial virtue and, apart from the broad moral that fidelity in love will ultimately triumph, there is nothing in the opera that would seem appropriate for the celebration of the birth of a Habsburg heir. But opera at the imperial court had a long history of concluding with an additional section at the end of the work, the *licenza*, that reminded audiences why the entertainment had been prepared, rather than drawing any moral from it. Here, a stock persona, La Felicità Pubblica (Public Felicity), descended from on high and in a recitative dedicated the entertainment to Karl ('Augusto Carlo'), his wife Elisabeth ('Augusta Elisa') and the young Leopold ('Leopoldo'), and then sang a noisy aria accompanied by trumpets and timpani, that revealed that the infant archduke was already displaying appropriate family virtues:

Nell'Augusto suo sembiante	In His August appearance
Già palesa il Regio Infante	The Royal Infant already shows
La Clemenza e la Pietà.	Clemency and Mercy.
E raccolto nel Suo volto	And together on His face
Con l'Onore sta il Valore	Are Honour and Virtue,
Con l'Amor la Maestà.	Love and Majesty.

A sequence of three dances (a *ballo*) was followed by an exultant chorus of praise, directed at the emperor:

Il piacer, che v'innamora	The joy which enraptures you
È un favor che vien dal Cielo:	Is a sign from Heaven:
Ed il Cielo anch'ei s'onora	And Heaven itself is honoured
Col valor del vostro zelo.	By the quality of your endeavour.

Angelica, vincitrice di Alcina was given four times in September and October 1716 and, as was typical of wider practice in the court, was never performed again. Annual milestones in the lives of members of the imperial family, birthdays and name days, were regarded as individual events that required a new work and only a period of mourning after the death of an emperor caused a halt in the steady unfolding of operas. That respect was not extended to infants, however. The begetter of *Angelica*, Archduke Leopold, died on 4 November, not yet seven months old; the predetermined schedule of new works continued to unfold and on 19 November another opera was performed for the first – and last – time, *Il Costantino*, to mark the name day of the empress.

By 1716, opera had featured in this way at court for the best part of a century and had become embedded in the dynastic ritual, as much a part of the Habsburg sense of inheritance as any outlook related to statesmanship and politics, and, inevitably, often inextricably linked to it. No doubt

Sir Edward Wortley Montagu would have reported the unfortunate death of the young Archduke Leopold as an event that reopened the issue of the absence of any male heir in the family, a problem that would soon assume European proportions. At the same time he would also have reported to the recently ensconced Hanoverian dynasty in Britain, in power for a mere two years, the strong sense of purposeful continuity that characterized the Habsburg dynasty, accumulated across five centuries. For successive generations of the family, music was not just, or even primarily a form of entertainment, it was an assertion of identity, helped by the fact that many emperors were themselves capable musicians.[4]

Three emperors: Leopold I, Joseph I and Karl VI

THE basic organization of the Habsburg court was established in the first half of the sixteenth century and, remarkably, was still in place in 1918 at the end of the First World War, when the last Habsburg ruler, Emperor Karl I, resigned as the empire disintegrated around him. There were four departments: Obersthofmeisterstab (High Steward), Oberstkämmererstab (Chamberlain), Obersthofmarschallstab (Marshall) and Oberststallmeisterstab (Stables). From the sixteenth century to the accession of Leopold I to the Habsburg throne in 1657 the total number of court employees across the four major departments grew to around 600; by the end of his reign in 1705 it had tripled, to around 1800.[5] Musicians were part of this growth. The Hofkapelle (literally the 'court chapel', but indicating the personnel as well as the place) came under the first department, that of the Obersthofmeister, alongside mounted guards and infantry guards, dining protocol, kitchen services, the wine cellar and lighting. Table 1 provides a comparative indication of the size of the Hofkapelle from around the middle of Leopold's reign, 1680, and the year of his death, 1705.[6]

During Leopold's reign the Hofkapelle more than doubled in size, reflecting the increasing presence of music in court life as well as changing musical fashions. At its head was a Kapellmeister, successively Johann Heinrich Schmeltzer (one year only, 1680), Antonio Draghi (1682 to 1700) and Antonio Pancotti (1700 to 1705). Theirs was as much an administrative role as a musical one of composition and direction; in fact, Draghi was first employed as a librettist and Pancotti as a singer. They reported directly to the Obersthofmeister. From 1697 there was a Vice-Kapellmeister too, initially Antonio Pancotti and then, when he, in turn, became Kapellmeister in 1700, Marc' Antonio Ziani (from 1700 to 1715). A major new development occurred in the 1690s. Whereas previously the musical repertory was provided by the Kapellmeister (especially Draghi) and those instrumentalists who also composed, supplemented by some music sourced from outside the court, during the last decade of the century five Court Composers (Hofcompositeurs) were appointed to work

Table 1 The growth of the Hofkapelle between 1680 and 1705

	1680	*1705*
Kapellmeister	1	1
Vice-Kapellmeister	–	1
Opera Intendant	1	–
Composers	–	5
Organists	3	5
Male sopranos	7	6
Male altos	3	6
Tenors	5	9
Basses	4	8
Female sopranos	–	2
Violins	10	20
Cellos	–	3
Violone	–	2
Theorbo	1	3
Lute	–	1
Oboes	–	6
Bassoons	1	3
Cornetts	1	3
Trombones	3	5
Trumpets	4	9
TOTAL	44	98

alongside the Kapellmeister and Vice-Kapellmeister: Carlo Agostino Badia (1672–1738), Johann Joseph Fux (1660–1741), Joseph Hoffer (c. 1666–1729), Franz Thalmann (fl. c. 1700) and Giovanni Bononcini (1670–1747). The increasing number of Italian operas that were presented at the court during Leopold's reign explains the employment from 1700 of two female sopranos, Anna Lisi and Maria Sutterin, the only women in the Hofkapelle. Church music continued to be sung by all-male forces, a group of singers that grew from nineteen to twenty-nine in Leopold's reign.

There was an even larger expansion in the number of instrumentalists at the court in this period, from twenty in 1680 to fifty-five in 1700. As with the number of singers, this should not be taken as an indication of the size of individual performing forces, particularly in the later period; they represented the number of available players and singers, and duties were shared. Also the court's generous practice of keeping on many of its musicians into old age, when they were no longer capable of performing as frequently, or even at all, reduced the numbers who were actually available.

Many employees developed more than one skill: some instrumentalists were composers, some violinists played the gamba, others the viola, cello players played the violone, oboe players could play the flute and, very unusually, Kapellmeister Draghi was also a poet; some of the musicians also served as copyists.

Jobs for life were complemented by a predilection to appoint and promote from within the court. Draghi went from singer and librettist to Opera Intendant before becoming Kapellmeister, and Pancotti went from singer to Vice-Kapellmeister before finally becoming Kapellmeister. Familial appointments were common too: three of the trombone players in the early 1700s were from the Christian family – Leopold, Hanns Georg and Christian – and three of the six oboists were brothers – Franz, Roman and Xavier Glätzl. Musical inheritance was further promoted by a system of court scholars, individuals identified at a young age for specialist musical training provided by members of the Hofkapelle who, surreptitiously, instilled appropriate courtly behaviour too. For instance Antonio Draghi's son Carl was an organ scholar for ten years before being taken on as a court organist in 1698; he was to serve until his death in 1711. While these inward-looking practices may have bred a certain complacency and insularity over time, from the court's point of view it also affirmed a tradition: musicians instinctively knew the system and could be relied upon to uphold its values. The performing musicians were serviced by two organ tuners and repairers who doubled as organ blowers, a lute repairer, two porters, a librarian and – a telling indication of the busy nature of musical life – an official, one Colmann Bamberger, who was responsible for booking additional players from outside the court as necessary.

There were many individuals central to musical performance at the court who were paid from budgets other than that of the Hofkapelle. The most important of these were the imperial Court Poet (Hofdichter) and the imperial Dance Master (Hoftanzmeister), who had equal standing with the Kapellmeister, the first providing most of the librettos for operatic works and the second responsible for training a complement of court dancers and choreographing their participation in operas.[7] The hierarchical structure of the court also gave trumpet and timpani players a different status from that of violinists, oboists and singers. While some were paid from the music budget, there were others who were attached to the mounted guards and still others who were attached to a wholly different department, that of the Oberststallmeister (Master of the Stables).[8] As well as having administrative responsibility for stables, horses and carriages, the Oberststallmeister had a ceremonial role, accompanying the emperor whenever he travelled on horseback or by coach; as part of the wider splendour of public ceremony a group of trumpets and timpani heralded key moments in the journey, such as imminent arrival and departure, and actual arrival and departure, an aural cue for the genuflection of any bystanders. The Oberststallmeister had a dedicated group for this purpose, who could also be called on to play with their Hofkapelle colleagues;

indeed, the Hofkapelle itself did not have a salaried timpani player and was entirely dependent on other musicians at court for this provision. This broad administrative division of trumpets and timpani players into two camps, the musical and the ceremonial, was to remain through to the second half of the nineteenth century; only in 1873, during the reign of Leopold's great-great-great-great-grandson, Franz Joseph, were all trumpet and timpani players finally incorporated into the Hofkapelle. Even more potent than idiosyncratic administrative traditions was the lasting symbolism of the sound of trumpets and timpani in C major in Viennese music, from the seventeenth century to the early nineteenth century, in opera, church music and, later, instrumental music.

Another characteristic of musical life at court that had a long-term effect on musical culture and style in the city was the nationality of the participants. Most of the instrumentalists were of German origin (in the broadest sense), while most of the singers and most of the Kapellmeisters and composers were of Italian origin, producing a daily working environment that was bilingual – though Germans were more likely to understand Italian than Italians were to understand German – and a musical style that was a synthesis of the two.

The huge number of courtiers employed at the Habsburg court plus a chronic shortage of space in the Hofburg itself meant that musicians did not reside there. Instead, rented accommodation, compulsorily acquired in the inner city, was provided free of charge, the court paying only a third of the normal rent to the owners. For the musicians this was not an inconvenience, since nowhere in the inner city was more than fifteen minutes away from the Hofburg. It also allowed them to participate in musical events outside the court, especially in churches like the Michaelerkirche, Schottenkirche and Stephansdom, and in convents like that of the Ursuline order.[9]

In comparison with other courtiers, the musicians were comparatively well paid, and in Leopold's time punctually paid, by a bureaucracy that was often short of money as well as creaking and tortuous. Through a system of petition the musicians could seek, with or without the support of the Kapellmeister, additional payments for all manner of reasons, such as duties that had been voluntary for a long time, to support a growing family, continuation of payment after they had retired, and a widow's pension following the death of the husband. All were considered, some directly by the emperor, and most were granted. For instance, Nicola Matteis (the composer of some of the ballet music for *Angelica, vincitrice di Alcina*), first entered court service as a violinist in July 1700 with an above-average pay of seventy florins. Court documents described him as 'the English violinist' ('der engelländische Geiger') and, just over a year later, he petitioned the court for expenses to travel back to England to bring his children to Vienna, in order to release them from 'un-Catholic hands' ('uncatholischen Hende'). He was given 100 ducats for this purpose, approximately three times his annual salary.[10]

Within the Hofkapelle, the range of pay was a wide one: the Kapellmeister in Emperor Leopold's time was paid 2,000 florins per annum; the court composers Badia and Fux were paid 60 florins per month; singers such as Badia's wife, Anna Lisi, could be paid as much as 120 florins (twice her husband's pay), while violinists were typically paid between 30 and 45 florins (all per month). Occasionally, the expected standard of behaviour was not observed. In 1687, for instance, the Obersthofmeister was obliged to issue guidelines to address particular recent failings in the provision of liturgical music: every musician was to appear punctually, unless previously excused; nobody was to leave before the end of the duty; the allocated part should be undertaken without demur, whether first or second; the Responses should be performed conscientiously and to time; the musicians should observe behaviour appropriate to a holy place and not deny the Kapellmeister his due respect; finally, disorder in the music service was no longer to be tolerated and disobedience would be punished.[11]

This admonishment was given in the name of the emperor himself, Leopold, not just a standard display of protocol but, as Obersthofmeister, Kapellmeister and disorderly musicians knew, a reprimand from someone who took a keen interest in the Hofkapelle, knew its personnel and, more generally, had an abiding interest in the patterns of human behaviour, his own and others. As the second son of Emperor Ferdinand III he was not expected to become emperor and had received an education that emphasized the scholarly and the spiritual, rather than the political and the military, preparing him for the traditional career in the church. As one of his most influential teachers, the Jesuit Philip Miller, would have noted with satisfaction, Leopold's character and interests had already been moulded when his brother, the heir, Ferdinand IV, died of smallpox in 1654. Aged fourteen, the new heir was fluent in four languages – German, Italian, Spanish and Latin – that is, the local language, the cultured language, the language of the Spanish branch of the family (including, later, Leopold's first wife) and the language of the religious, intellectual and diplomatic spheres. He was a skilled huntsman.[12] These abilities were commonplace amongst the Habsburgs. But he was also an enthusiastic and graceful dancer, a painter, and he had an interest in mechanical objects. Unfortunately for Leopold this wide-ranging artistic and intellectual outlook was not matched by an impressive physical appearance. To an alarming degree he had inherited the Habsburg physical characteristics of a protruding chin and bulbous lips, cruelly reported by the Ottoman ambassador shortly after he became the heir apparent:

One may doubt that with him the Lord God really wished to create a human being: he is a young man of average height, without a goatee, with slender hips, not exactly fat or corpulent, but not lean either ... His lips are swollen like those of a camel, and an entire loaf of bread could be fitted into his mouth. Also his teeth are large and white like those of a camel. When he speaks, spit always foams and trickles from his mouth and camel lips, as if he was vomiting, wiped away by the strikingly beautiful pageboys who stand on either side with giant red napkins. He seldom combs his hair and it is always untidy. His fingers look like lengthy gherkins.[13]

Although Leopold the emperor was supported and protected in his duties by all the accumulated authority of the Habsburg dynasty, Leopold the unprepossessing man constantly sought refuge in his interests. Chief among these was music, in which he indulged as a capable performer and composer, as well as a discerning listener.[14] He had learnt to play the organ and the flute, and was a confident singer. In an era when the theoretical and the creative were more closely bound than they were later to become, the young Leopold moved keenly from one to the other and, by the age of sixteen, had completed ten short works, mainly items of liturgical music. They were assembled by one of his teachers, the court organist Wolfgang Ebner, and kept in the court library (the cornerstone of the later Austrian National Library).[15] As imperial juvenilia they reveal a sturdy, if occasionally short-winded craftsmanship, but their retention by the court reflected a lifetime of active composition. In total, sixty-nine works are known, of which only two do not survive in the National Library; they included eight oratorios, more than thirty sacred works and contributions to more than twenty operas, ranging from single arias to whole acts.[16] Leopold's compositions were regularly performed alongside those of the court composers – in that sense he was himself a Hofkomponist – through to the 1740s and, sporadically, even into the nineteenth century. He was also a Kapellmeister manqué in the sense that he often took personal interest in musical appointments and, at rehearsal, continually impressed the performers with his acute hearing.

As well as routine access to the music library of the Hofkapelle Leopold maintained his own personal library of music for study purposes, 524 volumes located in his private quarters in the Schweizertrakt in the Hofburg and for that reason referred to as the 'Bibliotheca cubicularis' (library of the bed chamber).[17] In addition to twenty of Leopold's own compositions, it contained works by the court composers and compositions that Leopold had obtained from elsewhere, including music by Carissimi, Monteverdi and Alessandro Scarlatti. The volumes were uniformly bound in white pig's leather and featured a portrait of the emperor and his personal motto, 'Consilio et Industria' ('Consideration and Diligence'), on the front and the imperial double-headed eagle on the back.

Leopold's enthusiasm for music caught the attention of several early music historians, including Charles Burney, John Hawkins and Ernst Ludwig Gerber. In his *General History of the Science and Practice of Music* from 1776, Hawkins, the Englishman, gives him particular historical credit for spreading knowledge of Italian music north of the Alps.[18] In Vienna over a century later Guido Adler, the founder of musicology, wrote his pioneering study of music by early Habsburg emperors in which he recounted the still current anecdote that Leopold, on his deathbed, had summoned a few musicians to perform in an adjacent room.[19] Rather dryly, Adler remarked that the historical accuracy of this anecdote could not be established, but as a received truth that Adler nevertheless chose to repeat, it perpetuated an enduring image of the innate musicality of the Austrian imperial dynasty and, by association, its subjects.

Leopold was succeeded by his twenty-six-year-old son, Joseph. His upbringing, unlike that of his father, had always prepared him for public duty and his character could not be more different: impulsive, confident, assured, aggressive even.[20] At the same time, he inherited and willingly indulged a love of music, and, indeed, was reputed to be more naturally gifted in the art than his father. These seemingly incompatible attributes are reflected in his personal motto, 'Amore e Timore' ('Love and Fear'). His musical upbringing and training were similar to those of his father: he played the flute and the harpsichord, received theory lessons from Johann Jakob Prinner (who taught many of the Habsburg children) and Ferdinand Tobias Richter (one of the court organists), and began to compose. He was also a gifted dancer. Here the parallel with his father ceases. A bout of depression led him to destroy most of his compositions and only seven survive, of which the most substantial is a Marian antiphon, *Regina coeli*, for soprano, strings and organ.

In theory, the Hofkapelle, like the court as a whole, was not a permanent corpus of individuals that served successive emperors, but was the creative privilege of each new emperor, who could, if he wished, change its constitution entirely, even abolish it; in that way the court became the image of the ruler. Since, in 1705, the musical image was one that he had willingly inherited from that of his father, Joseph retained its constitution and most of its personnel. Over the six years of his reign the number of musicians continued to grow, towards and then over a hundred.[21] The most significant additional member was a third female soprano, Catherina Kaplerin, to share the burden of lead roles in Italian opera. Joseph was particularly fond of the music of Giovanni Bononcini and the composer quickly became the favoured composer, writing six stage works in six years. One of Joseph's few surviving compositions was an aria 'Si trova in tempeste', written for Bononcini's three-act opera, *Endimione*, first performed in 1706. While he was willing to indulge his musical tastes at court, Joseph very opportunistically placed a tax, the *Musikimpost,* on dance, music and theatre evenings in the city, in order to raise money for the imperial coffers, severely depleted by the War of the Spanish Succession.

After only six years as emperor, Joseph died of pneumonia in April 1711, his resistance undermined by smallpox and venereal disease. The succession fell to Joseph's brother, Archduke Karl, who, since 1703, had lived in Barcelona as the would-be King of Spain, where he had his own retinue of musicians.[22] Nine months were to elapse before Karl made a return to Vienna. During these nine months, his mother, Eleonora

Magdalena Theresia (the widow of Leopold I), acted energetically on
his behalf. Taking advantage of the principle that the personnel of the
Hofkapelle did not automatically continue in post, she disbanded the
entire retinue to make way for a formal review of its personnel, made more
difficult by Karl's wish to employ some of the musicians he had taken to
Spain. Apart from a few quick decisions, prompted by the need to have
sufficient musicians to maintain the church services, this was a process that
lasted several months through to 1712, when Karl finally arrived in Vienna.
The net result was that about a fifth of the personnel changed, bringing the
total numbers down to around eighty.[23] Nearly all the musicians who had
worked in Barcelona, mostly native Italians, were taken on, which meant
that many faithful members of the Viennese court lost their positions.
The most conspicuous was Giovanni Bononcini, who was not engaged
in any capacity; neither was his preferred librettist, Silvio Stampiglia.
Marc' Antonio Ziani, at the age of fifty-nine, was promoted from Vice-
Kapellmeister to Kapellmeister and Johann Joseph Fux, aged fifty-one,
was promoted from composer to Vice-Kapellmeister. Over a dozen new
singers were engaged to replace many who had served since the accession of
Leopold I. One tenor, Pietro Sanghi Garghetti, had been in post since 1674
and now was pensioned off at the age of seventy-three. The oldest person to
lose his position was a violinist named Michael Rausch, aged eighty-four;
he too received a pension. The make-up of the newly revitalized Kapelle
was broadly the same, with one notable exception. At the end of Joseph's
reign there were eight trumpet players: two years later they numbered
eighteen, more than a fifth of the total personnel, including five that Karl
had brought with him from Spain.

In temperament, Karl was more like his father than his brother: mild
mannered, rather unprepossessing in appearance, with the congenital
Habsburg hanging lower lip and a gait that was wholly at odds with his
status.[24] Unlike Leopold, however, this second son had never been destined
for the church; since the age of fourteen he had been the heir designate
to the Spanish throne, vying for that position with the French Bourbon
prince, Philip of Anjou, Louis XIV's grandson. Tension between the
Habsburg and Bourbon dynasties erupted in a European war in 1701, the
War of the Spanish Succession, which, as well as the particular issue of
the succession, contested the respective influence of the dynasties in the
Netherlands, the Rhineland, Bavaria and Italy. After thirteen years of
warfare, the final outcome was that the Bourbons became the new ruling
dynasty in Spain and the Habsburgs acquired the Spanish Netherlands in
compensation, as well as territories in Italy.[25]

Although Karl had spent the best part of ten years in Barcelona as the
self-declared heir of the king of Spain, and was deeply attached to the
country, his musical sympathies had been forged as a child at the Viennese
court in the 1690s. He was taught by Ferdinand Tobias Richter, his
brother's teacher, but a more enduring influence was that of Johann Joseph
Fux, then one of the court composers. His elevation to Vice-Kapellmeister

on the emperor's accession in 1711 renewed a happy musical relationship, further rewarded when Fux was made Kapellmeister in 1715, a position he was to hold until his death in February 1741, just four months after that of his imperial patron. During that time music at the Habsburg court reached a pinnacle of endeavour and significance that was unequalled in Europe, and was never even remotely to be equalled in later generations. Like his father before him, Karl was a willing participant too, habitually presiding at the harpsichord in opera performances; he almost certainly composed but nothing has survived.

By 1723 the number of musicians employed at court reached an all-time high of 127 and reflected Karl's interest and patronage over the previous decade (see Table 2).[26] The position of Hofmusik-Oberdirektor

Table 2 The personnel of the Hofkapelle in 1723

Hofmusik-Oberdirektor	1
Kapellmeister	1
Vice-Kapellmeister	1
Composers	3
Maestro di Concerti	1
Organists	7
Male sopranos	8
Male altos	4
Tenors	11
Basses	8
Female sopranos	6
Violins	26
Cellos	5
Violone	5
Gamba	1
Baryton	1
Theorbo	1
Lute	1
Oboes	8
Bassoons	4
Horn	1
Cornetts	2
Trombones	4
Trumpets	16
Timpani	1
TOTAL	127

was well-established and Prince Ludwig Pius of Savoy was the third incumbent. It was a position held by an aristocrat rather than a musician or administrator, typically for a few years, someone who represented the outlook of the emperor and tempered any disputes between the Kapellmeister and the Obersthofmeister. Over the decades the position became a pivotal one in Viennese musical life, determining, for instance, whether Mozart could give a public concert and dealing with Mahler's difficult tenure as music director of the court opera. When Fux became full Kapellmeister in 1715, he was given a salary of 3,100 florins, 600 florins more than his predecessor. There was now a vacancy as Vice-Kapellmeister. In a break with customary practice, Karl did not promote one of the two composers already at court, Carlo Badia or Francesco Conti, but sought the services of Antonio Caldara (1660–1736), someone with a growing reputation in Italy and elsewhere who represented Italian music at its most fashionable. Karl had first become acquainted with him in Barcelona, probably in 1708. The composer then returned to Italy, where he worked for the Duke of Mantua and Prince Ruspoli in Rome. It was a measure of the lure of the imperial Hofkapelle, as well as the personal interest of the emperor, that Caldara accepted the position of Vice-Kapellmeister in 1716; the salary was the same as that previously given to Fux but, in another break with tradition, the emperor allowed Caldara to be absent from court for long periods of time in order to accept commissions for dramatic works from other patrons. Between his appointment and his death in 1736 Caldara was to compose a total of forty-six stage works and thirty-five oratorios for the Habsburg court.[27]

Fux and Caldara represented the two contrasting aspects of musical style at the court in the early eighteenth century, the conservative and the progressive. Three further composers serviced the needs of the court. One was a survivor from the time of Leopold I, Carlo Badia, another was Francesco Conti (1682–1732), appointed by Leopold as a theorbo player in 1701 and promoted by Karl to the rank of composer in 1713. Finally, Giuseppe Porsile (1680–1750), a Neapolitan by birth, had worked as Kapellmeister for Karl in Barcelona; in Vienna he was first employed as a singing teacher to the dowager empress Amalia Wilhelmine, before becoming a Hofkapelle composer in 1720.[28]

As Table 2 indicates, there was a new position in the hierarchy, the Maestro di Concerti. As will become evident in the next chapter the occupant of this post, Kilian Reinhardt, had become an indispensable part of the administration, though his title was more impressive than his pay, a middling 720 florins; most singers and many instrumentalists were paid more, including his nephew, Johann Georg Reinhardt, one of the seven organists. As well as the general increase in the numbers of singers (from twenty-two at the end of Leopold's reign to thirty-seven) and instrumentalists (from fifty-five to seventy-six), two new instruments were represented: the horn and the baryton, a kind of gamba with sympathetic strings that, later in the century, Haydn's employer, Prince Nicolaus, played and for which Haydn was obliged to compose.

As before, the musical personnel did not include court employees who played a key role in the presentation of opera, such as the librettists, costumiers, fencing masters, painters and carpenters. Chief amongst these were the court poets who provided the librettos for the stage works of Caldara, Conti, Fux and Porsile. Pietro Pariati (1665–1733) joined the court in 1714 and remained there for the rest of his life. During his youth in Venice he had often worked with Apostolo Zeno (1668–1750), and the two renewed their friendship when Zeno followed Pariati to the Habsburg court in 1718. Zeno was another person who had worked for Karl VI in Spain. He remained in Vienna until 1729, when he was replaced by a second leading librettist, Pietro Metastasio. Of equal status to the court poets were the set designers. By 1723, the father-and-son team of Ferdinando and Giuseppe Galli-Bibiena, who had provided the spectacular staging for *Angelica, vincitrice di Alcina*, had been replaced by another team from the same family, Giuseppe and his brother Antonio Galli-Bibiena.[29]

Although the term Hofkapelle (or Hofmusikkapelle) was commonly understood as the musical retinue that served each emperor in turn, it was not the only musical retinue at the imperial court during the reigns of Leopold I, Joseph I and Karl VI. Two empresses who had outlived their husbands had their own musical retinues, part of the courtesy that entitled them to maintain their own court on the death of their husband; naturally, these courts, including the musical retinues, ceased to exist once the dowager empress, too, died. Leopold I's stepmother, Eleonora Gonzaga, had her own musical retinue of twenty-four for nearly thirty years until her death in 1686, while Joseph I's widow, Amalia Wilhelmine, had a retinue of about twenty-eight singers and instrumentalists during the whole of Karl VI's reign, until she died at the age of sixty-nine in 1742.[30] The only widow who did not take up this courtesy was Eleonora Magdalena Theresia, Leopold's third wife. She had never shown a particular interest in music, which helps to explain the enthusiasm with which she went about reorganizing the Hofkapelle pending the arrival of Karl VI. These small musical courts had personnel that overlapped with that of the imperial court or nurtured musicians that subsequently moved on to the imperial court, including two who reached the highest level. Antonio Draghi had joined the musical court of Eleonora Gonzaga as a singer and poet, and became its Kapellmeister before transferring to the imperial court. From 1711 to 1718, Fux was Kapellmeister at the court of Amalia Wilhelmine, a position he combined with his imperial duties, first as Vice-Kapellmeister and then Kapellmeister.

Music in a fortress city

WHEN Lady Mary Wortley Montagu arrived in Vienna in September 1716, she was obliged to wait a few days before being presented at court. She took the opportunity to explore the inner city and wrote her first impressions in a letter to her sister:

> This Town, which has the Honnour of being the Emperor's Residence, did not at all answer my Ideas of it, being much lesse than I expected to find it. The streets are very close and so narrow one cannot observe the fine fronts of the Palaces, thô many of them very well deserve observation, being truly magnificent, all built of white stone and excessive high. The Town being so much too little for the number of the people that desire to live in it, the Builders seem to have projected to repair that misfortune by claping one Town on the Top of another, most of the houses being of 5 and some of them 6 storys. You may easily imagine that the streets being so narrow, the upper rooms are extreme Dark, and what is an inconvenience much more intolerable in my Opinion, there is no house that has so few as 5 or 6 families in it. The Apartments of the greatest Ladys and even of the Ministers of state are divided but by a Partition from that of a Tailor or a shoe-maker, and I know no body that has above 2 floors in any house, one for their own use, and one higher for their servants.[31]

At the time of Lady Mary's visit, Vienna had a population of about 115,000 compared with over 600,000 in contemporary London and Paris. It felt crowded because most of the people lived in the inner city, an area easily traversed by foot, in any direction, in fifteen minutes. From the thirteenth century it has been a walled city, which in later centuries had spilled over into the suburbs, but with a marked differentiation between the two that was to define the social geography as well as the physical geography of Vienna for ever (see Fig. 1). The Hofburg, abutting the southern portion of the city walls, had been the principal residence of the Habsburgs only since the early seventeenth century, when Ferdinand II (Leopold I's great-uncle), who was raised in Graz, came to the throne. At that time the city walls were being rebuilt following two separate invasions by the Turks early in the previous century, a monumental building project that took 140 years to complete. It enveloped the city, including the imperial palace, so that it became literally a 'Hof Burg' (court fortress). Rather than a single wall, there were several, broadly concentric elements. Underneath a high inner wall was a deep dry moat and, on the other side a much lower outer wall that reached up to the natural level of the outside terrain. Beyond that was a large buffer area, with no buildings, that separated the inner city from the suburbs and which made any invading forces vulnerable to attack. To the north and east of the city the fortifications abutted the Danube and the river Wien respectively, a seeming strength but one that was compromised by the low water levels of both rivers.[32]

The fortifications were completed in 1672, well into the reign of Leopold I, and were put to the test eleven years later, in 1683, when the Turks laid siege to the city for two months from 14 July to 14 September. Leopold and the court had fled westwards along the Danube to a palace in Linz. While many inhabitants of the inner city fled too, thousands more from the suburbs were urged to seek comparative safety in the inner city, if only to avoid the pre-emptive fires that were started by Habsburg forces in the suburbs. Vienna was surrounded on all sides, but the fortifications just about held; they were literally undermined in and around the Hofburg, when Turkish troops, led by Karl Mustapha, excavated large caverns and filled them with gunpowder, hoping that the resultant explosion would breach the walls. With civilian assistance the defending forces held on, aided by unseasonably heavy rain, thunderstorms and an outbreak of scarlet fever. The siege finally ended when Austrian, Bavarian, Franconian and Saxon forces to the west and Polish forces to the north mounted a co-ordinated and sustained attack on the Turks, who hastily withdrew into Hungary and beyond.[33]

The repelled Turkish siege of 1683 is a landmark date in the history of Vienna. Had the fortifications not held, the city would have became an Ottoman stronghold on the north-western edge of its empire, and the Habsburg court, severely weakened in power and influence, would have relocated elsewhere, probably to Linz or to Prague. Although the Ottoman threat was to remain an intermittent one until the end of the eighteenth century, it was never again to threaten Vienna itself. In victory, Habsburg and Viennese self-confidence was reinforced, even though it could never have been accomplished without the military assistance of others – Bavaria, Poland, Saxony, even France. The development of the inner city, including the multi-storey buildings in white stone that Lady Mary Montagu was to comment upon and that had already begun to appear, grew apace, producing the predominantly Baroque cityscape that characterizes it to this day.

The Habsburgs cultivated the loyalty of aristocrats by, amongst other means, not taxing them if they built their principal palace in Vienna. In the decades following the Turkish siege, many new or extensively reconfigured palaces were built by aristocratic families in the vicinity of the Hofburg.[34] Here they could vie with each other for attention at court. Over successive generations, they produced a class of society that was to influence the development of the city for more than 200 years. Loyalty to the Habsburg court led naturally to a cultivated interest in music, which, with increasing momentum in the middle decades of the century, encouraged many aristocrats to employ their own retinue of musicians. Palaces built (or substantially altered) around 1700 by family dynasties that were to feature prominently in later music history included the Liechtenstein palace in the Minoritenplatz (completed in 1705); the Daum palace in the Herrengasse,

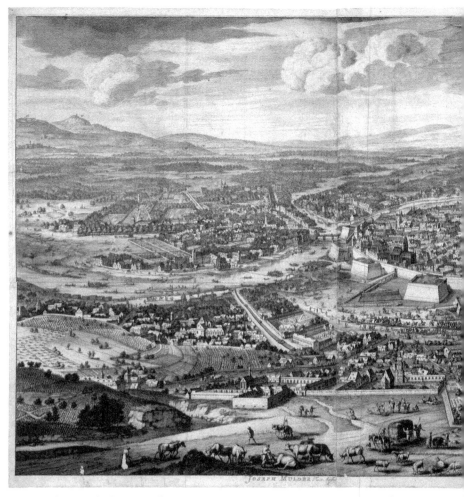

1 View of Vienna before 1683, from an engraving after Folbert van Alten-Allen (Amsterdam, 16

later acquired by the Kinsky family (1716); the Dietrichstein palace (1690), acquired by the Lobkowitz family in 1753, after whom the square was subsequently renamed; and the Schwarzenberg palace on the Neuer Markt (1705; demolished 1894). Especially interesting is the Esterházy palace in the Wallnerstrasse, two streets away from the Hofburg and completed in 1695. Above the gateway to the inner courtyard an inscribed tablet reveals how closely the family sought to identify itself with Habsburg endeavour, past and present.

> Praise to God alone. This house, once occupied by the Holy Margrave Leopold of Austria, was handed down in the course of time to the Esterházy noble family. It was acquired through the noble Prince of the Holy Roman Empire, Paul Esterházy, Palatine of the

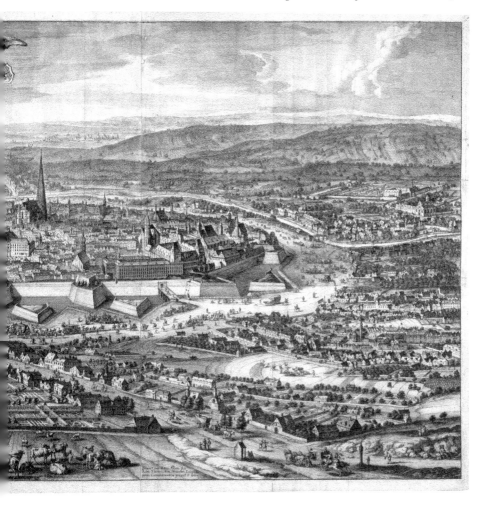

kingdom of Hungary, and re-built, from the ground up in this form, for the adornment of his family, in the year of our Lord 1695.[35]

The Margrave Leopold of Austria (1073–1136) was a notable benefactor of several ecclesiastical institutions, including Klosterneuburg to the north-west of Vienna, and was canonized in 1485; rather opportunistically, the inscription alludes to the Viennese fable that a hunting lodge belonging to the margrave had stood on the ground now occupied by the Esterházy Palace. Emperor Leopold (himself named after St Leopold, the canonized margrave) rewarded Paul Esterházy's loyalty with territory in Hungary, made him the designated Habsburg representative in the country (the Palatine), and awarded him the title of Prince of the Holy Roman Empire.[36]

Since victory over the Turks was readily projected as victory for Christendom over the infidel, churches were also part of this building boom in the late seventeenth and early eighteenth century.[37] Many churches in the suburbs had been destroyed during the siege and were built anew, entirely in the Baroque style. Within the city walls, however, none had been seriously damaged.[38] The most symbolic of them all, Stephansdom, whose Gothic spire dominated the city and for that reason was used as a watchtower (with an oversized megaphone to relay messages during the Turkish siege), was left untouched by the Baroque style. Vienna's oldest church, however, Peterskirche to the north of the Graben, was entirely rebuilt, a project personally supported by Leopold I; one of the people who worked on making sure that all aspects of its visual splendour – art and architecture together with colour and light – were fully co-ordinated, was Antonio Galli-Bibiena (1700–1774), a member of the same Galli-Bibiena family who worked on operatic productions at court.

At first, it seems surprising that the Hofburg itself was not extensively rebuilt. At the very beginning of Leopold's reign a new wing had been added, abutting the inner wall of the fortifications, and Karl VI added a complementary wing on the opposite side of the square and – not directly connected to the Hofburg – a new building to house the court library. Although substantial building projects in themselves, they did not bring a striking overall coherence to the imperial palace.[39] The confined space meant that it was difficult to present a distancing, commanding perspective; indeed, there was no obvious main entrance to catch the eye. Since musicians and other court employees had to be housed in the inner city and its streets were daily filled with people making their way to and from the imperial palace, on routine business as well as part of formal processions, there was a real sense that the whole inner city was an imperial residence.

In any comparison with the Versailles of Louis XIV, the Hofburg had little to offer and, conscious of this, Leopold I, Joseph I and Karl VI each developed plans for new, architecturally imposing residences outside the city. Ambitious, detailed plans for the development of the former hunting lodge at Schönbrunn were drawn up after its near destruction in the Turkish siege; Joseph I was particularly keen on the project and pressed ahead with the central portion of the palace and one wing, and it might well have been completed had he lived longer. His brother, Karl, however, was not enthusiastic and it languished until the reign of Maria Theresia. Instead, Karl devoted much of his reign to ambitious plans for a second new residence, to the north-west of the city rather than to the south-east, and one that showed the enduring influence of his years in Spain. The Augustinian monastery at Klosterneuburg was the oldest in the Austrian territories and, like many, had a commanding view of its surroundings, in this case the rolling hills up to the Kahlenberg and, in the other direction, across the Danube valley, the site of key battles in 1683. Still yearning after his time as the future king of Spain, Karl saw it as the Habsburg equivalent to the Escorial, an ostentatious palace located in a working monastery, with a church already rebuilt in the Baroque style. These plans remained unfulfilled and, with only one-eighth of the project completed, they were abandoned after his death in 1740.[40]

Music and Habsburg identity

WITH three successive emperors – Leopold I, Joseph I and Karl VI – who between them reigned as Holy Roman Emperor for a period of eighty-two years, from 1658 to 1740, and who presided over a continuing growth in musical personnel at court, as well as engaging directly with its practice, music in Vienna had a presence and a purpose that was inextricably linked with that of the dynasty itself. At one level it was a diversion, one in which the emperors, family members and courtiers indulged; in terms of repertoire, small-scale sonatas, most chamber cantatas, keyboard music and lute music may be seen as fulfilling that function only. But music of that type did not have the aura and wider significance that music for the church and music for the theatre had: their function was altogether grander and symbolic. Since it had evolved over a period of time, rather than drawn up at one particular moment, the nature of that grandeur and symbolism was complex and, indeed, often achieved coherence and credibility only through musical means.

One of the potent remarks attributed to Louis XIV, key to understanding the role of the monarchy in France, was 'L'état, c'est moi' ('I am the state'). No Habsburg emperor could have uttered such a remark because there was no clearly defined state for which he could be regarded as its embodiment. He might have said of Vienna itself 'I am the city' ('Die Stadt bin ich'), but beyond that there was no sense of uniform possession and little desire to seek one. The emperors in Vienna presided over two fractured entities. The hereditary lands (*Erblande*) consisted principally of the archduchy of Austria, the kingdom of Bohemia and the kingdom of Hungary, together with Moravia and Silesia. Here the Habsburgs exercised direct power, but there was no overall title, with each successive emperor assuming the historical title of Archduke of Austria, King of Bohemia and King of Hungary. From 1713 direct rule was also exerted in Lombardy, and two years later, in the Austrian Netherlands. The title of emperor came from a second, even more heterogeneous entity, the Holy Roman Empire, more precisely the 'Holy Roman Empire of German Nations', that is the legacy of Charlemagne's empire from the ninth century, not the Roman empire of antiquity, though successive Habsburg emperors conveniently muddied the distinction and drew considerable symbolic authority from association with the latter. This was an area that broadly covered German-speaking Europe, including many of the hereditary lands (Austria and Bohemia, but not Hungary), along with dozens of smaller archbishoprics, dukedoms, kingdoms, principalities and independent cities. Each new emperor was elected, but, as the largest holder of territory, the reigning Habsburg had always been chosen since the beginning of the sixteenth century. While the central bureaucracy of the empire was a distinct administrative unit in Vienna, it had little or no direct influence on the non-hereditary lands and the actual ceremony of crowning the new emperor, as well as his formal election, was held 370 miles away in Frankfurt. Nevertheless, it was this office, the Holy Roman Emperor, rather than more effectual ones of archduke or king, that was most commonly invoked on title pages of music performed at the court.

Neither the hereditary lands nor the empire remotely constituted a state as Louis XIV would have understood it, and the degree of allegiance to the Habsburg dynasty varied not only between hereditary and non-hereditary lands, but within both; the two kingdoms of Bohemia and Hungary, for instance, could not have been more different, the first unstintingly loyal, the second more restless and troublesome. Although German was the most prevalent language in all areas, there were large parts of the hereditary lands and the empire that spoke other languages: Czech, Italian, Magyar, Polish, even French. At the Habsburg court itself, particularly in Karl VI's reign, Spanish too was heard. Promoting the German language above all others was not a characteristic of the Viennese court or of the city in general.

The diversity of the population was a feature that had caught the attention of Lady Mary Montagu. She left Vienna with her husband in November 1716, when they travelled north to Hanover, staying en route in Prague, Dresden, Leipzig and Brunswick, before returning to Vienna at the beginning of January 1717. She drew on her experiences in those cities when she offered the following comments on Vienna:

> 'Tis true the Austrians are not commonly the most polite people in the World or the most agreable, but Vienna is inhabited by all Nations, and I had form'd to my selfe a little Society of such as were perfectly to my own taste and thô the Number was not very great, I could never pick up in any other place such a number of reasonable, agreable people.[41]

Music at court reflected this diversity and the lack of a politically determined focus on one language. Latin was the language of sacred music and Italian was the language of opera; German, when it was sung at court, was associated with simple songs and light-hearted comedies. It did not even begin to acquire equal status in music, sacred and secular, until the last decades of the eighteenth century.

For the Habsburg dynasty at the turn of the seventeenth century, the notion of a state and the appeal of linguistic nationalism were alien ideologies. Religion, however, specifically the Catholic faith, was at the very core of its identity. During the Reformation, large areas of the hereditary lands of Austria, Bohemia and Hungary had converted to Protestantism and, indeed, Vienna itself was mostly Lutheran in the early seventeenth century. To settle political conflict resulting from the early years of the Counter-Reformation, the Peace of Augsburg (1555) asserted the principle of *cujus regio, ejus religio*, that is, the religion of the people should follow that of the ruler. Passively, it enshrined religious tolerance between different territories, notably in large parts of the Holy Roman Empire, but more aggressively, it also enabled rulers to force their own religion on their subjects, in the process reasserting the much older principle of the divine right of kings. Within the hereditary lands, the Habsburg dynasty, working alongside the Jesuits in matters of faith and with compliant local magnates in matters of enforcement, spearheaded the Counter-Reformation. By the time Leopold I became emperor in 1658 most of the Austrian and Bohemian lands was firmly Catholic, as were large parts of Hungary too. The subsequent defeat of the infidel Turk was easily presented and understood as the legitimization of the Catholic faith, the often ruthless ways of the Counter-Reformation and the divine authority of the Habsburg dynasty itself. It is no accident that music title-pages habitually couple the word emperor (Imperatore) with the description 'Catholic Royal Majesty' ('Cattolica Reale Maestà'). As for the hereditary lands, they acquired a defining appearance that has endured to this day – opulently decorated churches, commanding monasteries, sensitively placed palaces and touchingly devout shrines to the Virgin Mary.

At the head of this religious, social and political order stood the Habsburg dynasty. The plastic arts of painting and architecture played their part in this all-enveloping identity, as did the carefully nurtured theatre of court ritual and ceremony. Music for the Catholic liturgy often related powerfully to these elements, but music's unequalled ability to move between the literal and the ineffable and, especially, to transcend the former with the latter, made it a particularly appealing and persuasive art form in Habsburg Vienna. Appropriately, it dominated artistic life at the imperial court.

CHAPTER 3

Catholicism, Ritual and Ceremony

The regulation of the liturgy

O NE of the longest serving members of the Habsburg Hofkapelle was
not a composer, singer or instrumentalist, but someone who had
started as a functionary, copying and distributing the performing parts
for the musicians, the Dispensatore delli Concerti, and who over half a
century became the central authority on the organisation and presentation
of sacred music at court: Kilian Reinhardt (1653/4–1729). He joined
the Kapelle of Leopold I in the year of the Turkish siege, 1683, quickly
making the transition from willing novice to efficient organizer.[1] As several
petitions from the late 1690s indicate, he felt that he was overworked and
did not always have the respect of the performing musicians, accusing
them of uncivil and coarse behaviour. His proposed solution reveals
something about court hierarchy and prejudices; Reinhardt felt that if he
were given the title of 'Musician' ('Musicus') that would elicit respect. This
was granted as well as the enhanced title of Maestro di Concerti.[2] By the
1720s Reinhardt's accumulated experience and detailed knowledge of the
workings of the musical court, particularly in the complex area of liturgical
music, was unrivalled, even by its Kapellmeister Johann Joseph Fux. As part
of a review of the membership of the musical court instituted by Karl in
1726 Reinhardt seems to have been required to document this knowledge.
The result was a handwritten volume of over 200 pages that indicates to the
last detail the role of liturgical music at the court: *Rubriche Generali Per
le Funzioni Ecclesiastiche Musicali di tutto l'Anno* (General Regulations on
the Role of Ecclesiastical Music during the Entire Year).[3] Written in Italian,
the language that guaranteed maximum distribution amongst musicians
and administrators, the volume has a lengthy dedication that indicates,
alongside the tortuous supplicatory formalities, its authority:

Holy, Catholic and Royal Majesty

If the scrupulous care that I have taken in the preparation of these
Rubriche, which I now most humbly present to Your Holy Imperial,
Catholic and Royal Majesty, will elicit your most clement acceptance,
I will rejoice greatly in that result and I will have realized the
ambition to which I committed myself when I set forth on this work.
There have been twelve most peaceful holy baptisms, seven most
august and serene weddings and nine imperial and royal coronations
that I have been able to attend, thanks to good fortune, and to which
I have been able to contribute with my most humble service. These

date from the times when the most august emperors, Leopold I and Joseph I, of glorious memory, reigned, and from the time when Your Holy, Imperial, Catholic and Royal Majesty, filled with good grace, began reigning, with the kindness of his supreme actions towards this, his native land. My advancing years, now amounting to very old age, enfeeble my intention to continue this service with the most faithful of zeal. Nevertheless, since on this occasion I can still flatter myself with the aforementioned product and purpose, to my dying days I will not fail at any time to execute every conceivable task in order to prove that I remain always bowed at the feet of your most Imperial, Catholic and Royal Majesty.

> Your most humble
> Kilian Reinhardt,
> rendered after 50 years
> of most faithful service

Both the title-page and the dedication reveal that Reinhardt had been collecting this information for fifty years. This may have been poetic licence, but if it was literally true, then Reinhardt would have started working at the court in 1677, in his mid-twenties. Whatever the precise length of service at court Reinhardt draws attention to his work on behalf of three successive emperors.

In the main part of the volume Reinhardt lists all the services in the Catholic liturgy that require music. With a nod to practicalities it starts on 1 January, rather than the beginning of the liturgical year, and since it lists moveable feasts alongside fixed feasts the list is broadly, rather than strictly, chronological. An appendix may be described as a list of para-liturgical occasions that have traditionally required sacred music, including religious processions, commemorative events, weddings, baptisms and funerals. Taking these two lists together and omitting occasional events, the number of church services during one year that required the services of the Hofkapelle easily exceeds 400. Making sure that the appropriate music was provided, together with the required personnel, was a huge task. Reinhardt's volume gives clear guidance throughout for each of these recurring services, indicating, where appropriate, those occasions where there was an element of discretion; in fact, discretion required more work than following prescriptive practice, since it involved discussion and decision-making. In addition to the differing musical requirements arising from the core Catholic liturgy, such as the time-honoured status of different feasts, Reinhardt's instructions were influenced by three other factors.

The first was the wider public role of court services in Vienna. While most services took place in the court chapel, the Hofburgkapelle, located in the centre of the imperial complex of buildings – where the congregation was a private one consisting of the imperial family, courtiers and occasional guests – there was an impressive tradition of presenting particular services outside the court in churches in the inner city and in the suburbs. With some latitude from year to year, Reinhardt's instructions list over thirty churches in Vienna that regularly included court services, to which can be added eight public squares in the inner city that were the locus of parts of services: a formidable demonstration of the indivisibility of religion and dynasty, the public and the court. There were annual visits to, amongst others, the Augustinerkirche, Jesuitenkirche, Michaelerkirche, Peterskirche and Stephansdom. With the exception of the Augustinerkirche and the Michaelerkirche, most of the churches were not in, nor adjacent to, the imperial complex, and processions to and from the churches, punctuated by trumpet fanfares and sometimes featuring vocal music too, were a regular and popular feature of street life in Vienna; later in the eighteenth century Charles Burney was told by a resident Italian that the Austrians were addicted to religious processions, 'portatissimi alle processioni'.[4] Reinhardt's volume documents the kinds of music required for this annual cycle of visits as well as practical details, such as where the musicians should stand at certain points in the services. Another complicating element that arose from the visits was that some of the churches had their own musical personnel that had to be accommodated. When the musical forces of the Hofkapelle visited Stephansdom they were regularly supplemented by musicians from the cathedral, forming a shared musical-cum-religious community.

The second major consideration that is factored into Reinhardt's *Rubriche Generali* was the court's broad division of feast days into three categories, informed by secular as well as sacred practice, with consequences on the lavishness of ceremony and, arising from that, the splendour of the music: Gala Days, Fleece Days and Ordinary Days. Gala Days were court festivals on the name days or birthdays of senior members of the imperial family, when courtiers were required to dress elaborately for all the related festivities – banquet and opera as well as church service. Some of the name days, pre-eminently that of Leopold (Feast of St Leopold, 15 November), were already important saint days that would have required appropriate musical celebration in church services for that reason; in such cases the complementary designation Gala Day merely provided additional affirmation. Fleece days were more exclusive and an aspect of court life that Karl VI had imported from Spain. Formed in the fifteenth century, the Order of the Golden Fleece had split into two branches early in the eighteenth century following the end of the Habsburg presence in Spain, the Spanish and the Austrian; the first sovereign of the Austrian branch was Karl VI. The order consisted of a fixed number of princes and noblemen who had given particular service to the church and to the Habsburgs. On Fleece Days its members wore their golden chain over a red costume speckled with golden embroidery. Reinhardt records nearly fifty church services as Fleece events (*Tosone*); they include the most important days in the church calendar – Christmas, Easter, Ascension, Whitsuntide and Corpus Christi – plus the twelve feasts of the apostles. Many of the associated services were held in the inner city, where the public was able to witness the accompanying procession to and from the church. Finally, Ordinary Days, by definition, were the most numerous, when courtiers would dress in their routine black and gold, and the ceremonial element was generally less ostentatious.[5]

The third and final factor that affected Reinhardt's planning was the annual pattern of residence for the imperial court, fairly fixed but liable to adjustment. It resided in the Hofburg only during the winter and early spring, from November to April; May to mid-July was spent in the summer palace in Laxenburg; and the remainder of the summer through to October in the Favorita, after which the pattern would begin again. From a logistical point of view the last of these palaces, the Favorita, was easily accommodated in the detailed planning. Located in the suburbs to the south-east of Vienna on a gently rising hill, it was visible from the Hofburg and could be reached on foot in forty minutes or so, less by horse and carriage. Laxenburg, however, was a hunting lodge in the fertile countryside fifteen miles to the south of Vienna, a couple of hours away from the Hofburg. There, church services were held in the palace chapel, occasionally in the local parish church, and were routinely supported by music, lavishly so for the more important dates in the church calendar such as Ascension and Pentecost. In terms of court ceremony Ordinary Days were the norm in Laxenburg and Fleece Days were generally avoided.

With all these considerations in mind – the religious, the ceremonial and the practical – Reinhardt gives detailed instructions for each service, or sequence of three or more related services: the church where the service is to be held, the degree of court ceremony involved, and the kind of music that is to be provided. He also notes those years when the practice differed substantially or where it had changed over the decades, especially between the reigns of Joseph I and Karl VI. Four particular examples will exemplify the varied role of music in the calendar of services and the administrative complications associated with presenting it in an orderly manner.

For the moveable feast of the first Sunday in Lent (Dominica I. in Quadragesima) two services were expected, mass and vespers, both held inside the court complex in the Hofburgkapelle. Because it was Lent, the degree of ceremony is indicated as Ordinary. Reinhardt very rarely prescribes the actual piece of music that is to be used, but lists the criteria for the choice. The music in both services is *a cappella*, as was traditional during Lent, but Reinhardt makes a distinction between that for the mass, which is to be without the support of an organ, and that for vespers, which is to have the support of basso continuo (organ and violone). Reinhardt's habitual term for the *a cappella* mass is 'Messa in contrapunta' (an indication of style) and he notes that the Gloria is not to be sung. He specifies the texts that are to be used for the introit ('Invocabit me'), gradual ('Angelis suis'), tract ('Qui habitat') and offertory ('Scapulis suis'); the responses are to be sung without accompaniment. Since the psalms that featured in a vespers service did vary a little, Reinhardt prescribes the ones for this particular ceremony: 'Dixit Dominus', 'Confitebor', 'Beatus vir', 'Laudate pueri' and 'In exitu Israel'. The Hymn is to be 'Audi, benigne conditor', and settings of the *Magnificat* and *Ave Regina* also are to be sung. The number of different items of music came to about nine; in practice, this figure was sometimes higher, since settings of individual movements from the mass and vespers were taken from more than one musical composition, forming a composite liturgical item. Finally, Reinhardt has a non-musical comment: the sermon in the vespers is to be given in Italian, not the routine Latin.[6] Because the venues for the church services were familiar to all the musicians, the Hofburgkapelle particularly so, Reinhardt very rarely provides information on the size and placing of the forces. The Hofburgkapelle was extensively rebuilt a century later, in 1802, when a musicians gallery was erected at the back of the church; it is difficult to be certain where the performers were placed in Reinhardt's time, but they were probably at floor level in front of the altar.[7]

    The fixed feast of the birth of St John the Baptist occurred on 24 June, for which Reinhardt prescribes the content of three related services: the first vespers on the previous evening, the mass in the morning and the second vespers in the afternoon. Unusually, two venues were involved: the first vespers service plus the mass took place in the church in the Favorita, and the second vespers was given in the church of the Barmherzigen Brüder in the northern suburb of Leopoldstadt, a church dedicated to John the Baptist; this was the only time that the court visited this church. Since, as detailed by Reinhardt, the second vespers was a shortened version of the service of the previous evening, the musical works could be the same; as always, Reinhardt specifies the text of the antiphons and the psalms that precede the hymn, *Magnificat* and *Salve Regina*, and for the mass service, the introit and the offertory; the gradual music on this occasion was to take the form of an instrumental sonata. The ceremonial status of the three services is described as Ordinary but the musical setting is one level up from the routine, solemn (*solenne*), that is musically generous works with trumpets and timpani. However, trumpets and timpani were not required in the second vespers. Reinhardt also takes care of one further complication. Occasionally, if Easter was rather late, the fixed feast of St John occurred during Corpus Christi, in which case both vespers were to conclude with a setting of the Litanie de Venerabili Sacramento and the mass was to include the Credo, a movement that was normally omitted on this feast day.[8]

    The most significant interruption of the residence of the court in the Favorita occurred every September, on the moveable feast of the naming of the Blessed Virgin Mary, the first Sunday after 8 September.[9] As one of several Marian days in the church calendar, it had always been celebrated with due reverence, but this particular Marian feast was loaded with additional significance for the Habsburgs and for the Viennese too. The moveable feast always occurred within four days of the anniversary of the defeat of the Turks on 12 September 1683 – the siege being, for many, a living memory of what had been a living hell – and became associated with that deliverance. As the Counter-Reformation unfolded from the late sixteenth century onwards the Habsburg family had increasingly invoked the Virgin Mary as the patron of its success, referring to her as the 'victor in all of God's battles', and the 'supreme commander of the Austrian family'. On one of the largest squares in the inner city, that of Am Hof, a strikingly tall and slender statue of the Virgin Mary had been erected in 1647. Looking eastwards, she is shown crushing the serpent's head under her foot; the dedication is to God, 'the most sublime emperor of heaven and earth through whom kings reign, and to the Virgin, bearer of God and the one conceived without sin, through whom princes reign, as the special ruler and patron of Austria'.[10] When the Turkish siege of Vienna was lifted in September 1683, the 'supreme commander' and the 'victor in all of God's battles' had magnificently extended the triumph of the Counter-Reformation to the defeat of the infidel. For the imperial court and the people of Vienna, the proximity of the victory to a Marian day was hugely meaningful. Above all other occasions this annual commemoration of the defeat of the Turks showed the indivisibility of the sacred and the secular. Music played its part.

The mass service was held in Stephansdom, where in September 1683 Leopold I had celebrated the *Te Deum* following his victorious return to the city. The court, the privy councillors, the clergy and the musicians assembled at the Augustinerkirche, from where they processed along the side of the imperial building, turned right into the Kohlmarkt, and continued along the full length of the Graben before veering to the left and entering the main door of the cathedral. A notably wide street in a city that contained many narrow ones, the Graben was bounded on both sides by high buildings that afforded the Viennese the best vantage point for the visual splendour of the processions. It was aurally splendid too. During the procession, an *a cappella* setting of the Litany of the Blessed Virgin was performed, its constituent movements preceded, separated and followed by fanfares (*intrate*), played by trumpets and timpani; these fanfares were not brief flourishes but outbursts of music lasting about a minute or so, typically for an ensemble of four trumpets, three trombones and timpani. It was on occasions like this that the numerous court trumpeters came into their own. The church service began with a *Te Deum* before moving to the mass, both sung by the combined forces of the Hofburgkapelle and Stephansdom, and with trumpets and timpani as part of the orchestral forces. The cathedral was the largest church in Vienna and, reflecting long-standing practice, the musicians were located in a gallery on the left hand side, directly opposite the complementary gallery reserved for the emperor.[11] Reinhardt does not actually specify that there was a return procession from the Stephansdom to the Augustinerkirche; probably this was taken for granted, together with the intermittent fanfares of trumpet and timpani.

Two months later, on 15 November, another religious service that was historically resonant took place, this time outside Vienna in the abbey of

Klosterneuburg. The date was the feast of St Leopold, the founder of the Austrian ruling household and the patron saint of the Austrian territories. His remains were preserved in the abbey. For Leopold I, the celebration of his name day embodied everything that was central to his being: his devout nature, his sense of inherited tradition and, linking the two, his unremitting responsibility towards his religion. Early in the reign of Karl VI, that sense of complete identification was enhanced even further when it was decided that Leopold's music should feature as much as possible in the feast day services, a practice duly noted by Reinhardt. The court travelled to Klosterneuburg on the previous day in order to attend the first vespers service that evening. As well as a reminder that the music should have trumpets and timpani, Reinhardt indicates that the service was a substantial one, more than two hours; as always he stipulates the texts of the antiphons, the psalms and the hymn 'Iste Confessor' (This Witness of the Lord), as well as indicating that the settings of the *Magnificat*, the *Salve Regina* and the Litany of the Blessed Virgin Mary should be sung. For the service the following morning, the mass should have trumpets and timpani but, once again, Reinhardt is keen to ensure that music has maximum presence in the service, adding the comment 'extended compositions' ('Compositione Lunga'). The second vespers service in the afternoon should be shorter, between thirty minutes and an hour, and contain only half the music from the first vespers.[12]

While the central purpose of Reinhardt's volume was a utilitarian one, the precise documentation of courtly and musical practice that had developed across fifty years, its pages readily communicate the all-pervasive culture that was being served and sustained. The emperor, his court, its composers, singers and instrumentalists, as well as the Maestro di Concerti himself, were inextricably woven into a pattern of duties that governed their existence, year after year, decade after decade. Although, in essence, the annual cycle was governed by religious observance it was also much more than that. All three emperors – Leopold I, Joseph I and Karl VI – willingly, if not instinctively, championed the role of music as part of a wider sense of character and authority. The first of these, Leopold, best illustrates that attitude, one that shaped the outlook of his two sons.

Leopold I and *pietas austriaca*

THE feast of St Leopold was not the only event in the annual cycle of church services that proclaimed the religious conviction of Emperor Leopold. On every anniversary of his death, on 5 May, there was a commemorative requiem service preceded by an all-night vigil, and followed immediately by a celebratory service. Reinhardt's instructions ensured that ostentation was abjured: the ceremonial aspect was Ordinary and the setting of the requiem was to be solemn, but with no trumpets and timpani. In many years, probably most, Leopold's own setting of the requiem text was used. During Joseph's reign the service took place in the Hofburgkapelle; from 1712 onwards it was held in the chapel in Laxenburg.[13]

A few weeks later, on Trinity Sunday (the Sunday after Pentecost), the liturgical service once more invoked the memory of Leopold. On 13 May 1686, when the court was in Laxenburg, severe lightning had struck the palace, but God working through Leopold had ensured that no one was injured. For this commemorative annual service of thanksgiving the full panoply of musical celebration was let loose: first an outdoor procession made its way around the palace during which the hymn 'Pange, lingua' was sung, its verses separated by trumpet and timpani fanfares; a *Te Deum* was sung in the church (with trumpet and timpani), followed by a mass. One comparatively small detail relating to the use of trumpets and timpani noted by Reinhardt indicates the sense of musical theatre that was to be enacted. The outside procession and the *Te Deum* were replete with the sound of trumpets and timpani; the mass, on the other hand, was to be a musical setting without trumpets and timpani. They do, however, appear once more, in a self-contained fanfare, a blaze of glory before the Sanctus.[14]

Even allowing for the lightning strike of 1686 this service seems excessively lavish, at odds with the theological complexity of the feast day of the Holy Trinity. But there were wider resonances, intended and unintended. At the time of the lightning strike a magnificently opulent monument proclaiming the majesty of the Holy Trinity was being built in the Graben, a project that took eleven years to complete. Instigated by Leopold following the plague of 1679 (hence Pestsäule), it shows the emperor kneeling in homage to the Holy Trinity, the source of his authority, the one that is also celebrated in Laxenburg. Soon after the building of the monument was begun the Turks laid siege to the city. Inevitably, the imagery on the monument became associated with the repelling of that evil too. Every religious procession from the court to Stephansdom passed it, including the one in September to mark the end of the Turkish siege, and part of the annual service held on the last Sunday in October, to give thanks for the end of the plague, was held at its foot. Lightning, the ungodly and the plague had all been overcome through the divine authority of the emperor.

In the wake of the Counter-Reformation, this all-embracing piety had already been identified by more than one writer as a key component of the authority of the Habsburg dynasty and had acquired a name, *pietas austriaca*. Initially, 'Austrian' signified the household rather than a geographical identity, but as its tenets took hold it was easily transferred to Austria the country; certainly, its social attitudes were to outlive the Habsburg dynasty and are apparent even in the twenty-first century. Building on the existing tenet of the divine right of kings, *pietas austriaca* articulated the relationship between the divine and the ruler but, crucially, moved from being just a theoretical concept to adumbrating a way of life for the Catholic ruler and his subjects. It gave complementary emphasis to the Holy Trinity, the cult of the Virgin Mary, the veneration of the eucharist (rather than the cross) and the communion of particular saints.[15] While it was easily invoked to justify wars – in that sense all wars led by the supreme commander of the army, Mary, were religious wars – it also emphasized more quiescent characteristics, particularly modesty and clemency. Leopold I, who would have known the term *pietas austriaca*, promoted its principles unstintingly, through private as well as public devotion – the building and rebuilding of churches with their richly symbolic art and architecture, the erection of public monuments – and through court ceremonial. For this gifted musician, music was an inextricable part of *pietas austriaca*, not a mere adornment and, in the same way as the concept in general influenced Austrian society long after it was first theorized, the nature of the liturgical music that it yielded also remained. The sacred music of Haydn and Bruckner, to name only two composers, is deeply imbued with its spirit.

Musical *pietas austriaca* manifested itself early in Leopold's life. The collection of Leopold's youthful compositions compiled by his teacher, Wolfgang Ebner, includes three Marian works: *Ave Regina* ('Hail, Queen of heaven, Hail, Lady of the Angels'), *Regina coeli* ('Queen of heaven, rejoice, alleluja') and *Salve Regina* ('Hail, Queen, Mother of mercy; our life joy and hope, hail!'). From a narrowly musical perspective, the comparative brevity of the texts did not stretch the capabilities of the teenage composer and they may have been chosen for that reason. At the same time, it is likely that, even at that age, Leopold was unable to isolate craft from subject matter. His Jesuit tutors had already inculcated Marian devotion into his being and the composition of these works was viewed by him as an act of devotion, however limited they were in their musicianship. The lingering sentiment of the last line of the text of the *Salve Regina* – 'O clemens, o pia, o dulcis Virgo Maria' ('O gentle, o holy, o sweet Virgin Mary') – typifies an entire personality.

As emperor, Leopold also promoted the veneration of St Joseph, the father of Christ, a promotion that was encouraged by dynastic concerns. Two would-be heirs to Leopold, Ferdinand and Johann Leopold, had not survived, the first dying at four months, the second at birth. In 1675 Leopold dedicated the Austrian hereditary lands to St Joseph and when, just three years later, another son was born he attributed the happy event to the workings of that saint. This future emperor was accordingly named Joseph, the first use of that name in the history of the Habsburg dynasty.[16] Leopold's musical works include a hymn, 'Te Joseph celebrent', for a vespers service.[17] Its date of composition is not known. It could have been written at the time of the birth. More likely, it was for a later occasion, the celebrations in Vienna in 1690 that followed Leopold's protracted political campaign to have the young Joseph declared King of the Romans, the future Holy Roman Emperor.[18] On 4 March the twelve-year-old boy made a ceremonial entry into Vienna; his name day was a couple of weeks later, on 19 March, which would have provided an appropriate occasion for the first performance of his father's work. Certainly, its largely unostentatious nature, set in the minor key and with sparing use of two concertante violins, would have made it suitable for Lent. By the time Reinhardt compiled his *Rubriche Generali,* the hymn was a standard component of the two vespers services on that feast day and continued to be sung up to 1741.

In total, forty sacred compositions are attributed to Leopold, covering almost the full range of liturgical music: a mass, a requiem mass, two settings of the *Salve Regina,* one *Stabat Mater,* ten hymns, and several motets and offertories.[19] The absence of a setting of a *Te Deum* is significant. Leopold's preferred musical response in sacred music was a reserved, melancholy one, not a jubilant one, and most of his output is set in the minor key. Undoubtedly his most affecting exploration of this aspect of his personality is a set of three movements ('Lectio Prima, Secundo, Tertia') that he composed in 1676 following the death of his music-loving second wife, Claudia Felicitas, aged twenty-two and after only three and a half years of marriage.[20] Designed to be performed during the three all-night vigils that preceded the funeral service, the three movements show a consistently sensitive control of instrumental and vocal sonority. The performing forces consist of two muted cornetts that play solo roles, four solo violas, a five-part vocal ensemble that sing chorally and soloistically, doubling instruments (two trombones and a bassoon), double bass and organ. With this low centre of instrumental gravity and set successively in C minor, E flat and C minor, the movements all make a journey from a slow instrumental introduction ('sonata') to a final section for voices only; in between, complementary paragraphs of music move between concertante writing for instruments and voices, recitative, homophony and imitation. In this work, Leopold provided the ultimate example of the interrelationship of the personal, the religious and the musical. Over succeeding decades it became a fixed part of Habsburg history too, performed following Leopold's death in 1705, the death of his third wife, Eleonora Magdalena Theresia, in 1720, and on similar occasions through to the end of Karl VI's reign.

Johann Joseph Fux: composer and theorist

REINHARDT worked alongside Fux from 1693 onwards, witnessing his steady rise through the ranks, from composer to Vice-Kapellmeister (1713) and Kapellmeister (1715), his favoured status under Emperor Karl VI, plus his wider presence in the city as Vice-Kapellmeister (1705–12) and then Kapellmeister (1712–15) at Stephansdom. He would have regarded him as the single most important composer of sacred music that had served the court, someone whose music was inextricably linked with its values. Fux's output of liturgical music extends to more than 405 works, probably the largest corpus of Catholic liturgical music by anyone in the period, most of which was prompted by the needs of the imperial court in

Vienna. It included nearly 100 settings of the mass, 116 motets, graduals and offertories, nearly seventy Marian antiphons, and forty-eight works for vesper services.[21] While sacred music by other composers, such as Giovanni Felice Sances, Antonio Caldara and Emperor Leopold, was a constant part of the repertory, Fux's music dominated, particularly as repeated repertoire items. With Reinhardt he formed a sustained partnership that defined the character and function of liturgical music at court.

Most of Fux's masses have identifying titles that link them with the circumstances that first prompted their composition, useful too in any general conversation between Kapellmeister, Reinhardt and emperor that needed to identify a particular work. Inevitably, the most common kind of title was one that featured a saint's name, indicating the name day on which the mass was first performed; to a certain extent that association held for subsequent performances, though practicalities sometimes led to masses being performed on other occasions and thus acquiring an alternative title. Saints celebrated in this way by Fux include Leopold, Joseph and Karl; the influence of Jesuit teaching at the court is indicated through masses dedicated to St Ignatius and St Aloysius; other saints associated with individual masses included St John, St Michael and St Ludmilla (the grandmother of St Wenceslas, the popular Bohemian saint). More individual are titles that evoke a particular human characteristic, especially those arising out of *pietas austriaca*: *Missa Charitatis* (affection), *Missa Confidentiae* (trust), *Missa Humilitatis* (humility), *Missa Temperentiae* (moderation), *Missa Constantiae* and *Missa Fortitudinis* (constancy and fortitude, the two components of Karl VI's motto). Tellingly, none of these masses has trumpets and timpani, deliberately projecting themselves as unostentatious, a meaningful alternative to the splendour of masses with trumpets and timpani. Beyond general sonority, it was very difficult for any one of these masses to promote a particular named quality consistently, given the contrasts of the text of the Ordinary, although standard musical responses to individual phrases such as 'Kyrie eleison, Christe eleison' and 'Credo in unum Deo' would naturally do so – humility for the former, fortitude for the latter. Nevertheless, for trained ears, like those of Leopold, Joseph and Karl, the extent to which individual masses drew attention to certain phrases and underplayed others was part of the listening and spiritual experience, a form of connoisseurship readily acknowledged in visual arts of the time but almost wholly unrecognized in music.

To gain a better appreciation of the relationship between the kind of music, its function within the church calendar and the wider symbolism of Habsburg authority and power, one can turn to Fux's treatise on musical composition, *Gradus ad Parnassum*, a compelling and unique source. Published in Vienna in 1725, the volume came to define Fux's legacy, a codification of compositional practice, especially counterpoint, that was to influence musical pedagogy for well over two centuries.[22] Fux's treatise was written in Latin; by the end of the eighteenth century it had been translated into English, German, French and Italian. This wider distribution removed the treatise from its immediate formative context, a staunchly Catholic court at the beginning of the eighteenth century, and it became widely regarded as a training manual that promoted technical fluency, an unfortunate misrepresentation of the original. For Fux, technical mastery was certainly important and the measured didacticism of the treatise is a core attribute, but the wider purpose of this mastery is equally apparent throughout.

Focussing on the means and forgetting the end has distorted appreciation of the volume. It was written by Fux, the skilled composer and equally skilled teacher, but very much in his capacity as Habsburg Kapellmeister. It was printed by Johann Peter van Ghelen, the court printer, and the costs were met by the emperor himself. In reality, it was the official view of the imperial court in such matters and when, two years later, it was followed by Reinhardt's manual on the practicalities of delivering church music, the emperor, Kapellmeister and Maestro di Concerti would have celebrated the interdependence of the two volumes, as well as their accumulated authority.

Fux's title, *Gradus ad Parnassum*, was taken from a very different manual, one on Latin versification that had first appeared in 1687.[23] To project the relationship between the attainment of artistic mastery and the patronage of the Habsburg court, the title-page is preceded by an elaborate engraving that shows the many steps that lead to Parnassus, contained within a larger frame that is replete with musical and Habsburg imagery (see Fig. 2). The pupil, who is carrying his portfolio of compositions, has negotiated a long path to Parnassus that was sometimes difficult (the threatening rock), but essentially civilizing (the standard use of a curve to indicate sophistication); his diligence and his role as an example to others is suggested by three figures at the beginning of their journey, one of whom seems to aspire to follow while the other two have fallen by the wayside or, at least, are resting. Apollo, the God of music and poetry, sets his lyre to one side in order to place a laurel crown (the traditional sign of immortality) on the head of the pupil, watched in the background by two groups of three muses. Above them is the winged horse, Pegasus, the favourite of the muses.

The outer frame places the achievement of the pupil in a wider context. At the central apex of the two frames, and overlapping both, is the imperial double-headed eagle, carrying a sceptre on the left (divine authority) and a sword on the right (military prowess); on its breast lies the court of arms of the Austrian household and it is nested underneath the crown of the Holy Roman Emperor. At the top of the frame, almost breaking the bounds of the frame itself, are various musical instruments: trumpets, timpani, harp, viola da gamba, cornett, lyre and organ. One of the trumpets even has the imperial banner attached. The music itself, a roll on the left (the score) and a sheaf on the right (the performing parts), are inserted between the instruments. At the foot of the engraving there are instruments associated with recreation – lute, viol and panpipes – together with masks that suggest music for the dance and the theatre; the format of the

2 Frontispiece from Fux, *Gradus ad Parnassum*, 1725

music manuscript, oblong and with only a few staves, also suggests dance music.

Most of the treatise is laid out in the form of a dialogue between the teacher, Aloysius, and his pupil, Josephus, an idealized series of lessons in which the teacher is nurturing and patient, the pupil keen and respectful. This could be viewed as reflecting some of the self-conscious virtues of the court, in particular humility and industry, but Fux identifies himself as the pupil, Josephus, and Aloysius as his teacher, a reverse of the expected relationship and a nice conceit on the commonplace view that a good teacher never stops learning, particularly from an industrious and capable pupil. Aloysius was a sixteenth-century Jesuit who was canonized a year after the publication of Fux's *Gradus* and, in using that name, the author may well have wished to ally himself with the authoritative nature of Jesuit teaching that was so prized by the Habsburg family. But it is another Aloysius that is specifically identified by Fux, Aloysius Praenestinus, that is the composer Giovanni Pierluigi Palestrina (1525/6–94). There could not be a more potent indication of musical lineage, one that was entirely in keeping with the history of the court in general.

During his lifetime, Palestrina was closely involved with the reforming tendencies in the Catholic Church that laid the musical foundations of the Counter-Reformation. Following the precepts of the Council of Trent, he revised several of the church's books of plainchant, and his *Missa Papae Marcelli* was probably composed as an exemplar of the strictures laid down by the council on intelligibility of text. When the then Habsburg Kapellmeister, Jacob Vaet, died in 1568, Palestrina was the first to be offered the job; he declined because he thought the music budget that Emperor Maximilian III was offering was insufficient.[24] Despite this snub, the music of Palestrina, especially his hymns, was performed in the imperial court throughout the seventeenth century and for much of the eighteenth too. For Fux the composer, Palestrina was a luminary, the 'light of light', a model for his own work and part of a general Italian musical inheritance that he, as an Austrian from Styria, had willingly joined. By placing himself squarely in the legacy of Palestrina, Fux was affirming the success of the Counter-Reformation and the role of music in the Catholic religion, and, as imperial Kapellmeister, the resolute contribution of the Habsburg dynasty to both.

Fux is quite clear about the main function of music:

> I judge that no one could doubt that, just as sacred things are above worldly ones in dignity, so music offered up for divine worship, destined to last eternally, is much nobler than other music, and special care should be given to it. And because God is the highest perfection, it is fitting that harmony offered in His praise should conform to all the rigour of the rules, attaining perfection insofar as human imperfection allows, and should be supplied with all suitable means of exciting devotion.[25]

Fux proceeds to divide his 'music offered up for divine worship' into three styles. His first is historically loaded, the 'Stylus a Capella'. Fux's account begins: 'It is well known that in early times the Divine Offices were sung by voices only.' Although it is not clear whether Fux is here referring to the singing of plainsong or to Renaissance polyphony, the point is the same: the absolute primacy of the human voice. 'So', Aloysius continues, 'in "a Capella" style very great care must be taken over the ease and naturalness of the singing.'[26] Aloysius recommends one of his own masses for study, humorously naming one by Fux (the *Missa Vicissitudinis*), even though he is nominally the pupil, before proclaiming Palestrina as 'the prince of this style'. Mastering the style, through study and practice, is the prime goal of *Gradus ad Parnassum*, 'for he who is strong in the understanding of these things comes close to the ability to do them'.[27] Thus sacred music at the imperial court is linked firmly to the Catholic inheritance, an aural equivalent to the lives of the saints or the recurring features of church painting and architecture.

Modern definitions of the term *a cappella* are not helpful when it comes to understanding its usage by Fux and others. Fux divides it into two types, voices alone and voices supported by other instruments. He hints at the difficulty of the first, in comparison with the second, and its privileged position at the imperial court: it 'is still kept up in as many cathedral churches as can do it: and in the Emperor's court, for forty years, through the singular piety of our most venerable monarch, and through reverence for divine worship.'[28] The second type maintains the primacy of the voice and the text but allows instruments to support them, a practice that Palestrina himself was familiar with in an *ad hoc* way, but which had become fairly routine in sacred music at the imperial court, as is evident from Reinhardt's *Rubriche Generali*. It could be the discrete support of organ alone, or with added strings doubling the appropriate voices, or, especially distinctive, an ensemble of cornett and two trombones doubling the soprano, alto and tenor lines.

Fux's *Gradus* does not relate musical style to the church calendar; this is where Reinhardt's *Rubriche* is revealing. In Advent and Lent, Reinhardt prescribes that certain services should be *a cappella* without instruments, other services *a cappella* with instruments, a distinction that may have been borne out of expediency: with so much music to perform, supporting voices with instruments was a sure way to deliver it with minimal rehearsal.

Like other composers who wrote sacred music for the court, Fux often used the description 'a capella' in the titles of his masses to indicate its style and, from that, the two periods of the year, Advent and Lent, for which they were suited. More common was the description 'missa in contrapunto', an indication of polyphonic ambition. Mastery of a style that had sprung from sixteenth-century Rome was for Fux the ultimate sign of devotion. Accordingly, his most complex *a cappella* mass was dedicated to Karl VI, the *Missa Sancti Caroli*, composed sometime between 1712 and 1718.[29] It was not intended to be performed on Karl's name day of 4 November – that was an occasion for a work with trumpets and timpani – but it was the ultimate display of musical learning which Karl, the literate musician, would have studied from the autograph manuscript. Perhaps it was presented as a tribute to the emperor when Fux became full Kapellmeister in 1715. Across the customary six movements of the Ordinary – Kyrie eleison, Gloria, Credo, Sanctus, Benedictus and Agnus Dei – Fux uses fifteen different contrapuntal matrices for the deployment of his four vocal parts, all clearly and proudly labelled. For instance, in the Kyrie eleison there are two interlocking pairs of voices that proceed in strict canon: the bass is answered a ninth higher by the alto, while the soprano is answered a ninth lower by the tenor. The Sanctus is a four-part canon, with the tenor answering the bass at the fifth, the alto answering at the octave and the soprano at the twelfth. The whole has a mathematical beauty that reaches back further than even Palestrina, to the concealed complexities of settings by medieval composers.

Thirty-one pages of the *Gradus ad Parnassum* are devoted to the 'Stylus a Capella' with eleven music examples. Fux's other styles, two in number, take up a mere six and a half pages between them, with only seven music examples. The 'Stylus Mixtus' is mixed in the sense that it embraces compositional outlooks that are more modern, that is vocal music which may include solo sections, duets and trios as well as choral sections, and independent instrumental writing in introductory, intermediary and concluding sections. Fux has reservations about this style. On the one hand the composer should 'have care to make the music pleasing to hear and filling the listeners' minds with delight'; on the other hand, there is a danger of impropriety: 'do not confuse this style with the manner of theatrical and dance music in the way that many do.'[30] Clearly this is why images of the theatre and the dance are relegated to the bottom of the frontispiece of the treatise, a long way from Parnassus.

Fux's third category is 'Stylus Recitativus', that is recitative or, as the author calls it, 'oratorical speech'. Fux is more sympathetic to recitative than he is to the excesses of the mixed style, probably because it, too, had a historical pedigree, in this case back to the early seventeenth century in the music of Monteverdi and others, and because by definition it privileges the text. He quotes several bars from his own setting of a psalm, 'Domine, ne in furore tuo arguas me' for voice with the accompaniment of strings and organ, pointing out that 'recitative can be introduced where in a speech of supplication we express our feeling to God'. In the remainder of this section, Fux acknowledges the power of the style in secular music too. 'Secular music is composed for the sake of refreshing the minds of the listeners, and diverting them to various emotions: the following are the feelings to be expressed in recitative: anger, pity, fear, force, anxiety, voluptuousness and love.'[31]

After this, the treatise rather rushes to a close, but not before Fux turns his attention once more to the tension between tradition and innovation in church music. Prompted by the young Joseph's knowing question, with supercilious parenthesis: 'What advice do you give about composing arias (as they are commonly called)?', Aloysius's reply is a diplomatic one, at least initially. Later, his real views are vividly expressed:

> What fixed advice would I give about an arbitrary kind of music which is subject to constantly changing taste? I by no means disapprove of the cult of novelty, but give it the greatest praise. For, if a middle-aged man were to enter today in a dress worn fifty or sixty years ago, he would certainly expose himself to the risk of being laughed at. Thus also music is to be adapted to the age. But I have never seen or heard someone tell of a tailor so enthusiastic about novelty that he puts the sleeves of a tunic at the thigh or knees: nor is there any architect so stupid that he puts the foundations of a building in the roof.[32]

Fux was sixty-five years old when *Gradus ad Parnassum* was completed, chronically suffering from gout. Older than the middle-aged man described by Aloysius, he was clearly conscious that his music was being overtaken by new developments and wished to assert the values of inherited tradition. While this tension between the progressive and the traditional is commonplace in musical history, it had a particular resonance in this time and place, the second decade of the eighteenth century in Vienna, since Fux's church music was not the product of an unfettered spirit but of an absolutist court. In that sense Fux, too, was an absolutist and, unfortunately for him and for the wider musical reputation of the imperial court, other parts of Europe, both Catholic and Protestant, had already developed a more musically liberating style of church music.

CHAPTER 4

Italian Opera and the Preservation of the Habsburg Dynasty

Opera, representation and identity

THE steady cyclical unfolding of the church year, from birth, to death, to resurrection, occasioned most of the music composed and performed at the Habsburg court. Opera also had a fixed role, similarly predictable in time, place and purpose. Although the art form never dealt directly with religion, it enjoined and celebrated virtues that were present in the Catholic liturgy at court, as well as sharing a basic theatricality. At one level, it could offer entertainment, but the control that the court exerted over its nature and development over the thirty years or more either side of 1700 meant that it had an identity that was entirely consonant with political and social values. In that, it was highly peculiar to Vienna.

Its principal language was, overwhelmingly, Italian and most of its practitioners, such as the composers Carlo Agostino Badia (1672–1738), Giovanni Bononcini (1670–1747), Antonio Caldara (c. 1670–1736), Francesco Bartolomeo Conti (1681–1732), Antonio Draghi (1634/6–1700) and Giuseppe Porsile (1680–1750), and the librettists Donato Cupeda (c. 1661–1704), Nicolò Minato (c. 1630–1698), Pietro Pariati (1665–1733), Silvio Stampiglia (1661–1725) and Apostolo Zeno (1668–1750), were attracted to the imperial court because of its long-standing cultural allegiance with Italy. Between them, these eleven individuals were involved in the composition of over 250 operatic works for the Habsburg court, works ranging in scope from one-act compositions, for a few soloists and a small orchestral ensemble, to five-act works, for the full resources of singers, chorus, dancers and large orchestra, and lasting five or more hours. One crucial characteristic of this repertoire was that it was a private one, for the court and its guests and, unlike church music, which willingly embraced the city in its familiar pattern of processions and services, the Vienna court opera did not get beyond the confines of the court, even on the grandest of occasions such as the performances of *Angelica, vincitrice di Alcina* in 1716. But operatic performances were not a secret: two court newspapers, the Italian *Il Corriere ordinario* and, from 1703, the German *Wienerisches Diarium*, regularly reported the operas that were performed and, of greater importance, the occasion that prompted the performance.

Unlike church music, which was a constant daily presence at the court, opera was presented only at specific times of the year. As was the practice in Italy, there was usually a new opera in Carnival (*Fasching*), the cold, grey weeks that preceded Lent, sometimes two; repeat performances were also given in the period. Name days and birthdays of the emperor and empress, and sometimes other members of the court, prompted new works every year but, given that these were specific occasions, designated as Gala Days, the associated opera was not usually given a repeat performance. Although the actual day of celebration was often moved a few days either side of the name day or birthday, this commitment to particular days of the year could result in a very uneven distribution of operatic performances and a strain on the musical and theatrical resources of the court. From the mid-1680s onwards five or six operas were typically given every year, reasonably distributed across the calendar: the birthday of Empress Eleonora Magdalena Theresia on 13 January; a Carnival opera; Emperor Leopold's birthday on 9 June; the name day of the empress on 22 July; and the name day of the emperor on 15 November. When the birthday of the heir, Joseph, was added to the sequence, 26 July, the Carnival opera was sometimes omitted to keep the number of new works at six or fewer per annum, something that also saved money, an abiding concern.[1] During the short reign of Emperor Joseph the pattern was a Carnival opera followed by the name day of Joseph (19 March), birthday of Empress Amalia Wilhelmine (21 April), name day of the empress (10 July) and birthday of Joseph (26 July); in addition, the birthday (1 October) and/or name day (4 November) of Joseph's brother, Karl, was usually marked by a new opera, filling the gap between July and the following Carnival. When Karl succeeded his brother as emperor, the annual sequence became a very lopsided one. The emperor and empress both had their birthdays and name days between August and November (birthday of Empress Elisabeth, 28 August; birthday of Karl, 1 October; name day of Karl, 4 November; and name day of Elisabeth, 17 November). As a result, in many years no operas were given between the end of Carnival in February and the end of August.[2]

In addition to these standard annual patterns, additional works were sometimes given, for name days of other members of the court and, more spectacularly, as part of the festivities associated with marriages, such as those of Joseph I to Princess Amalia Wilhelmine of Braunschweig-Lüneberg in 1699,[3] the future Karl VI to Princess Elisabeth Christine of Braunschweig-Wolfenbüttel in 1708,[4] and in 1716 the short-lived celebration of the birth of an heir, Archduke Leopold, *Angelica, vincitrice di Alcina*. While the death of an infant, even one destined to rule, was not a reason for a period of mourning, court protocol demanded a mourning period of up to a year following the death of an emperor. After the death of Leopold on 5 May 1705, no operas were performed until the following Carnival;[5] similarly, Joseph's death on 17 April 1711, barely a month after the performance of that year's name day opera, Bononcini's *Enea in Caonia*, put an immediate stop to the annual cycle and no operas were given for a whole year.[6] While those composers and performers primarily associated with church music continued in their duties, those who were almost exclusively associated with opera were able to leave Vienna temporarily while they waited to see the nature of the provision under the new emperor.

The tenacity with which the court held on to the practice of Carnival operas and operas for birthdays and name days is revealed by the ready acceptance of the practical consequences of having to present performances when the court was not resident in the Hofburg, but in the Favorita and at Laxenburg, occasionally elsewhere too. The presence of one, designated imperial opera house in Vienna that consistently supported and promoted the art form across the decades was not a characteristic. Instead, the court willingly expended substantial amounts of money on presenting operas in several locations, in purpose-built theatres, in small and large rooms that were modified for the purpose, and in the open air.

From early in Leopold's reign a former dance hall in the imperial complex had been converted into a theatre and was regularly used for Carnival operas. It had an unhappy early history. In 1683, when Turkish forces were already in the suburbs and the court had given the order for major buildings in those areas to be burnt, attention turned to how best to protect the inner city from imminent attack. Since the theatre was a wooden structure that abutted the defence wall, it was literally in the line of fire, one that might easily have spread to other parts of the Hofburg. A hurried decision was taken to demolish it. It was rebuilt but, for reasons that are not entirely clear, it was not used for several years, until 1697. Two years later an accidental fire led to its complete destruction. Under the direction of Francesco Galli-Bibiena, the celebrated theatre designer, it was once more rebuilt and became the principal venue for opera when the court was resident in Vienna.

Galli-Bibiena's theatre was a thoroughly modern one, using all his mastery of geometry to create a deep and natural perspective, spectacular stage sets of gardens and palaces, and, equally spectacular, swift changes of scenery. While the ground floor allowed members of the audience to sit on benches that faced the stage and others that ran at right angles to it, the three storeys of boxes had no seating. All this was designed to place the imperial family at its symbolic best. With individual seats they occupied two boxes opposite the stage, upper and lower, and were part of Galli-Bibiena's careful perspective, since the distance from the imperial boxes to the front of the stage was the same as that from the front of the stage to the back of the stage. Given what is known about similar theatres from the eighteenth century that survive, it was very likely also the best place for sound – direct, natural and clear. Social hierarchy was also figured into the design, creating the theatre of the theatre. Audience members on the ground floor were looked over by those in the boxes, while the standing occupants of the side boxes were able to look sideways in both directions, to the stage and towards the imperial box. This masterpiece of design and representation was used until the 1740s when it was converted back to its original use as a dance hall, this time for public use. As the Grosser

Redoutensaal it continued to play an occasional role in the city's musical history right up to the First World War.[7]

Next to the theatre there was a smaller room that retained its former function as a venue for dancing, while doubling up as a grand entrance hall into the theatre. In Karl VI's reign, it was occasionally used for opera performances, especially when the occasion did not warrant using the extensive resources of the main theatre. In the years following the Turkish siege, operas were also performed in various large rooms in the Hofburg. For the grandest of occasions, such as the marriage of Archduke Joseph and Princess Amalia Wilhelmine in February 1699, a courtyard within the imperial complex, the Burgplatz, was transformed into a natural theatre, the windows of the surrounding buildings becoming the equivalent of theatre boxes while, at the same time, offering some respite from the weather; no doubt the spectacular theatre of triumphant crowds and chariots drawn by real horses outshone any subtleties in the musical performance. For more routine occasions temporary theatres were sometimes erected in the gardens of the Hofburg.

When the court moved to Laxenburg, hunting was the main social attraction and opera performances of any kind were rarely given, helped in the reigns of Joseph and Karl by the convenience that no imperial name days or birthdays intruded into the pastime. The Favorita, however, in the outer suburbs in Vienna, was better placed to support opera and regularly saw performances, indoors and outdoors. Burnt to the ground during the Turkish siege, the palace was immediately rebuilt, including a medium-sized theatre whose auditorium measured approximately 100 × 50 feet, with probably a ground floor and a gallery. Here, for instance, operas celebrating the name day of Empress Amalia Wilhelmine and the weddings of two archduchesses were given – Maria Josepha to Crown Prince Friedrich August of Saxony in 1719, and Maria Amalia with Crown Prince Karl Albrecht of Bavaria in 1722.[8] As in the Hofburg in the inner city, other spacious rooms or lengthy galleries in the palace were used too. More entrancing was the open-air theatre in the gardens, built above a lake that was itself 300 feet in length and 62 feet wide. For operas with a pastoral or magical subject matter it was ideal, and it was here that Lady Mary Montagu attended a performance of *Angelica, vincitrice di Alcina* in 1716, an occasion marred only by the rainy weather that curtailed the performance. As the wife of the ambassador she would have had a designated seat but many people, as in the theatre in the Hofburg, had to stand for the duration of the performance. The rush to shelter from the rain and then to depart the gardens – 'the opera was broke off and the company crowded away in such confusion, I was almost squeezed to death' wrote Lady Mary – made for a rare break with protocol.

Opera attendance at the invitation of the imperial court was a complicated business, burdened with issues of propriety, precedence and status, and documented in all its minutiae by successive holders of the office of Obersthofmeister. Like the operas themselves, it was a predominantly serious and high-minded business, but could descend into the irrational and the comical. The fundamental consideration was status. On stage, status was acknowledged by the actions of emperors, princes and kings: their valour and beneficent deeds were rewarded, and the timely intervention of the gods enforced the essential righteousness of their actions. Similarly, the selection of the audience and where they sat according to precedent (established or concocted) reinforced the undisputed and undisputable quality of the ruler. For the individuals who were feted in the birthday, name day and wedding operas, it displayed their unimpeachable authority and integrity; for courtiers who attended the opera, it emphasized their collective self-worth as part of a reassuring hierarchy; and for those from outside the court, such as visiting royalty and resident foreign diplomats, it affirmed Habsburg power and prestige.

The emperor and the empress were the last to arrive and took their seats opposite the main stage, as if monitoring and commending the action. Here the difference in ceremonial between the sacred and the secular is a striking one. When the emperor and his guests attended individual churches in Vienna, such as the Augustinerkirche, Michaelerkirche and Stephansdom, they usually sat in a gallery to the right of the altar, very rarely in the nave. That way religious ceremony could be observed from close quarters but the centrality of the altar, the cross and the eucharist was acknowledged too. In the opera, however, the emperor and empress were central. They sat on individual armchairs on a slightly raised platform covered with red velvet and topped by a canopy. No one else had a canopy and a platform, but who was entitled to an armchair, as opposed to a chair with no arms, or a place on the benches, or no seating at all, was meticulously controlled.

Within the imperial family precedent and protocol were generally understood, but new members of the court and especially visiting dignitaries often caused knotty problems of precedence, solved by arcane expertise or ingenious invention. As direct representatives of their respective monarchs, ambassadors enjoyed the highest status. In the case of France, this was not always straightforward. Until 1701 the French had an envoy at the imperial court rather than an ambassador, a lower rank that had to be reflected in the allotted seating. Intractable problems of equivalence, between the hierarchies of varying foreign dynasties and between members of the aristocracy with similar sounding titles, were often resolved through the process of *incognito*, where individuals were invited in a personal capacity rather than a formal capacity or, alternatively, were formally invited to the dress rehearsal instead. When that proved unacceptable to the self-esteem of one or more individuals, the court sometimes resorted to the charade of sending formal invitations, having previously established that they would not be accepted.[9]

Although the Turkish siege of Vienna occurred between July and September 1683, the actual Turkish advance from their base in Adrianople had begun several months earlier, on 31 March; by 3 May they had reached

Belgrade. Leopold and his advisors were casually confident that the Turks could be halted in Hungary and, from there, repelled. But the imperial forces were slow to assemble and the Ottoman forces continued to advance.[10] Still, Leopold and his court maintained their routine. In June they were in Laxenburg, where on 9 June they celebrated the emperor's birthday with a new opera by Antonio Draghi, *La lira d'Orfeo,* given in the open air – a fable on the power of music, intended as a tribute to Leopold's own musicianship on his forty-third birthday. In fact, several years earlier Leopold himself had written an intermezzo, in Spanish, on the subject, *Orfeo y Euridice.*[11] Only the text and the ballet music of Draghi's work have survived. In this version of the myth, Euridice is not lost to the underworld; instead, the libretto focuses on Orpheus's ability to repel evil gods and belligerent human beings with the power of his lute playing, a gift directly bestowed by Apollo.[12] In real life, the infidel showed no signs of being repelled. As if oblivious to reality, Leopold went from Laxenburg to Perchtolsdorf for a spot of hunting, returning to Vienna only on 7 July. That was when reality struck and the immediate decision was taken to flee westwards, first to Passau and then to Linz. Although the siege ended in September, there was no name day opera for Leopold that year and the birthday opera for the empress, Draghi's *Gl'elogii,* was given in Linz in January 1684 because the Hofburg was not yet ready for habitation.[13]

In a general sense, all operatic works presented at the Habsburg court were about the emperor, or rather the emperor as an embodiment of certain values: integrity, valour, loyalty, compassion, and so forth. Greek heroes were the subject of some operas, such as Achilles the warrior (*Achille in Tessaglia,* given for the name day of the empress in 1681); Telemachus the son of Odysseus who went in search of his missing father (*Il Telemaco, overo Il valore coronato,* given for the emperor's name day in 1689),[14] and Themistocles, the Athenian politician who saved Greece from Persian rule (*Temistocle in Persia,* given for the emperor's birthday in 1681). There were a number of operas about individuals from Greek mythology with softer skills that were easily associated with Leopold: as well as Orpheus they included Apollo, the god of light, music and poetry (*Il tempio d'Apollo in Delfo,* given for the name day of the empress in 1682) and Ovid's Pygmalion, the sculptor who fell in love with a statue he had carved (*Pigmaleone in Cipro,* given for the birthday of the empress in 1689). Leopold's own contributions to opera, typically two or three numbers, tend not to be in works of an overtly heroic character, a self-knowing trait that was in keeping with contemporary accounts of him as someone who was not forceful or aggressive and, more broadly, someone who personified the attributes of *pietas austriaca* that were constantly promoted in liturgical music.

As well as being a competent composer, Leopold was a keen and capable dancer well into his fifties, presenting an elegant stage presence that belied his unfortunate personal appearance (see Fig. 3). He had established a troupe of dancers, usually eight in number and recruited from Paris, who

3 Emperor Leopold I in costume, by Jan Thomas, 1667

came under the guidance of a Hoftanzmeister, who, like the Kapellmeister, reported directly to the Obersthofmeister. The Hoftanzmeister also taught the imperial children to dance.[15] The one-act opera *La moglie ama meglio* (The Wife loves the Husband), composed by Draghi for Leopold's birthday in 1689 includes an aria by Leopold as its penultimate number, 'Dunque son nato'.[16] The opera was followed by a ballet in which five members of his family participated: his wife Eleonora Magdalena Theresia, the ten-year-old heir to the throne, Joseph I, two daughters, Maria Elisabeth (aged eight), Maria Anna (aged six) and the youngest of them all, the future Karl VI, who was just three.[17] Following the example of the imperial family, dancing, to a greater extent even than musical ability, was an expected social accomplishment at court, practised by all – ladies, gentlemen, pages and dwarves. In the largest of operas, such as *Angelica, vincitrice di Alcina*, the professional dancers were supplemented in the concluding scenes by capable amateurs, with everybody paying direct homage to the emperor.

During Leopold's long reign there was another dramatic genre, sacred rather than secular, which featured annually alongside Carnival, birthday and name day operas, the *sepolcro*. Usually written in Italian, the *sepolcro* was performed on Maundy Thursday and Good Friday in the Hofburgkapelle, where a representation of Christ's tomb was erected in front of the altar. The ultimate focus was reflection on the meaning of the crucifixion and the resurrection, prompted by the thoughts and actions of named biblical characters presented alongside those of allegorical figures, such as Faith, Sin, Death and Hope. At appropriate moments, the cast would provide some elementary acting, such as weeping, kneeling or carrying the cross, and, as in performances of secular works at court, the audience was provided with a printed libretto, in German as well as in the original Italian. Musically, these sacred dramas provided a striking contrast to the *a cappella* masses that occurred in liturgical services in the Hofburgkapelle during Lent; their importance within the performing traditions of the court is attested by their inclusion in Reinhardt's *Rubriche Generali*.[18]

Although Joseph I's reign was a short one – a few weeks short of six years – the energy and determination that were evident in his handling of the challenges that confronted the Habsburg court, especially the continuing War of the Spanish Succession, were also evident in his attitude towards opera at court, revealing the same flair, even daring. It was during his reign that the new opera house was completed in the Hofburg and the number of operatic works presented every year increased to an average of ten. Alongside facilities and expenditure there were initiatives in terms of personnel that signalled a new, determinedly international presence for Italian opera at court.

The first opera to be presented after the official year of mourning was a pastoral opera, *Endimione*, for the name day of Empress Amalia Wilhelmine in July 1706. Not without a touch of ironic indifference, given the womanizing ways of the emperor, it celebrated the happy marriage of the shepherd Endymion and Selene, the goddess of the moon; she was so smitten with him that she asked Zeus (Endymion's father) to grant him eternal youth (that, presumably, would have appealed to Joseph). It marked the debut of a new partnership of composer and librettist, Giovanni Bononcini and Silvio Stampiglia. At the age of thirty-five Bononcini was a composer who was regarded as a leading figure in Italian opera and whose works had been performed in Rome, Naples, London, Paris and elsewhere.[19] He had joined the musical court in Vienna in 1698, when a portion of his salary was paid by Joseph from his own funds, rather than from those of the Hofkapelle; clearly, Bononcini was to be associated with the new generation, rather than that of Leopold. In 1702, he was allowed to travel to Berlin, where he worked in the court of Queen Sophie Charlotte; during the year of mourning that followed Leopold's death, Bononcini returned to Italy where a new Carnival opera, *La regina creduta re,* was given in Venice. He had already collaborated with Stampiglia on over a dozen stage works: at Bononcini's behest Stampiglia, too, was engaged by Joseph I. During the next five years the pair completed six further works for the court, the main Carnival opera in each year plus, usually, either a work for the birthday or the name day of Joseph. The last of these works, *Enea in Caonia,* on the subject of the Greek hero Aeneus, was performed on the emperor's name day on 19 March 1711; less than a month later Joseph died. For the wider musical prestige of Italian opera at the court, as opposed to the long-standing preoccupation with self-representation, this early death cut short an operatic partnership that could have served it for many years, one that would have made Vienna one of the most forward looking centres of Italian opera in Europe.

Bononcini and Stampiglia seemed to have stayed in Vienna during the period of mourning following Joseph's death, dutifully and hopefully waiting with the other courtiers to find out if they were going to be engaged by the new emperor, Karl VI. In the event they were not. It seems that they had become too expensive to employ and were the victims of the dowager empress Eleonora Magdalena Theresia's emphasis on cutting costs. In this, she may have been supported by other, more conservative figures at court, such as Ziani, Fux and the increasingly influential Reinhardt. Bononcini and Stampiglia may even have been casualties of the prevalent mood; since the new emperor was much more like his father in manner – quiet, reserved and a poor conversationalist (he had inherited the camel lips) – he was also predisposed to preserve older traditions rather than continue with Joseph's more modern approach. Musically, it was a short-sighted decision.

For his part, Bononcini went on to pursue a career that took him to Paris and London, as well as back to his native Italy. While the imperial court performed only one more opera by him, *Alessandro in Sidone* in 1737, elsewhere his operas enjoyed a popularity that was independent of the presence of the composer. He was especially popular in London, where he was resident from 1720 to 1732, as a colleague of Handel, sometimes rival, in the Royal Academy opera company, the mainstay of Italian opera in the city. Although it enjoyed royal patronage, the London company was a commercial one and its performances were public ones; public, rather than private theatres were increasingly the norm in Italy too, in Venice, Rome, Naples, Milan and other cities. As the genre developed and its public popularity grew, Vienna as a centre of Italian opera became increasingly irrelevant. If Joseph, as the least cautious of the Habsburg emperors in the early eighteenth century, had allowed the genre to develop a public and commercial presence in the city, albeit one supported by the court, the history of opera in Vienna would have been a more dynamic and influential one in the early eighteenth century. He was certainly sympathetic. A castrato singer and poet named Francesco Ballerini, who was not formally a member of the Hofkapelle but another person who was paid from Joseph's private purse, petitioned the court for permission to erect a public opera house in Vienna, which would also serve the court. He was granted an imperial privilege, even a plot of land to the north-west of the Hofburg, but the nearby Minorite monastery and the city hospital objected on the grounds of noise and possible fire hazard. Nothing came of the plan and the permission lapsed on Joseph's death.[20]

Karl remained faithful to the tradition he knew. Only in the reign of Maria Theresia did court opera, in a new theatre, the Burgtheater, become a public form of entertainment, one managed at arm's length by the court but free, at last, to play its part in the evolution of the art form. By the 1780s it was able to support and enhance the career of Mozart, something that it had been incapable of doing for Bononcini. For the earlier composer there is a melancholy footnote to his career. Towards the end of his life, he returned to Vienna, where he was granted a pension by Empress Maria Theresia. It was not enough to live on and he was no longer at the forefront of operatic life. He died in the city in 1747, aged seventy-six and a forgotten figure.

After the death of Joseph I, a full calendar of opera performances at court did not resume until 1714, with a new group of composers providing the annual fare. From that year through to 1725, the Carnival opera was provided by Francesco Conti (1681–1732),[21] a competent enough composer but with limited experience as a composer of opera. He had joined the Habsburg court as a theorbo player in 1701, having previously worked for Cardinal Francesco Maria de' Medici in Florence, and it was as a player of that instrument that he earned his reputation, one enhanced by a visit to London in 1706–7. During Joseph's reign he composed two works, *Clotilde* for the 1706 Carnival (though it may not have been performed because of the period of mourning for Leopold I) and *Il trionfo dell'amicizia, e dell'amore* for the 1711 Carnival. On the basis of this very limited composing career, Conti was appointed one of two court composers in 1713, simultaneously maintaining his duties as a theorbo player. In addition to the annual Carnival opera, in most years Conti provided a second work, for one of the name days or birthdays.

Another indication of Karl's caution in the area of composition was his willingness to maintain the principle of advancement from within the court. Early in his reign Marc' Antonio Ziani, aged sixty or so, was promoted from Vice-Kapellmeister to full Kapellmeister; he composed one complete opera and one act of a second, multi-authored work before he died in January 1715.[22] Karl's favouring of Fux also had consequences on the operatic life of the court. His promotion to Vice-Kapellmeister in 1713 and Kapellmeister in 1715 was a clear demonstration of the primacy of church music, and his operatic contribution was usually restricted to composing a stage work for Karl's birthday. The first of these in his new position as Kapellmeister was a setting of the Orpheus story, *Orfeo ed Euridice* – like the earlier work of Draghi for Emperor Leopold, a tribute to the emperor as musician and as patron.[23] A one-act work with seven scenes, it was performed in a large room in the Favorita, an intimate piece that eschewed the spectacular scenic effects of opera presented in theatres or outdoors. There are six characters plus a chorus, and the story begins with Orfeo announcing his intention to journey to the underworld so that he can be reunited with Euridice. Eventually, it is Jupiter, in a gesture of magnanimity on his birthday, who commands Pluto to set Euridice free. The denouement comprises a chorus in elegantly poised minuet rhythms: 'No day has ever equalled the honour of this day. Never before today has Aurora [the goddess of the dawn] appeared more brightly' ('Non v'è giorno che contrasti suoi fasti a questo di. Più seren' in sino ad ora mai l'Aurora non uscì'). In the following *licenza* Amor steps forward to declaim, explicitly, the link between Jupiter and 'great Augustus' ('grande Augusto'), that is the emperor, before the chorus is repeated once more, this time with the focus switched on to Karl's birthday rather than the *lieto fine* of the plot.

One notable appointment by Emperor Karl went against the grain of caution, that of Antonio Caldara (c. 1670–1736). Born in Venice, he had been a chorister and cellist at St Mark's, worked for the Duke of Mantua and Prince Ruspoli in Rome, before becoming acquainted with Karl during his time in Spain.[24] Like Bononcini, he was an opera composer whose experience and ability were far greater than those of any of the composers already employed at the imperial court. Caldara travelled to Vienna in 1712 in the hope of gaining a position, but nothing came of it. Four years later, in 1716, following Fux's appointment to Kapellmeister, Karl appointed Caldara, rather than either of the two court composers, Badia and Conti, to the vacant position of Vice-Kapellmeister. Sensibilities required this gifted composer of opera to be slotted into a working pattern that did not offend Conti and Fux, who together had supplied most of the operas up to that point. Karl's solution was a diplomatic one: Conti continued to compose the Carnival opera and Fux, as Kapellmeister, remained the preferred choice for one-off occasions such as the birth of the male heir, Leopold, in 1716 and the wedding of Archduchess Maria Amalia and Crown Prince Karl Albrecht of Bavaria in 1722; for the most part Caldara was entrusted with the composition of works for birthdays and name days.

It was to take more than ten years and the declining health of Conti and Fux before Caldara became the undisputed senior composer of opera at the Habsburg court.[25]

A coronation in Prague (1723):
political unity and musical conservatism

THE political issue that preoccupied Karl for most of his reign was dynastic succession: who would follow him as ruler of the Austrian lands and, in keeping with long-standing precedent, as the elected Holy Roman Emperor?[26] As a young man, he himself had never expected to be the reigning emperor in Vienna and had, instead, enthusiastically embraced his position as King of Spain, with a court located in Barcelona, a staging post, he hoped, to the one he intended to establish in Madrid. The premature death of his brother, Joseph I, without a male heir, meant that the succession passed to Karl, a course of action previously agreed by the two brothers and their father, Leopold, in 1703. In fact, that agreement had gone a step further, dealing with the not-so-fanciful possibility of the complete absence of male heirs (at the time, Joseph had two daughters and had already lost a son, and Karl was not yet married). They agreed that if that possibility ever became a reality, then the succession should pass to the eldest female of the reigning emperor.

When Karl became emperor and moved to Vienna, he had already been married for three years, to Elisabeth Christine of Brunswick-Wolfenbüttel, but had no children. Two years later, there were still no children. In these vexing circumstances Karl decided that he should turn the private agreement into a public decree and in April 1713 issued the Pragmatic Sanction that allowed female succession in the Habsburg dynasty, fully realizing its incendiary nature. A female succession would have to be accepted by the territories directly ruled by the Habsburgs, those that chose the Holy Roman Emperor and, to maintain the newly configured balance of power that was emerging at the end of the War of the Spanish Succession, other major European powers. The emperor still had time on his side and when a son, Leopold, was born in 1716, he and his advisors must have hoped that the provisions of the Pragmatic Sanction could be put to one side. All this would have been in the minds of the audience that attended the celebration opera *Angelica, vincitrice di Alcina* later that year, only to be thrown into doubt a few weeks later when the infant Leopold died, just seven months old.

The empress was already pregnant with her second child, duly born on 13 May 1717, a girl christened Maria Theresia. When, a year later, a second daughter was born, Maria Anna, the provisions of the Pragmatic Sanction became a real concern once more. Within the court, opera played its part in these preoccupations. From 1721 a new occasion was often added to the annual cycle of opera presentations, the name day of Maria Theresia,

15 October (the feast of St Theresa of Avila), squeezed into the already congested autumn period between her father's birthday and her father's name day.[27] Relatively meaningless to the four-year-old Maria, this was the first time that an archduchess had been honoured in this way.

Meanwhile, Karl had embarked on his lengthy project of gaining wider political approval for the Pragmatic Sanction. In many ways, the most acquiescent territory was Bohemia. Prague, rather than Vienna, had been the main seat of the Habsburg dynasty as recently as the reign of Rudolph II (1576–1612); it had embraced the Counter-Reformation; and it lacked the rebellious tendencies evident in Hungary, ones that the Turks had managed to exploit. Many Bohemian aristocrats, such as the Collalto, Kinsky, Lobkowitz and Schwarzenberg families, who built new palaces in Vienna in the reigns of Leopold, Joseph and Karl, had summer palaces in the attractive countryside of Bohemia, while religious foundations founded by the Jesuits, Augustinians, Benedictines and Cistercians were as evident in the Bohemian kingdom as in the neighbouring Austrian archduchy. Like his predecessors, Karl dealt sympathetically with the longer historical inheritance of Bohemia, allowing it to maintain its status as a kingdom. When the assembled Bohemian and Moravian estates accepted the tenets of the Pragmatic Sanction in 1722, both sides willingly agreed that Karl should be crowned King of Bohemia in Prague the following year, a demonstration of shared identity and the first coronation for sixty-six years.

The ceremony was set for September 1723. Late summer and early autumn was already the busiest time in the calendar of the Habsburg court, with a number of sacred and secular celebrations, but, rather than a short visit of a few days to Prague in September, the court took the decision to be in residence in the Bohemian capital from July to mid-November, broadly the period they would normally have spent at the Favorita. For four months, Karl was to be demonstrably both the Holy Roman Emperor and the King of Bohemia, and many of the practices of the court that would have taken place at the Favorita and in the Hofburg were transferred to Prague. The coronation ceremony itself was to be held in the cathedral of St Vitus, Prague's equivalent to Stephansdom; the court was to be in residence at the castle, within walking distance of the cathedral, as in Vienna; and there were a number of short excursions to Brandeis (Brandýs nad Labem), a medieval castle ten miles to the north-east of Prague for hunting, equivalent to the annual visits to Laxenburg. The main celebratory opera, *Costanza e Fortezza*, was to be a huge spectacle, given outdoors in the late evening and benefiting from the experience of presenting works such as *Angelica, vincitrice di Alcina* in the gardens of the Favorita; and Fux, the court Kapellmeister, was to be its composer. Finally, while the main church ceremony was to be in the cathedral and others in the chapel of the castle, several services during the period were to be held in churches in the city, reflecting continuing practice in Vienna. In essence, Prague was to be the imperial capital for a few months.

On 4 June a notice in the *Wienerisches Diarium* reported that musicians, opera props, chaplains and servants were leaving that day for Prague, to prepare for the transfer of the court. The musical personnel were headed by the Music Director, Prince Ludwig Pius of Savoy, Kapellmeister Fux, Vice-Kapellmeister Caldara, court composer and theorbo player Francesco Conti (with his son, Ignace, a mediocre theorbo player who would never advance further than court scholar), Kilian Reinhardt, two organists, three female sopranos, six male sopranos, five male altos, five tenors, four basses, thirteen violinists, four cellists, two double bassists, one cornetto player, four oboists, two bassoonists, four trumpeters, two trombonists, one timpanist, one porter, one assistant, two organ tuners/repairers and a lute maker. Prince Ludwig, Fux and Caldara had a carriage each, the singers Rosa and Franz Borosini shared a carriage and the remaining personnel travelled in fifteen wagons. One wagon carried the orchestral instruments, another a chamber organ and several harpsichords, and, a striking indication of the busy schedule that lay ahead, two wagons were required for the music itself. Finally, seven wagons carried general luggage.[28] This wagon train would have taken approximately a week to travel to Prague; perhaps the individual carriages went separately and arrived sooner. The total number of musical personnel that were dispatched to Prague numbered sixty-nine, over half the available forces. The remaining instrumentalists and singers stayed in Vienna where, as a reasonably balanced body of performers, they were able to keep a reduced schedule of church services going, supervised by the most junior of the court composers, Giuseppe Porsile. No operas were given in Vienna during the absence of the emperor and empress.

According to the *Wienerisches Diarium* the emperor, empress and the two young archduchesses, Maria Theresia and Maria Anna, left Vienna on 19 June.[29] Theirs was a more leisurely journey that included a stay at Count Collalto's summer palace in Pirnitz (Brtnice) in Moravia, where the streets were decorated and, as was customary, the arrival of the imperial party was announced by trumpets and timpani.[30] By the end of the month they had arrived in Prague. A Marian day fell on 2 July, the Feast of the Visitation of the Blessed Virgin Mary. In Vienna, according to Reinhardt's *Rubriche Generali*, the first vespers and the mass were celebrated in the Favorita and the second vespers in the Jesuit church Am Hof, preceded by devotion at the foot of the Marian shrine in the square; in ceremonial terms it was an Ordinary occasion. For the first church service in Prague, this was upgraded to a Golden Fleece ceremony, attended by members of the order in their colourful robes. The first vespers were held in the castle chapel, the mass in the cathedral of St Veit and the second vespers in the church of St Nicolaus.[31] All these were within walking distance, if rather hilly, and it is safe to assume that processions to and from the castle and the churches took place. The feast of St Jacob (St James the Greater) took place on Sunday 25 July and this, too, was redesignated a Fleece service, probably because it represented a visit to the oldest church in Prague, St Jacob's on the other side of the Vltava river, in the so-called New Town.[32]

4 Galli-Bibiena's open-air theatre for *Costanza e Fortezza,* Prague, 1723

As part of this sensitive engagement with local Catholic traditions, the imperial court paid particular homage to John of Nepomuk, a fourteenth-century priest. According to popular Bohemian legend he had refused to divulge the confession of the wife of Wenceslas IV to the king, and was thrown, bound and gagged, into the river Vltava. Women of the imperial family had often entrusted themselves in prayer to this model priest confessor, a veneration that was practised throughout the Habsburg territories.[33] During her stay in Prague, Empress Elisabeth prayed at the tomb of John of Nepomuk in St Vitus cathedral on at least three occasions, each duly reported in the *Wienerisches Diarium.*[34]

Throughout July and August, work continued on building the open-air stage and auditorium for the coronation opera in an area below the riding school near the castle. Since January, there had been a new court theatre director, Giuseppe Galli-Bibiena, one of four members of that family who served the court. His design was on an unprecedentedly large scale, even for the Habsburg court and the Galli-Bibiena family, and was commemorated in a set of engravings.[35] As Fig. 4 suggests, the dimensions of the theatre were unconstrained.[36] It was 128 feet wide and 374 feet deep; especially eye-catching were the two onion-domed turrets either side of the stage, each over 70 feet high and easily read as a representation of Karl's motto and the title of Fux's opera, 'Constancy and Fortitude'. The proscenium was 56 feet wide, in front of which the orchestra sat in three elongated rows, an expansion of the typical seating arrangement in contemporary theatres, but to the point that it must have made ensemble difficult; at each end, there was a standing group of trumpets and timpani who feature extensively in the outer acts of Fux's opera, in left and right antiphony, and together. In the foreground, the engraving shows the raised dais with canopy on which the emperor and empress are seated and, to their side, the two archduchesses. Behind the dais the engraving shows only the first two of the twenty or more rows of the amphitheatre that contained the standing places. As in the theatre in the Hofburg in Vienna, seated accommodation was to the right and left, at right angles to the stage. Altogether, Galli-Bibiena's massive structure was reported to have held an audience of 4,000 people, though, as various details in the area around the raised dais of the emperor suggest, some of these people were servants and guards rather than invited guests.

Although Fux's opera was readily associated with the crowning of Karl VI as King of Bohemia, and was certainly remembered in subsequent decades as a coronation opera, in terms of the court calendar it was a birthday opera for the empress, Elisabeth Christine, one of twenty-five stretching from 1713 to 1740. Her birthday, on 28 August, initiated a particularly intense period of sacred and secular celebration that went on for nearly three weeks. It began very early in the morning of 28 August with a short one-act opera performed in the imperial quarters in the castle: *Il giorno felice: Componimento per Musica allusivo al glorioso giorno Natalizio della Sacra Cesarea, e Cattolica Reale Maestà di Elisabeth Cristina Imperatrice Regnante.*[37] The neutral sounding title 'Componimento' (literally, composition) tended to be used for short operatic works, probably presented with the minimum of stage action, in simple costume and with a small orchestra, in this case strings, two flutes and two lutes. It was probably directed by its composer, Porsile, who would have made the short trip to Prague to rehearse and present the work, before returning to Vienna to maintain the church services there. The particular charm of this 'felicitous day' is that the three singers (soprano, tenor and bass) were not members of the Hofkapelle, but capable amateur singers from elsewhere in the court, a lady (La Fraila Stirum), a priest (Abbate Leoparti) and a count (Conte Logi), who took the figurative roles of the Dawn, the Sun and Time respectively. All nine musical numbers in the opera are addressed directly to 'Elisa', and the technical ambition of the vocal lines shows no signs of limited capability, especially that of the tenor, Abbate Leoparti.

Towards eleven o'clock the imperial family and about fifty ministers and courtiers gathered together for the procession to the nearby church of St Thomas. Part of the Augustinian monastery, it replicated the role of the Augustinerkirche in Vienna. Kilian Reinhardt's instructions in his *Rubriche Generali,* that the music in the Augustinerkirche on that day should have trumpets and timpani and that there should be fanfares too, were almost certainly followed in Prague in 1723.[38]

After a banquet in the castle, the entire court attended *Costanza e*

Fortezza, which began shortly after eight o'clock and did not finish until one in the morning. Later that following day there was a mass service in St Vitus. In the few days between the birthday celebrations at the end of August and the coronation on 5 September several members of the nobility – Count Althan, Count Dietrichstein, Prince Eugen, Prince Lobkowitz and Prince Schwarzenberg – went on a hunting trip.[39]

The coronation service in St Vitus cathedral followed long-established tradition, appropriately reflected in the historical scope of the music, from Gregorian chant, through *a cappella* music, to fanfares and contemporary settings of the liturgy for choir and orchestra. The coronation was embedded within the mass service, between the epistle and the gradual, when the anointment of the new king was followed by the investiture, crowning, enthronement, oath of allegiance and *Te Deum*.[40] The *Te Deum* was a new setting by Kapellmeister Fux, the only detail of the music that was performed at the service that is known.[41] Set in the court's standard ceremonial key of C major, it is scored for soprano, alto, tenor and bass chorus and strings, with cornetto and two trombones doubling the upper three voices, and a group of four trumpets plus timpani. Declamatory words and phrases such as 'proclamant', 'Pleni sunt caeli et terra majestatis gloriae tuae' ('Heavens and earth are full of the majesty of thy glory') and, especially, 'Tu rex gloriae, Christe' ('Thou art the king of glory, o Christ') elicit jubilant bursts of trumpet and timpani writing. All these come from within the composition, exploding into the resonant spaces of the church. But there is a moment when trumpets sound from outside the composition, and the service itself reached beyond the walls of the cathedral to the entire city. The first part of the *Te Deum* is an extended paean to God and to Christ, followed by a section of prayer beginning 'Te ergo quaesumus, famulis tuuis subveni, quos pretioso sanguine redemisti' ('We beseech thee, therefore, to help thy servants, whom thou has redeemed with thy precious blood'). Between these two sections – Allegro then Adagio – Fux's score contains the instruction 'Toccata di Trombe', but no actual music. The trumpet flourishes came from another group of players, probably those who were most accustomed to providing ceremonial fanfares, cleverly identifying and nominating the particular 'servant' whose protection is sought. This was a signal for salutation from the congregation and the peeling of the cathedral bells, which, in turn, prompted the peeling of bells in every church in Prague. Only then did Fux's setting of the *Te Deum* resume.

The Sunday following the coronation ceremony was the fixed feast of the birth of the Virgin Mary; the first vespers service was held in the All Saints church within the palace complex, the mass in St Vitus and the second vespers service in the Church of Our Lady (the so-called Týn church), in the main square of the Old Town. It was during the mass service that Elisabeth Christine was crowned Queen of Bohemia.[42]

On 12 September, Karl attended a musical event organized by the Jesuit college in Prague, a performance of a melodrama specially commissioned from the Dresden court composer Jan Dismas Zelenka.[43] The final event in this concentrated period of private and public celebration was the annual service of thanks for the liberation of Vienna from the Turks in 1683. This coincided with the naming of the Blessed Vigin Mary – a moveable feast – and in 1723 it was held on 15 September in the cathedral of St Vitus (once more substituting for Stephansdom), with the full panoply of processions punctuated by trumpet fanfares, and the performance of a *Te Deum* as well as the mass.[44] Only after this event did the assembled nobility and other dignitaries begin to disperse and return to Vienna or to their country estates.[45]

The choice of subject for the birthday and coronation opera, *Costanza e Fortezza*, would not have been made by Fux, but by the court poet, Pietro Pariati, who had succeeded Stampiglia in 1714. He had provided librettos for all the regular occasions in the operatic calendar of the imperial court, often up to four or more per year, and had worked with all of its composers.[46] Most of his librettos are derived from Greek mythology and those for the birthday or name day of the empress were frequently on pastoral subjects. The choice of a heroic subject and one based on Roman history was, therefore, doubly unusual and, as such, inappropriate for the birthday of the empress. But the greater purpose was well served: the libretto deals with the resolute defiance of the Romans and, although individual actions within the story were easily associated with the bravery of Karl or the fidelity of Elisabeth, more important was the overriding sense of a unified empire that could withstand sustained assault. This was easily associated with Karl's motto 'Constancy and Fortitude' and that, rather than the name of a single Roman figure, was the chosen title of the work. Pariati had already written two librettos for Karl's birthday that dealt with particular virtues, immortal heroism (*L'eroe immortale*, 1717, set by Johann Georg Reinhardt) and wisdom (*La via del saggio*, 1721, set by Conti). *Costanza e Fortezza* was on a much larger scale and destined for a much larger audience.[47]

While Italian opera of the day often played out conflicting moral situations through the interplay of individual characters, the unprecedentedly large and acoustically unconfined venue in Prague meant that an opera that solely or mainly worked through aria and recitative would have had little or no impact. Pariati, Galli-Bibiena and Fux went for the grandest of stage spectacle, with chorus and ballet as well as individual arias. Each act concludes with a sequence of choral dances – the standard bourrée, gavotte, sarabande and minuet – repeated several times and with the chorus declaiming a text that emphasized the constancy of the Romans in Act 1 and their fortitude in Act 2.

Act 1 went even further in adjusting standard operatic practice at the court to suit the particular surroundings. It is dominated by choruses, individually quite short, but often repeated as many as six times, and using all the trappings of Habsburg ceremonial style: trumpets and timpani in C major, sometimes singly, sometimes in groups of four and, most arrestingly at the very beginning, as two alternating groups of four trumpets and timpani. Members of the Habsburg court would most readily have associated these sounds with the grandest of *Te Deum* settings by Fux, such as the one that was to be performed at the coronation a few days later. One musician who recorded his impressions of the occasion was the young Johann Quantz (1687–1773). At this stage in his career he was a jobbing oboist, working mainly in Dresden. He had travelled to Prague to witness the performance of *Costanza e Fortezza*, but landed up playing in the orchestra as one of the many extra musicians that were hired. Rather revealingly, he wrote that the style of the music was 'more church-like than theatrical', but because of that 'very magnificent'.[48]

This musical splendour worked hand in hand with Galli-Bibiena's expert and extravagant stagecraft. The battles between the Etruscans and the Romans in Act 1 are set on the banks of the Tiber. In the garden of the Favorita in Vienna, Galli-Bibiena would have been able to use the man-made lake; in Prague the commemorative engravings of the event indicate that Galli-Bibiena constructed a waterway as part of the staging. During the battles of the first act a wooden bridge was made to collapse into the waterway, with the ensuing fountain gradually transforming itself into a magic temple. Nymphs appear, assuring Rome of the protection of the gods. Fux responds to this wondrous *mise en scène* with an equally fundamental change of sonority, a recurring chorus of nymphs that is delicately scored for high voices, flutes and strings, with no double basses. The chorus gently urges Rome not to be afraid, particularly as it is the birthday of the goddess Vesta, an allusion to the empress's birthday and persona (Vesta, the daughter of Saturn and Rhea, was the goddess of domestic life). Even if the text was unintelligible in the open-air amphitheatre, the printed librettos presented to members of the audience would have made the point.

Act 1 is much the longest, with fourteen scenes followed by a ballet. Act 2, on the other hand, is closer to the normal flow of serious Italian opera at the court, with its alternation of recitative and aria; the few choruses, all sung by Etruscans, studiously avoid C major, trumpets and timpani. In fact, it is not until near the end of Act 3, the end of the opera, that this sonority returns, first as part of a bellicose chorus sung by Roman soldiers and then in the *licenza*. Following a recitative, aria, chorus and several dances, the final number in the opera is the grandest of minuets in C major, supported by the same two choirs of trumpets and timpani, stereophonically placed, that had opened the work three hours earlier. In the *licenza*, there were two texts, one addressed to the empress ('Elisa') and equating Prague with Rome, the other one to the emperor ('grande Augusto').

A Vesta il labbro, applaude,   The lips may praise Vesta,
ma Elisa, adora il cor.   But the heart adores Elisa.
E a Roma dessi laude,   May Rome be praised,

ma in quella si festeggia	But here in Prague
di Praga, di sua Reggia,	We celebrate His realm,
la gloria e lo splendor.	His glory and His splendour.
Grande Augusto, a tue corone	Mighty Augustus, for your crowns
Già dispone lieto il mondo,	The joyous world already prepares
Archi e Trofei.	arches and trophies.
Ed applaudano a l'impegno	And may the favourable Penatean gods
del tuo legno i Penati amici dei.	Praise the diligence of your rule.

Quantz's memory of the occasion was that the opera was performed by a hundred voices and 200 instrumentalists. Suspiciously rounded, these numbers were probably an impression rather than an accurate calculation. While the solo voices were all supplied from within the court, the choral forces were largely sourced from Jesuit schools and churches in Prague. Similarly, the instrumental forces that had left Vienna in early June, some thirty players, were topped up by local players as well as visitors to Prague, including Johann Gottlieb Graun, Tartini, Zelenka, as well as Quantz. Four thousand people were alleged to have attended the performance, but this may be an exaggeration. There was one repeat performance ten days later on 2 September; perhaps the figure of 4,000 reflects attendance at both. Ordinarily, the composer of the opera would have been expected to direct the performance from the harpsichord and, of course, Karl VI himself is known to have done so on many occasions. The nature of the occasion ruled out Karl as a participant; Fux, too, had to be ruled out because of his increasingly painful gout. Vice-Kapellmeister Caldara undertook the task but, to judge from the engraving of the theatre, because of the large forces and the distances between them, he seems to have done so standing up, as a primitive conductor, rather than discreetly from the harpsichord. Kapellmeister Fux was not forgotten. In a highly unusual relaxation of protocol, he was seated near the emperor, in a sedan chair that had been specially brought from Vienna.[49]

By the end of September, the wider political purpose of the court's stay in Prague had been achieved, but the previous decision to stay until mid-November meant that the remaining traditional autumn celebrations – birthday of the emperor, name day of the emperor and name day of the empress – were celebrated in Bohemia and Moravia rather than in Vienna. The new works provided by Caldara and Conti for these occasions could be presented with the normal resources of the court; perhaps some musicians were already dispatched back to Vienna. For some of the solo singers who had participated in *Costanza e Fortezza* – Anna Ambreville (soprano), Rosa Borosini (soprano), Giovanni Carestini (castrato), Pietro Cassati (castrato), Domencio Genovesi (castrato), Gaetano Orsini (castrato), Gaetano Borghi (tenor) and Christoph Praun (bass) – the continuing schedule of rehearsals and performances was a demanding one; three of them, Ambreville, Carestini and Praun, participated in all three operas in October and November.

The first of these occasions was the emperor's birthday on 1 October, celebrated in the castle in Prague with a new work by Caldara, *La contesa de'numi* (The contention of the gods).[50] Five named gods, Jupiter, Juno, Pallade (that is, Athena), Apollo and Mars, take it in turn to sing their praises. Described as a 'Servizio di Camera', like the earlier work for the empress's birthday it probably had little or no scenery, possibly some appropriate costumes and minimal stage action; it is, however, roughly twice as long with a total of sixteen numbers plus a *licenza*. For the most part, the orchestra is a small one, just strings, but Caldara reserves a moment of theatre for the *licenza*. In a recitative on behalf of the assembled cast, Jupiter offers 'humble tribute' to Karl, who, in the coronation service, had himself been described as 'Roman Jupiter'.[51] It is followed by an aria in C major with trumpet obbligato, an extended competitive dialogue between singer and instrument, 'Vivi, Regna, e godi in pace/Vita, Regni, e libertà' ('Live, rule and enjoy in peace/Life, realms and freedom'). In order to make this number a particularly memorable and climactic one, Caldara avoids the obvious; he does not use either the key or the instrument in the final chorus of the assembled gods, instead providing a measured minuet in B flat major.

Much of October was taken up with hunting visits to Brandeis before it was time to celebrate the emperor's name day, on 4 November.[52] Conti provided a work with the congratulatory title *Il trionfo della fama* (The triumph of fame), eleven numbers plus *licenza*.[53] Fame is joined in his temple by four other allegorical figures, Glory, Valour, Taste and Destiny, all of whom salute the emperor. They are supported by a chorus representing each of the four known continents, Asia, Africa, America and Europe, a display of worldwide praise. The work begins and ends with trumpeting choruses in C major, but it is an aria for Valour that catches particular attention. Sung by the bass Christoph Praun, it evokes the fear and terror of Asia and Africa when faced by the bravery of the emperor, 'L'Asia crolla, Africa teme/Dell'Augusto alto valor' ('Asia crumples, Africa fears/Augustus's mighty valour'). Karl the musician would readily have recognized its deliberately perverse use of C major, the antithesis of normal usage: no trumpets, no treble sounds at all, and no continuo; instead, supported by cellos and double bass, two solo bassoons compete with the voice in an extended, virtuoso depiction of abject trepidation.

A couple of days after the emperor's name day, on 6 November, the court began its journey back to Vienna,[54] a leisurely one that took just over a fortnight. En route it stayed two nights in Znaim (Znojmo), near the border between Moravia and Upper Austria, in a palace owned by the court (misleadingly called the Althan palace). It was here that the empress's name day was celebrated with a church service and in the evening an open-air performance of a new one-act work by Caldara, *La concordia de'pianeti* (The harmony of the spheres).[55] The libretto of Caldara's work, by Pariati, once more assembles a cast of gods, this time representing heavenly bodies – Venere (Venus), Diana (the moon), Giove (Jupiter), Apollo (the sun), Marte (Mars), Mercurio (Mercury) and Saturno (Saturn). They and a chorus of demigods offer their extended compliments to 'Elisa'. The title-page of Caldara's score makes it clear that the work was composed by the command of the emperor ('per Comando della Sacra Cesarea, e Cattolica Reale Maestà di Carol VI. Imperatore de' Romani Sempre Augusto') and it is left to Venus, the goddess of love, sung by Anna Ambreville – her fourth role in four months – to begin the *licenza* and to shift the emphasis from congratulatory gods to congratulatory members of the Hofkapelle, before the final chorus of the opera proper is repeated.

Tu sei cara, e pari guisa,	You are precious, and to me you appear,
Grand' Elisa, ai mortali e agli Dei.	Noble Elisa, similar to mortals and to Gods.
E così con doppio onore	So with multiple honour,
De la terra sei l'amore	You are Earth's love
E del Ciel l'amor tu sei.	And you are Heaven's love.

Unlike Caldara's name day work for the emperor, *La concordia de' pianeti* begins and ends with a chorus in C major, including the familiar sound of trumpets (four in number) and timpani. For the empress, the final chorus may have recalled her birthday opera, *Costanza e Fortezza*, since it too is set up as a minuet. Caldara's autograph manuscript describes the work as a 'Componimento Teatrale per Musicale'. That it was indeed a 'theatrical' presentation is revealed by the report in the *Wienerisches Diarium*. The work was performed in the open air in the small town of Znaim, specially lit for the occasion. A series of wagons, each drawn by eight horses, carried the musicians to the open-air venue where they formed a makeshift stage. The performance finished at nine o'clock and was followed by a meal.[56]

With this lavish and extended visit to Bohemia, Karl and Elisabeth, the newly crowned king and queen, had affirmed the power of the Habsburg dynasty, together with the sacred and secular values they shared with the loyal kingdom. Bohemia was to remain largely supportive of Habsburg rule well into the nineteenth century, a striking contrast to Hungary, which was more fractured in its loyalties and intermittently troublesome. For many musicians, the performance of *Costanza e Fortezza* lived long in the collective memory. When Charles Burney was writing the section on the Berlin court in his musical travelogue, *The Present State of Music in Germany, the Netherlands and United Provinces* (published in 1773), he digressed substantially to include a lengthy paraphrase of Quantz's account of the performance, beginning with a sweeping statement: 'History does not furnish a more glorious event for music, than this solemnity, nor a similar instance of so great a number of eminent professors, of any one art, being collected together.'[57] In Prague, it had left a physical mark too, Galli-Bibienia's open-air theatre surviving intact until the Seven Years' War, when it was destroyed by the invading Prussian army.[58]

At the beginning of the eighteenth century, Prague was a city that had much in common with Vienna, staunchly Catholic and enjoying a period of sustained prosperity that similarly manifested itself in the building of new palaces and the modernisation of churches. Lady Mary Montagu, too, had noticed its relationship with Vienna:

> those people of Quality who can-not easily bear the Expence of Vienna chuse to reside here, where they have assemblys, Music, and other diversions (those of a Court excepted) at very moderate rates, all things being here in great Abundance, especially the best wild fowl I ever tasted. I have allready been visited by some of the most considerable Ladys whose Relations I knew at Vienna. They are dress'd after the Fashions there, as people at Exeter imitate those of London. That is, their Imitation is more excessive than the Original.[59]

The long stay of the court in Prague in 1723 also drew attention to telling differences in its musical life, hinted at in Lady Mary's letter. While music in Vienna was overwhelmingly the province of the court, the absence of such a court in Prague, and the fact that the city was never to be part of the annual imperial schedule, meant that music was more varied in its presence and patronage in the Bohemian capital.[60] Since the turn of the century, visiting troupes from Italy had performed Italian opera in the city, either sponsored by local aristocracy or independently presented in hired halls. The theatre in Count Franz Spork's palace in the New Town became effectively a public theatre, with an annual season featuring the most fashionable operas from Venice, by Albinoni, Vivaldi and others, repertoire that could not be heard in Vienna. In the absence of a single dominant ruling family, the Bohemian and Moravian aristocracy had already started to employ small retinues of musicians headed by a Kapellmeister, to perform church music and the new fashionable forms of instrumental music. Most striking, a music academy had been established in Prague in 1713 to give concerts. Sponsored by the nobility they, too, were open to the public, either for a single concert or in the form of a subscription for a series of concerts. It was this animated mixture of aristocratic and civic musical culture that enabled Prague to contribute so many performing musicians to *Costanza e Fortezza* in 1723. Music in the Habsburg court in Vienna, on the other hand, for all its lavish expenditure and the continual involvement and interest of the imperial family, was increasingly inward-looking, conservative and cautious. Indeed, many of the characteristics of musical life in Prague, such as fashionable Italian opera, public theatres, aristocratic patronage and interest in new forms of instrumental music, were not to become evident in Vienna for many decades. Eventually, the imperial court enabled some of this, and certainly did not stand in its way. But its heyday as a direct patron of the art form was never to be replicated.

1800

CHAPTER 5

Court, Aristocrats and Connoisseurs

Mozart's coronation opera; Haydn's *Te Deum*

T HE last year of Mozart's life, 1791, began with the completion of a piano concerto, K595 in B flat, and concluded with the composition of the Requiem, unfinished at his death on 5 December. Many other works central to Mozart's legacy were composed during the year, including 'Ave verum corpus', *Die Zauberflöte* and the Clarinet Concerto. In contrast, a second opera from the same year, *La clemenza di Tito*, has always been rather marginalized, partly because as an opera seria, it seems at odds with the thrust of Mozart's operatic career – the three Da Ponte operas, *Le nozze di Figaro*, *Don Giovanni* and *Così fan tutte*, and the German singspiel *Zauberflöte* – and partly because it is not easily absorbed into the biographical narrative of a thirty-five-year-old composer who was overworked and under-appreciated. It has enjoyed a degree of rehabilitation in recent decades and the circumstances of its commission have been clarified, yet the very traditional nature of those circumstances and, from that, their influence on the work itself have been undervalued. Nearly seventy years separate the composition of Fux's *Costanza e Fortezza* and Mozart's *La clemenza di Tito*, but they do have much in common, features that demonstrate the longevity of certain outlooks in the imperial court and explain why the work stands apart from the remainder of Mozart's mature operas.

The wider political circumstances were even more acute than they were in the 1720s. When Joseph II, Karl VI's grandson, died in February 1790 Austria was faced with unrest on three different fronts. Joseph's chronic insensitivity towards Hungary risked insurrection in the country; together with Russia, Austria was involved in an unpopular war against the Turks; and the western part of the Austrian Netherlands had overturned their Habsburg rulers to form the United States of Belgium. Joseph was succeeded by his brother, Leopold II, a much more conciliatory figure who, in matter of a few months, defused tension in Hungary, secured a ceasefire in the war against Turkey and regained the Austrian Netherlands.[1] He recognized, too, the value of imperial tradition as an instrument of diplomacy. Joseph had never been formally installed as Holy Roman Emperor; neither had he been crowned King of Hungary or King of Bohemia. By September 1791 Leopold had attended all three ceremonies, in Frankfurt, Pressburg and Prague respectively, successfully re-establishing the centuries-old authority of the Habsburg dynasty.

Something of the eagerness to proceed with these dynastic rituals is evident in the musical preparations for the coronation in Prague.[2] The date of the actual coronation was set for 6 September, in the cathedral of St Vitus, with the first performance of an associated opera that evening. In early July neither the composer nor the subject matter of the opera had yet been determined. Unlike 1723, the arrangements were not directly in the hands of the imperial court in Vienna, but were the prerogative of the Bohemian Estates (representing the nobility and the church), presided over by Count Heinrich Rottenhan from the imperial court in Vienna. They, in turn, deputed the task to the impresario Domenico Guardasoni, who knew musical Prague, having intermittently managed the Italian opera company there. His signed contract of 8 July reveals how little had been done. Two operatic subjects (not specified) had been identified, to be set by a 'celebrated master'; if neither proved possible in the time that was available, then an old libretto by Pietro Metastasio, *La clemenza di Tito*, was to be set; Guardasoni was also to be paid for his efforts, even if they ultimately proved unsuccessful. He travelled from Prague to Vienna to further his plans. His first choice of composer was the proper one of the imperial Kapellmeister, Antonio Salieri (1750–1825), but he professed to be too busy to undertake a new opera in such a short period of time. Back in the 1720s, two further court composers would have been available (Caldara and Conti); now there was now only one, Mozart, who accepted. Hitherto his duties as Kammerkompositor had been restricted to directing private performances at court.[3] For Guardasoni and Mozart, it was a fortunate outcome, since both had collaborated on the premiere of *Don Giovanni* in Prague in 1787 and before that on performances of *Le nozze di Figaro* in that city. For this new coronation opera they took the easy option. Rather than waiting for a wholly new libretto to be written, Guardasoni commissioned the court poet Caterino Mazzolà to revise Metastasio's *La clemenza di Tito*, which Mozart proceeded to set in a matter of weeks.

The libretto had an impeccable Habsburg pedigree. It had been written by Metastasio, imperial poet since 1730, set by Antonio Caldara and first performed on Karl VI's name day in November 1734.[4] Like many of its predecessors, it celebrated the personal virtues of the Habsburg emperor – virtue, modesty and clemency – through the actions of a Roman emperor, Titus. The emperor is the target of an assassination plot led by the doubly vengeful Vitellia (daughter of the deposed emperor, whose love for Titus is unrequited) and the conflicted Sesto (a friend of Titus who is in love with Vitellia). In the panic and confusion of a deliberate fire in the Capitol, it is believed that Titus has been murdered. On learning that their beloved emperor is, after all, alive, the rejoicing of the Roman people is accompanied by the magnanimous pardoning of the plotters by Titus.

Guardasoni would have known something of the history of the libretto after its first performance at the imperial court in Vienna in 1734. Between that date and 1791 it had been set by over twenty composers, including leading figures such as Anfossi, Galuppi, Hasse, Holzbauer and Jommelli, often for royal occasions such as the name day of the Elector Palatine (Mannheim, 1757), the wedding of the Elector of Saxony (Dresden, 1769) and the birthday of the King of Portugal (Lisbon, 1771).[5] Apart from this pedigree, there was a very particular reason for its choice. Leopold, the new emperor, had been celebrated as a particularly sympathetic ruler of Tuscany for twenty-five years, dubbed Leopold the Wise and the Solomon of our Century, and often compared to the Roman Titus.[6]

How much of this rich allusive inheritance Mozart himself knew cannot be ascertained; even if he knew nothing it would not have taken Guardasoni long to explain. What is particularly interesting is how the composer's musical responses to the libretto often derive from imperial musical traditions. Like Fux's *Costanza e Fortezza*, Mozart's opera begins and ends in C major, the imperial key, flamboyantly coloured by the sound of trumpets and timpani. By 1791 the old specialist technique of playing in the highest register (*clarino*) had died out and Mozart's forces of two trumpets play fanfare figuration in the middle and lower ranges only (*trombe*), and, though they do not take the thematic lead, their rhythmic punctuation drives the music forward with great energy. The first public scene is set in the forum, where text, music and action are entirely traditional, binding the newest King of Bohemia to his cultural inheritance. A crowd has assembled to offer their annual tribute to the emperor. His imminent arrival is signalled by a trumpet and timpani fanfare, followed by a processional march and a chorus of salutation: 'O gods, guardians of the fate of Rome, preserve in Titus right, might, and the honour of our age' ('Serbate, oh Dei custodi della romana sorte, in Tito il giusto, il forte, l'onor di nostra età'). Titus's response to this public acclamation is an entirely modest one, an aria that stresses his generosity of spirit.

Del più sublimo soglio	With the highest office
l'unico frutto è questo:	this is the only satisfaction:
tutto è tormento il resto,	all the rest is misery,
e tutto è servitù.	everything is subjugation.
Che avrei, se ancor perdessi	What would there be left for me
le sole ore felici,	if I lost the only happy hours
ch'ho nel giovar gli oppressi,	in which I help the poor,
nel sollevar gli amici,	in which I help friends,
nel dispensar tesori	and in which I reward
al merto, e alla virtù?	merit and virtue?

It would be easy to associate these sentiments with Enlightenment values, particularly those of an enlightened despot, but the text is that of Metastasio, unaltered by Mazzolà,[7] and evokes earlier Habsburg values of modesty, virtue and the clemency of the title of the work. In Prague in 1791 they were addressed to Leopold II; they could just as well have been addressed to Leopold I. Mozart's response, nevertheless, emphasizes the individual rather than the position. It is lyrically generous, does not have the imperial trappings of trumpet and timpani, and, crucially, not even an orchestral introduction (a standard signifier of status in Italian and German opera of the time).

Mozart's opera had a notoriously mixed reception, its character and expected impact falling between several stools. Count Karl Zinzendorf, a connoisseur of Viennese opera in the 1780s, found it boring, probably because a serious opera on an old text did not fit with his preferred diet of comic opera. The alleged comment of the empress, Maria Luisa – 'porcheria tedesca' ('German muck') – was just the standard response of someone born south of the Alps (in her case, Spain) to an Italian opera written by a German.[8] More significant, if less memorable, is her documented response that as a grand opera it was not grand enough.[9] Coupled with a response of the courtier, Count Hartmann, that the staging and costumes did not match the festive occasion,[10] this points to its perceived failure as a Habsburg coronation opera. It is unlikely that there was anyone in the Prague theatre in September 1791 who had attended Fux's opera in 1723, but maybe the memory of the memory created an expectation that was difficult for Rottenhan, Guardasoni, Mazzolà and Mozart to fulfil.

The autograph of Haydn's *Te Deum* (Hob. XXIIIc:2) is lost and the precise circumstances surrounding its composition are not entirely clear. An invoice from a singer to attend a rehearsal of 'the new Te Deum' by Haydn is dated 5 September 1800,[11] which links it with the moveable feast of the Most Holy Name of Mary, the commemoration of the defeat of the Turks in 1683, which that year would have fallen on 9 September. Two later letters from Georg Griesinger to Breitkopf & Härtel indicate that the *Te Deum* was in some way connected with Emperor Franz's wife, Marie Therese.[12] She and her husband may have made a visit to Eisenstadt later in the autumn of 1800 when it could have been performed.[13] She had a consuming passion for all kinds of music, expressed in the many private entertainments that she organized at court in which a range of music – instrumental, opera, oratorio and sacred music – was performed, often featuring herself as a singer. Acquiring her own copy of the *Te Deum* fitted in with her eagerness to acquire the newest and best of church music. Whatever the precise sequence of events, Haydn's *Te Deum*, like Mozart's opera, links very clearly with older traditions, ones that the sixty-eight-year-old composer knew well. As a choirboy in Stephansdom, Haydn had experienced much of the pomp and ceremony of Habsburg ritual and he was at one time the owner of the autograph manuscript of a *Te Deum* in C by Fux, not the one performed in Prague in 1723, but an earlier one from 1706, scored for double choir and double orchestra (with a total of four trumpets).[14] Haydn's *Te Deum* is in the traditional key of C major and has three trumpets (not the customary two found in Haydn's liturgical music and those of his contemporaries). While the trumpet players at Eisenstadt and in the Hofburg in Vienna would have declared the florid writing in Fux's work unplayable, Haydn's *Te Deum* is coloured throughout by the sound of trumpets and they dominate the work at its conclusion, a rousing cacophony very reminiscent of earlier practices.

Music and the Habsburg dynasty, music and the Habsburg family

THESE two works by Mozart and Haydn demonstrate that composers at the end of the eighteenth century could evoke musical traditions from much earlier in the century, given the appropriate prompt. But they are exceptions in the respective outputs of the two composers; in both cases, other, more recent practices governed the bulk of music that they wrote in and for Vienna. There had been a fundamental change in musical patronage, a considerable weakening of the near-monopoly in which the court operated early in the century to a more pluralist environment in which the aristocracy, later joined by the bourgeoisie, played leading roles. Music at the imperial palace could still serve the old certainties of political and religious authority on occasions, but its presence within the court was now more likely to be as a form of diversion and private devotion rather than representation. It was still, nevertheless, a favoured art form sustained by inherited musical capabilities.

Emperor Franz II, Leopold II's son, who reigned from 1792 to 1835, was a capable violin player who from the 1780s had begun to amass a private library of music. It included works of all kinds, from operas to songs, from symphonies to dance music, but it had a special space for string quartets, the repertoire that sustained the emperor's favourite pastime of playing first violin in quartet performances. In these, he was joined by Joseph Eybler (Vice-Kapellmeister from 1804) and two enthusiastic and skilled amateurs, Count Rudolph Wrbna (director of the court theatres from 1807) and a highly decorated member of the imperial army, Lieutenant Field Marshal Johann Kutschera.[15]

For the first few years of his reign his uncle Elector Maximilian Franz (1756–1801) also lived in Vienna. Exiled from his court in Bonn because of the French Revolutionary Wars he cut a rather forlorn figure in Vienna, hoping to return to Bonn where he would have reignited the activities of his large musical retinue. One former member, Ludwig van Beethoven, would probably have returned with him to assume the post of Kapellmeister. The elector was certainly held in respect by his most famous courtier; Beethoven's First Symphony was to have been dedicated to him, but his death in 1801 thwarted that intention. At first, Beethoven could not think of a suitable replacement; eventually it was dedicated to Gottfried van Swieten.[16]

Emperor Franz had eight brothers who lived to adulthood, many of whom played leading roles in state affairs: archdukes Ferdinand (1769–1824), Karl (1771–1847), Joseph (1776–1847), Anton (1779–1835), Johann (1782–1859), Rainer (1783–1853), Ludwig (1784–1864) and Rudolph (1788–1831). The last named proved to be the most accomplished musician in the Habsburg dynasty since Leopold I in the seventeenth century. Born in 1788, Archduke Rudolph's initial musical training was entrusted to a court composer, Anton Teyber (1756–1822), but from 1802 onwards Beethoven was his teacher. The pupil and master relationship gradually changed to sustained adult friendship, with Beethoven dedicating no fewer than eight major works to the archduke – the Fourth and Fifth Piano Concertos, the 'Archduke' trio, the 'Les Adieux', 'Hammerklavier' and op. 111 Piano Sonatas, the *Missa Solemnis* and the *Grosse Fuge*. In earlier times the archduke might have formed his own musical court around Beethoven; a vestige of this form of patronage was his decision in 1809 to join Prince Kinsky and Prince Lobkowitz in providing an annual annuity of 4,000 gulden to the composer that enabled him to maintain his career in Vienna. At the same time the archduke continued to pay Beethoven for his lessons in composition and helped in other ways too, defraying the costs of copying the parts for the Seventh Symphony and arranging for a private run-through of that work and the Eighth Symphony in his apartments.[17]

As well as innate musicianship Rudolph shared with his great-great grandfather Leopold a deeply pious nature and a gentle manner, but not, thankfully, his disturbing physical appearance. Initially, like several of his brothers, the archduke was prepared for a career in the army, but at the age of seventeen his mild disposition and weak constitution prompted a change to one in the Catholic church. He was appointed co-adjutor to the Archbishop of Olmütz, in Moravia, with the expectation that he would succeed as archbishop in due course. When that happened in 1819, and the date of the enthronement was set for March of the following year, Beethoven wrote a lengthy letter of congratulation to his patron and pupil, at the end of which he floats the very traditional idea of writing a mass for the occasion. Beethoven's prose indicates too the continuing power of deference linked with the Catholic faith: 'The day on which a High Mass composed by me will be performed during the ceremonies solemnized for Your Imperial Highness will be the most glorious day of my life; and God will enlighten me so that my poor talents may contribute to the glorification of that solemn day'.[18] Had Beethoven fulfilled his intention it would have been the only work by the composer written for a traditional imperial occasion. In the event, the *Missa Solemnis* was not completed in time and an existing mass by Hummel was performed instead. Surprisingly, Archduke Rudolph's compositions show little interest in liturgical works, just fragments of a requiem and of some smaller works; instead his musical interests are thoroughly modern, Beethovenian even: piano music, a violin sonata, a clarinet sonata and a set of forty variations on a song by his teacher ('O Hoffnung').[19]

Like his eldest brother the archduke built up his own music library, starting at the age of thirteen. The several handwritten catalogues of the collection, regularly updated, suggest acquisitiveness as much as musical interest. From 1808 onwards one catalogue includes a summary of the number of composers in the collection, together with the total number of works.[20] In that year there were 2,000 pieces by 370 composers; by 1818 it had reached 6,700 pieces by 1,075 composers. The library contained all manner of music from the immediate Viennese tradition – works by Albrechtsberger, Diabelli, Dittersdorf, Gassmann, Haydn, Hoffmeister, Krommer, Mozart, Pichl, Pleyel, Salieri, Seyfried, Vanhal, Paul and Anton Wranitzky, and others. Indicative of Rudolph's wider musical horizons, there are also works by composers who never set foot in Vienna, such as J. C. Bach, Cannabich and Schobert. Finally, his interest in music of the past was not primarily of Habsburg composers, but was directed more widely, to Albinoni, J. S. Bach, Handel, Lully, Pachelbel, Rameau, Scarlatti and Vivaldi. One of the few older composers with Habsburg connections represented in the library was Palestrina, including the *Missa Papae Marcelli*. Unlike Franz's library of string quartets, this was primarily a library for study rather than for performance, the equivalent to Leopold I's Bibliotheca cubicularis.

As Franz's interests in string quartets and the archduke's interest in instrumental music suggest, opera was no longer at the centre of music-making in the court. The decisive move had occurred early in the reign of Maria Theresia. Opera was detached from the direct control of the Hofkapelle and transferred into the hands of an impresario who would supply the necessary music for the court calendar but would be allowed to make the court theatre a public theatre for the rest of the year; the musicians and theatrical personnel were still to be paid from the court which, together with the particular terms of successive leases to outside individuals, gave it a degree of influence. In extremis direct control could be re-established, which is what happened during the reign of Joseph II and Leopold II, but from 1794 onwards the court turned once more to devolved administration. The term Hoftheater was a blanket one for two public venues, the Burgtheater and the Kärntnertortheater, partly financed by the court, partly by the box office, and with the occasional support of individuals too. Joseph II's progressive reforms influenced opera in two particular ways. His aversion to court ritual and ceremony led him to cull the annual cycle of birthday and name days with associated festivities, replacing them with one general celebration on New Year's Day, the final nail in the coffin of the operatic culture that had flourished at the beginning of the century. Secondly, his promotion of German as the language of an assured urban society as well as of an efficient bureaucracy led him to establish a company devoted to opera in that language and, although it was dissolved after five years, a new and popular presence for German opera in the city had been securely established. By the beginning of the nineteenth century German had ousted Italian as the main language for opera.

Church music at court had taken the opposite trajectory. Whereas opera had become public, church music became more private during the second half of the eighteenth century. Subject to budget cuts in the reign of Maria Theresia, the annual cycle of visits to churches documented by Kilian Reinhardt for Karl VI was severely reduced, aggravated by Joseph II's banning of all church processions in the 1780s as part of his widespread reforms aimed at redefining the role of the church in society. Except for the grandest of occasions, church music at court was literally that – regular services for the benefit of members of the court with little sense of engagement with the outside world and with a less pervasive role in the projection of Habsburg identity. That outlook was complemented by a complete overturning of the principles of the Counter-Reformation. Freedom of worship for Protestants and other religious groups included the freedom to develop their own musical traditions. Joseph's loosening of the previous fundamental bond between church and dynasty in favour of churches and a multi-faith dynasty allowed a new toleration in music too, helping to foster the popularity of oratorio in particular.

Changes in the nature of church and operatic life at the imperial court had consequences on the make-up of the Hofkapelle. The orchestras of the Burgtheater and the Kärntnertortheater were fully established as separate entities, thirty-six players in the former in 1794, thirty-four in the latter, still paid from imperial coffers.[21] For the church services at court there was a choir of about two dozen with the last recorded male soprano (Georg Michael Schlemmer) and male alto (Anton Pacher) completing their long period of service, both over twenty-five years, in the 1790s.[22]

Throughout the period of constant reorganization the senior posts in the Hofkapelle had been maintained, along with the old security of employment for many of the individuals who held them. Assuring good relationships between the court and the musical life that it sponsored was still the responsibility of a music count, a position held between 1797 and 1818 by Count Ferdinand Küffstein, himself a capable violinist. The Kapellmeister was Antonio Salieri, who had lived in Vienna since arriving as a fifteen-year-old orphan. At the age of twenty-three he became a court composer and succeeded to the position of Kapellmeister in 1788. In the 1780s he composed five Italian operas for the Burgtheater and achieved a degree of international fame that dignified him and the imperial court. Although he is said never to have learnt to speak German fluently, this was a legacy of earlier times (there was no pressing need for him to do so); that he was content to march up the ladder of the Hofkapelle and remain in post as an infirm old man were long-standing traditions too. During the 1790s, as a composer Salieri was happy to retreat into court life, writing more and more church music for the Hofkapelle, while other composers took the lead in operatic life of the city and in musical life generally. In 1804 a Vice-Kapellmeister was appointed to assist him, Joseph Eybler (1765–1846), previously Kapellmeister at the Schottenkirche; he, in turn, succeeded Salieri as Kapellmeister in 1824.[23]

Despite continuing to uphold the tradition of Catholic church music in private and occasionally in public, retaining many of the purse strings that sustained opera in the city and indulging in music as a recreation, the court was now set apart from musical life in the city. Most of the leading

composers who lived and worked in Vienna were not employed by it
and their way of life was, instead, largely promoted and sustained by the
aristocracy. Indeed, the patronage of Archduke Rudolph was more akin
to that exercised by contemporary aristocrats than to that of any of his
ancestors.

The aristocracy as leaders of private and public taste in music

ONE of the most valuable sources on musical life in Vienna around
1800 is a volume compiled by Johann Ferdinand von Schönfeld,
Jahrbuch der Tonkunst von Wien und Prag (Yearbook of Music in Vienna
and Prague), published in 1796. It was an innovative volume. In the
preface the author explains why he embarked on the project. He wants
to document musical life in both cities, especially the individuals and
institutions closely involved: composers, performers, patrons, the court,
theatres, instrument makers, music dealers and publishers. With regular
supplements Schönfeld hoped that material would form the basis for a
'contemporary history of music of the Fatherland' ('eine vaterländische
Zeitgeschichte der Tonkunst'). No supplements ever appeared and readers
were denied a pioneering history. In the case of Vienna he was surprised
by the results of his own industry: 'who would believe that the number
of people in Vienna, who seem to have come together simultaneously to
bring the honour of music here to the highest degree, runs to over 200'.[24]
Prominent amongst them are the aristocracy, over sixty in number. Even
more interesting than the individual entries – short summaries of their
musical capabilities and enthusiasms – is a paragraph devoted to the nature
of the patronage, much changed in recent years:

> It was formerly the strong custom that our large princely houses
> possessed their own house *Kapellen* whose splendid genius was built
> by one person (an example of this is our great Haydn). It can only be
> a coldness for the love of art, a change of taste or economy plus other
> reasons that this laudable practice has disappeared, and one *Kapelle*
> after another has been extinguished, so that apart from that of Prince
> Schwarzenberg hardly any more exist.[25]

Schönfeld's example of Haydn can be expanded to support the general
truth of his assertion. Joseph Haydn was able to make his two visits to
London in the early 1790s only because of the severe and sudden reduction
in the musical life of the Esterházy court that had occurred when Prince
Nicolaus Esterházy died in September 1790. The opera troupe was
dismissed, as were most of the instrumentalists, leaving only a small group
of singers and players to maintain church services in Eisenstadt, plus Haydn
as Kapellmeister and the violinist Luigi Tomasini. As was the case in many
aristocratic houses, a wind ensemble (*Harmonie*) of eight players was later
engaged. There was some further *ad hoc* expansion of numbers in the

decade, but the unusually varied nature of the instrumentation of four of the six late masses that Haydn composed between 1796 and 1802 is largely explained by the variable number and kind of players available to him.

The other aristocratic household mentioned by Schönfeld, the Schwarzenberg family, had never formally employed a Kapellmeister, entrusting the organisation of musical life in Vienna and at its country estate in Krumau (Český Krumlov) in Bohemia to Ferdinand Arbesser, who seems to have been largely dependent on musically capable servants, topped up by the casual hiring of other performers. Only the *Harmonie* was regularly constituted.[26]

Understandably, it was easier for Schönfeld to lament the past than it was to explain the complexity of the present and, while 'change of taste' and 'economy' were factors in the decline of aristocratic Kapellen from their heyday a few years earlier, his first reason, 'coldness for the love of art', was not. Aristocratic patronage was pervasive, but its nature was now much more varied than it had been. The practice of one aristocrat supporting a group of musicians with an associated Kapellmeister across a number of years was in decline, replaced by aristocrats who supported music on a more *ad hoc* basis and, more novel and increasingly evident, who sometimes came together to support musical endeavours that none of them as an individual could afford, or chose not to afford. Some aristocrats in Vienna offered only occasional support for music, preferring to spend their money on other activities; others were active across a range of musical life; and one or two were consumed by that interest. For the composers and performers who were supported in this way it was not necessarily a less secure existence than before, since aristocratic retinues in the past had often been reduced in size, disbanded and, occasionally, reformed. To a certain extent the newer version of *ad hoc* patronage gave composers and performers increasing independence, even if not all of them relished the situation.

One of the best-known instances of multiple patronage was the publication by Artaria of Beethoven's set of three piano trios (op. 1) in 1795, the publication that marked a formal beginning to his career in Vienna. The title-page of the publication carries a dedication in French, to 'Son Altesse Monseigneur le Prince Charles de Lichnowsky'. Prince Lichnowsky (1761–1841) was a court councillor and chamberlain who had supported Mozart a few years earlier, until they fell out. He had never employed a Kapellmeister or an orchestra, but about a year before the publication of Beethoven's op. 1 he had begun to support a string quartet of four young players, led by Ignaz Schuppanzigh. At the same time he took Beethoven under his wing, giving him free accommodation and introducing him to further potential patrons.[27] It was almost certainly through his efforts that the initial run of the Artaria publication of op. 1 was accompanied by a lengthy list of subscribers, mainly aristocrats. Printed on two sides of a page at Beethoven's (or Lichnowsky's) expense, the 'Liste des Souscripteurs' constituted a clear statement of acceptance as well as of ambition (see Fig. 5).[28] Altogether, 125 subscribers pre-ordered 245 copies, the purchase of

Lifte des Soufcripteurs.

Mr. Franç.ᵗ d' Adlersheim.
Mdlle. Bab. d' Alméſſy.
Le Comte Appony. 6 Exemp.
La Bar. d' Arnſtein.
Mde. d' Arnſtein.
Mdlle. d' Arnſtein.

Le Baron de Baaden.
La Comteſſe Baſſewitz.
Le Général Bellegnayn.
La Bar. de Benzel.
Le Comte George Berényi.
Le Baron de Brann.
Mr. de Brann.
Mr. Joſ. Breindel. 2 Ex.
Mr. Bridi.
Le Comte Browne. 2 Ex.
La Comteſſe Browne.
La Comteſſe Brunswick.

Mdlle. Charlotte Chevaſſeux.
La Comteſſe Chaminska.
S. E. le Comte Csáky, Vice-Chancellier d' Hongrie.
Le Major de Cahn.
Le Comte Czerain. 2 Ex.
La Comteſſe Ant. Cziraky.

La Comteſſe Dalton. 2 Ex.
Le Comte Franç. Dietrichſtein.
Le Comte Maurice Dietrichſtein.

La Comteſſe d' Erdödy née Comteſſe Herberſtein.
S. E. le Comte Joſ. Erdödy. 3 Ex.

Le Prince Nic. Eſterhazy. 3 Ex.
La Comteſſe Joſ. Eſterhazy.

Mr. de Franck.
La Comteſſe Fries. 2 Ex.
Le Landgrave de Fürſtenberg.

Le Marquis de Gavré.
Lady Gilford, née Comteſſe Thuna.
Le Prince Graſſalkowitz. 3 Ex.
Le Conſeiller de Greiner.

La Comteſſe Hallberg, née Comteſſe Lichnowsky. 2 Ex.
Le Général Comte Louis Harrach.
La Comteſſe Erneſt. Harrach, née Comteſſe Dietrichſtein.
Le Comte de Hardenberg, Envoyé d' Hannove.
La Comteſſe Hatzfeld, née Comteſſe Zierotin. 2 Ex.
Le Comte de Haugwitz.
Mr. de Held.
Le Comte de Herberſtein Moltke.
Mdlle. de Henickſtein.
La Comteſſe Erneſt. Hoyos.
Mr. Paul Holff à l' académie du Génie.

Le Comte Etienne Illéshazy.

S. E. la Comteſſe de Kageneck.
La Comteſſe Karoly, née Comteſſe Waldſtein.
S. E. le Comte Keglevics.
La Comteſſe Kinsky, née Comteſſe Dietrichſtein. 3 Ex.
Le Comte Knutgl.
Mdlles. de Kurzbeck. 2 Ex.

La Baronne de Lang.
Le Prince Lichnowsky. 20 Ex.
La Princeſſe Lichnowsky, née Comteſſe Thunn. 3 Ex.
Le Comte Maurice Lichnowsky. 2 Ex.
La Comteſſe Henr. Lichnowsky. 2 Ex.
Le Prince Charles de Liechtenſtein.
Le Prince J. W. de Liechtenſtein.
La Princeſſe Liechtenſtein, née Comteſſe Manderſcheid.
La Princeſſe Liechtenſtein, née Comteſſe Fürſtenberg.
La Princeſſe Antoinette Liechtenſtein.
Le Prince de Ligne.
Mr. de Liechka. 12 Ex.
Mdlle. Ther. de Liechka.
Le Prince Lobkowitz. 6 Ex.
Lord Longford. 2 Ex.

S. E. la Bar. de Margelick.
Le Comte Marſchall.
Mr. Mentzl. 2 Ex.
S. E. la Comteſſe Metternick.

Mde. de Nevery.

S. E. le Comte Oginsky.
Le Bar. Ladis. Orczy.

Le Prince de Paar.
S. E. le Comte Palffy, Chancellier d' Hongrie.
S. E. la Comteſſe Pergen, née Comteſſe Groſchlag.
Le Bar. Joſ. Podmanicsky. 4 Ex.
Le Prince Joſ. Poniatowsky.
La Bar. de Puffendorf.

S. E. le Comte Raſoumoffsky, Ambaſſadeur de Ruſſie. 2 Ex.
S. E. la Comteſſe Raſoumoffsky, née Comteſſe Thunn.
Mde. de Riez. 3 Ex.

Le Comte de Salmour.

La Comteſſe Sauer, née Helſſenſtein.
Mr. Saunders. 2 Ex.
Mr. de Schaſfeld, Seigneur de Tarnova.
Mde. de Schoenfeld.
Le Prince Schwarzenberg. 4 Ex.
La Princeſſe Schwarzenberg, née Princeſſe d' Aremberg. 3 Ex.
La Princeſſe Schwarzenberg Douairière.
Mde. de Schwingenſchuh.
Mr. de Scio.
La Bar. de Schüttendorf.
Mr. de Selliers.
Mr. Siebe, pour Troppau. 6 Ex.
Le Bar. de Specht.
Mdlle. Ther. de Stettner.
Le Bar. de Stroganof. 6 Ex.
Mde. Stuard.
S. E. le Bar. de Swieten. 3 Ex.

Le Comte Rodolphe de Taaffe. 10 Ex.
Lord Templetown. 2 Ex.
Mr. Jean Thaul.
S. E. le Comte de Thunn.
S. E. la Comteſſe de Thunn, née Comteſſe d' Uhlfeld. 2 Ex.
S. E. la Comteſſe de Thunn, née Comteſſe Kollowrath, pour Prague. 22 Ex.
La Comteſſe Tischkiewitz, née Princeſſe Poniatowka.
Le Prince Troubetzkoi.
Mde. de Tschoffen.

Mde. de Wambold, née de Hangraben.
Le Comte Michel Wielhorsky.
Le Bar. Raym. de Weclar. 3 Ex.
Le Comte Rudolphe Wrbna. 3 Ex.
S. A. S. la Princeſſe de Wurttemberg, née Princeſſe Czartoriska.

Le Bar. Joſ. Zois.
Mr. Nic. de Zorcovics.
La Comteſſe Zychy, née Comteſſe Palffy.

5 List of subscribers to Beethoven's op. 1, 1795

multiple copies indicating a desire to extend meaningful financial support as well as wanting to have the music itself; if each subscriber had ordered only one copy, Beethoven's income would have been nearly halved. Prince Lichnowsky ordered twenty copies, his wife Princess Maria Christine a further three, his brother Count Moritz Lichnowsky two, and his sister Countess Henriette also two. Once the subscribers had received their copies, the publication was made available to the general public.[29] Most of the subscribers were from Vienna and its environs and many are included in Schönfeld's *Jahrbuch*, but the list also included some visitors to the city, such as Lord Longford (who was on the Grand Tour) and the young Anglo-Irish peer Lord Templeton (also probably on his Grand Tour), each of whom bought two copies.

A particularly important subscriber was 'S. E. le Bar. de Swieten', who purchased three copies. In his mid-sixties, Baron Gottfried van Swieten (1733–1803) was one of the most influential patrons of music in Vienna, a discerning figure responsible for fashioning musical tastes that were to leave a permanent mark on cultural life in Vienna.[30] His personality, though, was not to everyone's taste. Schönfeld's description in the *Jahrbuch der Tonkunst von Wien und Prag* slightly caricatures him: 'the patriarch of music. His taste is solely for the grand and the sublime.' Haydn, for whom Swieten prepared the librettos of *Die Schöpfung* and *Die Jahreszeiten*, commented on his early efforts as a composer of symphonies that 'they were as stiff as he was'.[31] Although he had served the Austrian court in various capacities for over twenty years Swieten remained something of an outsider. As a diplomat he had represented the imperial court in Berlin, Brussels, London, Paris and Warsaw before returning to Vienna in 1777. He was appointed President of the Imperial and Royal Court Library in that year, a position he was to hold until his death in 1803, and between 1781 and 1792 he was President of the Court Commission on Education. In the latter capacity Joseph II entrusted him with modernizing Austrian education at all levels. In a country that was still heavily influenced by the highly prescriptive teaching of the Jesuits, Swieten articulated views entirely consonant with the Enlightenment: education was something much broader than prescribed reading, it was for everybody, a participatory process in which each individual developed his or her interests, ones that would be for the betterment of society as a whole.[32] This was a long-term vision strongly articulated, one that might have accelerated the slow dissipation of the values of *pietas austriaca*, but its realization was thwarted by the changed political landscape of the early 1790s. When Leopold II became emperor, Swieten was removed from his position as President of the Court Commission, though he remained as President of the Court Library.

Music was a consuming interest. As a young man he had composed eight symphonies and some operas in French, and he was a competent singer; his diplomatic postings to North Germany and England led him to explore earlier music from those countries, works by Bach and Handel, music that was very different from the Viennese heritage of Caldara and Fux, which – very unusually in Vienna – he ignored completely. The stylistic and aesthetic differences of Bach's and Handel's music constituted the kind of educational challenge that Swieten welcomed. Back in Vienna, in his spacious apartment next to the gallery in the main reading room of the imperial library, he organized private gatherings of musicians to run through this material every Sunday from twelve to two o'clock. The participants spanned a couple of generations and included Salieri, Joseph Starzer, Anton Teyber, Joseph Weigl and Swieten as singers, while Mozart accompanied, sang and, as recollected by Weigl, corrected the mistakes of others.[33]

From these gatherings grew the idea of presenting full performances of major choral works from the past. To facilitate these performances Swieten elicited the support of members of the aristocracy, who underwrote the costs and supplied the performing venue, or both. Detailed records of their activities have not survived and it is likely that this was not a formally constituted society, though they were often referred to as the 'Associirte Cavaliers'. The term *Cavaliers* (or the Italian *cavalieri*) was a common one for the aristocracy in general, but the persistent use of 'associated' is significant, a coming together of individuals for a common purpose. The precise identity of these individuals from one year to the next is not known; it probably varied and, as the work of the consortium became more established, their number increased too. By 1801 the *Allgemeine musikal-ische Zeitung* reported that they numbered fifteen and referred to them as a Gesellschaft von Freunden der Tonkunst (Society of Friends of Music), though that was more a description than a label.[34] The article lists them as Count Apponyi, Prince Auersperg, Count Czernin, Count Erdödy, Prince Esterházy, Count Fries, Count Harrach, Prince Kinsky, Prince Lichnowsky, Prince Lichtenstein, Prince Lobkowitz, Prince Schwarzenberg, Baron van Swieten, Prince Trauttmansdorff and Count Zinzendorf; several of them had appeared on the subscription list of Beethoven's op. 1.

In 1788 Mozart had revised the orchestration of Handel's *Acis and Galatea* for Swieten, the success of which encouraged three further arrangements – *Messiah*, *Alexander's Feast* and the *Ode for St Cecilia's Day*. Repeat performances of the four works were given in the 1790s which, in turn, encouraged performances by other organisations in Vienna, especially for charitable purposes. *Messiah* and *Alexander's Feast*, in particular, became repertoire works in Vienna in the early decades of the nineteenth century, perfect examples of the long-term nature of Swieten's wider educational outlook. As a teacher, he had enthused and enlightened musicians, elicited the support of the aristocracy and expanded the musical interests of the wider public. Swieten's earnestness occasionally came to the fore. One anonymous anecdote reported that if Swieten encountered any member of the audience talking during a performance he would turn round and stare at them until they stopped. This was easily reported as schoolmasterish behaviour, but it was consonant with an increasing sense of seriousness, even of intellectual elitism, evident in certain areas of music-making in Vienna at the turn of the century.

As well as promoting an informed interest in old music, Swieten and his colleagues enabled Haydn to write his two late oratorios, *Die Schöpfung* and *Die Jahreszeiten*. Swieten was the author of the German text of both, encouraged Haydn in their composition and, through the Associirte Cavaliers, sponsored early performances. *Die Schöpfung* was completed in mid-January 1798 and Swieten and his colleagues set about preparing for its first performance. Ten (unnamed) aristocrats were to underwrite the costs, each contributing 50 ducats, which was equivalent to 225 gulden. Haydn was to receive a tenth of the total amount, 225 gulden. The remainder of the money went on preparing the performing parts, paying the performers, reimbursing Swieten's expenses and rewarding the military watchmen who looked after the arrival and departure of the carriages and sedan chairs. The first performance took place on 30 April 1798 in the palace of Prince Joseph Schwarzenberg, an elegant residence built in the early eighteenth century that looked northwards up the Mehlmarkt (Neuer Markt); more money had to be spent on compensating the flour and vegetable traders who normally occupied the square and who had to dismantle their stalls in order to allow access. Tickets were distributed amongst enquiring members of the aristocracy, creating a sense of expectation and cultural ownership that would have appealed to Swieten, further enhanced by the customary availability of the printed text and even by the fact that at the performances some members of the audience had to be accommodated in an overspill room where, for the most part, they could only hear the work through open double doors. Repeat performances were given a week later, on 7 and 10 May. The financial success of the undertaking allowed Haydn to be paid a further 450 gulden, bringing his total income from the oratorio to 675 gulden, almost as much as his annual income of 700 gulden at the Esterházy court.[35]

Plans for a subsequent fully public performance in the Burgtheater sometime in May 1798 had to be abandoned because a convenient date could not be found. Swieten, Schwarzenberg and Haydn returned to *Die Schöpfung* the following year. The main oratorio sponsored that year was Handel's *Messiah*, given in the Schwarzenberg palace across two evenings on 23 and 24 March 1799, but it was preceded by two performances of Haydn's oratorio on 2 and 4 March. Conveniently, these acted as dry runs for the public performance at the Burgtheater on 19 March, some of the costs of which were also underwritten by Swieten and his friends. Although this was a fully public occasion, with the normal ticket prices and the equally normal distribution of a free copy of the printed libretto, Swieten, the educator and the patriarch, could not resist guiding the potential response of the audience, crafting a convoluted 144-word announcement that appeared on the poster, suggesting that any applause between numbers would not be taken as a prompt for an encore, 'otherwise the true connection between the single parts, from the uninterrupted succession of which should rise the effect of the whole, would be necessarily disturbed'. Reports of the first performance suggest that the audience did not take Swieten's hint and applauded particular numbers; in keeping with his warning, however, none of the musical numbers seems to have been repeated.[36]

Building on the expectations aroused by the five semi-private performances that had taken place in the Schwarzenberg palace, the fully public premiere in the Burgtheater was an unparalleled success. As a venue for public music-making the theatre was not yet sixty years old and this occasion could claim to be the most significant premiere of any work in eighteenth-century Vienna, even more than the first performances of Mozart's *Le nozze di Figaro* and *Così fan tutte*: it was a moment when composer and work became public property, not at the service of the Habsburg dynasty, not for the private pleasure of one aristocrat and not primarily for the benefit of the composer. When, several decades later, a new opera house was built in the 1860s, the present Staatsoper, Haydn's oratorio was the only non-operatic work to feature in the opulent pageantry of the interior decoration.[37]

For Haydn in 1800 the reception of the work encouraged him to take the very unusual step of publishing the complete score of the oratorio at his own expense, a venture supported by the seeking of subscribers from home and abroad.[38] Many of Swieten's Associirte Cavaliers were among them, some ordering more than one copy: Count Apponyi (two), Prince Auersperg (two), Count Czernin (four), Count Erdödy (two), Count Fries (four), Count Harrach (one, plus a gratuity of 25 gulden), Prince Lichnowsky (one), Prince Lichtenstein (six), Prince Lobkowitz (six), Prince Schwarzenberg (six) plus Swieten himself (four).

With Swieten's death in March 1803, the consortium of noblemen lost its driving force and ceased to function. Its example, however, encouraged similar groups of aristocrats to come together to sponsor musical events, driven by the same high-minded principles: they were leaders of taste whose public altruism was gratifyingly acknowledged.

One of the most important was founded in 1807, to promote the status of the best of orchestral music: overtures, concertos and symphonies.[39] Known variously as the Liebhaber Concerte, Musikalisches Institut, Freunde der Tonkunst and Gesellschaft von Musikfreunden, it was initially led by the banker Joseph Banquier who enlisted the support of others, including Count Moriz Dietrichstein, Prince Lobkowitz and Prince Ferdinand Trauttmansdorff. A series of twenty concerts between November 1807 and March 1808 was performed by a reasonably consistent body of instrumentalists, a mixture of amateur and professional. Like many of Swieten's concerts in the Schwarzenberg palace, these were semi-private occasions, where the actions of a few encouraged the interest of the many. Seventy individuals were sought who could purchase any number of tickets, which could then be distributed to friends. The artistic ambition of the series was clear and very much in the Swieten tradition:

'Every concert must be distinguished by the performance of significant and decidedly excellent musical works, since the institute wishes to affirm the dignity of such art and to attain still higher perfection.' 'Significant and decidedly excellent works' ('bedeutender und entschieden vortrefflicher Musikstücke') were presented in a consistent format, a symphony as the first item in the programme and an overture at the end, the reverse of modern practice, with a concerto plus an aria or a second overture in between. 'Significant' also had a retrospective, hallowed feel to it. In the same way as Swietens's concerts looked back to Handel, these concerts looked back to orchestral works by Haydn and Mozart, presenting them alongside several by Beethoven, to create an ascendancy for these three composers over their contemporaries. The final concert in the series of twenty expanded its repertoire to oratorio, with a performance of Haydn's *Die Schöpfung*. The concerts were successful and tentative plans were made for a second season, plans that were abandoned because of the increasingly bellicose national mood that led to renewed hostilities with France.

Many of the salient characteristics of aristocratic patronage of music are clear. It was a participatory culture, an ambitiously discerning culture, and socially extensive, but was it also a reflective culture? Opinions and values can be deduced from actions, but actions were not routinely accompanied by words of comment and evaluation. Late eighteenth-century Vienna had never had the vivid public debate of musical events that readily occurred in London, Paris and elsewhere, and any move towards a more varied liberal intellectual climate that might have resulted from the reforms of Joseph II in the 1780s was thwarted by the nervous political climate of the 1790s. From early in the reign of Franz II censorship was ruthlessly applied. If Swieten the educator was pleased with the permanent broadening of the musical repertoire that ensued from his activities he might, also, have been disappointed that it did not result in much public debate. There was still only one newspaper, the *Wiener Zeitung,* which hardly ever offered comment; the main source for musical criticism were the weekly issues of the *Allgemeine musikalische Zeitung,* published in Leipzig, for which anonymous Viennese correspondents supplied regular reports on musical events in the city. While Haydn and Beethoven, for instance, are known to have read the journal, its wider influence in Vienna seems to have been limited.

The thoughts of one visiting composer and writer on music, Johann Friedrich Reichardt (1752–1814), are revealing. A native of Berlin, he spent the winter of 1808/9 in Vienna, where he was constantly impressed by the quality of music-making and the eager participation of the aristocracy but, as an experienced writer, he noted that the general environment was one of little intellectual debate. More than once he commented that polite society was reluctant to talk about literature, philosophy, politics and current affairs, a disappointing difference between Vienna and his home town. Coffee houses, which a century later were to be at the heart of public debate in Vienna, were remarkably free of it, according to Reichardt: there was good coffee and chocolate, but a poor selection of newspapers.[40]

One aristocrat who had regularly attended the Liebhaber concerts of the previous season was Count Johann Nepomuk Chotek, a Bohemian nobleman recently appointed by Emperor Franz to the post of Lower Austrian government advisor. He kept a diary in which he noted some impressions of the concerts, supplemented by comments written on the handbills that he assiduously kept. He certainly had opinions, on the works and on the standard of performance, but they are never expounded at length. 'Schön' is the standard word of approbation, applied to a Mozart symphony, a Cherubini overture and Beethoven's *Eroica* Symphony ('beautiful, especially the Andante'); for the more musically less ambitious items, such as an aria by Eybler and a set of variations by Devienne, Chotek's favourite adjective was 'alltäglich' (commonplace). An overture by Boieldieu elicits the dismissive comment 'noisy and in true French taste' and a violin concerto by Rode was not 'particularly beautiful' but was performed with an 'extraordinary degree of expression and with a beautiful tone'. Even allowing for the fact that these were summary comments entered into a private diary, they are consonant with the limited level of debate that Reichardt observed.

Chotek's diary reveals that he regularly attended Sunday mass before going on to the Liebhaber concert, usually in the Michaelerkirche, on court occasions the Hofburgkapelle and Stephansdom. One Sunday he was so engrossed in the service and associated ceremony to install new members of the Order of the Golden Fleece that he missed the opening item of the concert, Beethoven's First Symphony. Many, perhaps most, members of the concert audience regularly attended church services before the concert and the centuries-old blurring of the sacred and the secular may have conditioned their respectful attitude to music. Not many people articulated their understanding of the Catholic faith, especially in church: not many people articulated their understanding of music, especially in a concert venue.

One of the most striking examples of the new appetite of the aristocracy to support public (or semi-public) music-making was in the area of opera. From 1794 onwards the management of the two court theatres had been entrusted to Peter von Braun who, in exchange for an annual subsidy of 40,000 gulden from the imperial court, was given full responsibility for the management and artistic policy of the Burgtheater and the Kärntnertortheater – spoken plays, ballets as well as opera. To enhance his authority he was made a baron in 1795. In 1804, he added a third theatre to his responsibilities, the Theater an der Wien, a large modern building located to the south of the city walls, some fifteen minutes walk away from the Hofburg. With responsibility for three theatres, the baron had overstretched himself. Matters reached a head in 1806, when he concluded a contract with a consortium of nine aristocrats that effectively ended his period of management: the Theater an der Wien was purchased outright by the aristocrats and they assumed responsibility for the Burgtheater and the Kärntnertortheater. The commercial arrangements seemed to be very sound ones. The nine aristocrats formed a joint stock company to stabilize the running of the theatres, investing a total of 1,200,000 gulden between them. Princes Esterházy (investing 200,000 gulden), Lobkowitz (300,000) and Schwarzenberg (150,000) were the leading figures; the remainder of the stock fund was provided by Count Lodron, Count Zichy and three members of the extended Esterházy family. Financial commitment went hand in hand with management duties. Prince Esterházy was in overall charge; Count Pálffy looked after German plays; Prince Lobkowitz, opera and music generally; Count Zichy, ballet and finance; and Count Lodron, external affairs.[41]

With the ongoing Napoleonic Wars leading to significant and, eventually, uncontrolled inflation it was not the most favourable time to begin an artistic and financial venture of this kind. Five of the original nine aristocrats withdrew in 1810 and, eventually, Count Pálffy assumed sole responsibility. Throughout all this the imperial court kept a watchful eye through Count Rudolph Wrbna, the emperor's court theatre director. In a comic episode, of a kind that was to characterize imperial administration right through to the First World War, Pálffy wanted the title of kaiserliche–königliche Hoftheaterdirektor (imperial–royal court theatre director). He was allowed to use this title but was also told that he was to be subordinate to Wrbna as Obersthoftheaterdirektor (chief court theatre director).[42] Throughout the time that Baron Braun, the consortium and Count Pálffy ran the theatres the imperial court was absolutely unequivocal about one matter. It was never going to return the theatres to the direct control of the court.

Alongside the promotion of oratorio and orchestral music, and the maintenance of theatrical life in general, members of the aristocracy worked together on one further project, the shared patronage of Beethoven. The original circumstances that prompted the arrangement could not have been predicted; the swiftness of the response by Viennese aristocrats revealed their admiration for the composer and a good deal about the valued status of music in civic society as well as, more narrowly, aristocratic society.

In the autumn of 1808 Beethoven received an invitation to become director of music at the newly established kingdom of Westphalia, ruled by Napoleon's brother, Jerome Bonaparte. Beethoven was to move to Kassel, be given the very generous salary of 600 ducats (about 2,700 gulden), an orchestra, and the freedom to compose as he wished. In January 1809 the composer indicated that he would accept the offer, initiating a response from Viennese patrons anxious that he should stay in the city.[43] Only one aristocrat, Prince Nicolaus Esterházy, was capable of offering Beethoven a full-time position with similar terms but he was already committed to making his Vice-Kapellmeister, Johann Fuchs, full Kapellmeister on the death of Haydn (a succession that occurred later that year). His reluctance to get involved may also have been fuelled by residual resentment over the troublesome commission and performance of Beethoven's Mass in C in Eisenstadt in 1807. Baron Ignaz von Gleichenstein, a court official and a gifted cellist, had been working as Beethoven's secretary since 1806, itself a form of patronage. He was the likely author of a document that laid out the reasons why Beethoven should be persuaded to stay in Vienna and some ideas on how that might be achieved, a position statement that was to inform discussion with likely patrons.[44] The overriding criterion was one that was proclaimed on behalf of all composers, rather than Beethoven in particular – the freedom to compose 'really great works and, then, to be able to produce them in public'. After summarizing the terms of the offer from the King of Westphalia, Gleichenstein carefully exploits the national pride of the aristocracy:

> Beethoven's preference to reside in this city is so great, he is so grateful for the many proofs of good will which he has received and he cherishes such patriotic feelings for his second fatherland that he will never cease to count himself among the number of Austrian artists and will never choose to live anywhere else, provided that the advantages listed below are granted to him to a certain extent.

Four 'advantages' are then detailed, the qualifying phrase 'to a certain extent' suggesting that not all of them had to be met. First, Beethoven should be supported for life by one patron or, alternatively, patronage could be shared by several people; second, Beethoven's wish to be allowed to travel in order to further his reputation should be accommodated; third, he would like, ideally, to enter the service of the imperial court; fourth, the directors of the court theatres should guarantee him one evening a year at the Theater an der Wien for a benefit concert, in return for which Beethoven would participate in an annual charity concert.

Elements of three of the four 'advantages' are apparent in the contract that ensued, dated 1 March 1809. Three patrons agreed to contribute a total of 4,000 gulden annually (more than the offer from the King of Westphalia and nearly twice the amount that Fuchs was to receive as Esterházy Kapellmeister): Prince Kinsky, Archduke Rudolph and Prince Lobkowitz. The first, Ferdinand Kinsky, was an entirely new figure in Beethoven's life, who contributed 1,800 gulden. His Bohemian family had owned a palace in the Freyung in Vienna since 1784, but in the early nineteenth century it tended to divide its time between Vienna and Prague. Born in 1781, Kinsky had an active military career during the Napoleonic Wars and did not have the sustained interest in music that many of his fellow aristocrats had.[45] That came from his wife, Princess Caroline Kinsky (1782–1841), a capable singer who regularly acquired vocal music for a newly established library in their Prague palace.[46] The next highest figure of 1,500 gulden was contributed by Archduke Rudolph, Beethoven's favourite pupil and, most recently, the dedicatee of the Fourth Piano Concerto; this provided the entrée into the imperial court that the composer sought, though it was never to lead to a position at court. Prince Lobkowitz was the third patron. Although his contribution of 700 gulden was the smallest, in material terms he was the one who had the strongest record of supporting the composer to date. Lobkowitz had subscribed to six copies of Beethoven's op. 1, was the dedicatee of the op. 18 quartets and had sponsored private performances of the Third, Fifth and Sixth Symphonies, including the costs of preparing the orchestral parts. For this particular patron, contributing 700 gulden was merely a new element in a continuing pattern of support.

The contract achieved its central purpose of keeping Beethoven in Vienna and, over the next three years, the composer dedicated a whole series of major works to his patrons: the Mass in C to Prince Kinsky, rather than to the person who had commissioned it, Prince Nicolaus Esterházy (Breitkopf & Härtel, 1812); the 'Les Adieux' Piano Sonata to Archduke Rudolph (Breitkopf & Härtel, 1811); and the Fifth and Sixth Symphonies to Prince Lobkowitz (Breitkopf & Härtel, 1809). Princess Caroline Kinsky, too, received dedications, for two sets of songs, op. 75 and op. 83 (Breitkopf & Härtel, 1810 and 1811). The agreement allowed Beethoven to travel in order to further his career as long as he had the consent of the three patrons, a clause that was never activated. Only the wish that he be guaranteed a date in the Theater an der Wien for an annual concert was absent; the inclusion of Prince Lobkowitz, who looked after the musical affairs of the three public theatres, provided sufficient assurance that this was likely to happen. Despite a difficult history involving the premature death of Kinsky in 1812, the bankruptcy of Lobkowitz, delayed payments, renegotiated terms and even lawsuits, this agreement remained in force until Beethoven's death in 1827.[47]

Prince Nicolaus Esterházy and Prince Joseph Lobkowitz

FROM the 1790s through to the end of the Napoleonic period two individuals stood above the rest as tireless patrons of music, Prince Nicolaus Esterházy and Prince Joseph Lobkowitz. They were of similar age (Esterházy was born in 1765, Lobkowitz in 1772) and were two of the richest aristocrats in the Austrian territories, with extensive holdings of land in Hungary and Bohemia respectively, land that had been granted to them in the seventeenth century for their loyalty to the Habsburg dynasty during the Counter-Reformation and, in the case of the Esterházy family, the Turkish wars also. At the beginning of the nineteenth century that loyalty was innate and unquestioned, even though neither individual was active at the imperial court. At the same time as they collaborated as public patrons of music in Vienna they continued to spend money as private patrons in their own palaces in the city and on their country estates. Esterházy and Lobkowitz represented aristocratic patronage of music at its peak. They also figured in its demise.

The patronage of Prince Nicolaus Esterházy was the more traditional. When he succeeded his father as the reigning prince in 1794 the musical court was at a low ebb, a complement of a dozen musicians to maintain church services, a *Harmonie* of eight players, plus some military musicians. He exercised the traditional right to review the provision and, at first, reduced it even further, before beginning a long period of expansion, characterized by the desire to maintain and to improve the provision for church music, but in other respects rather arbitrary and unpredictable.[48] Wind players, in particular, were engaged, dismissed, and sometimes re-engaged in ensembles that were sometimes military, sometimes the very fashionable *Harmonie*. The emphasis on church music and the irregular constitution of the instrumental provision largely explain why Haydn did not write any symphonies in this late period.

The composer would have been astonished at an entirely new initiative that occurred in 1804, one that went against the grain of history. A Kapellknabeninstitut was established that was to train eight to ten choirboys, many from Vienna.[49] Choral music at the Esterházy court had always been sung by mixed forces. With this initiative the prince seemed to want to emulate the sonority of the Hofkapelle in Vienna, as well as its role in the life of the court. Opera received a new emphasis too. In the late 1790s it was provided by a travelling company, later by the enlarged retinue of musicians employed at the court supplemented by additional performers; there were even ambitious plans to build a new theatre attached to the palace in Eisenstadt. The repertoire mirrored that found in Viennese theatres, initially Italian opera followed by a decisive shift towards German opera, and paved the way for the prince's willing participation in the management of the court theatres in Vienna from 1806.

By 1808 the total number of musicians employed at the Esterházy court was over ninety, substantially more than during the 1770s and 1780s, when Haydn was at his busiest as Kapellmeister, the period traditionally viewed as the heyday of the court. However, as well as being untypical of wider practice it was soon to become wholly unaffordable. Following the French invasion and occupation of Vienna in 1809 the steady annual rise in inflation that had occurred over the previous years suddenly began to accelerate at an alarming pace. In 1811 the Austrian government was forced to declare the state bankrupt and to devalue the currency by 80 per cent, a desperate measure that only temporarily eased the situation.[50] Against this background Nicolaus Esterházy was forced to act decisively. He had already withdrawn from the theatre consortium in Vienna and in 1813 announced that musical personnel at the Esterházy court would be drastically reduced, from eighty to eleven, just five singers and six instrumentalists, who were to provide the music for the church services. Everybody else, including the boys of the Kapellknabeninstitut, the *Harmonie* and the singers and instrumentalists who had performed in the opera were dismissed.

Prince Lobkowitz's patronage of music was even more extensive than that of Prince Esterházy, though distinctively characterized by the casual employment of musicians rather than by a large, permanently constituted ensemble.[51] This was facilitated by a second characteristic. Whereas Prince Esterházy's retinue of musicians was based almost entirely in Eisenstadt, Prince Lobkowitz's musical activities were divided between Vienna, in the winter, and his country palaces in Bohemia, in the summer. In Vienna, Lobkowitz was able to draw on the musical resources of the city, to the extent that his palace became the pre-eminent centre for music-making. The prince had largely been brought up in the city, where two of his uncles were active patrons of music. A hip deformity meant that a military career was ruled out at an early stage and a distant father meant that he was largely brought up by his mother. As a cultured member of the aristocracy he spoke German, French and Italian, also a little English; more unusual, he was a fluent speaker of Czech, a diplomatic nicety that endeared him to many people on his Bohemian estates and indicative of an open-mindedness that characterized his sponsorship of music. As a musician, he was a competent violinist and cellist, and in adulthood possessed a pleasant bass voice.

On 2 August 1792 he married Princess Maria Carolina Schwarzenberg in the chapel of the Schwarzenberg palace in the Neuer Markt; a concert was given which included a substantial programme symphony by Anton Wranitzky on the subject of Aphrodite, the Greek goddess of love. Although the genre, a symphony, was thoroughly contemporary, its musical style, like that of Mozart's *La clemenza di Tito* and Haydn's *Te Deum*, often reaches back across the decades to earlier traditions. The allegorical subject matter, the home key of C major, the associated use of trumpets and timpani all culminate in an extended, often noisy 'Triumphlied'.[52]

When Lobkowitz reached the age of majority in 1797 he set up his own Kapelle, not a balanced orchestra of fifteen to twenty players, as would have been the case in earlier times, but an ensemble of five musicians, later expanded to seven; led by Wranitzky, it consisted of three violinists, two viola players and two cellists. Unlike the Esterházy court, church music was not a priority, but everything else was, from string trios to symphonies, from songs to operas and oratorios. Wranitzky was put in charge of employing the necessary additional players, a task that became so burdensome that one of the other violinists, Anton Cartellieri, who was also a singer, was put in charge of opera and oratorio from 1800; five years later, a third Kapellmeister was added, Joseph Rössler. The full-time complement never exceeded eleven individuals, of whom three had substantial administrative duties. As mentioned, winter was spent in Vienna, the summer months in Prague, Eisenberg (Jezeří) and Raudnitz (Roudnice). Some of the additional singers and instrumentalists hired in Vienna, who could number more than thirty for performances of symphonies and perhaps as many as sixty for performances of oratorios, moved with the court in the summer months, when they were supplemented by musicians from Prague and local amateurs, especially schoolteachers.

Lobkowitz's father, Prince Ferdinand Filip, had purchased a palace in the Spitalplatz owned by Count Althan. As a member of Karl VI's court he specially valued its proximity to the Hofburg, some three minutes away. Under Prince Joseph Lobkowitz the palace benefited also from its proximity to the Burgtheater and the Kärntnertortheater, and the sight of instrumentalists, singers and composers entering and leaving the palace must have been a familiar street scene in Vienna. The main salon on the first floor was converted into a small concert room, complete with eighteen benches that sat about thirty people; more people could be accommodated in adjacent rooms and the sound of the performance would have reached out into the broad central stairwell too. It was in this room that Beethoven's *Eroica* Symphony was given its first, private performance in 1804.[53] Much later in the nineteenth century, as this event entered the collective historical memory, the room became known as the 'Eroica Saal', and the role of its early sponsor prompted the renaming of the square from Spitalplatz to Lobkowitzplatz.

The *Eroica* was only one work by one composer amongst literally hundreds of works by dozens of composers that were supported by the prince. When Reichardt visited Vienna in the winter of 1808–9 he documented in full his experiences of the city, including the centrality of the Lobkowitz palace. There were afternoon concerts, such as those given by the Schuppanzigh quartet, evening concerts at which, for instance, the young Archduke Rudolph played, a song recital that began at nine o'clock and finished at midnight, and a concert performance of a new opera by Reichardt himself, *Bradamante*, at which the audience included Beethoven, Clementi, Leopold Kozeluch and Salieri. More distinctive was the use of the palace as a venue for rehearsal and practice. 'At any hour one can organize rehearsals as one pleases in the best and most favourable of circumstances; often several rehearsals and practice sessions are held at the same time in different rooms.' Reichardt's summary description of the palace was enthusiastic and neat: 'a veritable seat and academy of music'.[54] Apart from Anton Wranitzky, Beethoven and Reichardt, the many composers who benefited from this patronage included Eberl, Haydn, Hummel, Krommer, Paer, Reicha, Spohr, Weigl and Anton Wranitzky's brother, Paul Wranitzky. In essence, Lobkowitz was a potential patron for all composers who were resident in Vienna or were visiting the city. When he was given responsibility for musical events in the court theatres in 1806 as a member of the consortium who now ran them, this seemed an entirely appropriate extension of his musical domain, from the private and semi-public to the fully public.

Concerts, opera performances and trial runs of new pieces, such as Beethoven's Fifth and Sixth Symphonies, continued on the country estates in the summer. As in Vienna, concert rooms were built in Raudnitz and Eisenberg. Lobkowitz's spending seemed limitless: performers, preparation of performing parts, travelling expenses, new instruments, specialist instruction, new music for the library and old music from Swieten's estate (including the original score of Mozart's arrangement of Handel's *Messiah*). Arising from his duties at the court theatre he also purchased the struggling firm of Kunst- und Musikalienhandlung, which had the monopoly for publishing music performed at the court theatres.

This lavish, carefree support could not be sustained. He began to borrow money from fellow members of the nobility and he seemed oblivious to the fact that the value of all money was being eroded by increasing inflation. In 1813, the same year as Prince Esterházy drastically reduced the size of his Kapelle, Prince Lobkowitz presided over his last musical event at his palace in Vienna. Like the Austrian state itself, Lobkowitz was declared bankrupt and his affairs were put into administration. Beethoven, whose stipend of 700 gulden had been stopped in 1812, was not sympathetic, calling him a scoundrel (*Lumpenkerl*) and activated legal proceedings against the prince to get his stipend restored. This pivotal figure in Viennese musical life withdrew from society and died in December 1816. In later decades, as Beethoven's music reputation became central to the Viennese inheritance, Lobkowitz's reputation too was salvaged. But his story was ultimately a tragic one: the last and most indulgent of aristocratic patrons to support music in Vienna who died just as musical life in Vienna was finding new ways of promoting itself.

Women play and sing their part: a forgotten history

In his preface to *Jahrbuch der Tonkunst von Wien und Prag*, Schönfeld indicates that though his volume is in part a directory he also sees it as a means of elevating the status of music and musicians. The volume begins with a short section of two pages headed 'Special Friends, Patrons and Connoisseurs in Vienna' ('Besondere Freunde, Beschützer und Kenner in Wien') and Schönfeld explains his criteria for inclusion in this exclusive group: 'in this category we include those patrons who have not only celebrated, supported and made known individual musicians in all kinds of ways, but have given music a new strength and lustre which is especially important, since music is so little paid in comparison with other popular amusements'.[55] Schönfeld's list of twenty-one elite patrons does not contain Prince Lobkowitz because he had not yet made his mark on Viennese musical life. Prince Nicolaus Esterházy is not listed either, probably because his musical activities at the time were located in Eisenstadt rather than in Vienna. Swieten is listed but, oddly, not his colleague Schwarzenberg. The most startling characteristic of this select list, however, is the inclusion of six women, nearly a third of the total number: Countess Maria Anna Gillford, Countess Hatzfeld, Princess Lichnowsky, Fräulein von Martines, Baroness Buffendorf and Countess Schönfeld (no relation).

Countess Maria Anna Gillford (1769–1800) had married the Irish peer Richard Meade, the second Earl of Clanwilliam. She had been a subscriber

to Beethoven's op. 1, ordering one copy, which suggests that she may have
been a pianist, but Schönfeld draws attention to other musical capabilities
in the directory part of the volume: 'one of our best amateur guitarists, an
instrument she plays with tender feeling, delicacy and taste. Her singing is
melting, soulful and harmonious, with pleasant modulation and method.'[56]

Princess Maria Christine Lichnowsky (1765–1841), who had married
Prince Carl Lichnowsky in 1788, was the elder sister of Countess Gillford.
It is clear that she was well regarded as a notable musical patron in her own
right. She had subscribed to three copies of Beethoven's op. 1, also to the
first printed edition of *Die Schöpfung*.[57] In 1801 Beethoven dedicated the
piano arrangement of his ballet music, *Die Geschöpfe des Prometheus*, to her
and it is her abilities as a pianist that Schönfeld chooses to emphasize: 'a
good artist, she plays the fortepiano with expression and feeling'.[58]

The most capable woman was Marianna von Martines (1744–1812),
a well-known figure in musical Vienna since the 1750s. A protégé of
Metastasio, she had received theory lessons from Haydn (possibly keyboard
lessons too) and counterpoint lessons from Bonno.[59] She composed over
sixty works – keyboard music, arias, liturgical works and oratorios. By the
1790s she was a favoured teacher of singing too. Schönfeld's summary is a
fulsome one:

> One of the most eminent connoisseurs amongst our numerous
> dilettantes. She sightreads, accompanies from the score, is a splendid
> singer, very grammatical in composition and execution, her taste is
> principally for the old Italian manner. For a livelihood, and out of a
> love for the arts, she has, to all intents and purposes, her own singing
> school in which she trains excellent singers ... She has composed
> masses and very many arias, which occasionally approach the
> Jommelli style, and is in every respect a great champion of music.[60]

For Schönfeld, the importance of women as patrons of music in Vienna
is self-evident, something that he does not need to comment on specifically.
At the same time, the volume rarely details the nature of that patronage;
instead, the details that are given emphasize their qualities as musicians,
usually as singers and pianists. There is, nonetheless, a clear implication
that these women often worked independently of their husbands (if
they had one). This ties in with wider evidence: the active musical life of
Empress Marie Therese as a performer, collector and patron; Prince Marie
Hermenegild Esterházy's continuing interest in the music and well-being
of the court Kapellmeister, Joseph Haydn; the fact that Prince Kinsky's
patronage was very likely the result of his wife's interest in music; the
frequent inclusion of women on subscription lists; and, not least, the
number of works, especially piano music and songs, that were dedicated to
them, not as an act of condescension, but as an act of esteem that was on a
par with that accorded to men. Further evidence of the hidden history of
women in music in this period will emerge in the next two chapters.

CHAPTER 6

Demand, Aspiration and
the Ennobling of the Spirit

Music in the market place

MUSIC publishing arrived comparatively late in Vienna in comparison with much of Europe. A distinctive presence in Amsterdam, London, Paris, Venice and elsewhere since the end of the seventeenth century, it did not become an influential part of musical life in Vienna until the last couple of decades of the eighteenth century. It was not because music printing as a craft was unknown but because musical life itself did not require it. The musical activity of the imperial court was serviced by handwritten manuscripts (scores and parts) and since, for much of the century, the operatic repertoire was a private one, there was no tradition of issuing extracts in printed form, as in London, or printing complete operas, as in Bourbon France. In Vienna, the financial case for printing large-scale works, such as operas and church music, was not a viable one and, for all music, the general efficiency of manuscript copying, whether it was replacing a lost second oboe part for a Dittersdorf symphony or providing performance material for an entire opera by Paisiello, meant that there was little incentive to turn to printing. In the middle decades of the eighteenth century music dissemination was overwhelmingly through manuscript copies, and the steady supply of sonatas, quartets, concertos, symphonies, operas, masses and so on that was produced sustained an entire musical culture. Printed music was known, but it was often imported from elsewhere in Europe, such as Nuremberg and Paris, sold in bookshops in Vienna and only occasionally supplemented by material produced locally.[1]

The decisive shift from dissemination by manuscript to dissemination in printed form occurred in the latter decades of the century. It was not a case of a new technology replacing an old one at the service of an unchanged musical environment, rather it coincided with fundamental changes in musical taste which, at first, it was able to promote and accelerate and, subsequently, also to mould. Patrons of music, at court or from the aristocracy, were influential in shaping musical taste; so, increasingly, were the commercial instincts of publishers.

The pioneering firm also proved to be one of the most enduring: Artaria, a name that figures prominently in Viennese musical life from the late eighteenth century to the First World War.[2] The family came originally from Blevio on the eastern shores of Lake Como, part of the Habsburg territories in northern Italy, before moving north of the Alps, first to

Mainz and then to Vienna, working as printers and dealers of fine art. The decisive moment for music occurred on 12 August 1778 when Pasquale Artaria advertised their first item of music in the *Wiener Zeitung*, a set of three trios for two violins (or flute and violin) and cello by Paolo Bonaga (otherwise unknown). By the mid-1790s over 500 music items had been published; ten years later the number had doubled. Located in the main thoroughfare from the Hofburg to the Graben, the Kohlmarkt, Artaria was the principal publisher in Vienna of the music of Haydn and Mozart, and played a part in Beethoven's early career too, including the op. 1 piano trios, the op. 3 string trios, the op. 5 cello sonatas and the op. 12 violin sonatas. But the works of these three formed only a very small part of Artaria's total activity; alongside other composers based in Vienna, such as Albrechtsberger (1736–1809), Eberl (1765–1807), Förster (1748–1823), Gelinek (1758–1825), Gyrowetz (1763–1850), Krommer (1759–1831), Vanhal (1739–1813) and Anton Wranitzky (1761–1820), the catalogue featured music by composers who lived elsewhere, such as Boccherini in Madrid (1743–1805), Clementi in London (1752–1832) and Pleyel in Italy, Strasbourg and Paris (1757–1831).

Artaria's pioneering example encouraged the setting up of other music publishing firms, some founded by family members or ex-employees of Artaria. For both, friendly cooperation, rather than ruthless rivalry, characterized their relationship, with some firms purchasing some of the stock of the parent company in order to hasten a viable presence in Vienna. The first of these break-out firms was set up in 1798 by Tranquillo Mollo, a former employee, joined for a while by Domenico Artaria; their shop was located across the city in the spacious square of Am Hof. To get the business off the mark they had purchased plates of a serial publication by Artaria, the *Raccolta delle migliori Arie, Duetti e Terzetti scelti da varie Opere rappresentate nel Reggio Imperial Teatro di Vienna trasmessi per il Clavicembalo o Fortepiano* (Collection of the best Arias, Duets and Trios chosen from various operas performed in the Royal Imperial Theatre in Vienna arranged for harpsichord or piano), typically arrangements of the overture plus seven or more of the vocal numbers. In this way some of the most popular Italian operas from the time of Joseph II and Leopold II were still available to a domestic public – Martín y Soler's *L'arbore di Diana*, Paisiello's *La molinara*, Salieri's *Axur, rè d'Ormus* and Mozart's *Così fan tutte* and *La clemenza di Tito*.[3]

At about the same time as Mollo was establishing his firm, another former employee, Giovanni Cappi, was setting up his business.[4] Cappi was from the same area as the Artaria family, Blevio on Lake Como, and was taken on by the firm in Vienna, first as an employee, later as a partner; Giovanni's sister married a member of the Artaria family, Carlo, who was in charge of the branch firm in Mainz. When Cappi set up his own firm in 1801 he took another employee from Artaria as his partner, his nephew Pietro Cappi, and opened his business across the road from the parent firm of Artaria, in the Michaelerplatz.[5] He also set up his own serial publication of operatic music, differently organized from the one that Mollo had inherited from Artaria. Beginning in October 1806, the *Musikalische Wochenblatt* was a subscription series that came out once a week and, rather than selected numbers from one opera, contained arrangements from several, typically three of four numbers, three for voice and piano plus a single instrumental movement such as an overture or a march. Serial publications of music often began with high hopes before faltering. Cappi's *Musikalische Wochenblatt* was a notable exception: it appeared regularly throughout the year, including the summer months when many of its purchasers lived in the countryside, and maintained that schedule for four years, through to the autumn of 1810, including the period when Vienna was occupied by the French.[6]

The Bureau d'Arts et d'Industrie was a third publishing firm that was established at the turn of the century, one that was wholly independent of Artaria, at least in terms of personnel; in terms of location, however, it initially chose to be near Artaria and Cappi, in the Kohlmarkt, before moving to the Hoher Markt in 1805.[7] When the firm was founded in May 1801, Austria had recently signed the Treaty of Lunéville with France, the beginning of a three-year period of nervous peace. Using French for its commercial name was a nod to current political sensibilities as well as to its traditional usage on title-pages (as on Beethoven's op. 1); in later years, when hostilities resumed, the firm usually used the German formulation Kunst- und Industrie-Comptoir.

More important than their name was their outlook on music publishing. Two of its founder members, Joseph Schreyvogel (1768–1832) and Joseph Sonnleithner (1766–1835), were representative of an emerging element in the artistic life of Vienna. Both were skilful authors who, rather than pursuing wholly independent artistic careers, devoted a substantial portion of their working lives to administrative duties. Both, at various times, served as the secretary of the court theatres, a position that enabled them to supervise the repertory of spoken drama and opera, while simultaneously acquiring a substantial degree of administrative authority. Neither was an aristocrat, but members of an emergent educated bourgeoisie which was beginning to shape aspects of artistic life. Joseph Sonnleithner was to become one of the most influential musical figures in Vienna in the opening decades of the nineteenth century. This sense of artistic and intellectual ambition, coupled with a commitment to the means by which it could be promoted, can be seen in the published output of the Bureau d'Arts et d'Industrie. As with other music publishers at the beginning of the century, there was the expected output of contemporary piano and chamber music, but there was also a clear wish to broaden musical taste. Sonnleithner had acquired the discriminating interest in older music that had characterized Swieten and his circle. Alongside the latest piano music by Beethoven, Eberl, Hummel, Wölfl and others, the firm published Bach's Goldberg variations and no fewer than ten volumes of sonatas by Domenico Scarlatti. Equally notable, the Bureau d'Arts et d'Industrie was the only publisher in Vienna to issue symphonies in the first decade of the century, including Beethoven's Second, Third (*Eroica*) and Fourth, an expensive undertaking that shared the same high-minded agenda that was to motivate the organisers of the Liebhaber Concerte in 1807–8.[8]

If the Bureau d'Arts et d'Industrie was discerning, then the firm of Eder was unashamedly populist.[9] It was housed in a building on the Graben near Stephansdom, 'Zur goldenen Kreuze', familiarly known as the 'Elefantenhaus' because of the carved image of an elephant on the side wall, a remembrance of the first elephant seen in Vienna. The animal was brought from Spain to the city by Archduke Maximilian in 1552; it was a popular attraction but lived for only a year. The 'Elefantenhaus' housed one of Vienna's most popular coffee houses and it was in this building that Eder had his shop. Like Artaria, Bureau d'Arts et d'Industrie, Cappi and Mollo, Eder not only sold music but other goods too. While Artaria and the Bureau d'Arts et d'Industrie specialized in engravings and maps, Eder's store was more akin to a modern gift shop, selling books, games, visiting cards, paint pots and brushes, and presents for name days and the New Year.[10] Printed music formed part of this miscellany and concentrated on the lightweight and the topical: songs for children, the latest dances, patriotic songs, marches, and variations on popular melodies. But it was here, too, that Beethoven's three sonatas of op. 10 and the *Sonata pathétique* were made available.

Artaria and Cappi had emerged from the family trade of engraving, and the Bureau d'Arts d'Industrie from the broad intellectual horizons of its founders. A further publisher, the Magazin de Musique, arose from the ambition of one composer, Leopold Kozeluch (1747–1818).[11] A successful pianist, teacher and composer, in the 1780s he set up his own business, initially focussed entirely on his own music, especially piano music. Later, the music of other composers was published, never on the scale of the output of Artaria and Cappi, but with a continuing emphasis on piano music. During the 1790s the firm traded from two addresses – the first in Bräunerstrasse, the second in the Dorotheergasse – adjacent streets that went from near the Augustinerkirche up to the Graben. From 1800 onwards publications from the firm were sporadic and ceased entirely in 1802.

From this survey of six of the most active music publishers in Vienna around 1800 it is clear that the nature of these businesses was quite different from later industrialized practices. Rather than three separate entities in three different locations, printer, publisher and retailer were often one and the same thing, and the word publisher (*Verleger*) had subtly different connotations.[12] It was still used in the literal sense of the word, the 'person who presented' the item for sale, but it did not necessarily imply that it was printed but was used for handwritten items too. Accordingly, Artaria and others continued to offer the occasional manuscript. Since many named businesses also sold music from other firms in addition to their own, as well as non-musical items, 'music publisher' (*Musikverlag*) was not in common use; much more typical was *Kunsthandlung*, that is a shop for artistic goods. Even that is misleading, if it implies a degree of exclusivity. Many of these outlets were placed in close proximity to the principal thoroughfares of the city, the Michaelerplatz, Kohlmarkt and the Graben, and were meeting places for composers and performers, amateur and professional, local and visiting. In one hundred years musical works had become items of public trade in Vienna in a way that would have startled Leopold I, Kilian Reinhardt and Fux.

These six firms were by no means the only publishers of music in Vienna around 1800: a comprehensive account would have to take account of several other firms, large and small, the practice of self-publication and the intermittent publication of music by book publishers.[13] At the same time distribution through manuscript copies was still common. The sheer extent of the musical market, manuscript and printed, is best appreciated by looking at the activity of one further figure, the music dealer Johann Traeg.

Born in Gochsheim in Lower Franconia in 1747, Johann Traeg and his family moved to Vienna in his early thirties.[14] He was a professional music copyist, certain to make a decent living in the city. But he was not content to be a jobbing scrivener and over a period of twenty years or so established himself as the central figure in the musical commerce of the city. Unscrupulous copyists who worked for individuals and institutions would often make additional copies for themselves, pirate copies of sonatas, quartets and symphonies that they would sell for personal profit. Traeg legitimized this process, amassing a collection of master copies of musical works of all kinds from which he then provided copies on demand. There was nothing clandestine about his business; he regularly announced new acquisitions of instrumental music, songs and dances in the *Wiener Zeitung*, less frequently church music and opera. As his collection expanded he offered music for hire too and could also provide the musicians for private concerts or similar social occasions. Something of the busy nature of musical life in Vienna is evident from the concluding sentence of one of these advertisements: 'In order best to respond to these commissions I ask that at all times the request be received before midday'.[15] He had started his business from the family home, on the first floor of the Pilatisches Haus next to the Peterskirche. As the business expanded Traeg moved four times during the 1780s, always within the inner city: to the Rotenturmstrasse, Wipplingerstrasse, Salztorgasse and, finally, Singerstrasse. The last address was dedicated entirely to the business, with the family moving out to Wieden in the suburbs to the south of the city. In response to the increasing presence of music publishing in Vienna, notably Artaria, Traeg began to print music in 1794, the beginning of an eleven-year period of transition that eventually led to the firm concentrating on printed music rather than manuscript music. Traeg's son, also Johann, joined the firm in 1803 and took it over after the death of his father in 1805.

In 1799 a substantial printed catalogue of the complete stock of the firm was issued, comprising over 350 pages.[16] This was a cumulative catalogue that included old and new music, manuscript and printed music, as well as material that Traeg was selling on behalf of foreign publishers, notably André of Offenbach and the newly conjoined firm of Breitkopf & Härtel based in Leipzig. Ostensibly, the catalogue was meant to encourage potential purchases, but Traeg may have had other motives for its preparation. Since his accumulated stock in the Singerstrasse was a vast one, a complete catalogue provided much needed order for Traeg and his workers; customers entering the shop with the catalogue in their hand could ask to see an item rather than browsing aimlessly or searching abortively. Many of the items were being sold at reduced price, especially the older manuscript stock, so there may have been an element of trying to maximise sales from items that were no longer as attractive as they once were or which, in the interim, had become available in print. In his foreword to the printed catalogue Traeg indicates that any suggestions for its improvement would be welcomed and that supplements would be issued from time to time. In the event, only one supplement was issued, a catalogue of sixty-seven pages that appeared in 1804, listing the works acquired since the first catalogue.[17]

Between them, these two catalogues issued by Vienna's major music dealer, Traeg, detail nearly 14,000 compositions by some 800 composers, far more than the output of any one publisher and far more than survives in any one library. While there is some overlap with the print catalogues of major publishers in Vienna, it is not a considerable one, and if one is seeking a figure that would represent the total amount of music that could be purchased in the inner city around 1800, then it would be reasonable to push that figure upwards, to beyond 16,000. The layout of Traeg's catalogue does, however, help to establish a sense of the market. The type of music was more important than its composer; accordingly Traeg's two catalogues were divided by genre and associated performing forces. From this pattern, one can form a clear impression of what Traeg's priorities were, what kind of music sold best. Three areas stand out: piano music, music for voice and piano, and string quartets.

Behind closed doors: piano, song and string quartet

WHEN Mozart decided in 1781 that he would give up his post as Konzertmeister and organist in the archiepiscopal court in Salzburg in favour of a freelance existence in Vienna, he wrote an excitable letter of reassurance to his father: 'It is perfectly true that the Viennese are people who like to shift their tastes, *but only in the theatre*; and my special thing is too popular here not to allow me to support myself. Here is certainly the land of the piano [*Klavierland*].'[18] For once, Mozart was not exaggerating. As a pianist in *Klavierland*, he gained immediate access to musical society, a base for a wider musical career that was not dependent on one patron. Teaching the instrument went hand-in-hand with composing for it, the one feeding the other; by the end of the year Artaria had issued its first publication of music by Mozart, six sonatas for piano and violin (K376, K296 and K377–80). Although Mozart's subsequent career in Vienna was a much broader one, including chamber music for strings, symphonies and seven operas, keyboard music of all kinds formed a continuing presence in his output: six sonatas for solo piano, three for piano duet, nine sets of variations for piano, one for piano duet, two fantasias, one funeral march, one suite and several more single movements. To these could be added versions for keyboard of many of the orchestral dances that he composed annually from 1788 onwards; they were published by Artaria and, though it has always been assumed that they were not prepared by Mozart, there is no evidence either way; he would certainly have known about them and realized their value in further enhancing his popularity. The term 'piano music' (*Klaviermusik*) would have also embraced works that included one or more string instruments, in addition to the lead instrument; in Mozart's case, as well as the debut publication of six violin sonatas, there were four further violin sonatas, two sets of variations for violin and piano, five piano trios and two piano quartets, a total of nineteen works.

The popularity of Mozart's piano music did not die with him in 1791. *Klavierland* was continuing to grow apace and helped to nurture the composer's posthumous reputation in Vienna. Alongside the continuing availability of authentic works by the composer, there was the occasional wholly inauthentic work and many arrangements. One of the first ventures of the new firm of Breitkopf & Härtel, established in 1796, was to prepare an *Œuvre complettes* of Mozart's output, beginning with keyboard music. Between 1798 and 1806, sixteen hefty volumes were issued, all readily available in Vienna.[19]

The young Beethoven was another composer who traversed *Klavierland* with enthusiasm. For the first ten years or so of his career in Vienna he pursued a dual existence as a pianist–composer, before incipient deafness shifted the emphasis towards composition. Of the thirty-seven works published with an opus number up to the First Symphony, twenty-two involved the piano, either alone or in combination with other instruments. Indicative of the burgeoning market for printed music is that they were issued by three different publishers: ten solo sonatas (op. 2, Artaria; op. 7, Artaria; op. 10, Eder; op. 13, Eder; op. 14, Mollo), a sonata for piano duet (op. 6, Artaria), three piano trios (op. 1, Artaria), three violin sonatas (op. 12, Artaria) two cello sonatas (op. 5, Artaria), a quintet for piano and wind instruments (op. 16, Mollo), a trio for clarinet, cello and piano (op. 11, Mollo), and one horn sonata (op. 17, Mollo).

Publishers in Vienna had developed a fairly consistent practice of not giving opus numbers to sets of variations, an indication of the mostly limited compositional ambition of such works. They were often topical in their appeal, using well-known themes, especially from operas and ballets that were performed in Vienna. Beethoven was perfectly willing to engage in this process as a composer and, very likely, as a teacher and performer too. As Table 3 details, no fewer than eight popular theatre works in the 1790s were plundered by Beethoven for themes for sets of variations.[20] The original composers would not have objected because the variations could only increase the appeal of the stage work, and their publication complemented any arrangements for piano of numbers from the opera that were published, by Artaria and others. Together, stage performances of the original opera (or ballet) plus private performance of piano arrangements or sets of variations on particular themes constituted a continually unfolding tale of musical fashion that linked the salon to the theatre. For the performer of variations, there was the repeated pleasure of hearing the favoured theme, even when it was teasingly embroidered with decoration; for the teacher and the pupil it also constituted perfect didactic material,

Table 3   Sets of variations on opera and ballet
themes produced by Beethoven in the 1790s

1795 Traeg	Nine variations on 'Quant' è più bello' from Paisiello's *La molinara* (WoO 69); dedicated to Prince Lichnowsky. Paisiello's opera enjoyed international success following its first performance in Naples in 1788. At first, the opera was performed in Vienna in the original Italian, from 1795 through to 1832 in German. By 1800 the German version (*Die Müllerin*) had been performed eighty times in Vienna. A keyboard reduction of the overture was available from Artaria.
1796 Artaria	Twelve variations on 'Menuett à la Vigano' from Haibel's *Le nozze disturbate* (WoO 68). Joseph Haibel's ballet was first performed in Schikaneder's Theater auf der Wieden on 18 May 1795. In August 1795 the Magazin de Musique had issued a set of six variations on the same theme by Johann Lickl. A fortnight after Beethoven's variations were published in February 1796, Artaria issued a third set of variations on the theme, by Joseph Gelinek.
1796 Traeg	Six variations on 'Nel cor più non mi sento' from Paisiello's *La molinara* (WoO 70). Beethoven's second set of variations on a theme from this opera (see above), this time the popular duet. In addition to the overture, the duet was included in Artaria's serial publication, *Raccolta delle migliori Arie* (1790; from 1801, Mollo).
1797 Artaria	Twelve variations on a Russian Dance, derived from a folksong and used in Paul Wranitzky's *Das Waldmädchen* (WoO 71); dedicated to Anna Margarete von Browne-Camus. Between October 1796 and April 1797 Wranitzky's ballet received twenty-seven performances at the Kärntnertortheater. Beethoven's variations were published in April 1797; in July 1797 the Magazin de Musique published a set by Joseph Lipavsky. In January 1798 Artaria published a set of variations on the theme by Heinrich Eppinger.

developing finger technique, the capacity to project a variety of moods and, more surreptitiously, inculcating the patterns of harmony and syntax in common practice.

More often than not, the title-pages of published piano music contained a dedication. Never a random or casual matter, it represented a process of social exchange within a constantly changing network of musicians and patrons, one that engendered a sense of collective well-being. In Beethoven's case, three different types of homage are evident. The op. 2 piano sonatas and the op. 12 violin sonatas were dedicated to Haydn and Salieri respectively, a gesture of thanks to two teachers on one level, but on a different level an act of deference, the first to a commanding international figure, the other to the imperial–royal Kapellmeister. By associating

1798 Traeg	Eight variations on 'Une fièvre brûlante' from Grétry's *Richard Cœur-de-Lion* (WoO 72). This haunting melody, a *romance* sung by the minstrel Blondel in mock archaic style, occurs throughout Grétry's opera. Although Grétry's opera had been performed in German in Vienna in 1788, its selection as a theme for a set of variations was prompted by its inclusion in a ballet by Joseph Weigl, *Richard Löwenherz, König von England*; the ballet was performed thirty-two times in 1795.
1799 Artaria	Ten variations on the duet 'La stessa, la stessissima' from Salieri's *Falstaff* (WoO 73); dedicated to Anna Luise Barbara von Keglevicz. This comic opera, Salieri's last successful stage work, was first performed on 3 January and received five further performances before this set of variations appeared at the end of February.
1799 Hoffmeister, followed by Eder	Six variations on the trio 'Tändeln und Scherzen' from Süssmayr's *Soliman der Zweite* (WoO 76); dedicated to Countess von Browne-Camus. Including the premiere, on 1 October 1799, Süssmayr's singspiel received twenty-eight performances at the Kärntnertortheater during 1799 and 1800; Beethoven's variations were published by both firms in December 1799. A keyboard version of the overture was published by Cappi in 1807.
1799 Mollo	Seven variations on 'Kind, willst du ruhig schlafen', a quartet from Winter's *Das unterbrochene Opferfest* (WoO 75). Since its premiere on 14 June 1796 Winter's singspiel had become a repertoire work, receiving thirty-one performances by the time Beethoven's variations were published in December 1799.

himself with these figures Beethoven indicated his ambition, as a master of musical style and, indeed, as a possible future imperial–royal Kapellmeister. Notwithstanding these two notable examples, dedications from one composer to another were comparatively unusual. The second characteristic is the acknowledgement of continuing patronage; Prince Lichnowsky, the dedicatee of the piano trios of op. 1 in 1795, received the dedication of the set of variations on 'Quant' è più bello' from Paisiello's *La molinara* later in the same year and the *Sonata pathétique* (op. 13) in 1799. The third element is a pointer to the social milieu that supported the performance of piano music.

Three publications of piano music were dedicated to Countess Anna Margarete von Browne-Camus: the variations on a theme by Wranitzky (Artaria, 1797), the op. 10 piano sonatas (Hoffmeister, then Eder, 1798) and the variations on a theme by Süssmayr (Hoffmeister, then Eder, 1799). In 1790 she had married Count Johann von Browne-Camus and the couple moved from Russia to Vienna in the winter of 1794–5. He was one of Beethoven's most consistent supporters, described by him as 'a leading Maecenas of his muse', and the recipient of four dedications: the op. 9 string trios (Traeg, 1798), the op. 22 piano sonata (Hoffmeister, 1802), the variations for cello and piano on Mozart's 'Bei Männern, welche Liebe fühlen' (Mollo, 1802) and the Gellert songs (op. 48; Artaria, 1803). Nothing is known about his musical abilities or those of his wife; if she did play the piano, then the three piano sonatas of op. 10, in particular, show her to have been a very capable performer.

Baroness Josephine von Braun was the wife of Baron Peter von Braun, the person who was responsible for running the court theatres from 1794 to 1807, including the granting of any free evenings for concerts. Since the baron was known to be reluctant to hire out the theatre for concerts, perhaps the dedication of the op. 14 piano sonata (Mollo, 1799) to his wife was intended to smooth the way for Beethoven's debut benefit concert, given at the Burgtheater the following April. She also received the dedication of the op. 17 horn sonata (Mollo, 1801) and the string quartet arrangement of the first of the op. 14 sonatas (Bureau d'Arts et d'Industrie, 1802), both unusual works to dedicate to a woman. While it is impossible to divine the personal dynamics of that relationship and relate them to the norms of social etiquette of the time, these unusual dedications suggest that the husband was the vicarious target. Indeed, a letter written by Carl van Beethoven to Breitkopf & Härtel on behalf of the composer in 1802, following Baron von Braun's refusal to give Beethoven a free evening in the Burgtheater for a concert, makes that intention clear: 'it must really vex him to see himself treated so unworthily, especially since the Baron had no cause, and my brother has dedicated several works to his wife.'[21]

Prince Carl Lichnowsky's mother-in-law, Countess Maria Wilhelmine von Thun-Hohenstein, is one patron who is known to have played the piano. As well as a subscriber to the op. 1 piano trios she was also the dedicatee of the trio for piano, clarinet and cello, op. 11 (Mollo, 1798). Finally, the only female patron of Beethoven who was also a pupil was Countess Anna Luise Barbara von Keglevicz, a young lady from a Hungarian noble family; her father had subscribed to Beethoven's op. 1 and she was the dedicatee of the op. 7 piano sonata (Artaria, 1797) and the variations on 'La stessa, la stessissima' from Salieri's *Falstaff*, both of which require a mature technique. Her musicianship may be judged from the fact that, as the recently married Princess Odescalchi, she received the dedication of the First Piano Concerto in C major (Mollo, 1801).

The main alphabetical listing in Schönfeld's *Jahrbuch der Tonkunst von Wien und Prag* is headed 'Virtuosen und Dilettanten von Wien', short summaries of the musical attributes of individuals from the singer Johann Adamberger through to Baroness Katharina Zois. 'Virtuosen' is not used in the familiar sense of dazzling performers, but equates with 'professionals', those who earn their living from music and, from that wider usage, includes composers such as Albrechtsberger, Haydn and Salieri, as well as performers. At the same time, there is a very clear social filter in place. Only those 'Virtuosen' who are known in the exclusive world of private music-making are listed; jobbing musicians from the Hofkapelle or the theatre orchestras are entirely absent. The nuances of the second element of Schönfeld's heading are equally telling. 'Dilettanten' indicates amateurs, but with no pejorative sense whatsoever; while their social status meant that they did not pursue music as a paying career, their musical accomplishments were often, if not routinely, of a high standard. That Schönfeld includes the professionals and the amateurs – 'Virtuosen und Dilettanten' – in the same list, rather than in two separate lists, points to a fundamental characteristic of musical life in Vienna around 1800. The professional and the amateur mixed freely in private society, with the former gaining social standing and patronage while the latter was able to enhance his or her musicianship. That it was often a fairly informal environment is suggested by an observation made by Reichardt. As a North German, he noticed that the Viennese aristocracy often addressed each other by their first names and used the familiar 'Du' in conversation: 'This alone gives a rather cordial and genial [etwas Herzliches und Gemütliches] feel to society, of a kind that one seldom finds in the great houses of other countries and cities.'[22]

Reichardt had also noted the musical proficiency of many of the women and it is not surprising that over thirty female amateurs are included in Schönfeld's list. Countess Rombec 'plays the fortepiano masterfully, with precision, taste and ease, to the extent that she is to be considered amongst the greatest mistresses of this instrument', while Baroness Anna von Saffran is 'one of the most eminent of Kozeluch's pupils, plays the fortepiano with great delicacy, accuracy and feeling, and sightreads with endless skill.'[23] Many daughters from the emerging professional classes are included, such as the unnamed daughter of Ignaz von Sonnleithner (Joseph's brother and a lawyer) and Caroline von Greiner, daughter of Franz von Sales, councillor in the Austro-Bohemian chancellery. But one figure stands out, Maria Theresia von Paradis.[24]

Born in 1759, the daughter of a court lawyer, she lost her sight at the age of three. With the imaginative and dedicated support of her parents she learnt to play the piano and the organ, and was a proficient singer; she also learnt several languages, played cards and danced. During the early 1780s she went on a European tour, performing in Berlin, Brussels, London and Paris, accompanied by an old friend of the family, a pensioned court official named Johann Riedinger. Mozart wrote a concerto for her to play in Paris, probably K456 in B flat. From the mid-1780s she devoted herself more and more to teaching and to composition; her works included a handful of stage works, several cantatas, concertos as well as piano music. On a journey to Prague in 1789 she met Schönfeld for the first time and they became life-long acquaintances. His evaluation of her piano playing is an enthusiastic and detailed one, and he never mentions her blindness.

> Her touch is that of a master and not of a student; she makes demands on herself that are neither sleight of hand nor bursts of noisy speed, rather they are nourishment for the spirit and the heart. One praises in particular the following qualities in her artistry: feeling, taste, nuance, clarity and precision. She is especially strong in the so-called pearly style (*giuoco granito*) in which all the notes in a scale have equal power, roundness of tone, clarity and velocity. She uses Tempo Rubato sparingly and for a purpose. In adagio movements her notes float almost like a voice in song.[25]

From her house in the inner city, which she shared with Riedinger, she developed a teaching practice that was active until a few weeks before her death in February 1824. On Sundays during Advent and Lent her pupils, mainly young women, but also some men, gave concerts to invited guests and, with the assistance of friends and relatives of the pupils, the repertoire expanded well beyond solo piano music to embrace piano duets, piano trios, piano quartets and vocal numbers, all, as one commentator wrote, for 'the ennobling of taste' ('die Veredlung des Geschmacks').[26]

As these concerts in the Paradis household across thirty years exemplify, private concerts devoted entirely to solo piano music were not a feature of musical life in Vienna around 1800. Much more prevalent was the mixing of piano music with vocal music, an aspect of musical life in Vienna that has been underplayed, a victim of a later historical narrative that, for the sake of convenience, separated them. Since the songs of Haydn, Mozart and Beethoven form only a small part of the respective output of those composers, music historians were able to put them to one side to concentrate on their achievement as composers of symphonies, quartets, concertos, operas and, of course, solo piano music. This, in turn, has allowed Schubert, who composed over 600 songs, to gain a biographical and musical identity as the first composer to devote himself wholeheartedly to the genre. But Schubert did not emerge from nowhere. Vocal music, of all kinds, was a constant feature of private music-making and the ability to sing in society with assurance was as prized as the ability to play the piano.

In his list of professionals and amateurs in Vienna, Schönfeld comments on the musical abilities of two daughters of a court official, Charlotte and Sophie von Alt: 'The former plays the fortepiano with great precision, the latter sings with a very pleasant voice.' If that entry suggests a degree of reserve, the very next entry for Katharina Altemonte is unbounded in its enthusiasm:

> Fräulein Altemonte, a real musical genius. Her sincere Italian singing is very beautiful, full of feeling, flexibility and correct method. Her particular strengths are in the *Adagio*, and in *Recitative* she is excellent, all of which makes her one of our foremost dilletantes. She reads music so well that she can accompany from a score at sight. She sings all kinds of music masterfully; whoever has heard her at the keyboard accompanying herself will be enchanted by her singing, for there she is able to use her frequent *Tempi rubato* with freedom. She sings sentimental songs not only with great judgment but also with enthusiastic feeling.[27]

Later in the alphabetical sequence Schönfeld has five successive entries for members of the extended Henikstein family.[28] Joseph von Henikstein, a merchant and banker by profession, is a bass singer, a cellist and also plays the mandolin; his wife, Elise, is a singer; Karl plays the violin and the viola, also the mandolin; and Johann, who also plays the violin and the viola, and has just begun to sing bass. Of all of the family members it is Josepha that elicits the most fulsome praise:

> Amongst the many accomplishments possessed by this lady, music is certainly not the least, for she has brought this beautiful art to a particular degree of perfection. She reads very well, has a splendidly cultivated taste, and, though she doesn't have the strongest of voices, she contributes very clearly to trios, quartets, quintets, choruses and finales (of which she sings a lot). Her tone and technique are fine, rich and correct. In addition, she has the even greater advantage that she is able to accompany and direct vocal pieces of all kinds.

From these representative comments, much can be deduced about the nature and role of vocal music in private concerts. As in piano music women often took the lead, though both sexes would join in any group singing. Very often the women would also accompany themselves at the piano, rather than having a separate accompanist. This practice is reflected in the wording of many title-pages of published music of the time, which often use the phrase 'songs to be sung at the piano' ('Lieder beim Clavier zu singen' or 'am Clavier zu singen'), rather than 'songs with piano accompaniment' ('mit Clavier Begleitung'). The sense of ownership that resulted from one singer–pianist, such as Katharina Altemonte, Josepha von Henikstein and Maria Theresia von Paradis, was a distinctive one, and rather different from the sense of partnership that later came to characterize the singing of lieder. Composers, including Haydn, Mozart and Beethoven, often facilitated this practice by doubling most or all or the vocal part with the right hand of the piano part. Other Viennese composers who contributed to this pre-Schubert repertoire included Gyrowetz (1763–1850), Kozeluch and Steffan (1726–97), and the popularity of the genre may be judged from Traeg's catalogue of 1799, which includes close to 1,500 songs.[29] The performing repertoire was even larger, since extracts from opera and oratorio were sung too, as the comments on Altemonte and Josepha Henikstein suggest. This was the market directly served by serial publications like Artaria's *Raccolta delle migliori Arie, Duetti e Terzetti* and Cappi's *Musikalische Wochenblatt*.

Iconographic evidence of this private musical world is as elusive as detailed verbal reports. One of the most charming is a coloured print from 1793 (see Fig. 6). It shows an unknown lady seated at a fortepiano, the focal point for an ensemble of two violin players (or violin and viola), a flautist, a cello player and a male singer. It could represent a performance of an aria from an opera (such as Papageno's first aria in *Zauberflöte*, though Papageno is very self-effacing); alternatively, it could be a composite representation of the performers who typically participated in a social-cum-musical-occasion. As well as the centrality of the woman, who might well have sung at the keyboard too, the engraving reveals another aspect of music-making in Vienna around 1800: orchestral instruments – here violin, cello and flute – were usually played by men, hardly ever by women. This points to a different arena within private music-making, one that was as popular as piano playing and singing, but which was a largely male domain: the playing of string quartets.

In Schönfeld's *Jahrbuch der Tonkunst* the list of professionals and amateurs in Vienna who play string instruments – violin, viola, cello and double bass – exceeds fifty. Only three are women, all otherwise unknown. Mademoiselle Bayer 'is a distinguished virtuoso on the violin. She presents an agreeable bow stroke and plays sonatas and concertos with taste and skill'; Demoiselle Brunner is 'a clever violinist, in quartets as well in concertos'; and Fräulein Josephine von Dornfeld 'plays the violin very agreeably'.[30] The remainder are all men, including aristocrats, such as Count Apponyi, Count Ferdinand Küffstein and Prince Lobkowitz, court officials such as Gottlieb Demuth, a doctor (Knobloch), and a police official (Löwenau); professional players include Franz Clement and Peter Fuchs, and some composer–violinists are listed too, such as Gyrowetz, Krommer and the Wranitzky brothers. As the entry on Demoiselle Brunner exemplifies, Schönfeld's comments often home in on the particular aptitudes of the violinist, as a concerto soloist, a leader of a quartet or as a director of an orchestra. Heinrich Eppinger, a dilettante, is 'one of our leading violin players, particularly in concertos and quartets ... His tone is really pleasant and pleasing, and he has a lot of facility.' The composer and violinist Franz Krommer is described as a 'very skilful violinist, not only in

6 Private performance depicted by Johann Söllerer, Vienna, 1793

quartets and concertos but as a director of a large ensemble'.[31] The most fulsome praise is reserved for a young man barely in his twenties, Ignaz Schuppanzigh (1776–1830):

> This young man seems to have given himself over entirely to the service of Apollo. Everything that can be called good music is an attraction for him, without giving preference to any one instrument, piece or master. His particular instrument is the viola, which he plays extremely well; lately, perhaps following his own taste, he seems to have given preference to the violin, which he plays with feeling, grace and true artistry, in concertos as well as in quartets. In addition he likes to direct a full ensemble, which he does with precision, nuance, sensibility and fire. He is, therefore, known throughout musical society, is popular and sought after. Accordingly, it is particularly to his credit that he is obliging and agreeable in a way that will earn him even more friends.[32]

Apart from a period of seven years spent in St Petersburg, from 1816 to 1823, Schuppanzigh was a constant presence in Vienna from the mid-1790s until his death in 1830.[33] Especially associated with Beethoven, he deserves his own narrative rather just being consigned to a supporting role in the career of one composer. He participated widely in the musical life of Vienna, as director of the orchestra in the early morning concerts at the Augarten in spring and early summer, and leading the orchestra in many benefit concerts, but it is his contribution to the development of the string quartet that especially distinguished his career. He was not a lone figure in favouring the medium, as Schönfeld's *Jahrbuch* indicates, but he worked alongside patrons, composers, publishers and other performers to establish an unprecedented status for the genre and for himself as a specialist practitioner.

Prince Carl Lichnowsky was an early patron. At the age of sixteen Schuppanzigh was engaged along with three other youths, Louis Sina, Franz Weiss and Nicolaus Kraft, to play quartets at his regular concerts on Friday mornings. It was here that Schuppanzigh first met Beethoven; at the Bonn court Beethoven had regularly played the viola in the orchestra, and now paid Schuppanzigh for some violin lessons. From that time through to the following decade he together with five or six regular colleagues built up a reputation as quartet players; they are known to have played in the Lobkowitz palace as early as 1799,[34] when the performances might have included quartets from Beethoven's op. 18. From this position of emerging authority and standing Schuppanzigh undertook a major new initiative in 1804–5: four public subscription concerts, devoted primarily to the quartets of Haydn, Mozart, Beethoven, Eberl and Bernhard Romberg. Public subscription concerts of any kind were a rarity in Vienna at the time and most concerts were single events for the benefit of an individual or a named charity. In a tentative process that suggests the cautious opening out to a paying public of what had hitherto been hitherto private occasions, the lunchtime concerts were initially held in a private house in the Heiligenkreuzhof, in the north-east of the inner city beyond Stephansdom, before transferring to a public venue more often associated with dancing, a large room in the hotel 'Zum römischen Kaiser' in the Renngasse, directly opposite the Kinsky palace. As well as commenting on the novelty of the event, the subsequent brief report in the *Allgemeine musikalische Zeitung* hints at the high level of care and discrimination in the undertaking: the concerts were given after the works had been rehearsed (in other words they were not exploratory *prima vista* performances) and the authority of Schuppanzigh, in particular, was evident, someone who knew how to 'penetrate exactly the spirit of the works and to bring out their fire, strength, alternatively also their delicacy, tenderness, humour, charm and playfulness'. The journal also gave the names of the other members of the ensemble: Schuppanzigh's pupil Joseph Mayseder (second violin), Anton Schreiber (viola) and Anton Kraft (cello).[35]

The concerts continued for three more seasons, though next to nothing is known about them until the last season when four concerts were given in as many weeks in November and December 1807.[36] At least one of Beethoven's latest quartets, from op. 59 (dedicated to Prince Razumovsky), was given. Two reports from earlier in the year that related to private performances of these quartets attest to their challenging nature and their elite appeal to connoisseurs. 'They are deep in concentration and marvellously worked out, but not universally comprehensible' said the one, while the second hinted that their appeal was being broadened: 'Beethoven's newest, difficult but substantial quartets are giving ever more pleasure; the amateurs [*die Liebhaber*] hope to see them soon in print.'[37]

Schuppanzigh's performances of one or more of the set in his public concerts at the end of 1807 were given from manuscript parts; a month later they were published in Vienna by the Bureau d'Arts et d'Industrie, a firm already associated with printing works of reach and ambition.

Perhaps in the wake of the success of Beethoven's new quartets, 1808 marked a new stage in Schuppanzigh's career. The ensemble was now sponsored by Prince Razumovsky, who occasionally played second violin in it, an agreement that lasted until 1816, when Schuppanzigh and his colleagues were dismissed, according to one report for no apparent reason.[38] It was then that he embarked on a concert tour that took him to St Petersburg. Although Razumovsky had first call on Schuppanzigh and his colleagues, particularly when it came to the performance of new works, the musicians were free to work elsewhere. For four seasons, from 1809–10 to 1812–13, Schuppanzigh did not present public concerts of quartets, but revived the practice from the 1813–14 season onwards. One report on the concerts of the following season reveals very clearly the heightened degree of appreciation:

> A select company of people takes great pleasure in them. Mozart, Haydn and Beethoven are the order of the day. It is impossible to imagine, particularly in the case of the last composer, more perfect performances than one hears here. This precision, unanimity and insight into the spirit of musical art can only be attained through respect and love towards the composer.[39]

These comments expose an increasing emphasis on composer and their authored works – the quartets of Haydn, Mozart and Beethoven – whereas the popularity of piano music usually privileged performance rather than authorship. This focus on the message rather on the medium was also reflected in publication practices. A good deal of piano music was published in the knowledge that there was an insatiable market for it with topicality often a factor; publication of quartets, on the other hand, frequently took place some time after actual composition and, at its most elitist, made an artistic virtue of avoiding (or, at least, transcending) topicality.

From the early 1790s the practice had grown up of an aristocratic patron commissioning a set of quartets, which were owned by him in the form of manuscript parts (sometimes score) for a period of time before being released back to the composer, who would then distribute them for his own benefit. Typically that distribution was through publication, when the loop was closed with a dedication to the original patron; at this point the composer might be rewarded with further payment or a gift, such as a snuffbox. It represented a modification of the long-standing practice of a patron owning the music of his Kapellmeister, the product as well as the person. The new practice suited everybody. The composer was financially supported by someone of social and musical status, he could refine the work following the private performances, and was free to benefit from

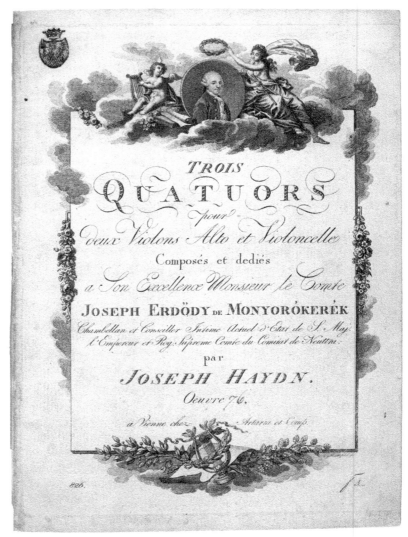

TROIS

QUATUORS

pour

deux Violons Alto et Violoncelle

Composés et dediés

a Son Excellence Monsieur le Comte

JOSEPH ERDÖDY DE MONYORÓKERÉK

Chambellan et Conseiller Intime Actuel d'Etat de S. Maj.
l'Empereur et Roy Supreme Comte du Comitat de Neutra.

par

JOSEPH HAYDN.

Oeuvre 76.

a Vienne chez   Artaria et Comp.

7 Title-page of Haydn's op. 76, Artaria, 1799

the eventual publication of the work; the patron, for his part, spent considerably less money than under the previous system, felt fulfilled by his judgment, impressed his peers with that discrimination, and was rewarded by a dedication that was widely distributed. Finally, it gave both parties the freedom to seek similar relationships with others.

In the winter of 1792–3 Count Anton Georg Apponyi, himself a good violinist, commissioned six quartets from Haydn for 100 ducats (450 gulden)[40] and had ownership of them for one year before they were published in Vienna by Artaria in 1795–6, 'Composés et dediés a Monsr. Le Comte Antoine D'Apponyi'. One person who heard the quartets performed when they were owned by Apponyi was the then Count Razumovsky who, in a letter to a friend in St Petersburg, bemoaned the fact that they were not yet available for purchase; like everybody else he had to wait for their publication as opp. 71 and 74.[41] Similar arrangements were in force for Haydn's op. 76 quartets (commissioned by Count Joseph Erdödy, completed in 1797, but not published until 1799 by Artaria) and his op. 77 quartets (commissioned by Prince Lobkowitz, completed in 1799, published three years later in 1802 by Artaria). Similarly Beethoven's first set of quartets, op. 18, were performed in private at one or more of Lobkowitz's palaces in 1799 and 1800 before being published by Mollo in 1801.[42] It was precisely this process that characterized the composition of the 'Razumovsky' quartets and led to the correspondent of the *Allgemeine musikalische Zeitung* to point out the same sense of anticipation that Razumovsky himself had experienced over ten years earlier.

Publishers were not content to be the grateful final beneficiaries of this process, but played a part in promoting an elevated status for the quartet, including the same emerging sense of a historical tradition evident in the programmes of Schuppanzigh's concerts. When Artaria published Haydn's op. 76 quartets in 1799, as well as the requisite dedication to Count Erdödy who had first commissioned them he provided an unusually elaborate title-page (see Fig. 7). The wording of the title-page is contained within a frame that is edged by garlands of flowers (suggesting beauty) and supported in mid-air by clouds (suggesting transcendence); at the top of the frame there is an engraving of the composer himself with a laurel wreath hovering like a halo above his head. The inclusion of Haydn's image is a clear indication of the consummate and everlasting mastery of this composer in this particular genre. Some of the routine details of the symbolism recall the title-page of Fux's *Gradus ad Parnassum*, but Haydn and others may well have remembered the words of Austria's national anthem, 'Gott erhalte Franz den Kaiser', recently composed by him and used as the theme for a set of variations in the slow movement of op. 76 no. 3. The fifth and sixth lines of the first verse extol Emperor Franz; they could well describe the image on Artaria's title-page:

Gott erhalte Franz den Kaiser,	God preserve Franz the Emperor,
Unsern guten Kaiser Franz!	Our good Emperor Franz!
Lange lebe Franz den Kaiser	Long live Franz the Emperor
In des Glückes hellstem Glanz!	In the brightest splendour of his destiny!
Ihm erblühen Lorbeerreiser,	To him may bloom sprigs of laurel,
Wo er geht, zum Ehrenkranz!	Wherever he goes, into a wreath of glory!
Gott erhalte ...	God preserve ...

A year later, in 1800, Artaria took the unusual step of publishing a much older set of quartets for the first time in Vienna, op. 20 from 1772; it was dedicated to another quartet enthusiast, a civil servant in the Hungarian chancellery, Nikolaus Zmeskall (1759–1833), who played the cello and who was himself a composer of quartets. Finally, in 1810, shortly after Haydn's death, Artaria issued a collected edition of fifty-eight quartets by the composer (*Collection complette des Quatuors de Joseph Haydn*). Pleyel's earlier, and later more celebrated, collected edition of the quartets had been available in Vienna, but this publication by a Viennese publisher for the Viennese market defined Haydn's legacy for Lobkowitz, Razumovsky, Schuppanzigh and others even more strongly. Iconography once more played a part: on the second page of the first violin volume there was a bust of Haydn and, underneath, a lute with a wreath of laurel, on the third page a memorial stone with another bust of the composer, together with a grieving figure to the left and a burning urn to the right.[43]

Mozart, too, was part of this privileged and privileging agenda in the quartet medium. Between 1801 and 1806 Breitkopf & Härtel issued four volumes containing twelve quartets as part of the ambitious *Œuvre complettes* project.[44] As with Haydn's quartets, many connoisseurs would have owned earlier printed editions of individual sets, even manuscript copies, but the opportunity to own the output in one uniformly presented format was a notable stage in the canonization of these works and gave authority to the emerging sense of three pre-eminent composers – Haydn, Mozart and Beethoven.

Although increasingly evident in the first decades of the nineteenth century, this perception that the string quartet was the most challenging and, potentially, the most absorbing of all genres was not entirely new. As early as 1788, Dittersdorf hinted in a letter to Artaria that his quartets might sell better than those of Mozart 'because of the excessively constant artfulness' ('wegen der allzugrossen darinne beständig herrschenden Kunst') of the latter.[45] The gap between the artful and the routine in the genre widened in the following decades as composers like Gyrowetz, Krommer and the two Wranitzky brothers provided less demanding alternatives to the works of Haydn, Mozart and Beethoven. There was also the continuing practice of performing arrangements of movements from operas, ballets and oratorios. Traeg's catalogue of 1799 has entries for over forty items of this kind, music by Cimarosa, Dittersdorf, Gluck, Mozart, Paisiello, Salieri and others. Between 1807 and 1809, the years that saw the first private and public performances of Beethoven's 'Razumovsky' quartets, the publisher Chemische Druckerey issued twenty volumes of a serial publication, the *Journal für Quartetten Liebhaber*, devoted to arrangements for string quartets of music from contemporary operas and ballet, a repertoire that never featured in Schuppanzigh's concerts.[46]

The ever-increasing exclusivity of the genre reached an extreme point in Beethoven's quartet in F minor, op. 95. Composed in the summer and autumn of 1810, the 'Quartetto serioso', as Beethoven called it, was dedicated to Nikolaus Zmeskall, a long-standing friend. Zmeskall had not commissioned the work; rather, it was a tribute from a questing composer to a loyal connoisseur. The work was not published in Vienna for six years, not because Zmeskall held any rights to the work, but because Beethoven thought that the general public was not yet ready for it. In a letter to Sir George Smart, the composer wrote: 'The Quartett is written for a small circle of connoisseurs and is never to be performed in public.'[47] At one level, Beethoven is voicing a degree of nervousness about its possible reception; at another level, there is the self-congratulatory view that it belonged to connoisseurs only. Generations of commentators have willingly embraced this view on behalf of the composer but, in truth, Beethoven was only one Viennese amongst many who shared and promoted it.

Music in Vienna in 1808: the view of a patriot

IN May 1808 a new newspaper appeared in Vienna, the *Vaterländische Blätter für den österreichischen Kaiserstaat*. Like the long-standing *Wiener Zeitung* it was to appear twice a week, on Tuesdays and Fridays, but its remit and content were rather different. Four years after Franz had assumed the new title of Emperor of Austria and two years after he had formally relinquished the title of Holy Roman Emperor, there was a new focus on Austria as an imperial state, the 'österreichische Kaiserstaat' of the title. The publication was not so much a newspaper as a strictly controlled feuilleton, an attempt to educate its citizens about the empire and to nurture a sense of patriotism for the fatherland. Early issues contained an essay on the princely kingdom of Berchtesgaden, an account of life in the rich agricultural area of Marchfeld that lay between Vienna and Pressburg (Bratislava), the attempts to promote the Hungarian language in literature and in legal proceedings, and the setting up of a school for surgery in Prague. Every issue contained a list of exchange rates between the various parts of the empire, and between Vienna and other major cities. It listed recent notable arrivals in Vienna, overwhelmingly members of the aristocracy, but since their place of departure was usually also listed – typically one of their palaces in the countryside – that very conveniently encouraged a sense of Vienna as the focal point for the different parts of the empire.

The sixth and seventh issues (27 May and 31 May 1808) contained a substantial two-part article on music, a survey of its present condition in Vienna.[48] While some articles in the *Vaterländische Blätter* are signed, this one is not, but it was probably the work of Ignaz von Mosel (1772–1844).[49] Professionally, he worked as an official in the Obersthofmeisteramt, but he was a proficient amateur composer and occasional writer on music. Like Joseph Sonnleithner, he was one of those government officials whose enthusiasm for music was making him an increasingly influential figure. His first essay for the new *Vaterländische Blätter* is certainly not a complacent exercise in national pride. While it does its duty in praising the particular qualities of music-making in the city and the notable contribution of many individuals, it is also surprisingly critical, pointing out where Vienna could do better.

The article begins in the most positive way possible, noting how music's uplifting qualities are nowhere better demonstrated than in Vienna, where it unites all classes:

> If one believes that the culture of music is closely associated with the cultivation of the mind, then one would have many reasons to congratulate the inhabitants of this major city: in virtually nowhere else is this godly art so extensively pursued, loved so much and practised so ardently as here; nowhere has so many accomplished practitioners, on virtually all instruments, many of whom could be considered alongside the professors of this art, a few may even surpass them. On a daily basis music works miracles here, of a kind that can be attributed only to love; it makes all levels of society equal. Aristocracy, bourgeoisie, princes and their vassals, masters and their underlings, all sit together and, through the harmony of sounds, forget the disharmony of their standing.

After noting the importance of music in the raising of the young, it observes that there is hardly a house to be found that does not have evenings devoted to string quartets or to piano sonatas, to the extent that they have displaced card playing as a social pastime. After this curious observation comes a much more serious one: 'So much is done for so-called chamber music, but so little opportunity is afforded for full orchestras, symphonies, concertos, oratorios etc.' The recently completed season of Liebhaber Concerte, culminating in the performance of Haydn's *Die Schöpfung*, is commended and it is hoped that it can be continued in the following season. The associated costs of promoting 'great music pieces' (*grosse Musikstücke*) in public are certainly considerable – the author specifically mentions the fees to be paid to wind players (dilettante wind players were less common than string players), the costs of copying the music and of providing wax candles – but there is another reason why such works are not regularly performed in Vienna. 'Why, up to now virtually no musical institute, no musical academy, no conservatoire and the like has been set up, is difficult to fathom.' The presence of such an institution would greatly help the provision of 'great music pieces'.

After noting with approval the presence of German opera in Vienna, the article moves on to composers in the city. Mozart is much lamented and is yet to be equalled; Haydn, 'the pride of Vienna' ('Wiens Stoltz'), whose *Die Schöpfung* has already been mentioned, is celebrated for his quartets and symphonies, but 'lives now only as a person, no more as an artist'. Mosel then moves to make some complimentary remarks about Albrechtsberger, Salieri and Maximilian Stadler, before coming to Beethoven. He is 'an unfettered and anomalous genius, of a kind rarely encountered' ('ein Genie ungebunden und regellos, wie es einem solchen zukömmt'), who has made a few, not entirely successful attempts in large-scale vocal music (that is the oratorio *Christus am Ölberge* and the two versions of *Leonore*) and shown himself in several single arias and songs to be capable of true and deep feeling. As an instrumental composer, he is 'an inestimable acquisition for Vienna and, amongst those composers now active, undoubtedly deserves the first position'. May 1808, the month of publication, was an interesting moment to comment on Beethoven's standing in Vienna. With the recent publication of the 'Razumovsky' quartets his reputation in that genre as the worthy successor to Haydn and Mozart had been consolidated, and the season of Liebhaber Concerte that had just ended had allowed listeners to hear seven performances of his existing symphonies (Nos. 1–4) in as many months.[50] If the author had been writing a year later, following the first private and public performances of the Fifth and Sixth Symphonies, then the reservations he felt about the oratorio and the two versions of *Leonore* would have been balanced by an even more enthusiastic appreciation of Beethoven as a composer of instrumental music. That, in turn, would have given an even stronger emphasis on the primacy of Haydn, Mozart and Beethoven.

While Mosel's article in the *Vaterländische Blätter für den österreich-ischen Kaiserstaat* gives a coherent view of musical life in Vienna in 1808, together with its strengths and weaknesses, it makes no reference at all to the abiding, increasingly disruptive influence of international wars, the French Revolutionary Wars of the 1790s followed by the Napoleonic Wars, even though the fundamental reason for the founding of the paper was to nurture devotion to the fatherland at a time of deep insecurity. May 1808 lay between two invasions of Vienna by French troops, in 1805–6 and in 1809, but the city had lived with the threat since the early 1790s and was not to be relieved of it until 1814. Although marked by periods of nervous peace, this was the second longest war in the history of Austria and the first to penetrate Vienna since the Turkish siege of 1683. Music, like every other aspect of society, was deeply affected, resulting in fundamental changes that were to shape its presence in the city for the rest of the nineteenth century and beyond.

CHAPTER 7

Music, War and Peace

In tempore belli

THE fervour and excesses of the French Revolution were real enough, as were the territorial ambitions of Napoleon but, ultimately, the period of war from 1792 to 1814 was less about repelling an ideology and a new social order than maintaining a familiar principle, the balance of power in Europe. Although Vienna was twice occupied by Napoleon's forces, the city retained its status as the capital of an empire and when the wars eventually came to an end, it was in that city that the international powers gathered to settle the peace, the Congress of Vienna.

During this period of turmoil and real hardship, Vienna both lost an old empire, the Holy Roman Empire, and gained a new one, the Austrian Empire. The lexicon of identity changed too, with increasing use of Austria rather than Germany, imperial state (*Kaiserstaat*) rather than empire (*Reich*) and, a newly emphasized image, the fatherland (*Vaterland*). It was a period of severe adjustment and much the same could be said about the role of music. Music in the Habsburg capital had lost its place at the centre of imperial identity and a second shift was already perceptible, from the aristocracy to the increasing involvement of the cultured bourgeoisie. The financial hardships of the period certainly accelerated the weakening of the influence of the aristocracy but there was never a revolution, just a gradual process of democratization, with no political or philosophical baggage.

One of the complexities, often forgotten, of this era of survival from 1792 to 1814 was that it was not consistently marked by warfare. There were substantial periods when Austria was nominally at peace with France, roughly eleven years in total, and for a few months in the Russian campaign of 1812 actually fought alongside France. While Britain was a frequent ally during times of war, Russia was a more intermittent one. These patterns of war followed by peace, together with associated shifting sympathies towards Britain, France and Russia, left their mark on musical life in Vienna and helped to forge a sense of musical identity, real and manufactured, that went with the new fatherland.

1792–1799
The First Coalition to the Peace of Campo Formio

L EOPOLD II's skills as an international diplomat had been adeptly
deployed in 1790, the first year of his reign, settling disputes with
the Austrian Netherlands, Hungary and Turkey within months. Since
the relationship between Austria and France had been an amicable one
since the 1750s, personified by the marriage in 1770 of his sister, Maria
Antonia (Marie Antoinette), to Louis XVI, Leopold first tried to persuade
the king and queen to compromise with the demands of the National
Assembly. When they refused, Leopold joined Friedrich Wilhelm II of
Prussia in threatening force against France if the king was not restored
to power. For Leopold, it was a still a matter of gentle diplomacy, rather
than an inevitable commitment to war, but his hopes were dashed by the
increasingly belligerent confidence of the Legislative Authority in Paris.[1]
Entirely unexpectedly, on 1 March 1792 Leopold died from a respiratory
ailment, aged fifty-four, having served as emperor for just over two years.
He was succeeded by his son, Franz II, who, at the age of twenty-four, was
plunged into an international crisis. On 20 April, France declared war on
Austria and Prussia. To assert continuity and identity Franz quickly went
through the various traditional coronation ceremonies: in June, he was
crowned King of Hungary in Ofen; in July, Holy Roman Emperor in
Frankfurt; and in August, King of Bohemia in Prague. Expenditure was
kept to the minimum and there was no coronation opera in Prague. The
battle zone lay to the west in the Rhine valley and to the north-west in the
Austrian Netherlands, and both sides achieved notable victories without
producing a settled outcome. In Paris itself the revolution lurched forward
alarmingly with the execution of the king in January 1793, the declaration
of war against Britain and Holland in February, against Spain in March,
and the execution of Marie Antoinette in October.

1793 brought the first significant musical response in Vienna to the war.
It came from Maria Theresia von Paradis, the blind pianist and composer,
setting a text by her companion, Johann Riedinger: *Deutsches Monument
Ludwigs des Unglücklichen* (German Monument to the Misfortune of
Louis). Written for voices and piano, it was published in Prague and
Vienna by Paradis's acquaintance, Schönfeld.[2] The text is hopelessly prolix,
allowing no room for musical elaboration, but both it and Paradis's music
were the product of individuals who were well connected at court, and
they reveal many of the anxieties and outlooks of the time. The outrage
at the execution of Louis XVI is cast as a German issue, the responsibility
of the Holy Roman Empire, not specifically of the Austrian monarchy;
appropriately, the work – the *Deutsches Monument* – is dedicated to
Franz's wife, Marie Therese, 'Kaiserin der Deutschen'. Most of the fifteen
numbers are shared between named characters, Gallia the Guardian Spirit
of France and Teutonia, plus Religion, Honour and Destiny, all of whom
are appalled at the desecration of a country, its values, its religion and its

fate. But this is not just a forceful lament. Towards the end a new character appears, The Avenging Angel, who urges the mighty German people to war; they respond 'Yes, yes, we feel ourselves ready, we want to avenge blood with blood, we will not return home until we conquer the enemy' ('Ja, ja, wir fühlen uns bereit, wir wollen Blut mit Blut rächen, wir kehren nicht zurück nach Haus bis wir den Feind besiegen').

By the following January, Paradis had made an orchestral version of the work in readiness for two public performances to raise money for an entirely new charity for war widows and orphans. The first performance was held within the confines of the Hofburg, in the Kleiner Redoutensaal, on 21 January 1794 (the exact anniversary of Louis's XVI's execution); the second, three days later, in the larger venue of the Kärntnertortheater. The rest of the programme consisted of a 'new symphony' by Haydn (one of Nos. 93–8), an aria by Mozart and a piano concerto by Leopold Kozeluch, Paradis's former teacher, in which she played the solo part. The aria by Mozart and the role of Gallia in the *Deutsches Monument* was sung by Aloysia Lange, Mozart's sister-in-law. At the second performance a violin concerto by Franz Clement was played instead of the Kozeluch concerto.

A few weeks earlier Paradis had composed a much shorter patriotic work, a song for the New Year, destined for one of her private concerts, 'Auf die Damen welche statt Gold, nun Leinwand, für die verwundeten Krieger zupfen', a sprightly song of forty-two bars, written for those ladies who, instead of working with gold thread (one of the imperial colours), now prepare lint for wounded soldiers.[3]

During 1794 the patriotism presented in these two works by Paradis was bolstered by more repressive measures in Austria, designed to ensure a defiant and united front as part of the First Coalition alongside Britain, Holland, Prussia and Spain. Under Franz's rule foreigners had already been required to carry special passports issued by the police, secret societies (including the Freemasons) were prohibited, schoolteachers were required to promote the virtues of the monarch and censorship of all printed matter, including music, was considerably tightened.[4] In the summer of 1794 the police responded brutally to an alleged plot to unseat the Habsburg dynasty. Upwards of forty people were arrested, guilty members of the army were hanged and sympathetic civilians were given jail sentences of up to sixty years.[5] Beethoven was one person who witnessed events or, more likely, heard the rumours that circulated. In a business letter, dated 2 August, to the publisher Nikolaus Simrock in Bonn, he gives him the latest news, beginning with the weather:

> We are having very hot weather here; and the Viennese are afraid that soon they will not be able to get any more *ice cream*. For, as the winter was so mild, ice is scarce. Here various important people have been locked up; it is said that a revolution was about to break out – But I believe that so long as an Austrian can get his *brown ale* and

his *little sausages*, he is not likely to revolt. People say that the gates leading to the suburbs are to be closed at 10 p.m. The soldiers have loaded their muskets with ball. You dare not raise your voice here or the police will take you into custody.[6]

Beethoven's comments on the placid Austrians are all too easily interpreted as sympathy towards France and criticism of Austria. They are more appropriately read as casual ones, accepting rather than judgmental. Beethoven was a Habsburg loyalist, brought up in a court in Bonn ruled by Maximilian Franz, the brother of Joseph II and Leopold II, and someone who had written cantatas to commemorate the death of the first and the succession of the second. Indeed, in the same letter to Simrock Beethoven indicates his continuing desire to return to Bonn, where he would have resumed his position at court; it was only the decision by the French to invade that part of the Rhine in the autumn and Maximilian Franz's consequent departure that finally persuaded the composer that he should remain in Vienna.

As the Austrian state battened down the hatches, the land battles continued on the western and north-western fronts, a long way from Vienna, allowing the continuing indifference of the people that had caught Beethoven's attention. From the summer of 1796 onwards the mood changed and with it came a spate of musical responses, one initiated by the state (a national anthem), most by the opportunism of publishers. Since all public events and all printed matter were subject to the approval of the government that distinction was of no real consequence. Music and state were as one. The First Coalition had began to unravel, as Holland, Prussia and Spain signed separate peace treaties with France. This left Austria and Britain as the only remaining members of the coalition; Britain's involvement, however, was entirely a maritime one, which meant that on land Austria became the sole combatant. To add to the western and north-western fronts there was now a new, menacing southern front, as French troops under the command of the young Napoleon marched northwards through Italy towards the Tyrol, inflicting defeat upon defeat on Austrian forces. Vienna sensed the real possibility of a pincer movement closing in on the city, from the south and from the west. Music was about to play a full part in whipping up patriotic fervour.

The national mood was considerably helped by the unexpected success of Austrian forces in the west, led by its new commander, Archduke Karl (Franz's brother). During the summer of 1796 advancing French forces were halted and the Prince-Bishopric of Würzburg was liberated. The latter was brought to life in Vienna's salons in the following months by two descriptive piano pieces, one by Johann Baptist Vanhal (published by Eder in November 1796), the other by Ferdinand Kauer (sold by Artaria in April 1797).[7] When the archduke returned to Vienna a celebratory cantata for voices and piano was published, with music by Franz Süssmayr and text by Franz Huber, two colleagues at the Kärntnertortheater: *Eine kleine Cantate auf die Ankunft seiner königliche Hohheit des Erzherzogs Carl* (A small Cantata on the Return of his Royal Highness Archduke Carl).[8] It is one of those domestic publications that is to be sung around the piano ('zu singen beim Clavier'). A solo soprano and tenor set the scene, culminating in a broad duet in C major, marked Larghetto: 'Future generations will be amazed to hear what Austria's young hero did' ('Mit Staunen wird die Nachwelt hören was Oestreichs junger Held gethan'). Most of the work is taken up with a chorus of three voices (sopranos, tenors and basses), where everybody around the piano sings seven verses, Maestoso, extolling Karl's achievement. The final verse diplomatically brings the emperor into the picture:

So lange Franz regiert	As long as Franz reigns
Und Karl der junge Sieger	And Karl the young victor
Die tapfern Oestreichs Krieger	Leads the brave warriors of Austria
Dem Feind' entgegen führt,	Against the enemy,
Blüht Glück in jedem Stande,	Happiness rules in every way,
Herrscht Ruh im ganzen Lande,	Peace reigns throughout the land,
Und uns an Wohlstand gleich	And for us there is no realm
Ist auf der Welt kein Reich.	That can equal its good fortune.

In the four years that separate the cantatas of Paradis and Süssmayr, music and Vienna had moved from proclaiming allegiance to a wider Germany to allegiance to an increasingly self-defining Austria.

Süssmayr's music was at the centre of an extended public appeal to national pride in the winter of 1796–7. A lightly armed infantry regiment of volunteers was formed in Vienna, ready to take to the field. Between mid-September and mid-November, nine fund-raising concerts were held in the Grosser Redoutensaal, the Kärntnertortheater and a theatre in the northern suburb of Leopoldstadt. The concerts in the Redoutensaal contained a new patriotic cantata by Süssmayr, *Der Retter in Gefahr* (The Deliverer in Peril); the main supporting item on each occasion was a symphony by Haydn (probably the 'Surprise' Symphony, No. 94).[9]

Süssmayr's cantata is on a generous scale.[10] Scored for three soloists, chorus and an orchestra of flutes, oboes, clarinets, bassoons, horns, trumpets, timpani, side-drum and strings, its fourteen movements set a well-planned text designed to foster national resolve by Johann Rautenstrauch, the author of a popular biography of Maria Theresia.[11] Beginning with a Chorus of the Distressed, the cantata proceeds with a sequence of arias plus one trio, sung by a variety of allegorical and representative figures – the Spirit of the Fatherland, a young man who wishes to join the army, a young mother and a country girl – each of whom evokes and responds to the call to arms on behalf of Austria. The final chorus in C major asserts and proclaims their new, shared resolve: 'Rise, for God, for our Emperor, for the rule of law, for the Fatherland' ('Auf, für Gott, für unsern Kaiser/Fürs Gesetz, fürs Vaterland'). Any member of

8   Title-page of Süssmayr's *Der Retter in Gefahr*, 1796

the several audiences who wished to recapture this heady atmosphere at home with friends could later purchase a printed vocal score, the title page of which was adorned with military and musical images (see Fig. 8). One person who owned a copy was Archduke Rudolph, as indicated by the handwritten initial in the top right-hand corner.

Süssmayr was not the only composer who contributed to the cause of the volunteer regiment. From his store in the 'Elefantenhaus', Eder issued a march for the force by an unknown composer arranged for piano,[12] and Artaria published a song by Beethoven, 'Abschiedsgesang an Wiens Bürger' ('Farewell song to the people of Vienna', WoO 121). The text of the song was written by a young sub-lieutenant, six verses of bellicose rhetoric. In what is probably Beethoven's worst composition – it must have taken him all of twenty minutes to write – he responds with endlessly repetitive martial music and a good deal of unison writing.

It was during this period that plans for another song, one intended for the whole nation, came to fruition: Haydn's Volkslied (as he called it), 'Gott erhalte Franz den Kaiser'. The instigator of the project was Count Franz Joseph Saurau who, as deputy head of the police, had played a leading role in the suppression of the would-be dissidents in 1794.[13] He believed that Austria needed a song, much like 'God save the King' in Britain, that would be a focus for national pride. The text was commissioned from Laurenz Leopold Haschka (1749–1827), a dilettante poet in the employ of the state who responded with four verses, clearly modelled on 'God save the King'. They avoid the heady rhetoric evident in the patriotic contributions of Süssmayr and Beethoven, including the modish words *Österreich* and *Vaterland*; instead there is a measured, almost other-worldly depiction of the attributes of the emperor, neatly encapsulated by the recurring climactic couplet, 'Gott erhalte Franz den Kaiser/Unsern guten Kaiser Franz'. Haydn's response was similarly measured and heart-warming, a song that could be sung at the keyboard by one person (as Haydn himself was to do in his dying days) or by the largest of public gatherings. Of all the patriotic music produced in Vienna during the wars this was the most individual; it was also the most frequently performed, the most influential and the most enduring. Joseph Saurau deployed the full might of the imperial–royal administration behind its official launch. Two different printers were engaged to prepare multiple copies of a single page, music on the left, words on the right, that were to be distributed to theatres throughout the Habsburg territories with instructions that it was to be performed for the first time on Franz's birthday, 12 February 1797. A hundred years earlier the emperor's birthday would have elicited a new opera, performed in the privacy of the court, often ending with a ballet; on this occasion, the whole populace paid homage. Eder was the first publisher to capitalize on its success. Within three days of the official launch he was advertising the song, plus a set of variations for piano on the theme by Johann Georg Lickl, the first of many such works.[14] Over the course of the wars 'Gott erhalte' was constantly heard, in private and in public, for individual pleasure and for collective well-being.

Two months earlier, in December 1796, a very different work by Haydn had received its first performance in Vienna, a new mass, his first for fourteen years, to which he gave the title *Missa in tempore belli*. As well as being topical it reflected several hundred years of accumulated tradition. It was performed on St Stephen's Day (26 December), one of the highlights of the liturgical year, the celebration of the first martyr and the saint whose name is enshrined in Vienna's premier church, the Stephansdom. Haydn's mass was written for the Piaristenkirche in the Josefstadt, a suburb to the west of the city, where it is located in a square bounded by the monastery and featuring a Marian column showing the Virgin Mary trampling the infidel. The service in 1796 marked the entrance to the priesthood of one Joseph Hoffmann, son of a court official who was in charge of the budget for the war.[15] Set in the traditional C major, with the sound of trumpets and timpani much in evidence, Haydn's mass interrupts the traditional three-fold repetition of 'Agnus Dei, qui tollis peccata mundi' with drumbeats and insistent trumpet fanfares; the composer later told his biographer Georg Griesinger that the drumbeats should sound 'as if one heard the enemy approaching in the distance'.[16]

By the end of March 1797, French troops had, indeed, entered the Tyrol and Styria. A truce was arranged between Austria and France that led to the signing of the Peace of Campo Formio seven months later in October 1797. For much of this period between the truce and the treaty, Eder continued to issue patriotic war songs, marches and descriptive piano pieces, though once the treaty was signed the flow stopped. The ensuing winter and spring were uneasy ones, a mixture of relief and increasing recognition that the peace was unlikely to last. One of the key figures in Vienna's musical life, Paul Wranitzky, wrote a large-scale symphony to celebrate the Peace of Campo Formio, a work that traced recent history from 'The Revolution', through 'The Destiny and Death of Louis XVI' to 'Peace Negotiations' and 'Jubilation at the Restoration of the Peace'. But two days before its first performance in December the imperial censors indicated their disapproval, uncertain about the mixed messages that an apparent reconciliation with recent French history might send to imperial Vienna.[17]

Even odder was the history of the publication of six canzonettas by Haydn the following July (Hob.XXVIa: 31–6). Very unusually, Artaria's edition was a bilingual one, the original English in parallel with a German translation. One canzonetta presented problems. 'The Sailor's Song', originally composed by Haydn in London in 1794, is a rumbustious celebration of the limitless bravery of the British sailor, ending with the rousing couplet 'The Roaring Cannon loudly speaks/Tis Britain's Glory we maintain'. Since at the time of Artaria's publication Austria needed to be wary of celebrating the bravery of its former coalition partner, the German text tones down the rhetoric to a feeble 'To the roar of cannons beautifully sounds a lively little song' ('Zum Donner der Kanonen klingt/Ein muntres Liedchen wunderschön').[18]

It was Haydn, Habsburg loyalist and a devout Catholic, the personification of *pietas austriaca* and an enthusiastic Anglophile, who most tellingly explored the tensions of this uncertain period in 1798, between peace and war. In fewer than eight weeks in July and August he wrote a new mass, described as *Missa in angustiis*, literally 'Mass in straitened times'. It was destined for performance on that most patriotic of occasions, 9 September, the day when Austrians commemorated the defeat of the Turks in 1683. Trumpets and timpani are certainly to the fore, but Haydn avoids the traditional key of C major in favour of an opening movement, 'Kyrie eleison, Christe eleison', in a theatrical D minor; the minor key returns in the Benedictus to undermine the comforting nature of the text, grippingly so when three trumpets play an insistent fanfare against a full declamation of that text.

In the nineteenth century Haydn's work acquired the nickname 'Nelson' mass and was conveniently linked with Admiral Nelson's Mediterranean campaign in the summer of 1798, when the British fleet routed the French in the Battle of Aboukir. But news of that victory did not reach Vienna until after the composer had completed his mass. The emotive power of Haydn's work is far more subtle than the unfortunate nickname allows: general unease explored and, eventually, relieved through the age-old medium of a liturgical mass, the whole informed by inherited memory of war and victory.

The Battle of Aboukir did, however, capture the imagination of other composers. One of these was Vanhal (1739–1813), who composed a lengthy characteristic sonata (that is a sonata with a programme), 'dedicated out of respect to the Hero Sir Horatio Nelson'.[19] Across eleven printed sides of music Nelson's story is unfolded in a series of musical vignettes: his appointment as admiral of the fleet, his tracking down of the French fleet in the Mediterranean, the do-or-die loyalty of his sailors, the breaking of the enemy line, the destruction of the French fleet, the victory cries of the English and Nelson's heroic status at home. It concludes with a *Finale all'Inglese*, that is the popular Viennese contredanse, derived from the English country dance. It is easy to be dismissive of a work of this kind, but when one remembers that this music is primarily for the performer not the listener, someone who is caught up in the musical realization of the many descriptive headings, then its fascination is clear. It was certainly effective as propaganda, acclimatizing the Viennese to the shifting priorities of its imperial rulers.

Within a year music had moved from a position where it was not permitted to allude to war, to a position where it openly celebrated the defeat of the French by a former ally. This paralleled the progress of international diplomacy. Faced by the inevitability of further hostilities, Austria was already forming a new international partnership, the Second Coalition, consisting of Britain, the Italian states, the Papal states, Russia, Turkey and Portugal. Following the French invasion of the Rhine on 1 March 1799, the Second Coalition war broke out on 12 March.

1799–1805
The Second Coalition to the Treaty of Lunéville

THE inclusion of Russia in the Second Coalition had been the result of a considered diplomatic campaign by the Austrian Foreign Minister, Baron Franz Thugut, and the Austrian Ambassador in St Petersburg. It was cemented with the standard instrument of Habsburg diplomacy, a dynastic marriage, between Archduke Johann (one of Franz's brothers) and Alexandra Pawlowna, the Tsar's favourite daughter.[20] It took place in Russia in October 1799, followed by complementary celebrations in Vienna in January 1800. Paul Wranitzky wrote a new symphony, dedicated to the newly married couple. Rather than the pictorialism of the symphony that had followed the Treaty of Campo Formio, Wranitzky's latest work modified the content of the standard four-movement symphony to include Russian elements. In place of the expected lyrical slow movement Wranitzky presents a *Russe*, a measured dance in duple time, and instead of the minuet and trio the composer includes a *Polones* and trio; the polonaise, rather than a minuet, was the premier dance in Russia and the standard way to begin a grand ball (as, much later, in Tchaikovsky's *Eugene Onegin*).[21] Unusually the finale begins with a slow introduction, scored for wind instruments only, evoking the Viennese practice of *Harmoniemusik*, in effect a serenade to the married couple.[22]

Alas, this diplomatic nicety was already being overtaken by contrary events. During 1799 Austrian and Russian forces had gained considerable success on the battlefield, in the Rhine, Switzerland and Italy, but success led to disagreement between the main coalition partners, and in January, at the height of the wedding celebrations in Vienna, Russia withdrew its support. Maintaining the goodwill of Russia was still a diplomatic aim, one that occasionally surfaced in music. With the certain knowledge of the new Russian Ambassador in Vienna, Count Razumovsky, Beethoven dedicated his three violin sonatas, op. 30 (published by Bureau d'Arts et d'Industrie, 1803), to Tsar Alexander; similarly the inclusion of Russian folksongs in 1805 and 1806 in the 'Razumovsky' quartets (op. 59) formed part of a continuing process of nurturing goodwill between the two countries.[23]

The other principal member of the Second Coalition, Britain, was a long-standing ally and over the course of the wars was to gain a stronger musical presence in Vienna than did Russia. The success of Admiral Nelson's campaign in the Mediterranean, which effectively separated French forces in Egypt from those in Europe, had propelled him into a national hero in Austria, as well as in Britain. Joseph Haydn owned an engraving of the Battle of Aboukir as well as one of Nelson himself.[24] Nelson, together with his mistress Emma Hamilton, her husband Sir William Hamilton (the British Ambassador in Naples), her mother and the poet Ellis Cornelia Knight spent just over two weeks in Vienna in August and early September 1800, when they were received at the imperial court. They also visited the opera where they heard a performance of Ferdinando Paer's *La virtù al cimento*. On 3 September they travelled to the Esterházy palace in Eisenstadt. Although Nelson was not especially musical, Lady Hamilton was an enthusiastic and capable singer. Haydn wrote a new work for the admiral and her, *The Battle of the Nile*, a setting of verses from a lengthy ode of that name by Ellis Cornelia Knight. In Vienna a printed copy of Knight's ode, signed by Nelson, was presented to the imperial library.[25]

For Haydn, this was only the latest manifestation of his Austro-British identity. Earlier in the same year he had published at his own expense the full score of *Die Schöpfung*, a work conceived with equal regard to the German and English texts and now published bilingually, with a list of subscribers from both countries, headed by the imperial family in Austria and the royal family in Britain. Many of the composer's instrumental works, including the recent op. 76 quartets, were published more or less simultaneously in Vienna (by Artaria) and London (by Longman & Broderip). Clementi, the pianist–composer, joined the latter firm as a partner in 1798 and during visits to Vienna in 1799 and 1804 was able to cement the musical relationship between the two countries.[26] He was to hold the rights for the first English editions of many of Beethoven's works, such as the Violin Concerto, the 'Razumovsky' quartets and the Fifth

Piano Concerto, publications that played a key role in making Beethoven's music known in Britain.[27] In Vienna, three sets of variations by Beethoven on well-known English themes were available from the music shops: 'See the conqu'ring hero comes' for cello and piano (Artaria, 1797), 'God save the King' and 'Rule, Britannia', both for piano (Bureau des Arts et d'Industrie, 1804).

While Vienna and Nelson were indulging in mutual adulation in the summer of 1800, the course of the war had turned decisively in France's favour. Russia's withdrawal from the coalition was followed by the dismissal of Archduke Karl as leader of the imperial forces and a brilliant series of victories by Napoleon's troops in northern Italy. Nothing had been gained after nearly two years of war when Austria signed the Treaty of Lunéville with France in February 1801. That treaty was to hold for nearly five years, until September 1805. Musically, it permitted French musical taste to feature in Vienna, albeit at some remove and without affecting traditional loyalties, especially British ones.

Since 1794 the two court theatres, under the direction of Baron Peter von Braun, had consistently presented operas in German and in Italian. Neither the Burgtheater nor the Kärntnertortheater was exclusively associated with one language, which helped to promote parity of esteem.[28] There was, however, a clear and irreversible trend towards more and more performances in German, which included presenting popular Italian operas in German translation. In Vienna, Mozart's posthumous status as a composer of opera was based increasingly on *Die Hochzeit des Figaro*, *Don Juan*, *Mädchentreu* and *Titus* as well the two original German operas, *Die Entführung aus dem Serail* and *Zauberflöte*. For the composer it helped to promote a German persona and, within that, a Viennese one. The long cultural hegemony enjoyed by Italian opera in Vienna was rapidly becoming a thing of the past; Beethoven, for instance, never even contemplated writing an opera in Italian.

German opera was further promoted by the popular success of Emanuel Schikaneder's makeshift theatre, the Theater auf der Wieden, in the 1790s. In a major indication of its success, a new theatre was built a mile away, to the south of the inner city, in the rapidly developing area of Laimgrube. As Vienna's newest theatre, the Theater an der Wien asserted its independence: it was larger than either of the two court theatres, more comfortable and more accessible, with a dedicated sheltered entrance for carriages. Above the main portico there was a stone carving of Papageno, Schikaneder's most popular role in an opera, *Zauberflöte*, that had underpinned much of his company's success. Financially, the Theater an der Wien soon began to accumulate substantial debts and by 1804 it had been taken over by Baron Braun, later by a consortium of nobility.[29] Before handing over responsibility to Braun, Schikaneder initiated a wholly new taste in opera.

In March 1802 the Theater an der Wien gave the first performance in Vienna of one of Cherubini's most successful works, *Lodoiska*. A highly emotive tale of tyranny and false imprisonment overcome by unshakeable determination and heroism, the opera had received its premiere in Paris in 1791 and was the inspiration for a whole series of similar works, much later dubbed rescue operas, that fired the fevered imagination of the French in that decade. While Austria was at war with France, its government would not have allowed French opera to be presented on the Viennese stage. A year after the signing of the Treaty of Lunéville, however, it was appropriate to do so, but translated into German to suit prevailing taste in Vienna. In that way its storyline and projected values were easily embraced by the Viennese, and if their French origins were ever acknowledged it was the France that was now at peace with Austria, not the France of the revolution. The German *Lodoiska* was a sensational success. At the two court theatres Baron Braun quickly saw that he needed to respond to this new enthusiasm and visited Paris in order to gather further operas of this type. In August 1802 the Kärntnertortheater presented its first work by Cherubini, *Die Tage der Gefahr* (a translation of *Les deux journées*), followed by *Medea* (*Médée*). Over the next few years the Kärntnertortheater and the Theater an der Wien vied with each other to present other fashionable operas from Paris: Méhul's *Le trésor supposé*, *Une folie*, *L'irato* and *Héléna*, and works by Dalayrac, Le Sueur and Isouard, all given in German.[30] In the immediate wake of their staging, music publishers such as Bureau d'Arts et d'Industrie, Cappi, Mollo and Sauer issued versions for the domestic market – selected vocal numbers and arrangements for piano and for string quartet.

It was against this exciting new tradition of German translations of fashionable French operas that Beethoven embarked in 1804 on the composition of his first opera, *Leonore*. The original text came directly from the French tradition, Pierre Gaveaux's opera *Léonore ou L'amour conjugal*, first performed in Paris in 1798, but not yet heard in Vienna. It ideally suited Beethoven's ambition to write an opera in the French manner. Joseph Sonnleithner, secretary of the court theatres, provided the translation as part of the broad remit of that position. As it was being composed in 1804–5, the political relationship between Austria and France was becoming ever more tense. Fearing the possibility of an invasion, Austria signed a defensive pact with Russia in November 1804; the following April, Russia, Britain and Sweden concluded an alliance, the Third Coalition, which effectively meant that it was inevitable that Austria would become a member; it formally did so on 8 August 1805.[31] Once again, allegiances had changed quickly; in just over a year Austria had moved from a position of regarding France as a power that might be trusted, to membership of a coalition that was likely to be drawn into battle. The new opera season began in August and Beethoven's work was scheduled for performance in November.

Another major work by Beethoven was even more caught up in the shifting international diplomacy of the time, the *Eroica* Symphony. The composer had begun work on the symphony in the early summer of 1803, when diplomatic relations between Austria and France were at their most cordial: if France presented itself as a state that ensured stability in central Europe, then Austria was prepared to accommodate the loss of influence in the disintegrating Holy Roman Empire in order to maintain its sovereignty in the core Austrian states. It was in this trusting phase of the relationship that Baron Braun had travelled to Paris to explore the operatic repertoire there. Beethoven, too, became part of this would-be cultural entente.[32]

On the 18th of Thermidor, in the XIth Year of the Republic, that is August 1803, the famed Parisian piano maker Sébastien Erard recorded the delivery of a complimentary piano to Beethoven; as was the custom at the time, the gift was a demonstration of his admiration for the composer-pianist topped up by the expectation that he would recommend the instrument to others. More than one source indicates that Beethoven himself was contemplating a journey to Paris to further his career and that his new symphony would be dedicated to Napoleon; if that didn't work out, he would dedicate the work to Prince Lobkowitz. Spring 1804 may well have been pencilled in as a possible date to travel, but by then Austria was becoming an increasingly nervous ally. In May 1804 Napoleon proclaimed himself hereditary emperor of France; for its part Austria had already accepted the *de facto* weakening of the Holy Roman Empire, the source of its imperial title, and decided that it would use the core Austrian states for a new title to match that assumed by Napoleon; at the same time it did not formally renounce the old title. In August 1804, Franz II, Holy Roman Emperor, also became Franz I, Emperor of Austria.

This was not a meek defensive gesture but a resolute act of reconfiguration, duly emphasized in the public celebrations that took place across the new empire in December 1804.[33] The principal church service took place in Vienna on 7 December, not a formal coronation but a service of thanksgiving, with many of the old characteristics: a service at the Stephansdom attended by the court, brazen trumpet and timpani fanfares, a setting of the *Te Deum* and the Mass by the court Kapellmeister Salieri, the pealing of bells across the city and celebratory cannon fire. Alongside these very traditional elements associated with the Catholic religion there was a notable embracing of other faiths, very much part of a new Austrian identity. The Lutheran church in the Dorotheergasse held its own service of thanksgiving, as did the Greek Orthodox church and the Jewish community. Opera, however, did not play a part in this new representation and no new work was commissioned. By accident, Mozart's *La clemenza di Tito* (given, unusually, in Italian) was in the repertory of the court theatres and three performances took place in November and December, but on the eve of the main celebration a rescue opera was performed, Cherubini's *Die Tage der Gefahr*, and, on the day itself, an opera buffa, Mozart's *Così fan tutte* (in German).[34]

Beethoven's response, while nearing the completion of his symphony, to the news that Napoleon had declared himself emperor is one of the most familiar stories in the history of Western music:

He flew into a rage and shouted: 'So he, too, is nothing more than an ordinary man. Now he also will trample all human rights underfoot, and only pander to his own ambition; he will place himself above everyone else and became a tyrant!' Beethoven went to the table, took hold of the title page at the top, ripped it all the way through, and flung it on the floor.[35]

This account, by Ferdinand Ries, a pupil of Beethoven at the time, was not published until 1838, eleven years after the composer's death and, though he was generally a reliable witness, its tone may owe something to Romantic expectations of how the great composer might have responded. What is certainly true is that the abandonment of the idea of a dedication to Bonaparte set in motion the tried and trusted process of patronage and early performances in Vienna. Between May (the month Napoleon declared himself emperor) and October the work was rehearsed and performed in private in Lobkowitz's palaces in Vienna and Bohemia;[36] Lobkowitz would have paid for the parts, which were also probably used in two further private performances in Vienna in January 1805, one in the spacious apartment of Baron Würth, the other in the Lobkowitz palace. The first public performance took place in the Theater an der Wien in April. By now, the political outlook in Vienna would not have sanctioned a symphony dedicated to Bonaparte. All the contemporary accounts of these early performances simply refer to it neutrally, as a symphony in E flat; the title *Sinfonia Eroica* came into use only when the work was published in October 1806 by the Bureau d'Arts et d'Industrie.

Beethoven's response to the changing climate was certainly a realistic one, but that realism was the very quality that Austria itself had been forced to develop. Beethoven and Austria were as one, in first admiring Napoleon before doubting and, finally, despising him. This leaves one aspect of the mythology of the *Eroica* story and its creator to be questioned: that Beethoven's incipient republicanism had been dashed by his feet-of-clay hero. The truth was a more prosaic one. His actions were ones of a Habsburg loyalist: Franz was entitled to call himself emperor, Napoleon was not. The persistence of the view that Beethoven, the musical revolutionary, was also a political revolutionary is remarkable, and determines understanding of the *Eroica* Symphony to this day. Sustaining this myth was itself to become a feature of Viennese musical history, even when it was fundamentally at odds with Austrian reading of political history of the time. Astonishingly, the first account to question this received outlook and to relate the early history of the work to the unfolding of contemporary events appeared only in 1998, in a book by Thomas Sipe on the symphony.[37]

1805–1809
The Third Coalition to the Peace of Pressburg

O N 23 September 1805, an aggressive France once more declared war
on a defensive Austria. This time the war was to be much shorter –
three months – following by a lengthy period of peace, over three years.
The war was short because it was ruthlessly decisive. By early November,
Napoleon's troops occupied the suburbs of Vienna, with the new Emperor
of France ensconced in the summer palace of the new Emperor of Austria,
Schönbrunn. The premiere of Beethoven's *Leonore* went ahead on 20
November at the Theater an der Wien, attended by a mixed audience of
Viennese residents and invading French, both responding to the composer's
assimilation of French musical taste, the former regarding it as a local
tradition, the latter probably discomfited by the use of German rather than
French. On St Stephen's Day Austria and France signed a peace treaty at
Pressburg. Austria was humiliated. It lost considerable territories in western
Austria, southern Germany and Italy and the following August Franz was
forced to relinquish the title of Holy Roman Emperor.[38]

Cherubini's fortunes during this time were mixed, embarrassingly
so. Baron Braun's attempts to persuade him to travel to Vienna had
finally borne fruit in the summer of 1805, when he arrived in the city
with a musical gesture of friendship between Paris and Vienna. The
Paris Conservatoire, founded ten years earlier, wished to make Haydn
an honorary member and Cherubini had been deputed to deliver the
invitation in person to the composer. Since Haydn's French was very
limited, Cherubini gave him a translation and wrote a grateful letter of
thanks on his behalf, which Haydn signed.[39] That letter, however, was
not written until March 1806, eight months after the invitation had been
received, which may suggest a certain unease, even reluctance, on Haydn's
part, perhaps on Cherubini's part too.

Meanwhile, Cherubini had composed his first original opera for Vienna,
Faniska. It was a rescue opera with many parallels to his own *Lodoiska*, as
well as Beethoven's *Leonore*; Beethoven's librettist, Joseph Sonnleithner,
was also responsible for Cherubini's libretto. The first performance of
Cherubini's work took place at the Kärntnertortheater on 25 February
and proved an immediate and lasting success, with thirty performances in
1806 alone. Cherubini himself was lauded and one commentator described
the work as a theatrical experience unequalled since Mozart's time.[40] This
commentator and others make no reference to the French occupation and
the work, like Beethoven's *Leonore*, was evidently appreciated in Vienna as
the pinnacle of a local operatic tradition, now celebrated in the presence of
the master himself.

Cherubini's own position, however, was an uncomfortable one. In the
1790s he had been Napoleon's favourite composer of opera. Later their
relationship cooled, but both were in Vienna in the winter of 1805–6.
For a brief time Napoleon made his old acquaintance responsible for

music at the republican court in Schönbrunn,[41] presumably an offer the popular composer could not refuse. Despite being musically well regarded, including by Beethoven and Haydn, the politically rather compromised Cherubini decided to leave Vienna before the end of the operatic season. By 1 April 1806 he was back in Paris.

Napoleon had already left Vienna and, with the new Austrian empire firmly under his influence, he turned his attention to the Iberian peninsula, invading Portugal in November 1807 and placing his brother on the Spanish throne the following May, incidentally just over a hundred years after Karl VI had entertained the hope of ruling Spain. With the theatre of war now located in the Iberian peninsula, Austria embarked on a process of national rehabilitation and increasing self-confidence. It was during this period that the journal *Vaterländische Blätter für den österreichischen Kaiserstaat* was founded and there were signs of an emerging Fourth Coalition, consisting of Austria, Britain, Prussia and, less certain, Russia. It never materialized and in the winter of 1808–9 Austria suddenly found itself on a headlong course towards war, but with no allies.[42] Whereas a decade earlier the imperial authorities had worked hard to raise national pride, that now had a momentum of its own, a momentum that the court foolishly chose to ride rather than to define and control.

Music played its part. Heinrich von Collin (1771–1811) was a court official and also a successful poet and dramatist. His popular play on the Roman general, *Coriolan*, had inspired Beethoven to write his overture of that name, and, at the celebratory performance of Haydn's *Die Schöpfung* in March 1808, the poet presented the composer with a congratulatory poem in three over-wrought stanzas, beginning 'You have carried the world in your breast, decisively vanquished the gloomy gates of hell' ('Du has die Welt in deiner Brust getragen, der Hölle düstre Pforten stark bezwingen').[43] Later in 1808, Collin completed a set of eight jingoistic poems, published with the simplest of musical settings by Joseph Weigl, just a vocal line with bass.[44] By early March 1809 others had followed Weigl's example, including a young schoolboy, Franz Xavier Strumreiter, otherwise unknown.[45] Johann Friedrich Reichardt had heard Collin himself declaiming some of his verses with fervour, commenting that 'he lives and exists entirely for the honour and fortune of his nation'.[46] Beethoven, too, was caught up in this pre-war frenzy. He sketched a setting of the most emotive of Collin's poems, 'Österreich über Alles' (Austria above everything):

Wenn es nur will,	If it only wants to,
Ist immer Oest'reich über Alles!	For ever is Austria above everything!
Wehrmänner ruft nun frohen Schalles:	Men of the militia shout joyful calls:
Es will, es will!	It wants to, it wants to!
Hoch Oesterreich.	Mighty Austria.[47]

Beethoven never completed his song, probably because the setting by Joseph Weigl was quickly becoming a musical rallying point, temporarily eclipsing even 'Gott erhalte' in popularity. A concert at the Burgtheater on 25 March 1809 was nominally for the benefit of three popular singers, Ignaz Saal, Johann Michael Vogl and Carl Friedrich Clemens Weinmüller, but the whole occasion was taken over by patriotism. It began with a performance of Haydn's 'Military' Symphony (No. 100), now one of his most popular symphonies, and included no fewer than five settings of Collin's poems, by Gyrowetz and Weigl. 'Österreich über Alles' concluded the evening, each of the seven short stanzas greeted by applause and with the audience answering the call: 'It wants to, it wants to!/Mighty Austria.'[48] The concert was given again on 28 March, this time for the benefit of the poor who worked (or had worked) for the court theatres. A third performance of more or less the same programme was given in the Grosser Redoutensaal, and was packed to the rafters, with Weigl's setting of 'Österreich über Alles' once again a highlight. That was on Sunday, 2 April 1809. A week later Austria declared war on France.

1809–1813
The siege of Vienna to the Treaty of Schönbrunn

THE euphoria continued for a few more weeks with yet another presentation of the same programme, the fourth, on 16 April in the Grosser Redoutensaal.[49] By 25 April 1809 Napoleon's troops were advancing eastwards from Regensburg, along the Danube towards Vienna. The Austrian emperor gave the order that the city should be defended and for the first time since 1683 it attempted to maximize its appearance as a formidable fortress. Buildings just outside the main walls were taken down, gates were barricaded, bridges to the outer fortifications were demolished, and all firearms, lances, halberds and sabres owned by the theatres were requisitioned for use by a ramshackle citizen army, including women and children. The imperial family, including Archduke Rudolph, fled eastwards to Hungary. Beethoven remained in the inner city.

Haydn was in his house in the suburb of Gumpendorf. A day after the French forces arrived in the outskirts of Vienna they began bombarding the inner city and a stray cannonball fell in the courtyard. In an act of solace rather than defiance this most instinctively loyal of citizens, whose memories of imperial Vienna reached back nearly sixty years, maintained his customary practice of regularly playing 'Gott erhalte Franz den Kaiser'. After a three-day siege and with considerable damage to the inner city Vienna surrendered on 13 May 1809, the beginning of a six-month period of occupation. Fortuitously, neither the Burgtheater nor the Kärntnertortheater was damaged; the former resumed its planned programme immediately with a performance of Mozart's *Die Entführung aus dem Serail* on 14 May, the latter offering Cherubini's *Faniska* on 16 May.[50] With breath-taking opportunism and efficiency Cappi included an arrangement of Le Sueur's 'Napoleon's Coronation March' in the latest issue of the *Musikalische Wochenblatt*.[51]

Haydn died on 31 May, but his funeral service on 2 June in a local church in Gumpendorf was sparsely attended and the music poorly performed because of the restrictions on movement from the inner city to the suburbs. The later memorial requiem service, in the Schottenkirche in the inner city on 15 June 1809, made ample amends. Viennese and French shared the guarding duties, in and outside the church, Mozart's Requiem was performed by enlarged forces of professional and dilettante musicians and an old friend of the composer, Joseph Carl Rosenbaum, noted in his diary that 'Secretary of State Maret, several generals, staff officers and senior officers, and many other French were present. The whole of Viennese society appeared, for the most part in mourning. The whole was most solemn and worthy of Haydn.'[52]

Many of the palaces in the inner city, including those of Prince Esterházy and Prince Lobkowitz, were requisitioned by French military personnel. While some aspects of musical life, such as music publishing and private concerts, were much less active than usual, the French authorities were anxious that public operatic life should continue, partly to win over the native Viennese, partly to entertain the occupying French. It was for that latter purpose, rather than with any sense of cultural imperialism, that a theatre troupe from Hamburg, billed as the Gesellschaft französischer Künstler (Society of French Artists), was engaged in early June to perform comedy plays and operas in French in the Burgtheater on Sundays and Thursdays. The company left at the same time as the troops, having performed a substantial repertoire of fifteen operas between June and November 1809,[53] the first time opera in French had been heard in Vienna since the 1750s and early 1760s. Only five of these fifteen operas were new to Vienna (works by Dalayrac, Della Maria, Jadin and Solié); the others had already been performed in German translation in Vienna, including Dalayrac's *Adolphe et Clara* (*Die zwei Gefangenen*, Theater an der Wien, 1804), Boieldieu's *Le calife de Bagdad* (*Der Caliph von Bagdad*, Theater an der Wien, 1804) and Méhul's *Le trésor supposé* (*Der Schatzgräber*, Theater an der Wien, 1803). Apart from the unfamiliar language it did not amount to much of a musical invasion.

During the period of occupation and the immediately following weeks, to Christmas 1809, there was the customary clutch of charity concerts: a performance of Haydn's *Die Schöpfung* for charities in general (15 November) and the annual two performances in December by the Tonkünstler Societät to raise money for widows and orphans of musicians, when the composer's *Die Jahreszeiten* was the choice. The programme of an earlier charity concert for the theatrical poor, presented on 8 September, catches the modern eye. The first half consisted of Beethoven's Symphony in E flat (the *Eroica*), the second half a miscellany of works by Clement, Cherubini, Nasolini and Mozart, ending with the 'Hallelujah' chorus from Handel's *Messiah*.[54] The complete absence of any evidence, factual or anecdotal, to link this performance of the *Eroica* with a pro-French outlook did not prevent the great nineteenth-century biographer of the composer, Alexander Thayer, from suggesting that there might have been some link.[55] The prosaic fact was that it was just another performance of a work by Beethoven that was gaining some degree of popularity following the two performances in the 1807–8 Liebhaber Concerte.

The terms of the Treaty of Schönbrunn, signed on 14 October 1809, were not merely humiliating for Austria: they were vindictive. As well as initiating the war, Austria had fought valiantly and effectively to the north of Vienna for several months after surrendering the city, and two days before the treaty there was an assassination attempt on Napoleon in the inner courtyard of Schönbrunn. As punishment Austria had considerable territories of its new empire taken away, approximately a third, annexed by Bavaria, Italy, Poland, Russia and Saxony. In addition, it was required to pay war reparations of eighty-five million francs and to reduce its army from 750,000 to 150,000 troops.[56]

After an absence of eight months, the imperial court began to return to Vienna from the end of November onwards. Beethoven's response was to complete a piano sonata that he had begun for Archduke Rudolph, subsequently published by Breitkopf & Härtel with the descriptive title *Lebewohl, Abwesenheit und Wiedersehen* (Farewell, Absence and Reunion). To his annoyance, the firm also issued it with a French title-page, *Les Adieux, Absence et le Retour*. Beethoven pointed out that 'Lebewohl' was more personal than 'Adieux'.[57] He would have been even more annoyed had he suspected that posterity would prefer the doubly inappropriate French as the favoured title for the work.

A much more populist piano piece was written by Vanhal in response to the return of the emperor, *Die Feyer der Rückkehr unsers allgeliebten Monarchen Franz I. am 29ten November 1809* (The Celebration of the Return of our beloved Monarch Franz I on 29 November 1809).[58] On 29 November the court newspaper, the *Wiener Zeitung,* reported that the emperor had made a formal entrance to the imperial residence three days earlier, when he was greeted by jubilant crowds. At 10.30 a.m. on the morning of 29 November the emperor, members of the court already in Vienna plus representatives of the imperial and civic military attended a *Te Deum* service in Stephansdom. That evening every theatre in Vienna offered gratis entry to the public; at the Kärntnertortheater opera-goers were able to attend a performance of Cherubini's *Die Tage der Gefahr*.[59] Vanhal's piano piece was published by Ludwig Maisch on 13 January 1810. It was not a general work of celebration but, very unusually, if not uniquely, it gave a musical representation of the service of thanksgiving in the Stephansdom. The Catholic church service could now be conjured up at home by the Viennese.

The work is in three clear stages: outside the church, the service in the church itself, and outside the church once more. A Tempo Maestoso introduction sets the scene and leads to a march, representing the procession from the court to the Stephansdom. The arrival of the imperial party at the church is signalled by an 'Intrada', that is fanfare figuration for timpani (left hand) and trumpets (right hand) with a clear distinction between writing for low trumpets (*principale*, up and down a C major arpeggio) and high trumpets (*clarini*, melodic writing that goes up to top C, in the manner of Fux or Caldara). This is followed by a contrasting section headed 'Organist fugirt' (The Organist plays a fugue), a complete four-part fugue on a slow-moving subject that ends expectantly on the dominant; trumpet and timpani herald the beginning of the *Te Deum*, which is itself written into the work as a self-contained movement, with thematic material identified with the appropriate text ('Sanctus, Sanctus, Sanctus'). The following adoration ('Die kindliche Anbethung zu Gott') is set in a contrasting A major and leads to the final three sections of the service, another four-part fugue played by the organ, a repetition of the fanfares that had preceded the *Te Deum*, and a repetition of the 'Intrada' to signal the departure of the imperial party. Outside the church, Vanhal turns finally to the joyous reaction of the wider public, a lengthy 'Marsch der Zufriedenheit des Volkes' (March of Contentment of the People) in C major.

In another rapid change of national mood, within ten months politics had moved from the rampantly jingoistic to the more traditional assertion of the values of emperor, church and state. In continuing efforts to appease the French, the new Foreign Minister, Clemens Metternich, returned to that old instrument of Habsburg diplomacy, marriage. He persuaded Franz to offer the hand of his eighteen-year-old daughter, Archduchess Maria Luisa, to Napoleon, aged forty; father and daughter disliked Napoleon intensely and there was the additional affront of a marriage between a member of a hereditary imperial family and a self-proclaimed imperial parvenu. The wedding took place in Paris in April 1810 and Austria was spared the embarrassment of subsequent celebrations in Vienna attended by Napoleon. In keeping with these reservations there was a notably limited musical response from composers. Vanhal wrote a fantasia for piano that wished the young bride well on her marriage and departure from Vienna; Joseph Preindl (the Kapellmeister at Stephansdom) composed a celebratory hymn for voice and panmelodicon, a recently invented mechanical instrument; and Gyrowetz set a clunking text written by a captain in the imperial army, 'Die Wonne der Nationen' (The Joy of Nations).[60]

While the consequences of military defeat could slowly be accommodated, there was a more pernicious process at work that proved impossible to ameliorate. Nearly two decades of war had placed a huge burden on the Austrian economy: the costs of warfare, of occupying forces during the periods of truce pending a formal treaty and, most recently, the hefty financial damages required by the Treaty of Schönbrunn. Austria's response had been to print more of its paper currency, a five-fold increase between 1800 and 1811 that led to severe inflation, particularly in the cost of food and rent in Vienna, a situation cleverly exploited by Napoleon in the 1809 campaign when he distributed counterfeit currency. In February

1811 the imperial government declared the Austrian state bankrupt, announcing a new beginning for its currency at 80 per cent of its previous value. Inflation continued, almost leading to a second state bankruptcy in 1816; it was not until 1820 that economic stability was re-established.[61]

Inevitably, the stability of musical life was affected and its development thwarted. Haydn, a property owner who was comfortably off after his two visits to London, had been forced to ask for an increase in his pension from the Esterházy family, the value of Beethoven's generous annuity that had kept him in Vienna was undercut, the consortium of aristocrats that had supported the theatres from 1807 had unravelled, the enterprise of the Liebhaber Concerte of 1807–8 was not maintained and Schuppanzigh abandoned his subscription concerts for four years. Working through the persistent and resourceful Count Pálffy, the court somehow managed to maintain the schedules of the Burgtheater, the Kärntnertortheater and the Theater an der Wien.[62] Most public concerts in Vienna were for charitable purposes – the biannual concerts of the Tonkünstler Societät for its musicians, others for the poor of the theatre workers and for St Marx hospital. Benefit concerts for individuals broadened their scope to include readings by actors as well as the previous miscellany of musical items, the so-called musical–declamatory (*musikalische–deklamatorische*) concerts. Three music publishers, the Bureau d'Arts et d'Industrie, Eder and Mollo, suspended music publication for a while.[63] Private music-making, which was more dependent on social practice than ready finance, was the most resilient aspect of musical life in Vienna during the years of financial crisis.

1813–1815
The Fourth Coalition to the Congress of Vienna

THE three years from 1812 to the Congress of Vienna in 1814–15 saw a remarkable transformation in the self-confidence and international authority of Austria, one in which the diplomatic guile of Clemens Metternich first saw him maintain his embrace of France before, at a decisive moment in the summer of 1813, turning against his paper ally and joining the countries of the Fourth Coalition (Russia, Prussia, Sweden, Britain, Spain and Portugal) to achieve victory over the enemy. The ensuing lengthy peace conference in Vienna that shaped post-war Europe marked the rehabilitation of Austria as a diplomatic player.[64] It also coincided with a new beginning in the history of music in Vienna.

Before that, there was the eccentric and endlessly energetic figure of Johann Nepomuk Mälzel (1772–1838). Son of an organ builder from Regensburg, he had lived in Vienna through the war period, combining his inherited artisan capabilities as an organ builder with a flamboyant sense of showmanship to produce a series of mechanical musical instruments to entertain the public. He certainly knew how to keep abreast of changing circumstances, always placing himself on the winning side. In May 1809, just over a week into the war with France, Mälzel gave a concert in the Theater an der Wien in which his popular mechanical trumpeter played signals and marches associated with the Austrian military; a month later, six days after the surrender of Vienna, the concert was repeated in the Burgtheater, with the mechanical trumpeter now playing French military signals and a march. His most ambitious mechanical instrument was the panharmonicon, in which the sound of string instruments was reproduced by carefully calibrated organ stops, and that of wind and percussion instruments by direct mechanical action on real instruments. Its repertoire included popular and/or patriotic works, such as movements from Haydn's 'Military' Symphony, Cherubini's opera *Lodoiska*, and Handel's oratorio, *Alexander's Feast*.[65]

With the outbreak of war in 1813 Mälzel seized his opportunity once more, this time with the intention of gathering funds to travel to London to exploit British national fervour following General Wellington's notable victory in the Battle of Vittoria in Spain. A particularly graphic scenario was devised for a new work: rival military signals and rival national songs ('Rule, Britannia' and 'Marlborough'), the battle itself with cannon and musket fire, and a victory symphony that highlighted 'God save the King'. Beethoven, who had already composed piano variations on the two British tunes, responded willingly to Mälzel's invitation to include these elements in a musical narrative. Showman and composer also envisaged that the work would enjoy an existence that was independent of the panharmonicon, as a live orchestral piece.

Beethoven's orchestral version, *Wellingtons Sieg* (Wellington's Victory) was given for the first time at two charity concerts in the hall of the University in December 1813, to raise money for sick and wounded Austrian soldiers who had taken part in the recent Battle of Hanau. That particular battle had seen the defeat of Austrian and Bavarian forces, but the bigger picture was unprecedentedly encouraging. Following the earlier Battle of Leipzig, Napoleon was retreating westwards towards the Rhine and the Battle of Hanau was just a temporary setback for the coalition. Too many charity concerts in the past had been associated with military defeats and national deflation, whereas the charity concerts in December 1813 were a clear anticipation of victory. In these circumstances, Beethoven's work was as much an Austrian occasion, the triumph of the fatherland, as it was a British occasion, even though Austria is not even mentioned in the piece. The first half of the charity concert included an appearance by Mälzel's mechanical trumpeter, playing in a couple of marches, and, before that, the first performance of Beethoven's Seventh Symphony. That work had originally been composed in the winter of 1811–12 with not even a hint of a programmatic content. It was received with rapturous applause, as if it were a second victory symphony.[66]

The occasion propelled Beethoven to the forefront of Viennese musical life, the beginning of a fashionable presence that was to last through and beyond the Congress of Vienna, with multiple performances of *Wellingtons*

Sieg making that work more widely known than the *Eroica* Symphony. When it was printed in 1816 (by Steiner) it was offered in eight formats, catering for a variety of circumstances and venues: full score and complete orchestral parts, and arrangements for string quintet, piano trio, piano solo, piano duet, two pianos and wind band.

The collective sense of euphoria that was whipped up by this single piece of music was evident in a flood of other works by Beethoven and others that appeared in the months leading up to the end of the war and during the Congress of Vienna.[67] The allied entry into Paris on the last day of March 1814 was celebrated by a quickly thrown-together pasticcio at the Kärntnertortheater, *Die gute Nachricht* (The Good News), containing arrangements of music by Hummel, Kanne, Mozart and Weigl, to which Beethoven was asked to provide a new final chorus, 'Germania! Germania! Wie stehst du jetzt im Glanze da!' ('Germany! Germany! How splendid you now stand'). Although allied unity was acknowledged in successive verses devoted to Tsar Alexander, King Friedrich Wilhelm and Emperor Franz, ending the work with the Austrian Emperor assured its appeal to the Viennese. The composite work received six performances in just over three weeks in April and May. It was followed by the first performance of the final version of Beethoven's rescue opera of 1805–6, now billed as *Fidelio*. While the whole history of rescue opera in Austria had carefully avoided relating the operatic experience to specific contemporary events, part of the unprecedented success that *Fidelio* enjoyed in 1814–15 was because it was, finally, able to do precisely that.

Within a year Artaria issued two versions of *Fidelio* for the wider musical market: a piano score of the entire opera and an arrangement of eleven numbers as *Harmoniemusik*. As well as performing extracts from *Fidelio*, domestic music-making could respond to any number of topical works. The teenage Schubert wrote two songs, 'Auf den Sieg der Deutschen' ('On the Victory of the Germans') and 'Die Befreirer Europas in Paris' ('The Liberators of Europe in Paris') and Anton Diabelli wrote two piano pieces in the manner of Vanhal's characteristic works, *Siegreicher Einzug Franz des Allverehrten in Paris am 15ten April 1814* (The Triumphant Entry of Franz the Universally Revered in Paris on 15 April 1814) and *Glorreiche Rückkehr Franz des Allgeliebten in seine Residenz am 16ten Juny 1814* (Glorious Return of Franz the Universally Beloved to his court on 16 June 1814). The last work is one of many that concludes with a joyous quotation of Haydn's 'Gott erhalte Franz den Kaiser'; 'Österreich über Alles', on the other hand, seems to have been forgotten, too associated with the events of 1809. On Metternich's return to Vienna on 20 July, a month after the emperor, the architect of Austria's regained international status was honoured with a serenade, an open-air concert in the square outside his palace, starting at 11.00 p.m. and performed by nearly 200 musicians.[68]

While the emperor and his foreign minister, the *Kaiserstaat* and the *Vaterland* were feted by musical Vienna, nothing of musical consequence was directly organized by the court, something that remained true right through to the end of the Congress of Vienna.[69] A century earlier, a splendid new opera by a court composer would have been commissioned, performed in the open air in the presence of the heads of state, their ministers and their wives, its wider purpose driven home in a final *licenza*. The court no longer had the resources to undertake such a venture; the best it could offer was a performance of Gyrowetz's popular comic opera, *Aschenbrödel* (Cinderella), given in the private theatre in Schönbrunn on 22 January 1815; even that was outshone by the spectacular convoy of sleighs that transported the international guests on the specially illuminated streets from the inner city to Schönbrunn and back again. While assembled guests were invited to many public performances in the theatres in Vienna, apart from *Fidelio* the fare on offer was the standard one: several performances of Mozart's *Don Giovanni* (in the now customary German), charity performances of oratorios plus benefit concerts for Beethoven and for Spohr.

One work by Beethoven, *Der glorreiche Augenblick*, performed at the composer's benefit concert on 29 November 1814 in the Grosser Redoutensaal and in the presence of several heads of state, encapsulates this shift of emphasis from the court to the city.[70] The 'glorious moment' that is celebrated is that of the city, Vienna, loyal to its emperor certainly, but newly empowered too. The excitable chorus assumes the role of its people and, using the old Roman name for the city, proclaims its newly found confidence: 'Vindibona, Heil und Glück! Welt, dein großer Augenblick' ('Vindibona, hail and good fortune! World, your great moment').

A more musically specific harbinger of the future had occurred a couple of weeks earlier, on 16 November – a performance of Handel's oratorio *Samson* at the Redoutensaal, given by a new, highly organized and ambitious body, the Gesellschaft der Musikfreunde. Largely accidental in its origins, the society had emerged from an earlier glorious moment that was decidedly Viennese in its character. The story begins in 1811, when the self-worth of the city was at its lowest ebb.

A glorious moment, a new future, the Gesellschaft der Musikfreunde

IN February 1811 Ignaz von Mosel wrote a two-part article for the *Vaterländische Blätter* that expanded on one particular observation that he had made in his first article for the newspaper, the desirability of having a conservatoire in Vienna in order to raise musical standards.[71] It was not a casual repeat of the earlier remark, but a carefully worked-out prospectus for a conservatoire, covering the type of education (aesthetics of music and composition, as well as performance), funding (a mixture of state, aristocrat and private), accommodation (administration, teaching and library) and constitution (seventeen draft ordinances). It ends with a plea: 'May the development of this academy not just remain a pious wish.' Although

Mosel's plans did not produce an immediate response, they were not to be forgotten.

Less exalted and more immediately pressing, in the same month a group of aristocratic ladies founded a society to help the poor and needy in Vienna, the Gesellschaft der adeligen Frauen zur Beförderung des Guten und Nützlichen.[72] Blind, deaf and orphaned children were to be supported not just with money but with organized activities such as swimming and bee-keeping, with charity concerts raising the necessary funding. Princess Caroline Lobkowitz, Countess Maria Anna Dietrichstein and Fanny Arnstein were leading figures and they were encouraged and supported by Joseph Sonnleithner, a philanthropic extension of his work as secretary of the court theatres.[73] A new concert room holding some 300 people had been built by the piano manufacturers Andreas and Nanette Streicher in the Landstrasse, the main street to the east from Vienna. A concert in this venue on 16 April 1812 shows the energy, capabilities and ambition of this new society. With the exception of wind players all the participants gave their services for nothing. It began with Beethoven's overture to *Coriolan* directed by Schuppanzigh, but many subsequent items featured women as soloists: Charlotte Traunwieser sang an unspecified aria and Frau Gouhan one by Zingarelli; the exceptionally gifted Magdalene Kurzbeck played a piano concerto in B flat by Dussek; and Fanny von Haan and Baroness von Peirera performed a double concerto by the same composer.[74] The particular success of this concert encouraged Sonnleithner and the Gesellschaft to be even more ambitious.

The spa town of Baden to the south of Vienna had always been a popular summer residence, favoured by Mozart's wife, Haydn's wife and Beethoven, amongst others. Already disfigured by the invasions of 1805 and 1809, half the town, including 137 houses, was completely destroyed by a fire in July 1812.[75] By October, a plan had been formulated by Sonnleithner and the Gesellschaft der adeligen Frauen to raise money for the people of Baden, by means of a large-scale performance of an oratorio, Handel's *Alexander's Feast,* to be given by as many professional and amateur musicians as wished to participate. A preliminary announcement already hinted that the efforts of the society could lead to a permanent body for the promotion of concerts, for recreational as well as for charitable purposes.[76] Originally, the venue was intended to be the customary one for grand public occasions, the Grosser Redoutensaal, but the number of singers and instrumentalists who wished to participate and the size of the anticipated audience prompted a move to the imperial–royal Winter Riding School; Emperor Franz not only gave his permission but defrayed all the associated costs. The choral rehearsals took place in the Lobkowitz palace, the final rehearsal in the Rittersaal of the Hofburg.

The concert took place at midday on Sunday 29 November. The anonymous Viennese correspondent for the *Allgemeine musikalische Zeitung* forwarded an unusually detailed account to the journal,[77] reporting that there were 280 in the choir and nearly 300 in the orchestra, and supporting his statistics with a diagram of the layout of the forces, vocal forces in front, orchestral support mainly in the rear (see Fig. 9). Ignaz von Mosel directed the performance and the orchestra was led by Johann Tost, the violinist who had worked with Haydn at the Esterházy court, but who was now a successful business man.[78] The audience numbered 5,000 and included members of the imperial court and the aristocracy. The event was such a success that it was repeated on the following Thursday. Altogether the two concerts yielded a net profit of nearly 26,000 gulden, including a donation of 1,000 gulden from the emperor. The *Allgemeine musikalische Zeitung* reported that the proceeds were distributed in two ways – to the people of Baden, as originally intended, and to those areas north of the Danube that had suffered in the war of 1809.

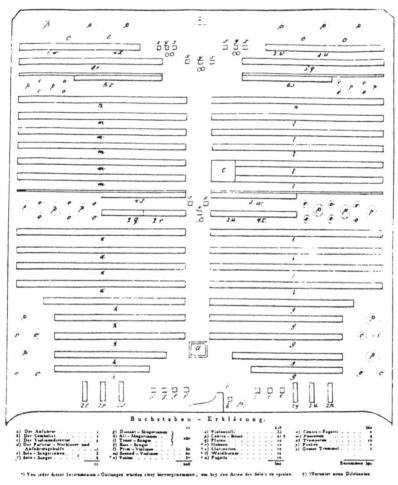

9 Stage layout for the performances of Handel's *Alexander's Feast* in the Winter Riding School in November 1812 (from the *Allgemeine musikalische Zeitung*)

The choice of work was a telling one. Swieten's Associerte Cavaliers had first made *Alexander's Feast* known in Vienna in 1791, one of four Handel works that Mozart reorchestrated for Swieten. Between that time and 1812 it was performed four times in Vienna, a key component of a local Handelian tradition, one that reflected and promoted wider British sympathies. In this spirit, the reviewer of the 1812 performance was pleased to note that the gargantuan forces had followed hallowed practice in London, though he muddled the name of the usual venue, 'Westmünsterhall' rather than Westminster Abbey. At a time when the notion of the Viennese Classical School based on the triumvirate of Haydn, Mozart and Beethoven was only intermittently apparent, Handel had a commanding presence in the musical life of Vienna; when Beethoven remarked that 'Handel is the greatest composer that ever lived', he was reflecting a Viennese consensus as well as uttering his own view. Because of its musical reach, the oratorio, not the symphony, was the pre-eminent genre in public concerts, with soloists, choir and orchestra, amateurs and professionals, all united in the presentation of a drama that had a compelling moral force. During the Congress of Vienna oratorio dominated public music-making; as well as Handel's *Samson* there were two performances of *Messiah* (*Der Messias*) and single performances of *Die Schöpfung, Die Jahreszeiten* and *Die sieben letzen Worte* by Haydn, and *Christus am Ölberge* by Beethoven.

Handel's full title for his oratorio, derived from Dryden's ode, was *Alexander's Feast: The Power of Music*. In Vienna the musical link between the two elements was strengthened by substituting the name of Alexander's minstrel, Timotheus, for his master. As *Timotheus: Die Gewalt der Musik,* the oratorio was perfectly suited to the occasion; medium and message were attuned in a way that not even Haydn's most popular oratorio, *Die Schöpfung,* could have done. From Mosel's perspective the power of music was something to be developed through systematic education, while the Gesellschaft der adeligen Frauen had demonstrated that there was a collective will to place the art form at the heart of civic life.

Joseph Sonnleithner (see Fig. 10) moved quickly to capitalize on the success of the two performances.[79] He recognized that this was not the moment for traditional top-down patronage and that any new organization had to capture the enthusiasm of the wider public. A register was placed in the Lobkowitz palace to record the names of those people who wished see a permanent music society in Vienna. The initial deadline of 15 December 1812 had to be extended and by early January there were 507 signatories. From these individuals a committee of fifteen people was chosen to draw up the statutes of the organization, which were to be presented to the emperor for his approval and tacit support. Initially chaired by Prince Lobkowitz, the committee included Count Anton Apponyi, Count Moriz Dietrichstein, Count Moritz Fries, Vinzenz Hauschka, Baron Nikolaus von Krufft, Ignaz von Mosel, Kapellmeister

10 Joseph Sonnleithner (1766–1835), by Alois Karner, c. 1820

Salieri, Joseph Sonnleithner, Johann Tost, Professor Johann Zizius and Baron Nikolaus Zmeskall.

Although this committee embraced a wide range of musical constituencies – the aristocracy, the rising professions of banking, commerce, government administration and university educators, plus professional and amateur musicians – one element was noticeably missing: the Gesellschaft der adeligen Frauen, the society whose endeavours had set the whole process in motion. Between the concerts and early December, a wide-ranging set of recommendations for the setting up of a dilettante society in Vienna had been drawn up, probably by Sonnleithner, indicating the many ways the Gesellschaft der adeligen Frauen could participate in the administration of such a society.[80] The document even proposed a name for the society, the Gesellschaft der oesterreichischen Musikfreunde, and suggested it should have a one-word motto, 'Harmonie'. Rather than harmony there was an emerging rift between the Gesellschaft adeligen Frauen and the new committee. While the committee was happy to take on board many of its ideas (and quite a few reflected shared views anyway), others were rejected, and the earlier society and its leading figures were not even mentioned in the founding statutes. Meanwhile, the Gesellschaft der adeligen Frauen had decided to maintain an independent existence; it continued to organize charity concerts through to the mid-1820s before finally languishing.

Sonnleithner's committee took over a year to complete its work, ninety-six statutes on forty-eight printed pages, finally approved by the emperor on 30 June 1814. The document is a model of clarity and organization, a lasting tribute to the professional skills of Sonnleithner.[81] The organization was to be called the Gesellschaft der Musikfreunde des österreichischen Kaiserstaates, the reference to the 'imperial state' denoting the particular support of the emperor. Archduke Rudolph was named as protector; Prince Lobkowitz would almost certainly have become the first president but, after his bankruptcy had forced him to withdraw completely from Viennese society, that position fell to Count Apponyi. Sonnleithner became the first secretary, working tirelessly, and without payment, for the organization until his death in 1835. The statutes begin with what would now be called a mission statement: 'The promotion of music in all its branches is the central purpose of the society.'

Over the months of deliberation, the musical priorities had both changed and expanded. With Mosel's clear influence, the first aim was now the establishment of a conservatoire, following the examples of Paris in 1795 and, even more of a stimulus, Prague in 1808; it was to train pupils of both sexes, a recognition of the talent and latent ambition of women in Vienna and a residual nod to the influence of the Gesellschaft der adeligen Frauen. Concerts to bring 'classical works' (*klassische Werke*) to the public were to be organized on a regular basis; here, 'classical' was used in two intertwined senses, historically revered (as in the works of Handel, Haydn and Mozart) and of an appropriate musical standard (for new works). A journal was to be established that included accounts of music promoted by the Gesellschaft, reviews, portraits of individual composers and performers, and lists of members who participated in the main concerts. A music library was to be set up that would eventually be open to the public as well as to the members of the society. Finally, as a focus for these activities, the Gesellschaft would need a dedicated building.

There were to be three types of members, practitioners (professional and dilettante), enthusiasts for music and, by invitation, honorary members (both practitioners and enthusiasts). The bureaucratic structure was a pyramid. At the base was an elected group of fifty representatives who, in turn, elected twelve individuals on to a council that worked with the protector to oversee the work of the society; the council was to be chaired by the president, elected for a term of six years. Permanent committees were to be established to run public concerts, concerts for members of the society only, the conservatoire, the library and the journal. Members paid a monthly subscription and women would have the same rights of membership as men.

Within three years, a period that coincided with the end of the Napoleonic Wars and the beginning of the Congress of Vienna, musical Vienna had set up an organization that harnessed the enthusiasm of a broad range of society for music and prepared a template for its development in the post-war era. Above all, it had a new sense of enthusiasm and purpose, borne out of the optimism of the time. Nevertheless, in much the same way as the Austrian Empire as a whole and Vienna in particular took several years to recover from the travails of war, the Gesellschaft der Musikfreunde des österreichischen Kaiserstaates was not able to realize all its aims immediately. The conservatoire was established in stages – vocal section in 1817, violin teaching in 1819, cello, piano and music theory in 1820, and most other orchestral instruments from 1821 onwards through to the early 1830s; oddly, as if turning its back on earlier traditions, a timpani teacher was not appointed until 1907.[82] Similarly, its concerts did not begin to shape musical life in the city until the 1820s and, at first, showed a disposition to place oratorio at the core of its activities rather than the symphony,[83] including persistent but ultimately futile attempts to persuade Beethoven to write a new oratorio. The library began its work immediately, acquiring its first autograph, Haydn's vocal canons 'Die zehn Gebote', as a gift from Griesinger in December 1814, and its first large historical collection, the library of the North German lexicographer Ernst Ludwig Gerber, in 1819.[84] A music journal (as opposed to a monthly newsletter) was never established by the Gesellschaft, though some of the ideas were taken up by others in Vienna, when the *Allgemeine musikalische Zeitung mit besonderer Rücksicht auf den österreichischen Kaiserstaat* was founded in 1817. Immediate plans to have a dedicated building came to nothing, and it was not until 1831 that the conservatory, the concert hall and the library could be housed in a dedicated building, located in the Tuchlauben in the inner city to the north of the Graben.

The Gesellschaft united the vision and energy of key individuals, notably Mosel and Sonnleithner, with proven aspects of musical life in the city, such as the strength of the oratorio tradition and the demonstrable enthusiasm for public concerts. It showed an awareness of musical life in other cities, notably London and Paris, also Leipzig and Prague. Its most salient characteristic, however, was an unspoken one, amounting to what might be called a silent evolution at the end of the Napoleonic period. While the Gesellschaft was supported by the imperial court and some of its most active members were drawn from the aristocracy, they did not control it. Patronage had shifted decisively from the dutiful emperor and the enlightened aristocrat to a confident independent institution, one that was to be a constant musical presence in Vienna.

1900

CHAPTER 8

Vienna, City of Music

Documenting the musical world

ONE of the annual rituals for many musicians and lovers of music in Vienna at the end of the nineteenth century was the publication in December of the latest version of *Fromme's Musikalische Welt*. Carl Fromme was a printer, publisher and bookseller with an imperial and royal warrant, 'K. u. k. Hof-Buchdruckerei und Hof-Verlags-Buchhandlung', based in the Trattnerhof on the Graben, who had developed a lucrative business in creating diaries for particular professions and occupations such as the clergy, doctors, lawyers, farmers and the fire service. The one for the 'musical world' had first appeared in readiness for 1876 and maintained its schedule of annual publication through to 1901 under the same editor, the music critic and writer Theodor Helm. Bruckner, a personal friend, is one musician who is known to have used it. Typically consisting of up to 400 closely printed pages and measuring 12 × 7 centimetres, it was designed for the pocket, with a sheath on the side to hold a short pencil. Commonly referred to as the 'blue book', it was a mine of information, an exhaustive documentation of the musical environment in Vienna and of the wider society that supported the art.[1]

In common with Fromme's other diaries, it lists all statutory holidays, important days in the Protestant, Greek, Jewish as well as Catholic religious calendar, exchange rates, postage rates and the alternative names for the months of the year: Eismonat for January, Weinmonat for October and so on. For the imperial family, dates of birth are given for the extended family, over two dozen living individuals. There are two lengthy lists of living composers, one for the *Vaterland* and one for abroad; for Vienna itself an alphabetical list of musicians of all kinds is given plus their addresses, useful at a time when the postal service would deliver on the same day in the inner city and foot messengers lingered on street corners waiting to deliver material even more quickly by hand. There were other musical lists: composers who had recently died, books on music published in the past year, opera premieres abroad, music journals in the German language, music critics in Vienna, and newspapers that regularly included musical criticism. Towards the end of the volumes there were several sides of printed staves for musical jottings and further pages for written notes. Finally, the inside cover had a pocket to hold visiting cards.

At least as useful as any modern electronic device, it also provided an annual chronicle of musical life in Vienna, a detailed picture of the environment in which the purchaser of the diary worked and, for those avid enthusiasts who retained the diaries, a narrative of its development across the years. Based on the concert season from August to July, rather than the calendar year from January to December, Theodor Helm first presented an overview of the productions of the imperial–royal court opera theatre (k. k. Hofoperntheater), followed by noteworthy events in concert life. For the latter, but never for the former, full details of individual concerts are given – date, venue, performers and programme – covering orchestral, choral and chamber concerts, plus song recitals and piano recitals. From year to year the lists grew longer, the editorial work more demanding. Theodor Helm was dependent on others to supply the basic information and in the preface to the 1901 volume he complained that this voluntary cooperation was not always forthcoming. After twenty-six years that volume was to be the last in the series.

Three years later, in readiness for 1904, Carl Fromme began once more to issue annual volumes, but in a revised format. Rather than *Musikalische Welt* it was now called *Musikbuch aus Österreich: Ein Jahrbuch der Musikpflege in Österreich und den bedeutendsten Musikstädten des Auslandes.* As a book, it discarded the element of the working pocket diary and was, instead, intended for the desktop or the shelf, larger in size, sturdy and decorated with fashionable Secessionist artwork. The more ambitious format was complemented by a new degree of authority: it now had the financial support of two imperial ministries, Culture and Education, and Foreign. As the preface to the first volume indicated, the accuracy and comprehensiveness of the volumes – Helm's concern – could now be safely assumed. Ten volumes appeared between 1904 and 1913, with three successive editors: Richard Heuberger (music critic and composer), Hugo Botstiber (Secretary of the Gesellschaft der Musikfreunde, later Secretary of the Akademie für Musik und Darstellende Kunst) and Josef Reitler (music critic).[2]

The most obvious change to the content was the discarding of the general information at the beginning of Helm's volumes – postage costs, foreign exchange rates, religious holidays and so on – plus the editor's general survey of music in Vienna in the previous season. There was a new opening section, 'Musicological Matters' (*Musikwissenschaftliches*), three or more short essays on subjects as varied as documents on musicians at the imperial court from the seventeenth century onwards, Brahms's library and Wagner's residences in Vienna, all easily understood by an eager lay audience.[3] The two remaining sections, Musical Chronicle and Musical Statistics, replicate the content and format of equivalent sections in the *Musikalische Welt.*

While the decisive move from diary to yearbook can be read as a move from the utilitarian to the monumental, both publications are the products of a broad musical establishment, in the sense that a vast amount of musical activity is presented in a largely consistent format, one that promoted a sense of shared identity. The nature of that identity was complex in certain respects, straightforward in others; some of it echoed characteristics that had first emerged a century previously, others were newer developments that had emerged in the intervening years. Although the volumes proclaim their loyalty to the Habsburg dynasty and, in the case of the *Musikbuch aus Österreich*, were directly supported by the government, very little of the musical activity that is documented was directly promoted by the imperial court and, accordingly, very little of it could be seen to be promoting the Habsburg dynasty in the manner of music around 1700 and, to a certain extent, around 1800. While there was some sense of music projecting a national identity, that of Austria, a process that had begun during the Napoleonic period, 'Austria' was now a rather contested term. As in all aspects of political and social life at the time, it contained a tension between a pan-German outlook and a more defined Austrian outlook and, within the latter, a further tension between nationalist outlooks in various parts of the empire, notably in the Czech and Hungarian territories. *Vaterland* was a term that was still encountered, most obviously as the title of the widely read Catholic newspaper, *Das Vaterland*,[4] but the sense of loyalty to a new empire that it signalled in Napoleonic times was often replaced by ironic usage, the focus of sentimental, uncritical attachment to something that was best not defined.

If notions of imperial and national identity are fitful or illusory in musical life in Vienna around 1900, the idea of a city identity – Vienna as a major centre for music – is palpable. The pages of the *Musikalische Welt* and the *Musikbuch aus Österreich*, despite the diplomatic title of the latter, constantly project this characteristic, most forcibly through the sheer amount of musical activity they document, plus the number of individuals and institutions that promote that identity. They also managed a sleight of hand, by placing the art form at the centre of that identity rather than to make it subservient to an overarching civic identity: music was more important than Vienna. There was a particular historical force here. Music had lost its dependence on court patronage and, even more so, on the aristocracy, but instead of falling to the city, patronage fell to its inhabitants, the burgeoning middle classes, to organize and support, through a proliferation of institutions and organizations, a process that had begun with the founding of the Gesellschaft der Musikfreunde in 1814. The most striking aspect of music in Vienna around 1900 is how it managed to sustain a presence between state and city, a sufficiently independent force that still drew on the former but increasingly projected the latter. Alongside that, a new expression entered the lexicon, *Musikstadt Wien*, Vienna, city of music.[5]

The fervour with which the Gesellschaft der Musikfreunde had been founded early in the nineteenth century was not enough, on its own, to maintain a significant presence, and its successful history was closely tied with the development of the city as a metropolis. Between 1800 and 1900 the population of Vienna grew from 250,000 to close to two million.[6] Its social geography changed fundamentally from the late 1850s onwards, when Emperor Franz Joseph sanctioned plans to demolish the old city walls so that the inner city could connect with the suburbs, a gesture of openness borne out of a new self-confidence rather than pragmatism.[7] The walls had existed for 300 years, defining the character of the city; within less than thirty years Vienna fundamentally changed its appearance and transformed its character. Rather than allowing the city and the suburbs to creep towards each other across the Glacis, the open area of land originally designed as a military buffer zone, the planners filled the space with a broad boulevard, the Ringstrasse, on which institutional buildings of all kinds were erected. One of these was a rather old-fashioned idea, located slightly apart from the Ringstrasse – a new Catholic church, the Votivkirche, completed in 1879 and built to commemorate the failed assassination attempt on Emperor Franz Joseph in 1853. Others were governmental: the national Parliament (1882) and the Rathaus (1882); one was legal, the Justice Palace (1881); one was educational, a new building for the university, previously housed in the inner city (1884); two were museums, the Art History (Kunsthistoriches) Museum (1881) and the Natural History Museum (1881); one was a theatre for spoken drama, the Hofburgtheater (1886); and two were musical, the opera house (1869) and a building to house the Gesellschaft der Musikfreunde (also 1869). Along the length of the Ringstrasse and in nearby streets, new palaces were built for the more moneyed members of society – merchants, architects, engineers, bankers, lawyers and others who sustained public life in Vienna. In complete contrast to the inner city, this area was never to become claustrophobic, with parks, such as the Volksgarten, Burggarten and the Stadtpark, and large open squares, like the Heldenplatz and the Schwarzenbergplatz, providing an unprecedented sense of space in the city. Beyond the Ringstrasse lay the suburbs where most of Vienna's population resided.

Vienna was already becoming a destination for travellers. Fig. 11 reproduces a map of the city, from a travel guide written by Karl Baedeker for tourists from Germany, Britain and America.[8] The extent to which the inner city is dwarfed by the suburbs is clear, as is its central position: the metropolis radiates from the centre across the Ringstrasse to the ever-expanding suburbs. There was, nevertheless, still a sense of inner and outer, reinforced by the division of the city into numbered administrative districts, beginning with eight in 1850, rising to nineteen in 1890 and twenty-one in 1910.[9] The inner city including the Ringstrasse was the First District, and other districts acquired a sense of identity too: Leopoldstadt, the Second District, was a reasonably well-to-do, mainly Jewish district; Josefstadt, the Eighth District, was where many government officials lived; Währing and Döbling, in the Eighteenth and Nineteenth District respectively, had many newly built villas in an undulating landscape; and Brigittenau, the Twentieth District, was one of the newest, characterized by factories and crowded workers' apartments.

An astonishing 65 per cent of the population in 1910 had been born elsewhere.[10] During the latter part of the nineteenth century the city acted as magnet for internal migration within the empire (or former parts

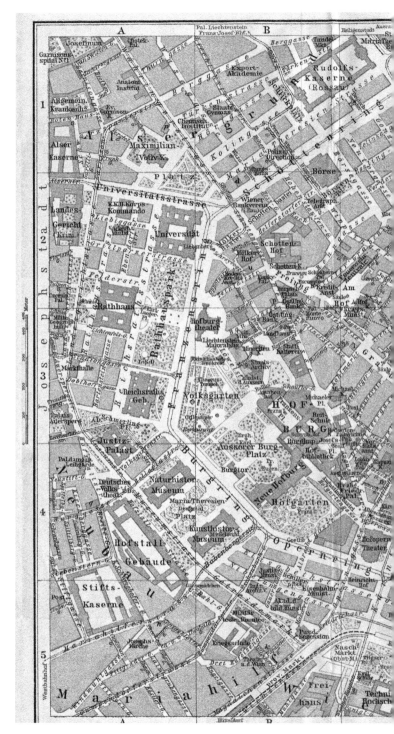

11 Map of Vienna
from Baedeker's
Austria-Hungary,
1911

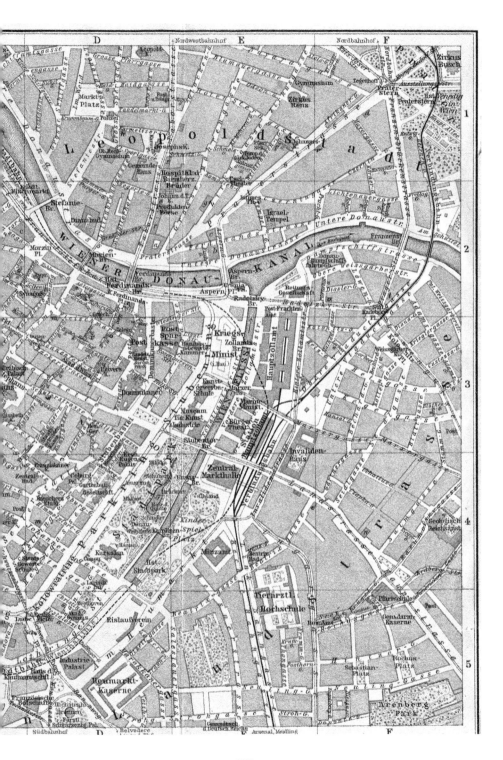

of the empire), from Upper Austria, Styria and the Tyrol, from Bohemia, Moravia, Hungary and Italy, and from distant Poland, Ruthenia (Ukraine) and Rumania. In the new national Parliament on the Ringstrasse twelve languages were sanctioned for debate and the streets of Vienna were a linguistic babble. While German was a lingua franca accepted by all, in music its status was an even more lofty one: it had now completely replaced Italian as pre-eminently the language of music. Alongside the German-language operas of Wagner, Humperdinck, Marschner and Weber, the Italian operas of Mozart, Rossini, Leoncavallo and Verdi were usually performed in German at the court opera.[11] It is against this background that Janáček, a fervent speaker of Czech whose music was very deliberately shaped by its speech patterns, willingly accepted that the first of his operas to be presented at the court opera in Vienna, *Jenůfa* in 1918, would be given in German.[12]

German was the predominant language of the song recital and of the many large-scale choral works that were performed in concerts. Swieten, the Associirte Cavaliers and the Gesellschaft der Musikfreunde had developed a tradition of performing large-scale choral music that grew substantially during the nineteenth century. Haydn and Handel maintained their popularity, supplemented by choral works by Bach, Brahms, Mendelssohn and Schumann. Choral singing boomed in the second half of the nineteenth century, from the male chorus of the Schubertbund to the large forces of the Singverein (organized by the Gesellschaft der Musikfreunde) and its rival, the Singakademie. A participatory culture open to all, choral singing played a notable part in integrating many migrants into a German-speaking culture.

While language acted as a unifying force in music, there had been a major change across the nineteenth century in religious toleration. The Habsburg dynasty had gradually opened up a gap between itself and the Catholic Church, so that it was no longer at the centre of dynastic identity, a considerable slackening of old drawstrings that helped to promote religious plurality. When the Austro-Hungarian Empire was formally constituted in 1867, articles 14, 15 and 16 of the constitution enshrined this outlook, the final negation of the Counter-Reformation: 'complete freedom of conscience and of belief is guaranteed to everyone'; 'every legitimately recognized church and religious society has the right to organized, public religious practice'; and 'those who belong to an unrecognized religious society are permitted observance at home, as long it is otherwise neither illegal nor morally offensive'.[13] At the same time as religious tolerance nurtured repeat performances of works like Bach's *St Matthew Passion*, Brahms's *German Requiem* and Mendelssohn's *St Paul*, there was a latent nervousness about performing Catholic music in the concert hall; that repertoire was still largely performed as part of standard liturgical practice and not as concert music.

Jews and those of Jewish descent had always willingly bought into the pre-eminence of the German language and German-speaking culture in the city and since the music of Bach, Handel, Haydn, Mozart, Beethoven, Schubert, Schumann and Wagner formed the mainstay of that tradition and that of Chopin, Dvořák, Elgar, Liszt and Smetana was embraced within it, there was a ready identification with the art form. Commerce and the medical and legal professions had a high percentage of Jewish employees, between 40 and 50 per cent, as did the free press.[14] Although meaningful statistics for the musical profession, encompassing administrators, critics, publishers and teachers as well as composers and performers, are not readily available, the number of prominent individuals in Vienna's musical life in all these areas who were Jewish, or of Jewish descent, is striking and significant: Guido Adler (musicology), Friedrich Buxbaum (cellist), Hugo Botstiber (administrator and scholar), Julius Epstein (piano teacher), Carl Goldmark (composer), Julius Korngold (critic), Gustav Mahler (conductor and composer), Arnold Rosé (concertmaster in the Vienna Philharmonic Orchestra and leader of the Rosé Quartet), Heinrich Schenker (theorist), Arnold Schoenberg (composer), Oscar Straus (operetta composer), Josef Weinberg (music publisher) and many more. While the Austrian constitution promoted religious toleration, society increasingly saw Jewishness in terms of race and, worse, appearance, rather than religious practice; consequently when individuals formally rejected the religion of the synagogue in favour of Protestantism (sometimes Catholicism), it made little difference to any prejudice, snide or vicious, feared or actual.

Institutions and venues in the First District

THE direct role of the Habsburg family in the patronage of music had weakened considerably across the nineteenth century. Having been a family that was highly interested in the art form and that had produced many very capable practitioners, the Habsburgs became a family that was not especially interested in music and quite incapable as musicians. Franz Joseph was more a man of the theatre and of fine arts and played no active part in the proliferation and expansion of musical life in Vienna during his long reign, though his all-consuming sense of duty fed a passive appreciation of the presence of music, one that he was happy to promote with government support and to acknowledge with public appearances.

The Hofkapelle still existed as a body of individuals, listed annually in *Fromme's Musikalische Welt* and in the *Musikbuch aus Österreich*. In 1907, for instance, there was a Kapellmeister, Karl Luze, one assistant, a court organist and two piano teachers for the boys; the choir had twenty members, the orchestra numbered thirty-eight (a pool of potential players rather than a regularly constituted ensemble); finally, there was an organ tuner, a stage manager and an archivist who also acted as the singing teacher for the boys.[15] As was the case at the beginning of the century there was a link with the personnel of the imperial opera house, itself financially supported by the court. Most of the instrumentalists were drawn from the orchestra of the opera house and received additional payment for their work in the Hofkapelle, where they were given a uniform. Typically, there were over seventy sung services a year, though an increasing number were sung with organ accompaniment rather than with orchestral forces. Most of the repertoire dated from the late eighteenth century onwards.[16] Anton Bruckner, a nineteenth-century personification of the older values of *pietas austriaca*, was familiar with this musical legacy from his time at the monastery of St Florian and at Linz Cathedral and willingly joined the Hofkapelle as an unpaid organist when he moved to Vienna in 1868, later volunteering for further duties as a deputy archivist and assistant singing teacher; only in 1878 was he put on the payroll as court organist, remaining in post for fourteen years.[17]

The imperial family did respond positively to one new musical trend in the nineteenth century. In 1846 Johann Strauss (the father) was honoured with an entirely new title, Imperial–Royal Court Music Ball Director (k. k. Hofballmusikdirektor), later given to two sons in turn, Johann and Eduard. Their collective international fame far surpassed that of any other Viennese musician, native or resident, in the nineteenth and early twentieth centuries and all three rejoiced in the title. The actual duties were limited, mainly to the Carnival season, when they chose the music for the court balls and directed the musical ensemble. There were two balls, one a formal state occasion for 2,000 people (where not much dancing took place), the other a more intimate occasion for 700 people personally invited by the emperor.[18]

Plans for a new court opera house in Vienna, to replace the Burgtheater and the Kärntnertortheater, predated the Ringstrasse project and, since it was readily acknowledged that there was not sufficient room in the inner city, it provided some impetus for that later project. It was the first building to be completed and opened on 25 May 1869 with a performance of Mozart's *Don Giovanni* (in German), attended by the emperor. Located near the site of the old city gate, the Kärntnertor, it confidently faced outwards onto the Ring and, with a capacity of about 2800, it was considerably larger than either of its predecessors. The public areas mirrored the new sense of space occupied by the theatre, constituting a form of theatre in themselves, especially the entrance hall, the broad, very graduated central staircase and the reception rooms on the first floor. Marble statues of the seven liberal arts (architecture, dance, music, painting, tragedy, poetry and sculpture) were complemented by bronze figures representing comedy, drama, fantasy, heroism and love. Frescoes by Moritz von Schwind depicted scenes from *Die Zauberflöte*. He was also responsible for the depictions of scenes from musical works – one oratorio and fifteen operas – that had figured in the history of the former Burgtheater and the Kärntnertortheater between 1786 and 1869: Beethoven's *Fidelio,* Boieldieu's *Die weisse Dame*, Cherubini's *Der Wasserträger*, Dittersdorf's *Doktor und Apotheker,* Gluck's *Armida,* Haydn's *Die Schöpfung,* Marschner's *Hans*

Heiling, Meyerbeer's *Die Hugenotten*, Mozart's *Die Zauberflöte*, *Don Juan* and *Die Hochzeit des Figaros*, Rossini's *Der Barbier von Sevilla*, Schubert's *Der häusliche Krieg*, Spohr's *Jessonda*, Spontini's *Die Vestalin*, and Weber's *Der Freischütz*. Underneath each scene was a bust of the relevant composer. Elsewhere in the opera house, two members of the Habsburg dynasty were honoured for their role in the history of opera in the city: Leopold I as the founder of a musical tradition, and Maria Theresia as the person who had opened the court opera to the public. The retiring room for the present emperor, the Kaisersaal, was decorated with frescoes that depicted seven scenes on various aspects of love in Mozart's *Figaro*. All in all there are close to 200 artistic representations of individuals and works in the opera house; designed as an opulent as well as an unending visual celebration, across the decades the artwork gradually accumulated the character of an unchanging museum.[19]

By the early 1890s a certain easy contentment had pervaded the opera house as a performing venue, the fault of a challenging schedule, a lassitude amongst the leading musical figures and an administrative structure that had not essentially changed since the beginning of the century. The season ran from mid-August through to mid-June, with almost nightly performances plus the occasional matinee performance, producing a total number in excess of 250. The company was run on a repertory basis, usually fifty or so works per season, many of which were available year in, year out, with the precise number of performances shaped by public demand and emerging practicalities rather than an inflexible predetermined schedule. The repertory reflected wider European operatic tastes rather than initiated them, with many operas, such as Bizet's *Carmen*, Leoncavallo's *I pagliacci* and Verdi's *La traviata* performed only after they had established a secure wider reputation. The repertory system, delivered by a regularly constituted company, also helped to maintain the preferred practice, especially towards the end of the century, of presenting operas in German.

Perhaps the most startling fact about the new opera house is its indifferent record on world premieres. Four operas by the Viennese composer Carl Goldmark (1830–1915) were given their first performance at the court opera house, with *Die Königin von Saba* enjoying regular performances, but it was not until 1916 that the opera house gave the premiere of a work that was to secure a permanent part in the international repertoire – Richard Strauss's *Ariadne auf Naxos*. From one year to the next the repertory was dominated by the operas of Wagner. Every season through to the First World War featured performances of his major operas – *Der fliegende Holländer, Lohengrin, Die Meistersinger, Tristan und Isolde* and the *Ring* cycle – and one of the most popular was *Tannhäuser*, which by 1894 had already notched up 200 performances.[20]

To sustain this arduous if unadventurous commitment, the musical forces employed by the court opera were unusually large: in the 1893–4 season the orchestra numbered 107, plus twenty-one stage musicians, and the chorus 117, in effect a double company that shared the schedule. The senior music staff consisted of a director, Wilhelm Jahn (in post since 1881), the court opera Kapellmeister, Hans Richter (in post since 1875), and two assistants, Johann Nepomuk Fuchs and Joseph Hellmesberger.[21] Because of a worsening eye condition Jahn's responsibilities were becoming almost entirely administrative and most of the conducting was done by Hans Richter. An acknowledged figure of international standing with a growing reputation in England, he was sometimes accused of not giving sufficient priority to Vienna and of working practices that ensured the schedule was routinely maintained rather than presented to the highest standards; difficult passages in all operas were adjusted to suit the under-rehearsed singers and orchestra, Wagner's operas were usually given in cut versions and those operas that Richter found uncongenial were dispatched with brisk tempi.

Director and Kapellmeister did not enjoy complete autonomy in administrative and strategic matters. As the imperial court opera, one that was funded by imperial coffers, it had a chain of command back to the Habsburg bureaucracy, even, in theory, to the emperor himself. The seventeenth-century post of Obersthofmeister was still in existence, held by three successive aristocrats at the turn of the century – Prince Konstantin Hohenlohe-Schillingsfürst, Prince Rudolf von Liechtenstein and Prince Alfred Montenuovo – and it was to these individuals that the opera house reported.[22] But the ensuing management was not particularly effective, characterized by indifference, prone to bureaucratic manipulation from within and open to the influence of outsiders, especially the press. Typically, its first response to the worsening situation in the opera house in the mid-1890s was a sticking-plaster solution in the shape of an additional conductor to help Richter. But as soon as news spread that a firebrand young conductor in his mid-thirties, Gustav Mahler, was interested in the post, the vacant post was changed to that of director, a replacement for Jahn. In the event, Mahler was first appointed to the position of conductor in April 1897 before succeeding Jahn as director in October. Despite being overlooked for the position of director, Richter continued to conduct at the opera for two further seasons, before resigning to concentrate on his position as conductor of the Hallé Orchestra in Manchester. During those two seasons, and under Richter's nose, Mahler injected a new sense of energy and unstinting devotion to the work of the opera house.[23] The intensity of rehearsals was exceeded only by that of subsequent performances. He made his debut with a searing performance of *Lohengrin*, soon forbade the practice of presenting Wagner's operas with cuts and began presenting the constituent operas of the *Ring* as a cycle rather than as individual works. For works like *Zauberflöte* he experimented with a much smaller orchestra and lavished unfamiliar attention on the delivery of the spoken dialogue.[24] While the energy he devoted to the preparation and rehearsal of individual works was superhuman, the repertory itself continued broadly in the same manner as before, a roster of fifty or so operas per year with any new works having already established themselves elsewhere; and so entrenched was the preference for presenting all opera in German that not even Mahler questioned it. He idolized Beethoven, Gluck, Mozart and Wagner and was sympathetic to Bizet, Charpentier, Smetana and Johann Strauss, but had a blind spot when it came to Italian opera, including Puccini and Verdi, preferring to entrust them to colleagues. For over a year he tried to persuade the court authorities to allow Richard Strauss's *Salome* to be added to the repertoire, but the ingrained nervousness of a Catholic court about a theatrical presentation of a biblical tale, especially one involving shocking sexuality, meant that permission was declined.[25] In the Vienna of Gustav Klimt and Egon Schiele this was an artistic aberration that was more about upholding the inherited values of an imperial and royal institution than it was about public morality.

A few minutes walk along the Ringstrasse in an anti-clockwise direction was one of Vienna's grandest hotels, originally designated as the Imperial and Royal Court hotel, but by the early twentieth century usually known as the Hotel Imperial. Behind the hotel stood the new building for the Gesellschaft der Musikfreunde, the Musikverein, a neo-Renaissance building formally opened by the emperor on 5 January 1870.[26] Entirely hidden from the Ringstrasse by the hotel, it did have an open aspect on the other side, towards the Karlskirche, though that was compromised by the decision to erect the building on a west-east axis rather than with an open view of the Karlskirche. Both the design and the varied purpose of the building remained faithful to the ideals of the founding fathers of the Gesellschaft der Musikfreunde: dedicated space for a conservatoire (the Konservatorium der Gesellschaft der Musikfreunde); an archive and library; and two concert halls, the Grosser Musikvereinsaal (for orchestral and choral concerts) and the Kleiner Musikvereinsaal (renamed the Brahms Saal in 1937). The former had a seating capacity of 1500 plus 500 standing places, the latter 600 seats plus standing room for 200.[27] The Grosser Musikvereinsaal, in particular, gave the feeling of an artistic temple, with its elongated shape, Doric columns, and serried nymphs that supported an upper gallery, while the standing area at the back of the hall encouraged a sense of detached, yet privileged observance of a ritual (see Fig. 12). Appropriately, the ceiling panels depict Apollo and the Muses. 150 years earlier Apollo and the Muses would have paid homage to a musical emperor; here they overlook a musical public that was equally self-regarding, on occasions even imperious.

The committee structure that had been set up in 1814 to oversee the work of the Gesellschaft der Musikfreunde had stood the test of time, particularly the idea of a president who chaired an executive council. The holders of these positions often held other influential posts too. In the 1890s the president was Baron Josef Bezecny, the Generalintendant of the court theatres, while the council consisted of Ludwig Bösendorfer (the renowned piano manufacturer and proprietor of a rival small concert hall, the Bösendorfersaal), Johannes Brahms, Johann Nepomuk Fuchs (also a conductor at the opera), Walter Gericke (director of concerts for the

12 Interior of the Grosser Musikvereinsaal, 1870, depicted by Johann Nepomuk Schönberg

Gesellschaft) and Baron Wilhelm Weckbecker (from the Ministry for Culture and Education). Since 1874 the conservatoire had also trained actors for the spoken theatre, but it was always a much smaller part of its activity, thirty-three in 1893–4 compared with 812 musicians.[28] Often casually referred to as the Vienna Conservatoire, it drew its students from across Europe and in areas such as violin playing had established a distinctive pedagogic tradition, in this case driven by three generations of the Hellmesberger family: Georg (1800–73), his son Joseph (1828–93) and his grandson, also Joseph (1855–1907). Its alumni included Guido Adler, Leopold Auer, Carl Flesch, Fritz Kreisler, Leoš Janáček, Gustav Mahler, Arthur Nikisch and Franz Schalk.

For the best part of a century the Gesellschaft had managed to exist as a private organisation, supported by its members, income from concert giving, hiring the two halls to outside bodies, fees for studying at the conservatoire and donations. Around 1900 long-standing misgivings about the ability of the Gesellschaft to maintain a viable conservatoire began to grow, not least from those who taught there who felt that they were underpaid. Guido Adler from the university was asked by the Minister of Culture and Education to draw up a plan for the possible takeover of the conservatoire by the state; Mahler had indicated his willingness to be the director of the new institution.[29] But the government dithered and in the end decided to subsidize the conservatoire with an annual grant, amounting to 60,000 crowns in 1904–5. The court returned more decisively to the issue in 1908. By now the Gesellschaft recognized the inevitability of a separation and agreed to the founding of a newly independent conservatoire from 1 January 1909, the Akademie für Musik und Darstellende Kunst, now dignified with the 'k. k.' appellation. It continued to use the Musikverein until new, more spacious premises were opened on the Heumarkt.[30]

A century after its foundation the Gesellschaft der Musikfreunde had lost one of its key components, but the other two, a venue for performance and the archive and library, had developed and adjusted to changing circumstances to the extent that the institution was able to maintain its commanding position in the life of the city. Support of ambitious amateur music-making was still very much to the fore. The choral society, the Singverein der Gesellschaft der Musikfreunde, was a large choir of some 300 members who rehearsed every Monday evening from seven to nine o'clock during the season in readiness for four subscription concerts plus two or more single concerts in the large hall of the Musikverein.[31] Successive concert directors of the Gesellschaft rehearsed and conducted the concerts: Walter Gericke, Richard von Perger, Ferdinand Löwe and Franz Schalk. Large-scale works from the nineteenth century characterized much of the repertoire – Brahms's *German Requiem*, Haydn's *Die Schöpfung* and *Die Jahreszeiten*, Mendelssohn's *Elijah* and *St Paul*, Schumann's *Das Paradies und die Peri* and Verdi's *Requiem*.

As in its founding years there was a consistent interest in the oratorios of Handel, including *Messiah* and *Judas Maccabaeus*, now topped up by the availability of the complete edition of the composer's works prepared by Chrysander between 1858 and 1894, with parallel German texts. In this way Viennese audiences became acquainted with more unusual works by this favoured composer: *L'Allegro, il Penseroso ed il Moderato* (performed 1897), *Deborah* (1898), *Hercules* (1907) and *Belshazzar* (1908).[32] Rather surprisingly, however, the 1912–13 season, the centenary of the monster concert that had set the foundation of the Gesellschaft in motion, did not include *Alexander's Feast*. Other works introduced to Vienna for the first time included Elgar's *The Dream of Gerontius* (in the German translation sanctioned by the composer, 1905) and Bach's *St John Passion* (1908).[33]

The Gesellschaft also supported an amateur orchestra for its members, though this seems to have found it difficult to sustain a meaningful presence. Since its main function was to accompany the Singverein, it had to be supplemented by professional players, usually from the opera, a continuation of the ready mixing of amateur and professional that had characterized public music-making in the city from the beginning of the nineteenth century. When, from 1901 onwards, the Singverein began using the new professional orchestra of the Wiener Konzertverein (of which more later) its status was further diminished and its repertoire tended to be of small-scale works.

From the days when Mozart had played his piano concertos in the Burgtheater in the 1780s, orchestral musicians from the court theatres had participated in public concerts on an *ad hoc* basis, necessarily few because they had to be slotted into the busy schedule of the theatres. It was not until 1842 that the players themselves, with the crucial support of the then court opera Kapellmeister, Otto Nicolai, decided that they would present themselves to the public as a concert-giving entity. Following Otto Nicolai's departure for Berlin in 1848 the concerts became rather intermittent until Carl Eckert established an annual pattern of subscription concerts in 1860, at first usually held in the Burgtheater. With the completion of the new opera house and the large concert hall in the Musikverein building, the orchestra was able to flourish as an opera orchestra in one venue and a concert orchestra in the other, tenaciously developing a presence in the musical life of Vienna until it too became an institution, the Vienna Philharmonic Orchestra, one that brought reflected glory to the other two – the opera house and the Musikverein.[34]

As the first page of the concert programme shown in Fig. 13 shows, the orchestra was routinely billed as the 'k. k. Hofopernorchester' and the occasion itself as a 'philharmonic concert'; in other words it was the concert that was philharmonic, not the orchestra. While, on the one hand, the billing was proper acknowledgment of the court origins of the orchestra, one that the orchestra was always anxious to maintain, it was also a description rather than a title. Other renowned orchestras, such as the Berlin Philharmonic Orchestra and the New York Philharmonic Orchestra, carried the name of the city in their title and gradually 'Wiener philharmoniker' came into casual use, though it was not formally used until 1908.[35]

The subscription concerts were always eight in number and typically took place between October and March, at 12.30 p.m. on Sundays in the Musikverein. The limited number of concerts, the precise dates and the starting time were all the consequence of duties at the opera house and, for some players, Sunday services at the Hofkapelle too, though the large complement of players employed by the court theatre helped to make it possible. A ninth concert was added to the sequence every year, a benefit concert to raise money for sick and ailing players; the concert was billed as the Otto Nicolai concert, in memory of the founding conductor. While practicalities ensured that the number of concerts could not easily be increased, their appeal can be judged from the fact that ticket prices were much higher than for any other concerts in the Musikverein: the 1907 edition of the *Musikbuch aus Österreich* gives a price range of 12 to 24 crowns for a subscriptions series of four concerts organized by the Gesellschaft der Musikfreunde in its own venue, but for the Philharmonic series the prices ranged from 24 to 64 crowns. For the British traveller of the time that equated to a price range of one to £3, or between $5 and $13 for the American visitor.[36] The operatic commitments of the orchestra meant that the orchestra did not give a concert outside Vienna until 1900 when, under Mahler's direction, it gave three concerts in Paris at the International Exhibition, an ambassadorial role for which it was duly thanked by the emperor.[37] Although a landmark occasion, the public back

PHILHARMONISCHE CONCERTE.

Sonntag, den 18. November 1900,

Mittags präcise ½1 Uhr,

im grossen Saale der Gesellschaft der Musikfreunde:

2tes Abonnement-Concert

veranstaltet von den

Mitgliedern des k. k. Hof-Opernorchesters

unter der Leitung des Herrn

GUSTAV MAHLER,

k. u. k. Hofopern-Director.

PROGRAMM:

L. v. Beethoven . . . . . . Ouverture zu: „Prometheus".

R. Schumann . . . . Ouverture zu: „Manfred".

G. Mahler . . . . Symphonie Nr. 1, D-dur.

Einleitung — Allegro commodo.
Scherzo.
Feierlich und gemessen.
Stürmisch bewegt.

(I. Aufführung in den Philharmonischen Concerten.)

Streich-Instrumente: Gabriel Lemböck's Nachfolger Carl Haudeck.

Programme unentgeltlich.

Das 3. Philharmonische Abonnement-Concert findet
am 2. December 1900 statt.

Verlag der Philharmonischen Concert-Unternehmung in Wien.
Buchdruckerei Wien, I., Dorotheergasse 7

13 Concert programme for the Court Opera Orchestra (Vienna Philharmonic Orchestra), 18 November 1900

home in Vienna would probably have noted that various members of the Strauss family and their respective orchestras had been travelling regularly in Europe and the USA for decades.

Following Nicolai's example the subscription concerts in the Musik-verein were conducted by members of the court opera staff – Richter from 1883 to 1898, Mahler from 1898 to 1901 and Joseph Hellmesberger from 1901 to 1903. Between 1903 and 1908 the concerts were conducted by a series of guest conductors, two or three per season, including Felix Mottl, Franz Schalk and Richard Strauss; from 1908, the new director of the court opera, Felix Weingartner, undertook the task. For those individuals who were both staff members at the opera house and conductors of the concert series, the situation was often a difficult one to negotiate. From its inception the committee of the orchestra had sought to have complete control over its appearances as a concert orchestra, while back in the opera house the same players were in a more traditional relationship, entirely beholden to the conductor in his role as director or Kapellmeister. Moreover, many decisions were taken by the concert orchestra as a whole in a secret ballot, as a kind of workers' cooperative, a process that could yield festering unease, occasionally open conflict, not only between conductor and players, but amongst the players themselves. Somehow, it worked, producing one of the world's most distinctive performing organizations. In essence, this is still the way the orchestra is run today.

Only the first of these conductors at the turn of the century, Hans Richter, regularly included a major concerto in the programme; the others preferred a mix of overtures, symphonic poems and symphonies. The repertoire was overwhelmingly Germanic or Slavic, with very little French music. The works of Beethoven, Brahms, Bruckner, Dvořák, Mendelssohn, Schumann, Schubert and Weber featured regularly in the programmes. At the same time the programmes were self-consciously enterprising, in the sense that almost every season contained four or five works that were new to the orchestra, by Liszt, Tchaikovsky, Richard Strauss and others, always clearly announced as such. There was a sense that unfamiliar musical works were being validated by the orchestra, and, consequently, by their audience too: they had passed the Philharmonic test. Indeed, that was quite literally the case, since the orchestra as a whole routinely voted on which new items of orchestral music should be accepted for performance.

First performances, as opposed to first performances in Vienna, were few and far between: for instance, only one of Mahler's nine symphonies was given its premiere by the orchestra, the Ninth Symphony in 1912, a year after the composer's death.[38] On occasions, the programmes were not only strikingly demanding, but produced some juxtapositions that seem odd to later audiences raised on different historical narratives. The second concert of 1906–7, conducted by Franz Schalk, contained two works that were new to the players, Elgar's *Enigma Variations* (a work that fitted naturally into any Austro-German embrace) and Tchaikovsky's Fourth Symphony; between them the strings of the orchestra played the *Grosse*

Fuge by Beethoven.[39] It was not only comparatively recent music that was introduced in this way, but works from earlier epochs. The main work in the opening concert of the 1910–11 season, conducted by Weingartner, was Schumann's Second Symphony, but it was preceded by two first performances by the Philharmonic, Bach's Suite in C major and Haydn's Symphony No. 1 in D.[40]

1900 saw the setting up of a second professional orchestra in Vienna that gave concerts in the Musikverein, one that was eventually to become the Vienna Symphony Orchestra. While the success of the Philharmonic concerts was clearly a spur, the impetus for this orchestra came from an individual whose contact with the operatic tradition in Vienna had been a brief and embarrassing one, leading him to forge a reputation as a concert conductor. Born in the city in 1865, Ferdinand Löwe had studied composition at the conservatory and had made a name for himself in Munich, founding the Kaim Orchestra, later renamed the Munich Philharmonic. In 1898–9 he was invited to conduct at the opera in Vienna, a wholly unsuccessful experience that led to his resignation, bizarrely compensated not only with a pay-off of 5,000 gulden but with the permanent title of Hofopernkapellmeister.[41]

Putting this episode to one side, Löwe set about carving out a very different presence in the musical life of Vienna, founding a rival concert orchestra to the Philharmonic. Löwe's first name for his new orchestra was a provocative one, New Philharmonic Orchestra, later changed to Wiener Konzertverein. Six subscription concerts were given in the first season, held in the evening on different days between January and March 1900, plus two single concerts, all in the Musikverein. The repertoire for this first season was a cautious one, consisting mainly of familiar works by Beethoven, Schubert, Schumann, Weber and Wagner.[42] The concerts proved popular and, without the logistical problem of fitting them around other playing commitments, the orchestra soon established an annual pattern of two interlocking subscription series of six concerts each, on Tuesdays and Wednesdays, running from late October through to April. Lower ticket prices encouraged a more broadly-based audience than attended the Philharmonic concerts on Sundays.

At the same time it carefully developed a different attitude to programming. Concertos and other works for soloists and orchestra were routinely included in the programmes, with eminent visiting performers such as Bartók in Beethoven's Fifth Piano Concerto (1903–4 season), Busoni in Liszt's A major Concerto (1905–6) and Casals in Schumann's Cello Concerto (1911–12).[43] There was also an eye for the kind of orchestral repertoire that was unlikely to feature in the Philharmonic concerts, including first performances in Vienna of Dukas's *L'apprenti sorcier* (1903–4), Debussy's *La mer* (1907–8), Sibelius's First Symphony (1907–8) and Delius's *Brigg Fair* (1910–11); there was also a continuing commitment to new works by Elgar: his *Enigma Variations* (1902–3), *Cockaigne* overture (1903–4), *Introduction and Allegro for Strings* (1905–6), First Symphony

(1908–9) and Second Symphony (1911–12).[44] The 1910–11 season was notable for a different reason: the presentation of a complete cycle of the symphonies of Bruckner, repertoire that had not always been favoured by the Philharmonic. If the Philharmonic represented a self-congratulatory establishment, the Konzertverein orchestra was very much a challenging, questioning new force.

Although the small concert room in the Musikverein was designed for the favourable presentation of instrumental chamber music, piano recitals and song recitals, it had a very active rival in the form of the Bösendorfersaal in the Herrengasse, in use as a concert hall since 1872, just three years after the Musikverein was opened. Located in what was formerly the riding school of the Liechtenstein palace, it had seating for 460 people with room for about 180 standing places; as the seating plan for the hall shown in Fig. 14 reveals, there were three rows of seating on the stage a few feet away from the performers, a lingering legacy of the private concerts of Maria Theresia von Paradis and others from much earlier in the century, where pianists, singers and quartets were surrounded by interested listeners.[45] For the audience seated in the rows of seats in the hall and those standing at the back, there was a sense that the focussed performers, together with the equally focussed listeners seated on the podium, represented an exemplary way of participation. A performance was routinely described as a 'song evening' (*Liederabend*) or a 'piano evening' (*Klavierabend*) rather than a 'concert' (*Konzert*), and that too suggested a degree of privileged intimacy.

Since the hall was owned by Vienna's leading piano manufacturer, one of its purposes was to promote the piano manufacturer, with piano recitals and song recitals as common fare, at least once a week during the season. They were usually single concerts rather than subscription concerts and often featured visiting pianists, such as Eugen d'Albert, Busoni, Dohnányi, Frederic Lamond and Anton Rubinstein; song recitals, on the other hand, were more likely to be given by local artists, such as Irene Abendroth, Selma Kurz and Marie Gutheil-Schoder. As a statistical summary of all piano and song recitals in the 1912 *Musikbuch aus Österreich* reveals, Chopin's works dominated piano recitals, followed by those of Liszt and Schumann, while the songs of Brahms and Schubert dominated song recitals, followed by those of Schumann, Richard Strauss and Wolf.[46] Mixed evenings of piano music and song were rare, but many song recitals embraced popular arias from operas and some piano recitals included works for piano plus other instruments.

For the Bösendorfersaal, even more distinctive was the association of the venue with instrumental chamber music, particularly string quartets. Towards the end of the 1890s, four quartet ensembles presented annual subscription concerts in the hall, often supplemented by additional, single concerts. The most venerable of these ensembles was the Hellmesberger Quartet, founded in 1849; three members of the family played at various times in the ensemble: Joseph (father, first violin), Joseph (son, second

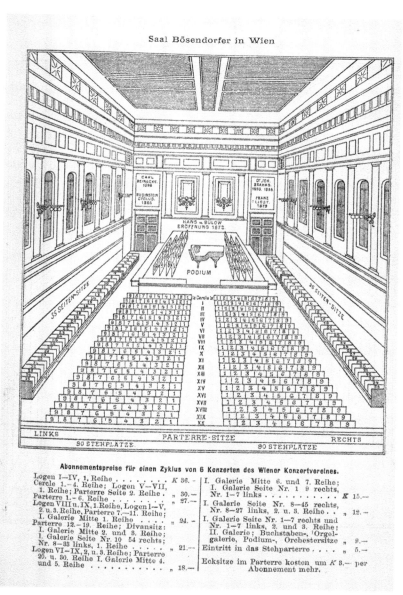

14 Seating plan for the Bösendorfersaal, 1908
(from *Musikbuch aus Österreich*, 1908)

violin, later first violin) and his brother, Ferdinand (cello). They were joined in 1883 by a new quartet founded by Arnold Rosé that, likewise, became an institutional presence in the musical life of the city, in this case until the Second World War when Rosé, a Jew – he was born Arnold Rosenblum – was forced to flee from Vienna, having been at the heart of musical life in the city for nearly sixty years.

In the 1890s there was little sense that the two quartet ensembles were in competition; the annual subscription concerts were held in alternate weeks with, judging from the programmes duly reported in the *Musikalische Welt*, an element of shared planning to avoid duplication of works, a natural extension of the cooperation that had to exist in order to accommodate their wider musical careers: playing in the opera and in the ballet, participating in the Philharmonic concerts, performing in the Hofkapelle, teaching at the conservatoire and, in Hellmesberger's case, conducting and composing too. Together, the two ensembles continually reinforced a core repertoire of the quartets of Haydn, Mozart, Beethoven, Schubert, Schumann, Mendelssohn and Brahms. Equally characteristic, and a clear consequence of the ownership of the venue by a piano manufacturer, the programmes always included one chamber work with piano, usually as a middle item – Schubert's 'Trout' Quintet, Schumann's Piano Quartet and Piano Quintet, the three piano quartets of Brahms and, a particular favourite, Brahms's Piano Quintet.

Two other quartet ensembles that appeared every season in the Bösendorfersaal during the 1890s offered a different perspective to the Hellmesberger and Rosé quartets. The first was an ensemble that always billed itself – rather clumsily – as the Bohemian Quartet from Prague. Established in 1891 by four former students from the Prague Conservatoire, including Joseph Suk as second violin, it made four trips to Vienna every concert season. Much of its repertoire mirrored that of the Hellmesberger and Rosé quartets, but each concert also included a Bohemian work, principally by Dvořák (Suk's father-in-law from 1898), Smetana and Suk himself; the chamber music of Tchaikovsky and Borodin was also more likely to feature in its concerts. While the name of the ensemble together with some of their repertoire indicated an identity that was different from the Viennese one of Hellmesberger and Rosé, these recurring visits by the Bohemian Quartet to the imperial capital were an act of comfortable assimilation rather than of studied difference.

The difference that distinguished a fourth quartet ensemble which presented annual subscription concerts in the Bösendorfersaal was gender: four women had founded the Damen Quartet in 1895 and gave three concerts per season, between February and March. The leader of the ensemble was Marie Soldat-Röger. Born in Graz, she had studied at the Berlin Conservatoire with Joachim and had already established herself as an international concert soloist, especially associated with Brahms's concerto. The cellist was Lucy Herbert-Campbell, an American born in Kentucky who had also studied in Berlin. The viola player was Natalie

Bauer-Lechner from Vienna; she was a student at the conservatoire at the same time as Mahler, who became a close friend and confidant, a relationship that ended abruptly in 1902 when he married Alma Schindler. Ella Finger-Balleti was the founding second violinist, later replaced by Elsa Edle von Planck.

Their programmes usually included two quartets plus a larger work for which additional players were engaged, perforce usually men. For instance, the first concert of the 1898 series featured Haydn's Quartet in D (op. 76 no. 5), Brahms's C minor Quartet (op. 51 no. 1) and Beethoven's String Quintet in C (op. 29), with Alfred Finger as the extra viola player. The second concert opened with Mozart's Quartet in B flat (K458), followed by Schumann's Quartet in A minor (op. 41 no. 1), and ended with Dvořák's Piano Quintet in A, with Richard Epstein as the pianist. The last concert was built round the celebrated clarinettist, Richard Mühlfeld, with performances of Brahms's Clarinet Trio (op. 114, with a certain Fraulein M. Baumeyer as the pianist) and the Clarinet Quintet (op. 115), separated by Beethoven's F major Quartet (op. 18 no. 1).[47]

Beyond the Ringstrasse

THE opera house, the Musikverein and the Bösendorfersaal all enjoyed the prestige of being located in the First District, but with the growth of Vienna to twenty-one districts by 1910 several new venues emerged in the suburbs. Financially and organizationally, they were sometimes quite precarious, often because they were less set in their ways, and characterized by commercial opportunism in some cases, social paternalism in others.

At the end of the eighteenth century Schikaneder's Theater auf der Wieden had created a new tension in the musical life of the city, between activity that took place in the inner city and that offered in his suburban theatre. When the Ringstrasse project was completed it had the effect of opening out the inner city to the suburbs, but with a boulevard to the south and the Danube canal to the north, there was still a clear sense of here and there, city and suburbs. Located in the Fourth District, the Theater an der Wien (Schikaneder's successor theatre) was now the oldest in Vienna. No longer run by the court, not even at arm's length, it had been owned by a series of theatre proprietors: Franz Launer, Alexandrina von Schönerer and Emil Ritter von Kubinsky. When the last named took over in 1900, there were suggestions that the theatre should be demolished, just a couple of years before its centenary; instead, it was extensively remodelled and still survives over a hundred years later.[48] It had its own musicians, forty-two in the orchestra and forty in the chorus,[49] and was the principal venue for operetta in Vienna. Between 1871 and 1897 the majority of Johann Strauss's sixteen operettas were first performed in the theatre and, in 1905, Lehár's most popular work, *Die lustige Witwe*, received its premiere there. Even though the theatre was an old one, both the auditorium and the stage were capacious and, because of that, it was a favourite venue for visiting opera companies. There was also a small concert hall in the Fourth District, a few minutes away from the Theater an der Wien, built in 1876 by a second prestigious piano maker in Vienna, Friedrich Ehrbar. Like its inner city equivalent, the Bösendorfersaal, it held about 500 people, including seating on the stage for chamber concerts.[50]

The Carltheater was located in the Second District to the north of the city on a broad avenue that led to the Prater. Opened in 1847, it enjoyed mixed fortunes through to the end of the century, primarily as a home for operetta, distinguished in subsequent years by a series of successful new works by Leo Fall, Lehár and Oscar Straus. Approximately half the size of the Theater an der Wien it, nevertheless, had musical forces of comparable size, thirty-two in the orchestra, forty-four in the chorus.[51]

Much smaller than either the Carltheater or the Theater an der Wien was the Josefstadt theatre, in the Sixth District. Its origins go back to the 1780s when a small theatre was erected in a particular spacious garden at the back of a house in the Kaisergasse (now Josefstädter Strasse), not far from the Piaristenkirche. In the 1820s the theatre was rebuilt and extended into adjacent properties; it was for this new theatre that Beethoven wrote his overture *Die Weihe des Hauses* (The Consecration of the House).[52] Seating approximately 600 people, the theatre was associated in the early years of the twentieth century with a particular form of musical theatre, the *Wiener Volksstück*, a light-hearted play with musical numbers on patriotic or sentimental themes. In a tradition that can be traced back to the early eighteenth century, part of the appeal was the appearance of a favourite actor, now Hansi Niese, the wife of the proprietor, Josef Jarno, as a stock character: a washing maid (in *Das Wäschermädel*), a servant who sees to everything (*Paula macht alles*) and, naturally, a musically gifted girl (*Das Musikantenmädel*). The musical limitations of the solo numbers are suggested by the size of the theatre orchestra, only twenty-eight (far fewer than at the Theater an der Wien), while the appeal of the crowd scenes is suggested by the size of the resident chorus, fifty-four (far more than at the Theater an der Wien).[53]

In the years before the First World War, two further venues were built outside the Ringstrasse, a second opera house and a second large concert building, respectively the Volksoper and the Konzerthaus. Although they can legitimately be seen as a response to a musical demand from a continually growing population that could not be satisfied by the court opera and the Musikverein alone, neither was originally conceived in those terms, but assumed that position once other plans had faltered. The origins of the Volksoper go back to November 1895, when a group of local politicians, influential members of the middle class and theatre professionals, drew up a proposal for a new theatre to serve the north-west of Vienna, the comparatively well-to-do Ninth and Eighteenth Districts. In a skilfully written, all-embracing prospectus they outlined their ambition for a theatre that was to be well equipped, affordable, dedicated to nurturing public taste (*Volksbildung*), was to contribute to the development of Vienna as a 'world city' (*Weltstadt*) and could be completed in time to celebrate the fiftieth anniversary in 1898 of Franz Joseph's accession to the throne, and would, accordingly, carry his name. A suitable plot of land had been identified, at the point where the Währinger Strasse (the principal road from the First District to the north-west suburbs) reaches the Währinger Gürtel (the outer ring road), a convenient intersection for the rapidly developing local train and tram service that served the affluent districts of Währing and Döbling, and encouraged easy access, too, from the inner city. The clear-headed nature of this vision allowed the emerging project to overcome financial difficulties and the inevitable petty wrangling, and it even managed to open on time, in the last month of the jubilee year, December 1898.[54]

While doffing its cap to the emperor, the Kaiserjubiläumstheater, as it was called, did not come under the jurisdiction of the court and was entirely dependent on commercial success for its future. Since the productions were to consist of spoken plays, it saw itself as complementing the new Burgtheater on the Ring, rather than the opera house, and was initially very successful. Five seasons later, in 1902–3, it reached a financial crisis and a new director, Carl Rainer Simons, was appointed. A Rhine-lander who had studied music and was experienced as a director and producer of opera, he slowly but deliberately shifted the emphasis across five seasons from the spoken word to opera, establishing the popularity of the latter at the expense of the former. It was during this time that the word Volksoper was added, rather cumbrously, to Kaiserjubiläumstheater, before eventually standing alone as the snappy title of the theatre.[55] With connotations of opera 'for the people' as well as 'of the people', it carefully cultivated an audience that liked to attend suburban theatres such as the Theater an der Wien for operetta as well as the court opera for Wagnerian music drama, encouraging it with affordable ticket prices. With Alexander Zemlinsky as its music director and with an orchestra of fifty-eight and a chorus of sixty-seven, it performed operettas by Heuberger, Lehár, Millöcker and Straus, and operas – always in German – by Bizet, Gounod, Lortzing, Mozart, Wagner and Weber.[56]

As the Volksoper began to establish itself as a major presence in the musical life of Vienna in the north-west, another venture, on the opposite side of the city in the south-east, was beginning to take shape. The *Volk* nature of these plans was even more striking, though they were ultimately to be considerably diluted. In January 1896, just two months after the first discussion about the new theatre in the north-west, plans were announced for an ambitious new building, a centre for sport and the arts that would act as an accessible home for all kinds of activities and a meeting place that would welcome everybody.[57] Evoking the ancient Greek ideal of the complementary development of the mind and of the body, it was to be called the Olympion, though it had something of the modern leisure centre about it too. The complex was to be built on an open plot of land on the Heumarkt in the Fourth District, which would have produced a building on a scale exceeding anything on the Ringstrasse, if the original idea had ever been realized. Although it proved too ambitious, some of its characteristics survived in the building that was eventually built on the site, the Konzerthaus. When the Olympion project was abandoned, two, more narrowly musical priorities drove planning over the subsequent years: the need for a second, large-scale concert venue in Vienna to supplement the Musikverein and, following the separation of the conservatoire from the Gesellschaft der Musikfreunde, the pressing need for accommodation for that newly independent institution, the Akademie für Musik und Darstellende Kunst.

Construction of the new building began in 1911 and was completed in October 1913. As well as being in the fashionable Art Nouveau style, the building presented a more accessible image than the Musikverein, a clear legacy of the original plans, with offices for various societies, several bars, cafes and dining rooms, a gourmet restaurant, a flower shop, a music shop and a shop for general provisions. A particular throwback to the Olympion project survives to this day, an adjacent ice-skating rink that can be viewed from inside the main building. Unlike the Musikverein, the entrance hall was a notably spacious one that served three concert rooms, the largest holding 1800, a medium-sized one 700 people, and the smallest 330 people. With efficient sound-proofing, three different concerts could be held simultaneously; alternatively, all three of the halls could be hired together for large-scale events like balls, conferences and exhibitions. The accommodation for the conservatoire adjoined the building on the other side to the skating rink, on the corner of Lothringerstrasse and Lisztstrasse, and included a purpose-built rehearsal theatre to complement the concert halls in the main part of the building.

Housed right on the cusp between the Fourth and the First District, the suburbs and the inner city, the Konzerthaus was able to look in both directions: it liked to project itself as less elitist than the Musikverein, yet it had taken on the challenge of presenting a musical presence that was a natural consequence of the success of the Gesellschaft der Musikfreunde. On 19 October 1913 the foundation ceremony took place in the presence of Emperor Franz Joseph, now eighty-three years old, who unveiled the coping stone. The associated concert was given by the augmented forces of the Konzertverein orchestra under their conductor Ferdinand Löwe and included a new composition by Richard Strauss, *Festliches Präludium,* an unremittingly noisy work for an orchestra of over a hundred players plus organ; it followed by a performance of Beethoven's Ninth Symphony.

It is unlikely that the emperor would have noticed that Strauss's work was in the old imperial key of C major, filtered through Wagner's *Die Meistersinger* as well as Strauss's own *Also sprach Zarathustra.* He may, however, have reflected on the much changed status of the emperor. Although the Akademie still enjoyed an annual grant from the court and, from that, its 'k. k.' appellation, the building itself, the Konzerthaus, like the Volksoper, was an initiative that had come from the people of Vienna and was funded by their efforts. It nurtured civic pride in Vienna as a musical capital – not so much of the Habsburg Empire, rather of German-speaking Europe.

On the façade of the building above the main entrance, on either side, Wagner's own rhyming couplet from the end of *Meistersinger* was inscribed: 'Honour your German masters, for then you will conjure up good spirits' ('Ehrt eure deutschen Meister, dann bannt ihr gute Geister'). 1913 was the hundredth anniversary of Wagner's birth and the many Wagner devotees who passed through the portico of the new building would have known the succeeding, triumphant lines too: 'And if you favour their endeavours, even if the Holy Roman Empire should dissolve into mist, for us there would yet remain holy German art!' The Holy Roman Empire had long gone and almost exactly five years later the Austrian empire, too, was to come to a pitiful end. Musical Vienna, however, never lost its addiction to holy German art.

CHAPTER 9

'Seid umschlungen, Millionen'

Otto Nicolai concert, 18 February 1900

THE annual benefit concert for the sickness fund of the Philharmonic Orchestra was held earlier than normal in the 1899–1900 season, between the sixth and seventh concerts in the subscription series rather than at the end.[1] The previous year Mahler had conducted a performance of his own Second Symphony; this year he chose Beethoven's Ninth Symphony, the first time he had conducted the work in Vienna. He assembled unusually large forces. Following the practice of doubling the wind instruments, the orchestra probably numbered over a hundred, but the choir was five times that size, drawn from the combined forces of the chorus of the court opera, the Singakademie, and the well-established amateur male choir of the Schubertbund.

Sheer numbers were useful throughout 'An die Freude', but the desire that the male voices should be powerful enough reveals a particular concern for a major turning point in the work: the moment when the choir and orchestra suddenly halt their singing of 'Freude, schöner Götterfunken, Tochter aus Elysium' and turn to a new text, 'Seid umschlungen, Millionen. Diesen Kuss der ganzen Welt'. The tempo changes from Allegro assai vivace to Andante maestoso, the key falls down from D major to G major, and tenors and basses, accompanied by cellos, double basses and bass trombone, declaim the new text to a new theme. Mahler's performances were vividly characterized by extremes of expression, ruthlessly controlled and delivered. Here the Andante maestoso marking was probably taken at a slower tempo than Viennese audiences were accustomed to and the contrasts of the subsequent Adagio ma non troppo, ma divoto were certain to have been delivered with maximum theatricality – *piano*, exaggerated swellings of tone, the beginning of a crescendo from *piano* that is turned back to *pianissimo*, followed by a crescendo to a full-toned *fortissimo*.

The hall had been sold out and the performance was so compelling that a repeat performance, with all the logistical problems of assembling the large forces once more at short notice, was organized for the following Thursday. As well as compelling, it was also controversial and, between the Sunday and the Thursday, Mahler had been subjected to vilification by much of the Viennese press, who supported their unease about the overtly expressive nature of the performance as a whole with detailed comments about Mahler's alterations to the score that enabled him to offer what was, in the view of one critic, a 'malicious misrepresentation'. Mahler was unrepentant and for the second performance prepared a printed defence of his outlook and methods, given free of charge to the audience. He invoked three reasons for his changes: first, that the new expressive range that Beethoven discovered in the Ninth Symphony could not be fully realized by the composer because of his deafness; second, that the limitations of trumpets and horns at the time meant that their use was compromised, a situation remedied in subsequent decades by improvements to those instruments; and third, that Mahler's interpretation was firmly in the tradition of Wagner's views about performances of Beethoven, especially the Ninth Symphony. These factors enabled Mahler to claim that he was 'constantly and solely concerned with carrying out Beethoven's wishes even in seemingly insignificant details, and with ensuring that nothing the master intended should be sacrificed or drowned in a general confusion of sound'.[2]

This minor scandal marked out the territory occupied by the conductor, the performers, the audience and the critics. Who were the prostrating millions of Schiller's text meant to be in awe of? Mahler maintained that it was the 'loving Father' of Schiller's text as set by Beethoven; Mahler's critics would have said that it was Mahler himself. The obvious truth was that neither was entirely true. Everybody worshipped Beethoven.

Beethoven and Wagner; Mozart and Haydn

THE annual subscription series of eight concerts presented by the Philharmonic Orchestra under Hans Richter and now Gustav Mahler routinely included three symphonies by Beethoven, mainly Nos. 3, 5, 6, 7, 8 and 9, with the Seventh Symphony being especially popular. When Mahler took over he seems to have embarked on a plan to cover most of the symphonies across two seasons, 1898–9 and 1899–1900, with the Ninth providing the climax in February 1900. To support this sequence there were a number of performances of other works by Beethoven. Thus the first concert of the 1898–9 season, on 6 November, featured performances of the *Coriolan* Overture and the *Eroica* Symphony, framing Mozart's G minor Symphony (K550). The fourth concert, on 18 December, included Beethoven's Eighth Symphony; the seventh concert, on 26 February 1899, the overture to *Egmont* plus Clärchen's two songs ('Die Trommel gerühret' and 'Freudvoll und leidvoll, gedankenvoll sein'), and the final concert, on 19 March 1899, was an all-Beethoven programme consisting of the overture to *Fidelio*, the Fifth Piano Concerto (with Busoni as the soloist) and the Seventh Symphony.[3] The first concert of the second season, on 5 November 1899, ended with the Fifth Symphony, the following one a fortnight later included one of the less frequently performed symphonies, No. 2. The third concert, on 3 December, ended with the overture *Die Weihe des Hauses*, and the fourth concert, on 17 December, with the *Pastoral* Symphony. Mahler then avoided Beethoven for two months, until the Nicolai concerts, focussing instead on works by Berlioz, Bruckner, Mendelssohn, Mahler and

Wagner. Likewise, after the two performances of the Ninth, there was no further Beethoven until the very last item in the final concert of the season, the overture *Leonore* No. 3.[4] This systematic presentation of Beethoven's symphonies concluded in the following season when Mahler conducted the First and Fourth Symphonies, weaker works he regarded as not representative of the composer.[5]

Beethoven's music enjoyed a similar presence in the programmes of the new orchestra in Vienna from 1900 onwards, the Konzertverein, but with a much increased presence of concertos, especially the Fifth Piano Concerto and the Violin Concerto, alongside symphonies and overtures. In comparison with the symphonies, Beethoven's opera *Fidelio* had always had a chequered history in Vienna in the nineteenth century. A resounding success when it was performed during the heady days of the Congress of Vienna, it was then only rarely heard, nowhere near as popular Mozart's *Don Giovanni*, the operas of Wagner and, in the 1890s, newer works like Bizet's *Carmen* and Humperdinck's *Hänsel und Gretel*. The court opera had a standard production that Hans Richter conducted about two or three times a season and Franz Schalk, Mahler's colleague from 1900, a few more. It was not until 1904–5, Mahler's eighth season as music director, that he conducted *Fidelio*. It was even more of an artistic statement than the performance of the Ninth Symphony had been.[6] Working with the celebrated theatre director Alfred Roller, also occasionally flatly rejecting his ideas in favour of his own, Mahler conducted a run of performances that even his many critics acknowledged created a unified vision of stage presentation and music, a Wagnerian vision of the work. This unremittingly elevated view of the work led to some major adjustments. Rocco's aria near the beginning of the work, 'Hat man nicht auch Gold beineben', was omitted, in Mahler's view too close to the world of singspiel, even operetta. Beethoven's overture, *Leonore* No. 3, a very familiar concert item, was strategically inserted between the end of the dungeon scene and the jubilant finale, which then became a heady amalgam of the finale of the Fifth Symphony (C major and the march) and that of the Ninth (the triumph of humanity).

The *Missa Solemnis* was a work that would have suited Mahler's gift for projecting dramatic contrast, local and large-scale. He never conducted it, citing the difficulty of getting a choir that could respond to his demands. It was something of a rarity on concert programmes in general in Vienna until Mahler's colleague, Franz Schalk, conducted four performances by the Singverein between 1906 and 1912. Even more striking is the intermittent presence of Beethoven's piano music. In his survey of the 1897–8 musical season in *Fromme's Musikalische Welt*, Theodor Helm drew attention to a rare event 'for serious lovers of music' (*ernste Musikfreunde*), the recital given by the visiting Scottish pianist and Beethoven specialist Frederic Lamond, devoted to five of his most challenging sonatas: the op. 110, the op. 111, the 'Hammerklavier', the 'Waldstein' and the 'Appassionata'.[7] Middle-period piano music by Beethoven, such as the last two works, cropped up reasonably frequently in mixed piano recitals but, as the comments in *Fromme's Musikalische Welt* suggest, Beethoven the composer of piano music did not feature prominently in his image around 1900, at least not in public.

This was in complete and absolute contrast to Beethoven the composer of string quartets. If one were to attempt to document the number of public performances of his string quartets in Vienna between the early 1890s and the onset of the First World War, it would soon reach into the hundreds. From their inception in 1849 the Hellmesberger Quartet had given Beethoven's works a central place in the repertoire, a tradition that was taken on by the Rosé Quartet. In the 1890s there was hardly a concert given by either of these ensembles that did not feature a quartet by the composer and, since there was clearly cooperation between the two ensembles on which works were played from one year to the next, a Beethoven devotee could easily become acquainted with the full complement of seventeen works across two or three years. In terms of individual works there is a marked emphasis on the three 'Razumovsky' quartets and the late quartets (op. 127, op. 130, op. 131, op. 132 and op. 135); on the other hand, ticking off all six of the op. 18 quartets was less easy.

As with the many performances of the composer's symphonies, Mahler's version of *Fidelio* and Frederic Lamond's one-off recital, there was a predisposition to emphasize the serious and the elevated in Beethoven's music, the Wagnerian as it were, rather than the genial and the entertaining. When the visiting Joachim Quartet from Berlin gave a series of three concerts in the Bösendorfersaal in the winter of 1896–7, the first of these was an all-Beethoven programme of a kind that no modern ensemble would undertake and, equally likely, no modern audience would welcome: the 'Harp' Quartet (op. 74), the F minor Quartet (op. 95) and the B flat Quartet (op. 130).[8] There was an unconscious acceptance, occasionally articulated, that quartets by other composers, from Haydn and Mozart, through Schubert and Mendelssohn, to Brahms and Dvořák, were best understood against the Beethoven template, a template that was itself a highly manufactured one. Exclusive, rarefied and with an element of discrimination that was tinged with self-congratulation, these qualities had first emerged in private a hundred years earlier, in the salons of the aristocracy and the performances of the Schuppanzigh quartet; they were now publicly accepted and constantly reasserted. Arnold Schoenberg was one young composer who was steeped in this environment: he played the cello in an amateur quartet and his first major composition was a quartet in D major.[9] Later, each of his four numbered quartets, from No. 1 (1905) to No. 4 (1936), was a determinedly fearless attempt to continue the tradition.

Wagner dominated the operatic repertoire in Vienna at the turn of the nineteenth century in the same way as Beethoven dominated instrumental music. Evident in different arenas, opera house and concert hall, the two traditions had a synergy, one that emphasized the elevated and the visionary, what Wagner called 'the artwork of the future' and what lay behind Beethoven's comment 'Art demands of us that we shall not stand still'. Through Wagner's writings, Vienna came to understand the composer's indebtedness to Beethoven, and, for many people, attending one of the many performances of *Lohengrin* in the court opera house, and one of the many performances of the B flat Quartet (op. 130) in the Bösendorfersaal on the following night, was a different experience only in physical scale, never in aesthetic reach. But who was controlling whom? If it was true that Haydn, Mozart, Schubert, Mendelssohn and Brahms were being valued according to Beethovenian criteria, it was also true that Beethoven was often appreciated according to Wagnerian criteria.

But this was not the complete picture. In the 1870s and 1880s Eduard Hanslick had led an anti-Wagner crusade based on the premise that Wagner's work was not true to the Beethovenian inheritance – the absolute music (Hanslick's term) of the sonatas, quartets and symphonies – and had set up Brahms as the true upholder of the tradition. By 1900, with some residual outbursts, polarized views of that kind were largely in the past, with conductors like Hans Richter, Mahler and, soon, Richard Strauss, regularly juxtaposing Beethoven, Brahms, Bruckner and Wagner in their programmes and composers like Schoenberg and Zemlinsky readily embracing both trajectories, interacting with both rather than regarding them as mutually exclusive. As Schoenberg wrote in his famous essay 'Brahms the Progressive', 'what in 1883 seemed an impassable gulf was in 1897 no longer a problem.'[10] Schoenberg may well have been thinking of the Otto Nicolai concert of 1897 that took place on 4 April, the day after the death of Brahms.[11] The scheduled programme was Wagner's overture to *Die Meistersinger*, Bach's Third Brandenburg Concerto and Beethoven's Ninth Symphony. As an act of homage to Brahms, Hans Richter decided to open the concert with a performance of Mozart's *Masonic Funeral Music* (K477), not as a diplomatic replacement for the Wagner overture but as an additional item.

The vitality of the Wagner tradition in Vienna was at odds with the composer's own experience of working in the city. On a visit in 1861 he was persuaded by the court opera to transfer the planned first performance of *Tristan und Isolde* from Karlsruhe to Vienna. Wagner first travelled back and forth to Vienna to witness preparations, then rented an apartment in the Hadikgasse in the Fourteenth District, before he gradually came to the conclusion that the invitation was being undermined by the duplicitous behaviour of the then Kapellmeister, Heinrich Esser, who simply did not like the work. For two seasons, the promised premiere kept on being postponed until, finally, the project was abandoned in 1864. Wagner left the city, referring to his experience as 'rotten, treacherous – and so crude'.[12]

Tristan und Isolde was not performed in Vienna until twenty years later, during the 1883–4 season, but from then through to the beginning of the First World War it was performed 128 times, an average of five performances per season.[13] The constituent operas of the *Ring* were performed with similar frequency, but all were outshone by the popularity of *Lohengrin, Tannhäuser, Der fliegende Holländer* and *Die Meistersinger von Nürnberg*. Schoenberg's statement that by the age of twenty-five he had heard each of Wagner's major operas twenty to thirty times is entirely credible.[14] Since the opera season ran from mid-August to mid-June the Wagner experience was a constant one, for many topped up in the summer by a train journey from Vienna to Bayreuth for the annual festival. As a service to its Viennese readers many volumes of *Fromme's Musikalische Welt* gave details of the operas and singers that had featured in Bayreuth the previous summer, and the volumes often divided their list of significant books on music that had been published in the previous year into two categories: Wagner, and everything else.

There were two specialist Wagner societies in Vienna, both affiliated to the parent organization in Germany, the Allgemeiner Richard Wagner-Verein. The older of the two, the Wiener Akademischer Wagner-Verein, founded in 1872, promoted private performances of extracts from Wagner's operas accompanied by piano plus the occasional curiosity by the master, such as his version of Palestrina's *Stabat Mater* for chorus and piano. Founded eighteen years later, the remit of the rival Neuer Richard Wagner-Verein was a wider one, devoted to Wagner the poet, the composer and the philosopher (in that order) and his significance for German art. Accordingly, as well as musical performances, it offered lectures on Wagner, including on his anti-Semitism, and only Germans could be members.[15]

One Wagner enthusiast in Vienna, a civil servant named Nikolaus Oesterlein who lived in the Alleegasse (now Argentinierstrasse) in the Fourth District, had amassed a collection of some 12,000 items associated with the composer – manuscripts, books, journals, pictures, photographs, busts, posters, tickets, programmes and so on – which he opened to the public. However, his attempts to gain private and public support for a dedicated Richard Wagner Museum in Vienna did not succeed and, a year before his death in 1898, the collection was sold to the city of Eisenach in Germany; as part of the Reuter-Wagner-Museum it remains the largest collection of Wagner items outside Bayreuth.[16]

When Mahler and Alfred Roller began their collaboration at the court opera in 1902–3, *Tristan und Isolde* was the first work to be presented, on 21 February 1903, part of the commemoration of the twentieth anniversary of Wagner's death. It was followed by a sequence of new Wagner productions designed by Roller: *Rheingold, Lohengrin* and *Die Walküre* conducted by Mahler, and *Siegfried* and *Götterdämmerung* conducted by Weingartner. Stage presentation of Wagner's final opera, *Parsifal*, outside Bayreuth was embargoed for thirty years after the composer's death. Many Viennese had made the pilgrimage to Bayreuth to see the work and some orchestral extracts, principally the Prelude to Act 1, had been played in concerts by the Philharmonic and the Konzertverein. The court opera in Vienna was one of the first to mount a production outside Bayreuth, on 14 January 1914, conducted by Franz Schalk, and the last Wagner production that Roller designed for the court theatre.[17]

Mozart's presence in Viennese concert life was an occasional, rather undefined one, and certainly nowhere near the cult status he was to enjoy in the city a hundred years later, at the end of the twentieth and the beginning of the twenty-first centuries. Hans Richter's concerts with the Philharmonic in the 1890s presented the occasional work such as the 'Paris' Symphony, and Mahler normally included one work per season, such as the G minor Symphony in 1898–9 and the 'Jupiter' in 1899–1900,[18] a practice that continued in the concerts conducted by Richard Strauss and Weingartner. Because the concerts of the Philharmonic hardly ever included an instrumental soloist, Mozart's piano concertos, violin concertos, horn concertos and the clarinet concerto were unfamiliar works. They were not much better represented in the programmes of the Konzertverein, even with their policy of featuring works with soloists; when the Symphonie Concertante for violin, viola and orchestra was performed in 1902–3 followed by two violin concertos in subsequent seasons, K216 in 1904–5 and K219 in 1906–7, these would have been novelties for many members of the audience;[19] a similar ignorance might have awaited even the D minor Piano Concerto (K466) when it was performed in 1909–10.[20] Chamber music concerts in the Bösendorfersaal and the small room in the Musikverein offered individual works from the 'Haydn' and the 'Prussian' Quartets, and, with an additional viola, some of the string quintets, but there were plenty of concerts that did not feature a single work by Mozart. Only in the opera house was Mozart's presence a constant one, with one or more of three operas, *Don Giovanni*, *Zauberflöte* and *Figaro*, performed every season; *Così fan tutte*, however, was a rarity.

1891 marked the hundredth anniversary of Mozart's death. The second subscription concert of the Philharmonic orchestra was doubly unusual in that the entire programme was devoted to the composer's music and featured a concerto: the *Masonic Funeral Music*, the B flat Piano Concerto (K595), the Adagio and Fugue in C minor (K546) and one of his last symphonies, K543 in E flat. In November and December the opera house gave performances of three rarely heard operas, *Die Entführung aus dem Serail*, *Idomeneo* and *La clemenza di Tito*. The Rosé Quartet also gave an all-Mozart programme in December: following a spoken tribute the ensemble (with an additional viola player and a guest pianist) performed the String Quintet in G minor (K516), the Piano Quartet in E flat (K493) and the A major Quartet (K464).[21] None of these commemorative events led to a permanent broadening of the repertoire and though there was another, similar focus in the next anniversary year, 1906, this, too, did not lead to a sustained resurgence of public interest in the composer.

One work by Mozart, however, had, become an honoured part of Vienna's musical life. In a tradition that can be traced back to the death of Haydn in 1809 and that of Schikaneder in 1813, Mozart's Requiem was often performed on memorial occasions for well-known public figures, sometimes in churches like the Augustinerkirche or the Karlskirche, sometimes in the Musikverein. The memory of Mozart himself was appropriately honoured in this way in 1891 and 1906,[22] while the death of Empress Elisabeth in 1898 and that of Karl Lueger, the popular mayor of Vienna, in 1910 were both marked by performances of the Requiem.[23]

Undoubtedly, the most familiar of works from Vienna's musical past was by Joseph Haydn: the national anthem, now played and sung in honour of the empire's longest serving monarch, Franz Joseph. The imperial army had over a hundred regimental bands,[24] who played it throughout the Habsburg territories on all manner of occasions. Shortly after Franz Joseph's accession it was provided with a new official text, by Joseph Seidl, one that adroitly linked the individual and the dynasty with the land, its integrity and destiny. Translations in seven official languages were ratified: Croatian, Czech, Hungarian, Italian, Polish, Rumanian and Slovak.[25]

Gott erhalte, Gott beschütze	God preserve, God protect
Unsern Kaiser, unser Land!	Our Emperor, our Land!
Mächtig durch des Glaubens Stütze	Mighty by means of the faith
Führ' Er uns mit weiser Hand!	He leads with a wise hand!
Laßt uns Seiner Väter Krone	Let us, by means of his fathers' crown,
Schirmen wider jeden Feind:	Shelter against every enemy:
Innig bleibt mit Habsburgs Throne	Fervently linked with the Habsburg's throne
Österreichs Geschick vereint.	United with Austria's destiny.

Uniquely amongst national anthems, 'Gott erhalte' had a comfortable place within the repertoire of art music too, as the theme for a set of variations in Haydn's own string quartet in C (op. 76 no. 3), accordingly dubbed the 'Kaiser-Quartett', often performed in the Bösendorfersaal and other small concert halls in Vienna. As a stand-alone movement it was also played with full string forces in orchestral concerts, not as a formal beginning or end but as an integral part of the programme, as in the Philharmonic concert on 4 December 1898 conducted by Mahler, where it followed Brahms's Second Symphony and Dvořák's symphonic poem, *Heldenlied*, and preceded Mendelssohn's overture to *Midsummer's Night's Dream*.[26] It even made a surprise appearance at the end of two marches by Johann Strauss, the *Rettungs-Jubel-Marsch* (1853) and the *Jubiläums-Marsch* (1898).

Haydn's melody provided a permanent backdrop for a general presence in Vienna's musical life that was more pronounced than that of Mozart. Many of the 'London' symphonies featured from time to time in the programmes of the Philharmonic Orchestra and those of the Konzertverein, supplemented by some rarities, such as No. 1 (1910–11, Philharmonic), No. 46 (1907–8, Philharmonic) No. 73 ('La chasse', 1896–7, Philharmonic) and No. 82 ('L'ours', 1905–6, Konzertverein),[27] while Haydn's name was honoured by association whenever Brahms's so-called *Variations on a Theme of Haydn* (op. 52a) were performed. The two choral societies, the Singverein and the Singakademie, kept *Die Schöpfung* and *Die*

Jahreszeiten in the repertoire, and the composer's quartets, especially from opp. 71, 74, 76 and 77, were regularly presented.

Apart from the national anthem, the quartets and the two late oratorios, there was another aspect of Haydn's output that had been a constant presence in Vienna since the composer's time: his liturgical music. Many of his masses together with smaller items of church music, such as the offertory 'Insane et vanae curae', were part of the standard repertory of several Viennese churches, including the Hofburgkapelle, Augustinerkirche, Michaelerkirche and Stephansdom, where they were often performed from manuscript parts that dated from Haydn's time. In a city that now officially embraced and generally celebrated religious diversity – Greek Orthodox, Jewish, Lutheranism and Muslim – these Catholic works represented a thread of religious and cultural history that went back to the Counter-Reformation and, for many people, continued to define who they were. This sense of personal identity through music was helped by the fact that Haydn's liturgical compositions hardly ever featured in the concert repertoire and, consequently, were not normally listed in the volumes of *Fromme's Musikalische Welt* or the *Musikbuch aus Österreich*.

These diverse strands in Haydn's reputation – the patriot, the Catholic, the composer of engaging instrumental music and the master of grand oratorio – were given a platform in 1909, the hundredth anniversary of his death. In a notable feat of coordination and organization, five quartet ensembles – Damen, Fitzner, Ondricek, Prill and Rosé – presented a complete cycle of Haydn's quartets between January and May. Similarly comprehensive, if less orderly, no fewer than thirty-two churches in Vienna, in the suburbs as well as the inner city, featured ninety-two liturgical performances of works by Haydn between January and June, that is from Epiphany through to Pentecost. Performances of *Die Schöpfung* and *Die Jahreszeiten* were given in the Musikverein and a third, earlier oratorio was resuscitated, *Il ritorno di Tobia*, performed in German rather than the original Italian.[28] At Guido Adler's behest, the third congress of the International Musical Society took place in Vienna at the end of May 1909. Although the scholarly aspect of the conference was much broader than Haydn, the whole occasion was given a focus by the centenary, with a celebratory mass in the Hofburg, concerts in the Musikverein, performances of two operas by Haydn translated from the Italian, *Lo speziale* (*Der Apotheker*) and *L'isola disabitata* (*Die wüste Insel*), plus visits to Haydn's house in Gumpendorf and to the Esterházy palace in Eisenstadt.[29]

Three days before the congress began, Adler wrote a publicity article in the Saturday edition of the *Neue Freie Presse*, a careful positioning of the event within the wider musical life of the city.[30] 'It's not that easy to bring art, scholarship and good fellowship (*Kunst, Wissenschaft und Geselligkeit*), the guiding principles of celebration, together under one banner' he writes before proceeding to argue that the scholarly side of the Haydn congress ought to contribute to a new awareness of Austria's musical inheritance.

Adler wanted to push the familiar sense of legacy back to the composer's antecedents, to the Renaissance and Baroque, so that Haydn's achievement could appear at the apex of a broad pyramid; to promote this idea, one of the concerts in the Musikverein presented music by Jacob Handl, Johann Joseph Fux, Gottlieb Muffat and Matthias Georg Monn from recent volumes of the *Denkmäler der Tonkunst in Österreich*.

Memorialization and monumentalism

WHEN Brahms died on 3 April 1897, the funeral arrangements were not undertaken by individuals but by an institution, the Gesellschaft der Musikfreunde. The composer had lived in Vienna since 1868 and was closely associated with the Gesellschaft as director of its concerts for three seasons (1872–5), an honorary member from 1876 and a member of the central committee from 1881. Many of his own compositions, notably his symphonies, were given their first Viennese performances in concerts organized by the Gesellschaft or, in the case of the Philharmonic concerts, housed by the society, and he had funded a composition prize. Above all, he had taken a particular interest in the development of the archive, visiting it regularly – it was only a few minutes walk away from his apartment in the Karlsgasse – to develop his knowledge and understanding of older music, donating money for its further development and leaving his considerable library as a bequest.[31] He, more than any other individual, embodied the values and the status of the Gesellschaft der Musikfreunde in Vienna.

The formal printed announcement of the death and details of the funeral arrangements were issued by the Gesellschaft on 4 April. At 2.30 p.m. on Tuesday 6 April the funeral cortege made its way from the Karlsgasse to the front entrance of the Musikverein, where members of the Singverein sang his valedictory part song, 'Fahr wohl', heard in absolute silence, except for the gently appropriate sound of bird song:

Fahr wohl, o Vöglein, das nun wandern soll;	Farewell, o little bird, that now shall wander;
Der Sommer fährt von hinnen,	Summer goes hence,
Du willst mit ihm entrinnen:	You wish to escape with it:
Fahr wohl, Fahr wohl, Fahr wohl!	Farewell, farewell, farewell!

From there the procession made its way into the inner city, behind the opera house, past the Lobkowitz square and into the Augustinerstrasse, before turning right into the narrow Dorotheergasse. On the left stood Vienna's Protestant church, established in 1783 in the reign of Joseph II. During the service the priest read the text that Brahms had chosen for the final movement of the German Requiem, 'Selig sind die Toten, die in dem Herrn sterben' ('Blessed are the dead, who die in the name of the Lord'). After the service the cortege made the lengthy journey

to the Zentralfriedhof, in the Eleventh District, to the south-east of
the city.

The physical location of the cemetery was certainly not a central one,
but since its opening in 1874 it had become central to Vienna's evolving
cultural memory. Built on an even grander scale than the Ringstrasse, with
a hugely imposing entrance and broad avenues that disappear into the
distance, it had designated sections for the Greek and Russian Orthodox
churches, Jews, Muslims as well as Catholics, and leading architects,
authors, bankers, literary figures, military personnel and surgeons
were buried there, their graves marked by grand, frequently oversized
monuments. As such, it was a cemetery of civic and national remembrance,
rather than personal remembrance, no more so than for composers. The
remains of Beethoven, Czerny, Gluck, Lanner, Schubert, Johann Strauss
(the father) and Josef Strauss were reinterred there and, in the absence of
any remains, Mozart was commemorated with a substantial memorial.
Brahms was buried in the same area, with a monument that looked
pensively across a lawn towards those of Beethoven and Mozart. It was
in this area that Brahms's friend from the Gesellschaft der Musikfreunde,
Richard von Perger, gave an address at the grave, recalling words uttered
by Franz Grillparzer at Beethoven's funeral almost seventy years to
the day: 'nicht verloren haben wir ihn, wir haben ihn gewonnen: denn
kein Lebendinger tritt in die Halle der Unsterblichkeit ein' ('we have
not lost him, we have won him: for no living person enters the hall of
immortality').[32]

Grillparzer's words, repeated by Perger, point to a sense of collective
ownership by the Viennese and admission into a musical pantheon that
was continually expanding. The 1890s, in particular, afforded several more
instances of this unfolding process. Suppé had died in 1895, Bruckner
in 1896 and Johann Strauss (the son) was to die in 1899. As well as graves,
there were conspicuous public monuments in Vienna to Beethoven (in
a square in the First District named after him, the Beethovenplatz), to
Haydn (in front of the parish church in the Mariahilferstrasse), to Mozart
(in the Albrechtsplatz behind the court opera, later moved to the nearby
Burggarten) and Schubert (the civic park in Heiligenstadt). Brahms
(Karlsplatz), Bruckner (Stadtpark) and Johann Strauss (Stadtpark) were
to join them in future years. The annual volumes of *Fromme's Musikalische
Welt* detailed these monuments as part of their list of notable places to
visit (*Sehenswürdigkeiten*), alongside houses in which composers had lived
and, of heightened interest, where they had died (*Sterbehaus*). For the
self-esteem of the Viennese, as well as the curiosity of visitors, there were
seven Beethoven houses, Brahms's *Sterbehaus*, Bruckner's house, Gluck's
Sterbehaus, Haydn's *Sterbehaus*, four Mozart houses, Schubert's birthplace
as well as his *Sterbehaus*, and Johann Strauss's house.

Milestones on the way to memorialization were a routine part of musical
life. As well as anniversaries of the birth and deaths of major composers –
Beethoven, Haydn, Liszt, Mendelssohn, Mozart, Schubert, Schumann and

so on – all kinds of anniversaries were celebrated in individual concerts: the twenty-fifth anniversary of the opening of the opera house (1894), the twenty-fifth anniversary of the opening of the Musikverein (1895), the thousandth concert in the Ehrbarsaal (1897), the hundredth anniversary of the national anthem (1897), the hundredth concert of the Rosé Quartet (1897), the fiftieth anniversary of the setting up of the Hellmesberger Quartet (1899), the tenth anniversary of Bruckner's death (1906), the tenth anniversary of Brahms's death (1907), the fiftieth anniversary of the Singakademie (1908), and the fiftieth anniversary of the first subscription concert of the Philharmonic Orchestra (1909).

In 1913, it was announced that one of the most revered musical venues in Vienna, the Bösendorfersaal, was to close. It was not so much its closure that affected the Viennese, but that fact that it was going to be demolished, denying memorialization. Stefan Zweig wrote movingly of the last concert on Friday 2 May, when the Rosé Quartet performed a suitably valedictory programme – Haydn's Variations on 'Gott erhalte' (from op. 76 no. 3), Schubert's String Quintet and the slow movement ('Lento assai e cantante tranquillo') from Beethoven's last quartet, op. 135:

> In itself this little concert hall, which was used solely for chamber music, was a quite unimposing, unartistic piece of architecture, the former riding academy of Count Liechtenstein, unpretentiously remodelled for musical use with wooden panelling. But it had the resonance of an old violin, it was a sanctuary for lovers of music, because Chopin and Brahms, Liszt and Rubinstein had given concerts there, and because many of the famous quartets had made their first appearance there; and now it was to make way for a functional building. It was incomprehensible to us who had experienced such unforgettable hours there. When the last bar of Beethoven, played more beautifully than ever by the Rosé Quartet, had died away, no one left his seat. We called and applauded, several women sobbed with emotion, no one wished to believe that this was a farewell. The lights were put out in the hall in order to make us leave. Not one of the four or five hundred enthusiasts moved from the place. A half hour, a full hour, we remained as if by our presence we could save the old hallowed place.[33]

A year earlier, in 1912, the Gesellschaft der Musikfreunde celebrated its centenary – it chose the year of the mammoth performance of Handel's *Timotheus* as the starting point rather than 1814, when it was formally constituted – and between 30 November and 7 December there was a series of celebratory events, concerts, a reception at court, a reception at the Rathaus, and the laying of wreathes of honour on the graves of musicians in the Zentralfriedhof and on Haydn's tomb in Eisenstadt. As well as the great and good of Vienna, the celebration attracted musical ambassadors from all over Europe who offered their formal congratulations, in many cases gifts too, at a dedicated reception.[34] The broad vision of the society had been maintained, sometimes carefully adjusted, to produce an institution without an exact equivalent in Europe: a concert venue, a promoter of concerts, a locus for amateur music-making, a conservatoire (until 1908–9) and the home of an archive and a library.

While the conservatoire had been taken over by the state and was soon to be part of the Konzerthaus complex, the archive and the library were still an essential part of the identity of the society, appropriately celebrated by an exhibition during the centenary celebrations. From earliest times it had responded enthusiastically to those individuals who wished to donate material or, alternatively, wished to donate money that could be used to purchase material. More distinctively, it benefited from being part of a society that was fully engaged in the everyday musical life of the city. While the imperial library continued, to a certain degree, to reflect the lofty outlook of a Habsburg administrative unit, collecting material that naturally belonged to them, such as the music and the records of the court theatres, the library of the Gesellschaft reflected the pluralism of musical life of Vienna in the nineteenth century. Brahms had epitomized this outlook as a pianist, choral conductor, collector, historian, musical editor as well as a composer, and his circle of close friends included two successive archivists, Carl Ferdinand Pohl and Eusebius Mandyczewski, as well as the concert director, Richard von Perger. When Brahms's extensive library was donated to the society following his death, in addition to his own music it included the autograph scores of Haydn's op. 20 quartets and Mozart's G minor Symphony (K550), early manuscript scores of Beethoven's *Missa Solemnis* and his op. 110 sonata, as well as smaller items, by, amongst others, Wagner.[35] This was not merely the act of a generous and grateful individual but a summation of many of the governing characteristics of musical life in the city.

With its tripartite organization of archive, library and collections the Gesellschaft der Musikfreunde was highly acquisitive, helped by its daily contact with performing musicians, local and visiting, and by the curiosity of its audiences. It had a substantial collection of musical instruments, from violins to Liszt's hybrid instrument, the piano-harmonium, and from natural horns to a Welsh crwth. But collecting went way beyond that, in effect including anything that had to do with music and musicians, with nothing being ruled out: batons, busts, clothing, death masks, ear trumpets, engravings, letters, locks of hair, medals, metronomes, minutes of committee meetings, paintings, passports, posters, programmes, sketches, spectacles and tuning forks. Today, traditional curators might describe some of this material as ephemera, more fashion-conscious curators as culturally rich signifiers of social history, but for many people in Vienna they were akin to holy relics. According to the Baedeker guide of 1911, admission was free to the various collections between September and July, on Tuesdays, Thursdays and Saturdays, from eleven to one o'clock.[36] Gaining access offered a complementary experience to attending a concert in one of the adjacent halls, the chance to come into contact – or, better still, near contact – with physical material associated with composers and performers. Stefan Zweig, once more, offers an insight into this mentality. He himself was not a musician but owned a portrait of Haydn together with a desk said to have belonged to Beethoven, and devoted much of his adult life to collecting musical manuscripts (also literary manuscripts), a fascination that was formed in pre-First World War Vienna:

> What I sought was the originals or the sketches for poems or compositions, because the problem of the creation of a work of art, both in its biographical and psychological forms, held my attention more than anything else. The mysterious moment of transition in which a verse, a melody, emerges out of the invisible, out of the vision and intuition of a genius, and is graphically fixed in material form – where else can it so well be examined and observed as in the tortured or trance-born manuscripts of the master? ... The sight of one of Beethoven's first sketches with its wild impatient strokes, its chaotic mixture of motifs begun and discarded, and with the creative fury, the superabundance of his genius, compressed into a few pencil strokes is physically exciting to me because it is mentally exciting. I can look at such a scribbled page of hieroglyphics with enchantment and love, as others gaze upon a perfect picture.[37]

One of the most obvious changes in the musical environment in Vienna that had developed during the nineteenth century was the amount of public debate it engendered. From next to nothing at the beginning of the nineteenth century it had become pervasive, even overwhelming. More than twenty daily newspapers, some of which appeared in more than one edition and could number up to seventy closely printed pages, included regular reviews of musical performances, often by long-standing and influential figures.[38]

The *Wiener Zeitung*, the official court newspaper, was still being published and had sprouted an evening edition, the *Wiener Abendpost*; its music critic was Robert Hirschfeld, who had studied philosophy and musicology at the University of Vienna and taught at the conservatoire. Appropriately for the court newspaper his music criticism was generally neutral in tone, a quasi-official outlook that was further promoted by the fact that he wrote programme notes for the Philharmonic concerts, a practice instigated by Richter for the 1893–4 season.[39]

Theodor Helm, the editor of *Fromme's Musikalische Welt*, was the music critic of the *Deutsche Zeitung*, a German nationalist paper that often promoted anti-Semitic views. Helm's musical sympathies were certainly German, as his enthusiasm for Wagner and for Bayreuth Festival in the pages of *Fromme's Musikalische Welt* reveal, but his musical commentary was never coloured by anti-Semitism. By the 1890s, Vienna's most famous music critic, Eduard Hanslick, was no longer as influential as he had been and many of his duties were undertaken instead by his deputy, Richard Heuberger. Like many others, Hanslick, Helm and Heuberger had long careers and, though the critics were often capable of stimulating public debate in a positive manner, their capacity to resort to the personal, even the vindictive, and to sow seeds of rumours often resulted in malevolent opinion rather than honest debate, as the biographies of Mahler, Schoenberg, Richard Strauss and Zemlinsky show.

In October 1909 Schoenberg, who the previous December had experienced the uncomprehending response of press and public to his Second String Quartet, wrote an article for *Der Merker*, 'About Music Criticism', in which he bemoaned the conservatism of the critical establishment and, more aggressively, its basic competence to judge. His real anger, however, was directed at the complete lack of moral integrity that characterized the press, compounded by its willingness to undermine and destroy:

> The reader attaches little importance to it any more, for one knows the motives at work in nearly all cases; one knows the trends, the personal friendships and enmities that are decisive. But something always sticks, in good or bad: praise and blame – ineffective in themselves, since everyone feels the lack of respect with which they are handed out – are transmuted into more commercially solid values; publicity is made for an artist, or animosity aroused against him, according to the relationship he allows the critic to have with him. And that is a kind of power, if hardly to be compared with the power of the almighty ones of former times, who could bestow and withhold appointments. Nowadays so much is pettier, and this is too – pinpricks where once there was a knife in the back. But it is cumulative; a thousand pinpricks paralyse as surely, perhaps, as a single knife-thrust killed. Perhaps this power is no more dangerous than the old kind, but it is more harassing.[40]

If the ever-deepening sense of historical legacy in Viennese musical life often smothered newer impulses, in a very different area, that of scholarship, it motivated a new, exploratory understanding of the musical past, one that had the concomitant effect of affirming the legitimacy of the present or, at least, of creating new narratives that informed understanding of the present. The authority of the process was certainly new, but the results played into standard cultural values. Here the leading figure was Guido Adler (1855–1941). As his involvement in the planned shake-up of the conservatoire in 1904 and in the 1909 Haydn conference suggests, he was not a marginal figure in the musical life of the city, but an endlessly energetic individual with a wide circle of sympathetic friends and supporters, one who seems largely to have avoided debilitating controversy and who maintained that status for over forty years, from the 1890s to his enforced retirement in 1938, following the annexation of Austria by Germany. Born in 1855, he grew up in Iglau, the same village as Gustav Mahler, five years his junior, though they seem not to have known each other at the time.[41] At the University of Vienna he studied law and then music history with Eduard Hanslick. From 1885 he was a professor at the German University in Prague, from where he began to formulate ambitious plans for the academic study of music, carving out a coherent discipline that would build on some existing practices.

Within Vienna itself there was a strong tradition of writing on various aspects of musical life from the mid-eighteenth century onwards, notably the large-scale biography of Haydn by Carl Ferdinand Pohl, concert life up to the late 1860s by Eduard Hanslick and the history of the Gesellschaft der Musikfreunde, also by Pohl.[42] In addition, there were, very obviously, the rich musical holdings of the imperial library and of the archive of the Gesellschaft that were waiting to be explored. Beyond Vienna, Adler was responding to the distinctive north German tradition of providing authoritative musical texts for the complete outputs of major composers from the past, principally Bach, Handel and Mozart. For a few years in the 1880s he hoped that musical works from the Viennese heritage might be published as part of a larger project devoted to German music history, but this proved too ambitious.

It was the publication by Breitkopf & Härtel of Leipzig in 1889 of three volumes of music by Frederick the Great that gave Adler a steer for his future work.[43] He formulated a plan to publish the musical compositions of three Austrian emperors, Ferdinand III, Leopold I and Joseph I, an imperial and musical legacy known to very few people, including members of the imperial court itself. An exploratory letter to the court elicited the response that such a venture would be welcomed and could be supported by the Ministry of Culture and Education. With this promised financial support Adler went ahead with the publication of two volumes of imperial music, while simultaneously planning the establishment of a permanent society that would plan a series of volumes, 'monuments of music' from Austria's past, the Gesellschaft zur Herausgabe von Denkmälern der Tonkunst in Oesterreich. By the end of October 1893 the statutes had been drawn up.[44] Based in Vienna – Adler was still working in Prague – the society had as its purpose the publication of music by composers from the past who were either born in Austria (that term was used in the current sense of those territories in the Empire that were not part of the kingdom of Hungary) or who had lived and worked there, plus musical works of significance for the history of music in Austria. Financially, the work of the society would be supported by subscriptions, income from other publications, subventions, gifts and legacies. As well as giving its formal approval, the imperial court, through the Ministry of Culture and Education, supported the society to the tune of 2,000 crowns per annum, gradually rising to 13,000 crowns in 1913.[45]

The administration of the society was headed by a management board (*leitende Commission*), and it is here that Adler's skills as a diplomat are at their most evident. Rather than populating the board with fellow scholars, he placed the work of the society firmly in the mainstream of musical life by recruiting, and filling later vacancies, from a range of constituencies.[46]

The first chairman was Eduard Hanslick, succeeded in 1897 by Baron Josef Bezecny, a financier with an interest in the arts who was also president of the Gesellschaft der Musikfreunde; he, in turn, was succeeded by Laurenz Mayer, a Catholic cleric, and Count Max Wickenbrug, head of the Ministry for Culture and Education. Another career civil servant on the board was Baron Wilhelm Weckbecker, who served for over forty years. Brahms was a founder member, a natural extension of his interest in older music and his experience as an editor, as was Hans Richter. The latter was succeeded by Mahler, who inherited the committee position of the imperial court's most eminent musician; although Mahler admitted to being rather bored by the historical priorities of the society he continued to give his tacit support through to his death in 1911.[47] Scholars from disciplines other than music included Emil von Ottenhal, Professor of History at the University of Innsbruck, and the Germanist Josef Seemüller and the theologian Heinrich Swoboda, both from the University of Vienna. A crucial, irreplaceable long-term member was the printer and publisher Carl August Artaria, grandson of Domenico who had headed the family firm in Beethoven's time; the firm had given up publishing music around 1860 but reactivated its expertise in order to produce the *Denkmäler* volumes. Artaria also acted as the treasurer. As close personal friends, Adler and Artaria were the two who drove the business of the committee, the latter readily deferring to the scholarly judgement of the former.

Between 1894 and 1913 forty-one volumes appeared, covering music from the fifteenth century to the end of the eighteenth century, from the Trent Codices to Albrechtsberger; twelve of these volumes were edited (or co-edited) by Adler himself. The content of the volumes stood apart from the standard repertoire of Viennese musical life – Handel, Haydn, Beethoven, Brahms, Wagner, Bruckner and Richard Strauss – but the implicit wider outlook was that the music of today gained cultural legitimacy because it built on centuries of similar achievement in Habsburg Austria. The opening sentence of the general preface to the first volume, signed by Adler, Artaria, Brahms, Hanslick, Richter and other members of the management board, alludes to this wider agenda: 'In Austria, where from time immemorial music has been cultivated with ever-increasing participation, where the artistic judgment of ruling dynasties found the strongest resonance in the natural talent of the people, there lies an extremely rich legacy of glorious music from the past.'[48]

To the modern reader the grandiose tone of these comments may seem at odds with the nuts and bolts of scholarly presentation that are displayed in the rest of the volume – informative preface, illustrations, impeccable musical typography and critical reports – yet they were of their time, a sincere attempt to foster a sense of allegiance. Drawing attention to the role of dynastic patronage as well as the musical riches of the past led naturally to the content of the first volume: the music of one of the Habsburg court's most notable musical servants, Johann Joseph Fux. It presents an edition of two works, the *Missa Sanctissimae Trinitas* dedicated to Leopold I, together with a reproduction of the handwritten letter of dedication, and the *Missa Sancti Caroli* (the *Missa Canonica*) dedicated to Karl VI on his name day, again with a reproduction of the dedication.

This initial volume was followed by a further four devoted to the music of Fux, culminating in 1910 with the edition of *Costanza e Fortezza*, the coronation opera that had helped secure the future of the Habsburg dynasty in the eighteenth century. Two volumes were given over to another large-scale Habsburg opera, Cesti's *Il pomo d'oro* (intended to celebrate the marriage of Leopold I and Margarita Teresa in 1666, but first performed on the empress's birthday two years later) and one volume to the church music of Caldara. From later in the eighteenth century there are two volumes devoted to instrumental music by Albrechtsberger and Michael Haydn, one to 'Precursors of the Vienna Classics' (Reutter, Wagenseil, Schlöger, Starzer and the Monn brothers), and one to Umlauf's *Die Bergknappen* (1778), a pioneering work in the development of opera in German in Vienna.

When Hanslick retired from his post of professor at the university in 1896 Adler had put himself in pole position to succeed him, as a recognized scholar in his own right, the instigator of the already successful *Denkmäler* project and a skilled administrator who was widely connected in Viennese society. Not surprisingly, the obvious choice was not to the taste of everybody and it took two years for Adler to be confirmed in post.[49] He immediately established the Institute for Musicology, an organization that was to realize his plans for a new discipline, first expounded in an article written over ten years earlier.[50]

Characterized by a robust intellectual framework, musicology was to be divided into two parts. The first was 'Historical Musicology', the study of music in defined epochs, together with their peoples, empires, nations, regions, cities, schools and individuals. The second, complementary part was termed 'Systematic Musicology', a theoretical framework that sought to rationalize the nature of the art – harmony, rhythm, melody, instrument, pedagogy and aesthetic. Adler's early training as a lawyer is evident not only in the clarity of the framework but in the whole approach to its associated working methods, one in which dilettantism was to be replaced by accuracy of description that would lead ineluctably to secure conclusions. In this, there was also something of the proficient Habsburg bureaucrat in Adler, the successor to Ignaz von Mosel, Joseph Sonnleithner and others who had fashioned views on the nature of musical life at the beginning of the nineteenth century.

The *Denkmäler* project was a key product of this scholarly thinking. At the same time it linked more broadly with other projects supported by the court that created a similar sense of collective identity for the diverse peoples of the empire, notably the twenty-four volumes of *Die österreichische-ungarische Monarchie in Wort und Bild* (The Austrian-Hungarian Monarchy in Word and Picture), a lavishly illustrated encyclo-paedia that appeared between 1885 and 1902.[51] The popular appeal of that project together with the scholarly standing of Adler's *Denkmäler* volumes provided the impetus for another ambitious project sponsored by the court, *Das Volkslied in Österreich*.

Initiated by the music publishing firm of Universal Edition and set up in 1904 it, too, received financial support from the Ministry of Culture and Education. From that year onwards the *Musikbuch aus Österreich* gave details of its committee structure every year, an ever-expanding and elaborate one that, by 1911, occupied four densely printed pages.[52] A central committee that guided the project from Vienna had twenty-five members (including, for a while, Guido Adler), from which a smaller executive committee of nine was drawn. Hungary had refused to cooperate on the grounds that the kingdom of Hungary was not part of Austria, but almost every other part of the empire had its own working committee, often two: German folk music in Bohemia, German music in Gottschee (Slovenia), German folk music in Carinthia, German music in Moravia and Silesia, folk music in Lower Austria, folk music in Upper Austria, folk music in Salzburg, German folk music in Styria, German folk music in the Tyrol, Italian folk music in Dalmatia and the Adriatic coast (Küstenland), Italian folk music in South Tyrol, folk music in the Ladin language, Rumanian folk music, Czech folk music in Bohemia, Czech folk music in Moravia and Silesia, Polish folk music, Ruthenian folk music, Serbo-Croat folk music and Slovenian folk music. These nineteen working committees had over 160 individuals.

A staggering 300 volumes of folksong were planned with a publication schedule of two a year, a project that would have taken 150 years to complete, to the middle of the twenty-first century. Not surprisingly, the whole enterprise soon became riddled with tensions: between individuals, between regions, between languages and, above all, between Vienna and almost everybody else. Leoš Janáček was one figure who worked assiduously for the project, as chair of the working committee for Czech folk music in Moravia and Silesia, and as a collector and editor. By 1913 galley proofs of a substantial volume of Czech folk music had been prepared, but the whole project collapsed when the empire collapsed five years later.[53]

Johann Strauss dedicates a waltz to Brahms

ON 25 November 1891 Johann Strauss (the son) sent a letter to his publisher Simrock in Berlin,[54] indicating his intention to write a waltz that was to be dedicated to Brahms. One of his oldest and closest friends, Brahms had introduced the Waltz King to Simrock, initiating a lasting business relationship. In subsequent correspondence Simrock forwarded a suggestion for a title for the new waltz, 'Seid umschlungen, Millionen'.[55] The sentiment of Schiller's text was clearly appropriate, the knowing resonances even more so. With a sense of mischief as well as

15 Title-page of Johann Strauss's 'Seid umschlungen, Millionen', 1892

genuine admiration, Strauss was going to write a concert waltz whose title owed its familiarity not to Schiller but to Beethoven, the composer who had determined Brahms's path and with whom he was, to his irritation, sometimes simplistically compared. As Strauss contemplated the content of his new waltz he was approached by Princess Pauline Metternich, the wife of Clemens Metternich's grandson and an influential figure at the imperial court, asking him to compose a waltz for a major international exhibition, devoted to music and theatre of all kinds, that was to be held in the Prater in the early summer of 1892.[56] Strauss agreed and, always the opportunist, proceeded to compose 'Seid umschlungen, Millionen' for the exhibition as well as for Brahms.

The new waltz was first performed, in Brahms's presence, at a concert given by Eduard Strauss's orchestra in the Musikverein on 27 March 1892, the brother having agreed that Johann should direct this particular item. As was often the case with concerts given by members of the Strauss family, there was a capacity audience. The new waltz was rapturously received, had to be repeated twice, and soon came to be known as 'The Millions Waltz' ('Der Millionenwaltzer').[57] To coincide with its many performances during the international exhibition Simrock, as was customary, published the waltz in several versions: for large orchestra, small orchestra, military band, solo piano, piano duet, piano and violin, and piano and flute. The title-page, sanctioned by composer, vividly portrays the circumstances of its composition and reception (see Fig. 15). Above an image of the exhibition space in the Prater, a central figure is seen carrying the whole world – not a straining male Atlas, rather an energetic Terpsichore, the muse of the dance, who effortlessly propels the waltzing world across the page. The dedication to 'Johannes Brahms' appears discreetly in the top right-hand corner. Potential purchasers, the millions of amateur and professional musicians across the world, are invited to recognize, admire and celebrate musical Vienna and two of its leading figures, Strauss and Brahms.

From Johann Strauss to Richard Strauss

The Waltz King turns to operetta

JOHANN Strauss's waltz, 'Seid umschlungen, Millionen', was not the last time that Strauss and Brahms were linked together in a public manner. On 3 June 1899 Johann Strauss (the son) died at his home in Igelgasse in the Fourth District, exactly two years and two months after Brahms's death. The funeral arrangements were strikingly similar. Strauss had converted to the Protestant faith in order to marry his third wife, Adele, and the funeral service was held in the same church in the Dorotheergasse, attended by individuals as different in outlook and profession as Karl Lueger, the mayor, and Gustav Mahler, the director of the court opera. Following the service the funeral cortege made its way towards the Gesellschaft der Musikfreunde where, as in Brahms's funeral, the Singverein sang that composer's 'Fahr wohl'. The horse-drawn procession then made its way to the Zentralfriedhof, where Strauss was buried in a plot immediately adjacent to that of Brahms. At a memorial concert in the Musikverein on 25 October, Strauss's birthday, the Singverein, accompanied by an orchestra drawn from the court orchestra and conducted by Richard von Perger, performed Brahms's Requiem.[1] The affecting waltz rhythms of 'Wie lieblich sind deine Wohnungen' could never have sounded more appropriate.

As two long-standing figures of the musical establishment, Strauss and Brahms had the affection and admiration of the Viennese public, but the nature of the affection and, arising from that, the appeal of their personal friendship was founded on a contradiction. Brahms was an outsider, from Hamburg, who had become an insider; Strauss, on the other hand was a Viennese, one of us, but for much of his career had been outside the mainstream of musical life in the city.

Born in 1825 in the suburb of St Ulrich (later incorporated into the Seventh District) to a family that could trace its Viennese roots back to the middle of the previous century, Strauss had lived in Vienna all his life. With his father, Johann, and his two brothers Josef and Eduard, he had established Viennese dance music – the waltz, the polka and the march – as a constant, highly idiomatic presence in the social and musical life of the city, not only as music for dancing but as dance music to listen to, outdoors and indoors. The Viennese pedigree of the music was constantly affirmed by the titles of many of the dances: political events such as the 1861 election (*Wahlstimmen* Waltz), celebrations such as the 1888 jubilee (*Kaiser-Jubiläum* Waltz), the pleasures of life such as drink and gossip

(*Champagner* Polka and *Tritsch-tratsch* Polka), the rapidly changing urban landscape (*Demolirer* Polka) and the unchanging pleasures of the surrounding physical landscape (*Geschichten aus dem Wienerwald* and *An der schönen blauen Donau*, both waltzes).

In a way that is unequalled in the history of music, the output of the Strauss family provided an unfolding narrative of the life of a city for the best part of a century. For the rapidly growing population it helped fashion an identity that was comforting and inward-looking. At the same time it was also the most persistent and widely disseminated of musical exports. All the members of the Strauss family were inveterate promoters of their music abroad, travelling regularly to St Petersburg, Paris, London, New York and Boston, as well as cities closer to home. These cities were usually treated to newly composed dances that sometimes pandered to local topics, but the real appeal to international audiences was that it was a greeting from Vienna, *ein Gruss aus Wien*.

It was Johann Strauss's first wife, Henriette 'Jetty' Treffz, who persuaded him to turn his hand to the composition of operetta, partly to avoid the constant international travel, partly because it was financially more lucrative. Between 1871 and 1897 he wrote sixteen operettas that gave a new focus to an already popular form of music theatre, with much of the musical content reflecting Strauss's long experience of the dance: ambience, personality and storyline were all articulated through marches, polkas and waltzes. Not all of the works were successful, but two, *Die Fledermaus* (1874) and *Der Zigeunerbaron* (1885) were overwhelmingly so, at home and abroad. Whether successful or not, the operettas provided a ready source for new waltzes that could then be sold independently. Johann Strauss's brother, Eduard, never wrote a stage work, instead devoting himself to the continuing lifestyle of composition for balls, concerts and international tours. Although ten years younger than Johann, he maintained this existence for only two years after his brother's death, giving his last concert in New York in February 1901. There was no sign that the music of the Strauss family was becoming less popular; on the contrary it had established an existence and momentum of its own. For Eduard, however, it had become a burden and he retired from musical life. He died fifteen years later, in 1916.

Even though the music of the Strauss family, whether for balls, the concert hall, the summer pavilion or the stage, was a constant and vital part of the musical calendar in Vienna, it was at the same time separated from the rest of music-making in the city. A clear manifestation of this is its virtual absence from the annual volumes of *Fromme's Musikalische Welt* and the *Musikbuch aus Österreich*; the home addresses of Johann and Eduard Strauss are dutifully listed every year, as is Eduard's imperial title of Hofballmusikdirektor; otherwise their names and their music are rarely mentioned. To a certain extent this was a product of an elitist aesthetic that sought a division between the 'serious' and the 'popular' or, to use the terms that were already gaining currency in Vienna at the end of the nineteenth century, between *Ernstmusik* and *Unterhaltungsmusik*.

But it was emphasized by topography too: that which was routinely performed in the inner city and that which belonged to the suburbs. A century after Mozart and Schikaneder had exposed the hypocrisy of the divide in *Zauberflöte*, it continued to affect the perception of the value of operetta and dance music. As well as the main homes of operetta, the Carltheater and the Theater an der Wien, most dance halls, like those in the Dianasaal, Dommayer's Casino and the Sofiensaal, were in the suburbs.[2] The separation sustained a sense of difference, for the benefit of both: operetta was a business run by entrepreneurs, opera was an art form supported by the court; operettas were often newly composed, operas were hardly ever first performances; the subject matter of operetta was often topical, that of opera invariably historical or mythological; and audiences were socially diverse at the operetta, more exclusive at the opera.[3]

While the Strauss concerts in the Musikverein indicate an enthusiastic acceptance by the mainstream of musical life, the really telling signal was the inclusion of *Die Fledermaus* in the repertoire of the court theatre from 1894 onwards, the fiftieth anniversary of Strauss's professional debut as a violinist and of his first waltz; at this point it is mentioned in *Fromme's Musikalische Welt*.[4] The fact that the operetta was able to maintain a presence in its repertoire was due to the support of Gustav Mahler.[5] The sense that operetta did not quite belong to the inner city remained, however, even when *Der Zigeunerbaron* joined the repertoire of the court theatre in 1910. A few years later Alma Mahler recalled her and Gustav's enjoyment of a performance of Lehár's *Die lustige Witwe* in the Theater an der Wien, followed by a furtive visit the following morning to buy the music at the Doblinger music shop (in the inner city), where Mahler pretended to engage the manager in a discussion about sales of his own music while Alma searched for Lehár's music.[6]

Schoenberg was another serious musician who valued the music of Strauss. He wrote perceptively about the nature of that appeal, making a comparison with Mozart that is not to that composer's advantage; in so doing he reveals something fundamental about Mozart's reputation at the time, that a work like *Zauberflöte* was best understood as a serious work rather than a comic one:

> Real popularity, lasting popularity, is only attained in those rare cases where power of expression is granted to men who dwell intensely in the sphere of basic human sentiments. There are a few cases in Schubert and Verdi, but many in Johann Strauss. Even Mozart, when, in *The Magic Flute*, he temporarily abandoned his own highly refined artistic style of presentation in favour of the semi-popular characters he had to portray musically, did not fully succeed; the popular parts of this opera never attained the success of the serious parts. His stand was on the side of Sarastro and his priests.[7]

As well as the continuing popularity of operettas such as *Die Fledermaus* and *Der Zigeunerbaron*, the years after Strauss's death saw the presentation of pasticcio operettas built around the composer's dance music. As early as 26 October 1899 – a day after the memorial concert in the Musikverein – a new operetta of this kind, *Wiener Blut*, was presented at the Carltheater.[8] Librettists of operetta were very skilled at providing rhyming texts to the regular musical phrases of pre-existing dances, also organizing the results into a reasonable narrative. *Wiener Blut* was followed by three further posthumous operettas prepared from Strauss's dance music, *Gräfin Pepi* (1902), *Reiche Mädchen* (1909) and *Der blaue Held* (1912). Music by other members of the Strauss dynasty was treated in a similar way, such as *Frühlingsluft* (1903) and *Das Schwalberl aus dem Wienerwald* (1906), both based on music by Josef Strauss.[9]

As well as new works from the Strauss family, there was a new theatre to perform the operettas, the Johann Strauss-Theater in the Fourth District, not far from the former summer palace of the Habsburgs, the Favorita. Holding just over a thousand seats, the theatre opened on 30 October 1908 with a spoken tribute to the composer, followed by a performance of a waltz by the orchestra and a performance of *1001 Nights*, a reworking of the composer's first operetta, *Indigo und die vierzig Räuber*.[10] To fill out this burgeoning posthumous image, members of the Strauss dynasty sometimes appeared as named characters in the plots of operettas, with and without their music, operetta about operetta. The ghost of Johann Strauss appears magically in *An der schönen blauen Donau* (1903), his father and mother (Anna) are the leading characters in *Im Paradeisgartl* (1913) and his father is a major figure in *Die tolle Therese* (1913).[11]

In the years immediately following the death of Johann Strauss there was a danger that his dominant personality, and that of the whole family, would smother the efforts of younger composers. On 30 December 1905 that changed for ever, when a new operetta by Franz Lehár, his sixth, was performed for the first time, at the Theater an der Wien. *Die lustige Witwe* (The Merry Widow) was not an immediate success, with some people dubbing it *Die traurige Witwe* (The Sad Widow) and the composer himself doubting that it would get beyond fifty performances.[12] Sixteen months later, performances in Vienna had passed the 400 mark, and when it was followed by other successful new operettas by him – *Der Graf von Luxemburg* (1909), *Eva* (1911) and *Endlich allein* (1914) – not only was Lehár's reputation enhanced but an abiding historiographical division was created, one that neatly obliged everybody: the Golden Age of Offenbach, Suppé and Strauss, and the Silver Age of Lehár, Oscar Straus and Leo Falls.

Old Vienna, New Vienna

THERE was another division that characterized operetta, one that was keenly felt by Viennese society in general: a willingness to juxtapose images from the city's past alongside allusions to the present. While it is difficult to think of an opera from the nineteenth century that is set in Vienna, including historical Vienna, it was a favourite location for operetta, with at least fifty-four examples between 1899 and 1914. To these may be added earlier operettas on musical figures from the city such as Haydn, Mozart, Schubert, Lanner, Schikaneder and on the supposed composer of the popular melody 'Ei, du lieber Augustin' (an anonymous folk harpist from the seventeenth century).[13] Other operettas, like *Der Zigeunerbaron*, are partially set in Vienna, and still others, though they may be described as taking place somewhere else, are inescapably about the city and its people, such as *Die Fledermaus*, set 'in a spa near Vienna' (which could only mean Baden), and *Die lustige Witwe*, set in Paris.

Some of these operettas refer to present-day Vienna and include scenes in the salons of the aristocracy, imperial offices, dance halls, a particular Gasthaus, public gardens such as the Stadtpark or against the backdrop of the Danube or the Kahlenberg, a physical and human environment evoked by dance music. An increasing number, however, are set in Vienna's past, casually anachronistic in detail but engagingly misty-eyed in sentiment. Probably the oldest setting is that of *Die Türken vor Wien* (1903, music by Ernst Reiterer), a commemoration of the Turkish siege of 1683, described as a 'historical portrait in two parts with song and dance'. The first scene, 'A day of horror (July 1683)', takes place in 'an open square within heavily fortified Vienna'; the second scene, 'Karl Mustapha's overthrow (12 September 1683)' is set in 'the Grandvizier's magnificent marquee in the Turkish camp'.[14] A more favoured historical era is the first part of the nineteenth century, especially the period between the end of the Napoleonic Wars and the Revolution of 1848, that is two or three generations ago and easily remembered as the good old days.

There was a small cluster of terms in use for this period, each slightly different in its resonances. The first was *Vormärz*, literally pre-March, that is March 1848, the beginning of a period of revolution that momentarily threatened the very existence of the empire and – more of a historical gloss – one that was saved only by the accession of Emperor Franz Joseph, an exemplary emperor who continued to serve his people. The term therefore denotes a period immediately before the present, while also validating it. The second term was *Biedermeier*, from the literary figure of Gottlieb Biedermeier created in 1850 by the Swabian author Ludwig Eichardt, a pious (*gottlieb*), honest (*bieder*) and comfortably bourgeois individual who led an untroubled, contented lifestyle.[15] Finally, there was the very prevalent term *Alt-Wien* (Old Vienna), one that had similar connotations to *Vormärz* and the Biedermeier period, but focussed on images of Vienna as a place. When Leopold Sonnleithner used the term in

1853 for his account of musical life in Vienna around 1800, it was reasonably neutral in its associations, denoting within living memory.[16] Gradually *Alt-Wien* became more and more nostalgic in tone, even escapist, and certainly more a matter of the heart than of the mind.[17]

Much of that remembrance was fed by the transformation in the physical appearance of the city that had occurred in the second half of the century, most obviously the large-scale changes brought about by the Ringstrasse project. But there were changes in the inner city too that fed into the culture.[18] The old Burgtheater, the court opera theatre from the middle of the eighteenth century, where many of Mozart's operas had been performed, where Haydn gave the first public performances of *Die Schöpfung* and where Beethoven had given his first benefit concert, was demolished in 1888 to make way for the new entrance to the Hofburg. The demolition of the old Kärntnertor, two adjacent gateways to the south, and the building of the new opera house led to the redevelopment of the entire area between the Kärntnerstrasse and the Lobkowitz palace, including the demolition of the Schwarzenberg palace. At the very centre of the inner city, the area around the intersection of the Graben and the Kärntnerstrasse had become something of a bottleneck and the much loved 'Elefantenhaus', from where Eder had run his music shop at the beginning of the century, was demolished to ease congestion.

Operetta often invoked the physical ambience of old Vienna.[19] *Wiener Blut* was set in three different locations during the Congress of Vienna: the summer villa of the fictitious Count Zedlau in Döbling, the grand reception room of another fictitious character, Count Bitowski, and, entirely anachronistically for 1815, the Casino garden in Hietzing where Johann Strauss (the son) had often directed his dances. Oscar Straus's operetta, *Mein junger Herr* (1910), is also set in aristocratic surroundings, this time in 1830, and the surrounding views are also specified – the Schottentor, the city walls and the Glacis. As an idealized physical environment *Alt-Wien* was celebrated in an especially spectacular manner in the International Music and Theatre Exhibition of 1892, where a life-size set, made out of wood, reproduced an entire square in the inner city, the Hoher Markt, as it was in the seventeenth century.[20] Although Johann Strauss seems never to have invoked an old building in his dance music or in his operettas, he was an unprecedented master of nostalgia for the landscape around Vienna, something from the past that helped to deal with the present. Two of his most popular waltzes, *Geschichten aus dem Wienerwald* and *An der schönen blauen Donau*, are typical in presenting that nostalgia as if in a framed picture: the introductions take the listener to the picture, the series of waltzes ponder it, and the coda sections summarize, distance and dissolve the image.

Since dancing rhythms pervade all operettas, whether in the foreground, as part of the action, or in the background, as an indication of atmosphere, they always project Vienna as a place where conflict is easily resolved, even if it is actually only pushed aside. The tensions of Strauss's most ambitious operetta, *Der Zigeunerbaron*, are projected on a larger canvas than normal: the relationship between the two parts of the Austro-Hungarian Empire as determined in the *Ausgleich* or Compromise of 1867. That 'compromise' successfully contained separatist views for a few decades by giving Hungary parity of status with Austria within an overall empire that was still ruled from the Kaiserstadt of Vienna, a solution that might equally have been devised by an operetta librettist as by a Habsburg bureaucrat. The degree to which the *Ausgleich* diffused tensions can be judged by the success that Strauss's Austro-Hungarian operetta enjoyed in the two capitals, Vienna and Budapest, through to the First World War.[21]

The first two acts are set in Banat (the area of open plains in south-east Hungary), in an unspecified gypsy village, allowing for plenty of local colour: threatening and benign gypsies of all ages, an oafish pig farmer, excitable treasure hunting and a drinking-cum-recruiting song on behalf of the army. Sándor Barinkay is an exiled Hungarian nobleman who has returned to his roots and falls in love with a gypsy girl, Saffi, who then discovers she is the daughter of a Turkish pasha. Barinkay is accompanied by a commissioner from Vienna, an Italian named Conte Carnero, who proceeds to debunk the imperial standing commission on morality, still active in the Vienna of Strauss's day. But rather than the present, the story is set in the middle of the eighteenth century, during the reign of Maria Theresia, who had skilfully cultivated the loyalty of Hungary, topped up with references to earlier wars with the shared enemy, the Turks.[22]

This mix of personalities and nationalities, allusive political commentary and garbled history might well have defeated some composers, but Strauss's music not only relishes this diversity but gives it a focus, with waltz rhythms playing a carefully planned role. Following the overture they are rarely heard in Act 1, except briefly to exaggerate the carefree youth of Barinkay. In Act 2, however, a new waltz is associated with a succession of pleasurable moments – the true love of Barinkay and Saffi, the discovery of the treasure, the irrelevance of the morality commission and, the most sustained, the anticipated journey back to Vienna, when all the leading characters (local and visiting) plus a chorus of soldiers and gypsies (the rulers and the ruled) sing an extended chorus of praise to the Kaiserstadt:

So voll Fröhlichkeit,	With so much joy,
Nach dem Kampf und Streit,	After the trouble and strife
Zieh'n auch wir in die lustige	We, too, will enter the merry
Kaiserstadt ein,	Kaiserstadt,
Wo so frisch und kühn,	Where, so fresh and dashing,
Flotte Weisen sprüh'n;	Lively tunes sparkle;
Dich erfüllt, ach, die	You are filled with
Lust nach Gesang,	Longing for song,
Weib, und Wein.	Women and wine.
Wo bei Lichterglanz	Where with bright lights
Und Gesang und Tanz	Song and dance

Uns in Lust, ja im	In desire, yes in
Jubel die Nächte vergeh'n.	Pleasure, we'll spend nights.
Wo die Rebe blüht,	Where the vine blooms,
Und heiß die Liebe glüht,	And flaming love burns,
Und alle Menschen das Leben versteh'n.	And everybody understands life.

Clearly, it is not the Vienna of Maria Theresia that is being invoked; in that sense it is new Vienna rather than old Vienna. Even more clearly the operetta is not a sustained allegory in the manner of a serious opera from around 1700, where the contemporary relevance of Greek mythology or Roman history was understood, even before it was pointed out in the *licenza*. This is a more fluid relationship with the past, one where old and new are not experienced as moments in history, but both contribute to a state of mind that is neither wholly escapist nor wholly self-deluding.

Since the appreciation of *Der Zigeunerbaron* in Vienna was not as a single, one-off work, but part of a continuing musical tradition that related naturally to wider cultural values, the sense of genre was as strong in this repertoire as it was, say, in the string quartet in concerts in the Bösendorfersaal. But, while that repertoire was overwhelmingly canonic, operetta was more impetuous, with new works constantly being added to the genre to be performed alongside *Der Zigeunerbaron* and *Die Fledermaus*. This, in turn, had an effect on changing the balance of the old and the new; as Johann Strauss and his music folded their way into history both became more susceptible to *Alt-Wien* outlooks. Karl Kraus made the crisp remark that '*Alt-Wien* was once new':[23] the added truth was that *Alt-Wien* had never really existed, it was always contemporary and constantly adjusting itself.

Lehár's *Die lustige Witwe* does not pretend to be set in the past, but it does pretend to be set in Paris, a conceit that allows it to emerge as a comment on modern Vienna. Baron Mirko Zeta, ambassador for the state of Pontevedro, wants to ensure that a rich widow from that country, Hanna Glawari, marries a fellow countryman, Count Danilo Danilowitsch, in order that Pontevedro can continue to benefit from her wealth. True love runs its customary tortuous course and Pontevedro is saved.

The name Pontevedro was a last-minute change to the libretto, substituted for Montenegro at the request of the imperial censor.[24] If any member of the audience remained uncertain about whether Paris really represented Vienna or that Pontevedro was Montenegro down an early telephone line, then the unfolding narrative contains any number of references to Austria and the Balkans, including the occasional phrase in Serbian. Baron Zeta is named after Montenegro's largest river and Danilo was the name of the current crown prince. Any visiting member of the audience who had their Baedeker guide to Austria-Hungary with them and turned to the section on Montenegro would encounter many of the same names.[25] The state was chronically poor and had a difficult relationship with the imperial capital.[26] While his state was suffering Count Danilo himself enjoyed a lazy, dissolute lifestyle, a bureaucrat in the imperial capital. He announces his presence with a homage to the *Vaterland* and, especially, to his favoured nocturnal haunt, Maxim's:

O Vaterland, du machst bei Tag	Oh Fatherland, by day
Mir schon genügend Müh' und Plag!	You cause me enough toil and trouble!
Nacht braucht jeder Diplomat	Night is needed by every diplomat,
Doch meistenteils für sich privat	Though mostly for private matters.
Um Eins bin ich schon im Bureau,	At one I'm already in the office
Doch bin ich gleich drauf anderswo,	Though soon afterwards, somewhere else,
Weil man den ganzen lieben Tag	Because one doesn't want to be
Nicht immer im Bureau sein mag!	All day always in the office.
Erstatte ich beim Chef Bericht,	If I have to report to the boss,
So tu' ich meistens selber nicht,	I usually don't do it in person.
Die Sprechstund' halt' ich niemals ein,	I never have meetings,
Ein Diplomat muss schweigsam sein!	A diplomat must be silent!
Die Akten häufen sich bei mir,	Documents pile up on my desk,
Ich finde, 's gibt zu viel Papier,	I find there's too much paper,
Ich tauch' die Feder selten ein	I seldom dip my pen in ink,
Und komm' doch in die Tint' hinein!	Yet I'm always in a spot of bother.
Kein Wunder, wenn man so viel tut,	No wonder, if one has so much to do
Dass man am Abend gerne ruht,	That one likes to rest in the evening,
Und sich bei Nacht, was man so nennt,	And by night allows oneself so-called
Erholung nach der Arbeit gönnt!	Recuperation after work!
Da geh' ich zu Maxim,	So, I go to Maxim's
Dort bin ich sehr intim,	Where I'm well known.
Ich duze alle Damen,	I'm friendly with all the ladies
Ruf' sie beim Kosenamen.	And call them by their pet names.
Lolo, Dodo, Joujou,	Lolo, Dodo, Joujou,
Cloclo, Margot, Froufrou,	Cloclo, Margot, Froufrou,
Sie lassen mich vergessen	They let me forget
Das teure Vaterland!	The dear fatherland!

Born of the same cynicism as the trio in *Der Zigeunerbaron* that mocked the work of the imperial morality commission, this is much more explicit, exposing a cheap eroticism that was widespread in contemporary Vienna, at all levels of society.[27] In his memoirs, *The World of Yesterday*, Stefan Zweig devoted an entire chapter, 'Eros Matutinus', to the social and psychological characteristics of this not-so-hidden aspect of the city before the First World War. Its hierarchical structure, its rules, as well as the sheer numbers who were engaged in its practices, led Zweig to an uncomfortable comparison with that other constant in Habsburg Vienna, the army:

This gigantic army of prostitution, like the real army, was made up of various branches, cavalry, artillery, infantry and siege artillery ... In the ranks of prostitution the siege artillery was the group which had

occupied certain streets as their quarter ... The cavalry or infantry
was made up of the roving prostitutes, the countless girls who sought
their clients on the streets ... But even these masses did not suffice
for the steady demand ... They wanted love at their ease, with light
and warmth, with music and dancing and an appearance of luxury.
These clients had their 'closed houses' or brothels. There the girls
were assembled in a so-called *salon*, furnished in counterfeit luxury,
some in evening gowns, others in unreticent négligées. A piano player
supplied the music: there was drinking and dancing and conversation
before the pairs discreetly retired to a bedroom.[28]

Throughout Lehár's operetta, Maxim's and the sound and sight of
marching are closely allied: a septet in Act 1 sung by men that establishes
the certainties of conquest; a fashionable cakewalk in Act 3 that begins
the cabaret; and, finally, the full-blown, heavily accented march that
accompanies the much anticipated appearance of Lolo, Dodo, Joujou and
friends. The imperial censors, who always worked from a submitted libretto
rather than from the musical score, were not in a position to comment
on the association between music and image, and did not object to any
of these scenes. Neither, it is safe to assume, did contemporary audiences:
celebration rather than discomfort was the accepted response. This was an
operetta that held up a mirror to contemporary society, current Vienna
rather than old Vienna.[29] Given the frankness of the presentation, parallels
are easily made with other art forms, customarily labelled expressionistic,
such as paintings by Klimt, Kokoschka and Schiele, and the plays of Arthur
Schnitzler, most pertinently *La ronde*, the source for Berg's opera, *Lulu*.
At the same time it represented an expansion of generic practice in the
medium of operetta, which ultimately sanctioned it and, for that reason,
made it only momentarily shocking. Nevertheless, the ease with which it is
achieved is disturbing.

Die lustige Witwe contains many more waltzes than *Der Zigeunerbaron*,
dances performed as part of the action, dances that infiltrate the unfolding
of the narrative and, throughout, a skilful balance between the sentimental
recall of an earlier waltz melody and the presentation of a new one. One
waltz serves as a musical emblem of the nascent love of Danilo and Hannah
Glawari, two Pontevedrians enveloped in the magic of Vienna. It is first
heard at the end of Act 2, following Danilo's statement that he is off to
Maxim's, when it immediately defuses his man-of-the world bravura.
Above several repetitions, Danilo and Hannah exchange pleasantries before
joining in the dance while also humming the melody. At the end of Act 3,
the desensitized world of Maxim and the civilizing world of the waltz are
brought into close juxtaposition. It is the previously heard, word-less waltz
that begins the process of transcendence. In the first run of performances
this thematic recall proceeded as before, that is with no sung text by the
lovers. The popularity of the melody encouraged the addition of a text,
verbalizing Danilo's falling in love and, even more tellingly, the irresistible

workings of the waltz. In conventional operatic terms it is a love duet, but, unlike many examples that could be heard in the court opera, it arises out of a dance and maintains that crucial sense of sensuous physical movement:

Lippen schweigen,	Lips say nothing,
's flüstern Geigen:	Violins whisper:
Hab mich lieb!	Love me.
All die Schritte	All the steps
Sagen: Bitte	Say: Please
Hab mich lieb.	Love me.

Led by Johann Strauss and Lehár, operetta had developed into an art form whose aesthetic was contemporary, constantly evolving and Viennese. The situation in the self-appointed central tradition of concert music and opera was less clear. It was Viennese in the sense that the sheer number of musical events that took place in the city made it one of the most musically active in Europe, if not the most active, but musical works themselves as well as their composers hardly ever attracted the adjective 'Viennese'. Because two giants from the past still dominated the repertoire, Beethoven and Wagner, music was much more likely to be discussed according to ideologies defined as German, as the inscription to the doorway above the new Konzerthaus suggests.

Pan-Germanism in music took many forms, as it did in contemporary politics, and its shifting criteria could be used to exclude as well as to embrace. Mahler's difficult career caused him to utter the well-known remark, reported by Alma Mahler, that he was 'thrice homeless: as a native of Bohemia in Austria, as an Austrian amongst Germans, and a Jew throughout the world.' Guido Adler, who could have uttered the same sentiments, spent his entire professional life rationalizing the musical past so that it could be understood by the present. The *Denkmäler* volumes sought to present an 'Austrian' identity rather than a Viennese or pan-German one, derived from centuries of imperial rule and support, but he also established the term 'Viennese Classical School' for the combined output of Haydn, Mozart and Beethoven. However, the term did not gain currency until after the end of the Austrian empire, when what was formerly regarded as Austrian or German was easily devolved on to one grateful musical city.

If serious music was at odds with light music in its sense of being Viennese, it also lacked much of the in-built energy of the latter. The 1911 edition of the *Musikbuch aus Österreich* reprinted an article by the critic Dr Robert Kanta that had first appeared in the *Zeitschrift für Musik und Theater*, a largely statistical survey of song recitals, piano recitals and violin recitals given in the 1909–10 season: sixty-seven lieder recitals with music by 125 composers, fifty-seven piano recitals with music by 400 composers and twenty-one violin recitals with music by sixty-three composers.[30] Despite this abundance of music-making, Kanta is highly critical of its tired programming. 'The entire season has the countenance of an average man (*das Antlitz eines Dutzendmenschen*); agreeable, pleasant and mostly tedious impulses determine its nature.'

The contrast with other art forms is striking. Progressive writers at the end of the nineteenth century, including Arthur Schnitzler, Hermann Bahr and Hugo von Hofmannsthal, had formed themselves into a group called Jung-Wien precisely to tackle the *Dutzendmenschen* complacency of contemporary literature, advocating frank exploration of the human condition, real and psychological.[31] More publicly evident was the activity, across eight years from 1897 to 1905, of the Vereinigung Bildener Künstler Österreichs (Association of Austrian Fine Artists), better known as the Secession. The driving force was Gustav Klimt, who organized a sizeable group of forty or more architects and painters, including Josef Hoffmann, Alfred Roller and Otto Wagner, to produce, display and promote modern art that showed a complete break – a secession – with the past. Elitist in its principles and accessible in its practice, the society was also highly organized. It enjoyed the generous support of businessmen (such as Karl Wittgenstein), politicians (such as Karl Lueger) and even the imperial court. It was not inward-looking, but sought to make Vienna aware of modernist thinking in art, architecture and design from elsewhere in Europe in a magazine, *Ver Sacrum*, that ran to twenty-four issues, and through the presentation of regular exhibitions that were much anticipated. A dedicated exhibition space was built in the Friedrichstrasse to the south of the Ring, the Temple of Art, a modern-looking white villa that contrasted with the large edifices on the Ring. Above the door, in the distinctive gold lettering of the Secessionist movement, stood its motto, 'Der Zeit Ihre Kunst: Der Kunst Ihre Freiheit' ('To each Epoch its Art: To Art its Freedom').[32]

Music never managed to create a society that was its equivalent in artistic vision, efficient organization and public impact, a disparity that was pointedly highlighted by the musical theme of the fourteenth Secession exhibition, held in April and May 1902. It was built around the display of a new statue of Beethoven by Max Klinger, transported from Paris to Vienna for the event. Unlike existing sculptures of the composer in Vienna, this monument was to be placed within the Temple of Art, as the focal point of a wider artistic experience. A brooding marble figure that sat on a large bronze throne, it drew on familiar Beethovenian images of heroism and divinely inspired creativity, and in that way communicated readily with the Viennese. But the monument was not to be appreciated in isolation. Also on display in adjacent rooms were a dozen or so complementary items – mosaics, marquetry, decorative objects, engravings, paintings and frescos – created by the members of the association as a response to the central feature.

Chief amongst these was the Beethoven frieze by Gustav Klimt, three double panels that evoked the transfiguring images of the Ninth Symphony – liberation, joy and brotherhood – not so much on behalf of Beethoven, but as a prompt for an alternative, more intimate exploration of these qualities. The third panel drew on the section in the finale, 'Seid umschlungen Millionen, Diesen Kuss der ganzen Welt', especially the kiss, which in Klimt's decorating hands emerges as an erotic gesture rather than a beneficent one.[33]

There were no responses of this alternative, probing kind from the musical world of Vienna to the Beethoven legacy. Indeed, at the time of the exhibition itself, the musical profession had first proved itself indifferent and, then, inadequate to the occasion. A performance of the Ninth Symphony by the Philharmonic Orchestra conducted by Mahler was planned to coincide with the opening ceremony but, fuelled by an ongoing dispute with the conductor, it was scuppered by the orchestra, who claimed that the performance could not be fitted into a busy schedule.[34] The day before the opening of the exhibition, Max Klinger was given a private viewing; he entered the main hall to the sound of the 'Seid umschlungen' section of Beethoven's score, arranged for six trombones by Mahler. Imposing enough as background music, it was also an embarrassingly feeble response from the most relevant art form of them all.

When one looks for underlying reasons why progressive composers in Vienna were unable to come together effectively in the manner of Jung-Wien or the Secessionists, one aspect of received musical history is not helpful, the term 'Second Viennese School'. As a term it was an obvious sequel to the first Viennese School, established by Adler, and came into general use long afterwards to describe a limited group of composers who had been taught by Schoenberg from 1904 onwards, principally Berg and Webern; but they were never formally constituted as a radical group. That formulation has also masked the efforts of a wider group of composers in 1904–5 to promote new music that quickly proved to be unsuccessful. Zemlinsky and Schoenberg were the principal figures behind the Vereinigung der Schaffenden Tonkünstler in Wien (Association of Creative Musicians in Vienna), a name clearly modelled on Klimt's Vereinigung Bildender Österreichs. Mahler was the honorary president, and Berg and Webern were key figures alongside Schoenberg and Zemlinsky; Guido Adler was an ardent supporter, but Heinrich Schenker declined to get involved.[35] Although ambitious enough, they did not have the cohesion or the organizational capability of the Secessionists. A series of concerts presented in the Musikverein in 1904–5 was a mixed success artistically: Richard Strauss's *Symphonia Domestica* and a variety of songs by Mahler were well received, Schoenberg's *Pelleas und Melisande* was not. Financially, the concerts were a disaster and it was for that reason that the society was effectively wound up in March 1905, before the end of the first season.[36]

A crucial difference between the Secessionists and the failed musical association was that members of the latter did not really want to secede, artistically or professionally. They were all, to a greater or lesser extent, bound up with the establishment, and transforming musical taste from within was always going to be more difficult than establishing a new independent presence. Mahler and Zemlinsky were at the head of the court theatre and the Volksoper in Vienna, and their work as conductors regularly took them elsewhere, while Schoenberg, Berg and Webern found themselves constantly indebted to Arnold Rosé, a stalwart of the musical establishment, for his support. Musically, all these composers sought to build on an inherited tradition, principally Beethoven, Brahms and Wagner, rather to reject it. That was the paradox that characterized their situation: the constant annual display of musical tradition in Vienna fed their aesthetic as composers but also frustrated the willing acceptance of their works.

On 21 December 1908, in the Bösendorfersaal, the Rosé Quartet presented an unusually challenging concert that included two first performances alongside a much-loved work by Beethoven. The concert began with the first performance in Vienna of a work by an unfamiliar composer, Paul Juon (1872–1940), a German composer of Russian origin now working in Berlin, his Rhapsody (op. 37) for piano quartet. It was followed by the premiere, from manuscript parts, of Schoenberg's Second Quartet; Beethoven's 'Harp' Quartet completed the programme.[37] Suspicious of the new and impatient for the familiar, the audience became restless and increasingly disruptive; what ensued was widely reported in the press as a news item, one that avoided any critical engagement with the music:

> The contest between those applauding and those hissing, which traditionally accompanies every Schoenberg novelty, was particularly bitter on this occasion. The second movement was interrupted by a howl of laughter from Schoenberg's opponents, who were called to order by barbed comments from his many disciples. After the third movement, in which a vocal part (Frau Gutheil-Schoder) is added to the string quartet, vehement cries of 'Stop' from the neutrals mingled with the row from the opposing factions. When the members of the Rosé Quartet later sat down to play the first movement of Beethoven's Quartet in E flat major, Op. 74, there was demonstrative applause.[38]

Just over four years later, on 31 March 1913, in another establishment venue, the large hall in the Musikverein, a second major performing organization, the Konzertverein orchestra, was involved in an even more disorderly event. Promoted by the Akademische Verband für Literatur und Musik (Academic Society for Literature and Music), the orchestra, conducted by Schoenberg, were to perform music by Schoenberg (the first Chamber Symphony), Mahler (*Kindertotenlieder*), Berg (the premiere of the *Five Altenberg Songs*, op. 4), Webern (Six Orchestral Pieces, op. 6), Zemlinsky (*Four Maeterlinck Songs*, op. 13) and Wagner (the prelude to *Tristan und Isolde*). The audience was restless during the Schoenberg and derisory during the Berg; shaking his fist Webern became involved in a verbal altercation with some members of the audience, the tumult grew, a senior member of the police who was present mounted the podium to call for calm, but to no avail, and the concert was abandoned.[39]

It is possible to exaggerate the importance of so-called scandal concerts such as these. The innate conservatism of the musical public was matched by an equally assured right to be frank in its judgment, whether preconceived, considered or of the moment, and disruptive behaviour of this kind was at one end of a spectrum that went from the peaceful sit-in at the end of the last concert in the Bösendorfersaal, frank discussion between works, whispering during the performance, booing while also applauding, impatient jangling of house keys (large ones), to ostentatious walking out during the concert. Later, musical biography routinely presented the composers as unfair victims and the occasions as hard-earned badges of honour; more rarely do they mention that difficult premieres like those of Schoenberg's First Quartet and *Verklärte Nacht* were followed by performances that were reasonably well received.

Richard Strauss and the future operatic ideal

SEVEN months after the aborted concert in the Musikverein, the Konzertverein orchestra took part in a much happier event, the opening of the Konzerthaus, its new, permanent home, the concert that began with a new work by Richard Strauss, the *Festliches Präludium*. It is not known if the Konzerthaus contemplated asking anybody else to write a new work. Certainly the choice from living Viennese composers would have been a rather circumscribed one. Mahler had died two years earlier. The elder statesman of resident composers was Carl Goldmark, now in his mid-eighties and, although many of his works were familiar in the opera house as well as the concert hall, he would have represented the past rather than the future. Zemlinsky's period in charge of the Volksoper had ended in 1911 and he was now living and working in Prague, harbouring not especially fond memories of musical politics in Vienna. As the recent abandoned concert in the Musikverein had demonstrated, Schoenberg, Berg and Webern would have been too risky. Even though he was not Viennese, by birth or by residence, the choice of Richard Strauss was not a surprise one and certainly not contentious. He had emerged as a commanding figure in the musical life of the city, somebody who represented the success of the present and a possible pointer to the future.

Strauss was just thirty when he first began to be noticed in Vienna in 1895. The Berlin Philharmonic Orchestra made a brief visit to Vienna in April of that year, giving three concerts in the Musikverein; Strauss conducted the first one, Felix Weingartner the second and Felix Mottl the third.[40] Some unflattering comparisons were made between the visiting Philharmonic and the local Philharmonic, comparisons that played some part in the gradual undermining of Hans Richter's standing in Vienna.

Richter, however, was a persuasive advocate of Strauss's music in his last three seasons as conductor of the subscription series, giving performances of *Till Eulenspiegel, Also sprach Zarathustra* and *Don Juan*. Mahler was more ambivalent about Strauss's music, conducting only one work, *Aus Italien*, during his three-year tenure as conductor of the subscription concerts.[41] For the Philharmonic Orchestra itself, with its policy of voting on the choice of new works, Strauss soon became a much favoured composer. Several works new to Vienna, like *Macbeth, Ein Heldenleben* and *Don Quixote* were performed, as well as repeat performances of *Don Juan* and *Till Eulenspiegel*; conductors included Felix Weingartner, Felix Mottl, Karl Muck and the young Bruno Walter. Richard Strauss himself did not conduct the Philharmonic Orchestra until the summer of 1906, when Karl Muck had to withdraw from a concert in Salzburg because of illness.[42] At three days notice Strauss took over the programme: Mozart's overture to *Zauberflöte*, the Symphonie Concertante (K364) and Bruckner's Ninth Symphony. This led to his engagement to conduct two subscription concerts in the following season.

His debut was on 16 December 1906 when the programme included Weber's *Oberon* overture, Mozart's G minor Symphony (K550) and the *Eroica* Symphony; the second concert, on 3 March 1907, featured Liszt's *Les préludes*, Brahms's Fourth Symphony and Strauss's own *Also sprach Zarathustra*.[43] The success of these concerts marked the beginning of an association between Strauss and the Philharmonic Orchestra that was to last through to his death in 1949. Strauss's tone poems were also featured in the programmes of the Konzertverein from 1902–3 onwards and the young Wilhelm Backhaus was the soloist in the performance of the *Burleske for piano and orchestra* in 1907–8.[44] Altogether, Strauss was the most frequently performed of living composers in the concert hall, one who was able to avoid comparison with the giants of the symphonic tradition – Beethoven, Brahms and Bruckner – because of his endlessly resourceful devotion to a different genre, the symphonic poem. He was the inevitable choice to write a new work for the Konzerthaus.

Strauss was also beginning to acquire a growing presence in the opera house. His second opera, *Feuersnot*, had achieved a respectable twelve performances in the court opera between 1902 and 1905, conducted by Mahler and Schalk.[45] Mahler very much wanted to present *Salome* too, but was thwarted by the imperial censors, who did not regard it as a suitable subject for the court opera; a visiting opera troupe from Breslau performed it in May 1907 in the Deutsches Volkstheater, a theatre normally associated with plays, where it fully lived up to its controversial reputation.[46] But, with an increasing sense of a bracing challenge accepted, *Salome* was the surprise success of the 1910–11 season at the Volksoper, with twenty-one performances in four months.[47] *Elektra*, too, was in the process of establishing itself. Premiered in Dresden in January 1909, it was first performed in Vienna two months later, in March 1909; near the end of the 1910–11 season, on 9 April 1911, Strauss made his debut in the pit of the court opera, conducting a performance of the work.[48] But, while Strauss was becoming more and more involved in the musical life of Vienna, he was not yet Viennese, not yet a Brahms and certainly not a Johann Strauss. It was the librettist of *Elektra*, Hugo von Hofmannsthal, who provided that final, crowning element.

Hofmannsthal was a native Viennese, born in the Landstrasse in the Third District in 1874. He first met the composer in Paris in 1900. For Richard Strauss, a Bavarian who was then chief conductor at the Royal Opera in Berlin, Hofmannsthal must have represented a comparatively unfamiliar type. A member of the Jung-Wien group, he embraced cultural-cum-political sympathies that were sharply Austrian rather than pan-German, someone who instinctively looked eastwards rather than westwards, to the territories of the empire that were to be sympathetically ruled from Vienna, rather than those that might figure in a wider German-speaking empire obligated to Berlin. For Hofmannsthal, that was the entirely natural outcome of a historical tension that had been resolved a hundred years earlier, when the Holy Roman Empire was dissolved and the Austrian Empire created.

A Habsburg loyalist, he enjoyed, rather than suffered, several periods of military service in the 1890s and, in the same year as he met Strauss, responded enthusiastically to the suggestion that he might join a new government department, a Kunstamt, to centralize and promote the sponsorship of culture, an initiative that came to nothing. Had the Kunstamt been set up, Hofmannsthal would have found himself working with Guido Adler on his *Denkmäler* project, and also on the court-sponsored *Das Volkslied in Österreich*. He would have been fascinated by the linguistic variety of the folk songs and their role as rich cultural identifiers. He himself was a proponent of Austrian German, including Viennese dialect, as a legitimate medium for literary expression.

His social views were comfortably old fashioned, with a deferential view of the role of the aristocracy in Austrian life, as leaders in the military, as private patrons of the arts and, not least, as the builders of the many urban and country palaces that graced the Habsburg territories. He lived in Rodaun, then a small village seven miles to the south-west of Vienna, one that effortlessly proclaimed its heritage. Laid to waste during the Turkish siege of 1683, it had the key twin characteristics of a small castle and a Catholic church rebuilt in the Baroque style. Hofmannsthal's house was from the same period, two stories high and with an inner courtyard. Built for Prince Trautsohn in 1724, it was later purchased by Maria Theresia, who then presented it as a gift to her confidante, Countess Charlotte. Hofmannsthal, too, had an aristocratic confidante, someone who was also a poet, Countess Thun-Salm. To her, he wrote simply of Rodaun and the house: 'This is Austria.'[49]

The same may be said of the libretto he was now working on for Richard Strauss, that of *Der Rosenkavalier*. Set in Vienna in the early years of the reign of Maria Theresia, its appeal could not be more compelling for

Hofmannsthal.[50] It was also one that tapped into a wider reverence for this monarch. One of the largest monuments on the Ringstrasse was unveiled in 1888 for the empress, in the park that lies between the Natural History Museum and the Kunsthistorisches Museum, from then on named the Maria-Theresien-Platz. Over sixty foot high, granite and bronze are marshalled to show a seated Maria Theresia, her right hand in an open gesture of greeting, while her left hand grasps a sceptre and the Pragmatic Sanction in the form of a scroll. She is surrounded by four allegorical figures representing Strength, Wisdom, Justice and Clemency. Equestrian statues of four field marshals – Count Joseph Daun, Baron Ernst von Laudon, Count Ferdinand Traun and Count Andreas Khevenhüller – look confidently to the four corners of the imperial and royal dominions. On the plinth itself four groups of individuals are presented: ministers, advisors, the military, and art and science. The last group shows Maria Theresia's doctor, Gerhard van Swieten, the numatist Joseph Eckel, the historian Georg Pray and three composers – Gluck, Haydn and Mozart – with Haydn casting a watchful eye on the child Mozart.[51]

Hofmannsthal and Strauss's *Der Rosenkavalier* is not an ossified representation of the eighteenth century. Rather it draws on the familiar poetic licence of *Alt-Wien*, an image of a time and place that is productively fuddled by the 150 years that followed; in particular, it is the world of operetta that provided a meaningful entrée into the work. Old Vienna is the locus, especially aristocratic Vienna, the interiors of the palaces are where most of the action takes place, and the behaviour and attitudes of the aristocracy are affectionately lampooned, not least in the linguistic variety of the text, featuring a song in Italian, gratuitous and affected French phrases, faux ceremonial German as well as Viennese dialect. The oafish behaviour of Baron Ochs (the German word for 'Ox') has as much in common with that of the pig breeder, Zsupán, in *Der Zigeunerbaron* as with Falstaff in Verdi's opera or the Count in *Le nozze di Figaro*. Likewise, the ready eroticism of the work would not have perturbed those who had enjoyed *Die lustige Witwe*, including the morning-after-the-night-before scene that begins Act 1 and the private room in the Gasthaus (with piano) that is the tawdry setting for Act 3. The morality police (*Sittenpolizei*) make an extended appearance in Act 3 to investigate the goings-on, only to leave when endless and deliberate confusion thwarts them.

The ease with which *Der Rosenkavalier* could be seen as an ambitious crossover from operetta is suggested by the reverse process that happened within days of its first performance in Vienna. On 16 April 1911, eight days after the first night in the court theatre, a new work was presented in the Ronacher theatre in the Prater, *Der Veilchenkavalier*, cobbled together from various pieces of music by Joseph Hellmesberger.[52] The literal meaning of the title, 'The Knight of the Violet', had a further connotation, alluding to *Veilchenfresser* or lady-killer. Unfortunately, the work has not survived, but as with all parodies it would have only sharpened appreciation of the original.

Last, but most obviously of all, *Der Rosenkavalier* is indebted to operetta in its extensive use of the waltz, a completely anachronistic evocation of the reign of Maria Theresia. The idea of making that dance, rather than the historically correct minuet, central to the action seems to have originated with Hofmannsthal: 'Do try and think of an old-fashioned Viennese waltz, sweet and yet saucy, which must pervade the whole of the last act'.[53] Strauss did indeed do this. Baron Ochs likes to sing along to this, his favourite waltz, and it features throughout his clumsy attempt to seduce 'Mariandel' (that is Octavian in disguise) in Act 3. Its opening phrases are similar to those of a waltz by Josef Strauss, the appropriately named *Geheime Anziehungskräfte (Dynamiden)* – Secret Powers of Attraction (Dynamite) – from 1865.[54] Whether this was deliberate or accidental on Strauss's part is immaterial; it is one of dozens of potential allusions in the opera – in the text and in the music – that would have triggered fertile associations in the minds of listeners.

One of the standard expectations of a waltz in an operetta is that it should signal sociability, especially between two potential lovers. Baron Ochs's recurring waltz is notable for the fact that it never elicits a favourable response. When first heard it has a text that is more about his coarse behaviour than the course of true love, more 'me' than 'you', and certainly no mention of 'us':

Mit mir, mit mir keine Kammer 　dir zu klein.	With me, with me there's no room 　too small for you.
Ohne mich, ohne mich jeder Tag 　dir zu lang.	Without me, without me every day's 　too long for you.
Mit mir, mit mir keine Nacht 　dir zu lang.	With me, with me no night's 　too long for you.

When, at the end of Act 2, Ochs is depicted eagerly anticipating his assignation with 'Mariandel', Strauss presents the waltz theme without a text and in such an exaggerated way that it becomes a complete distortion of sensibility; the full orchestra of over a hundred players are instructed to play the recurring upbeats with an exaggerated scoop and the shrill trills of the woodwind on each downbeat are a mocking comment on the missing words, 'me', 'me', 'me'.

In Act 3, when Ochs is finally alone with 'Mariandel', normative patterns of behaviour associated with waltz rhythms are cleverly turned on their head by the deft responses of 'Mariandel': first she refuses a glass of wine – 'Nein, nein, nein, nein! I trink' kein Wein' – and when Ochs's favourite waltz is played she says that it makes her weep and she had better make her excuses and leave. During the course of Act 3, Strauss recalls this waltz theme and many other waltz themes in a manner reminiscent of the final acts of operetta, but they are not associated with the denouement of the plot, a potent denial of a cliché. Instead, there is an extended, luxuriant trio for three voices (Sophie, the Marschallin and Octavian) followed by a duet (Sophie and Octavian), which avoids a closing scene with everybody on stage, another characteristic of operetta. It is this careful selection of musical and dramatic techniques from operetta that distinguishes the work. As Hofmannsthal wrote to Strauss shortly after he had begun working on the libretto: 'The third act will be the best of all, I hope; a little spiced to start with, then broadly comic, only to end on a note of tenderness.'[55]

In the same letter Hofmannsthal elaborates further on the issue of creative ambition in the work: 'True and lasting success depends upon the effect on the more sensitive *no less than* on the coarser sections of the public, for the former are needed to give a work of art its prestige which is just as essential as its popular appeal.' For Strauss, this was probably a welcome affirmation of a personal credo, for he had always shown himself to be adept at appealing to both constituencies, though the extent to which they needed to be kept in balance is exceptional in *Der Rosenkavalier*. The ideal here was something else that resonated with the Viennese, Mozartian opera, not so much as the product of the Italianate musical culture of the eighteenth century, but as a product of the standard performance practice from the early nineteenth century onwards of presenting it in German.

The atmosphere of *Der Rosenkavalier* – the interior of palaces, masters and servants, intrigue and disguise, good and bad behaviour – was easily related to productions of *Don Juan* and *Figaros Hochzeit* (see Fig. 16). In a letter written to Roller, to help him design the sets and the costumes for the new opera, Strauss succinctly lists the main characters, noting familiar equivalents: the Marschallin is the Countess (Strauss uses the German *Gräfin*, not the Italian *Contessa*), Octavian is Cherubino (*Page* not *paggio*), and Sophie is Susanna (spelt by Strauss in the German form, Susanne).[56] The parallels with Mozart's opera are certainly evident, but it is not a historicist exercise, much less a neo-classical one; instead each character reflects the morality of modern Vienna. The ageing lovelorn countess bares her fate in the manner of Countess Almaviva, but she also sleeps with the servant; Octavian, a female singer dressed as a man who is then disguised as a woman, has the self-confidence of someone from a cabaret (as in *Die Fledermaus* and *Die lustige Witwe*) rather than the adolescent confusion of Cherubino. But it is another Mozartian quality that helps to elevate *Der Rosenkavalier* above operetta, the sheer beauty of the human voice, especially the female voice. In the celebrated trio of relief and reconciliation at the end of the work Strauss does something that Mozart did not do in *Figaro*, or indeed in any other opera: he writes a trio for the three leading sopranos, the thoroughly modern Countess, Cherubino and Susanna.

When Hofmannsthal and Strauss were nearing the end of their joint work on *Der Rosenkavalier* they had an exchange of correspondence about the most appropriate label for the work. Hofmannsthal came up with the suggestion 'Comedy for Music', the matter-of-fact heading he had written on the manuscript of the libretto, though, for that reason, he was worried that it might imply that it was still waiting to be set to music. Ever the

16   Stage set for Act 2 of Richard Strauss's *Der Rosenkavalier*, by Alfred Roller

pragmatist, Strauss agreed to the suggestion enthusiastically: 'it's clear and new and free! And to hell with all wisecracks!'[57] The ensuing title page read 'Der Rosenkavalier. Komödie für Musik von Hugo von Hofmannsthal. Musik von Richard Strauss.' Even here, as Hofmannsthal must have known, there was a reference to eighteenth-century practice. 'Comedy for Music' is simply a variant of *dramma per musica*, the standard term for opera seria at the time, used for instance by Metastasio, court poet in Maria Theresia's time.

Together, Hofmannsthal and Strauss had created a work that celebrated a wide cultural inheritance: political, topographical, social, moral, linguistic as well as musical. As a modern opera about Vienna it also brought some of the divergent trends evident in the city's theatres together – the musical apparatus of Wagnerian music drama, the Mozartian performing tradition and the escapist world of operetta. In that sense it offered a way forward for opera in the city. But, while the Viennese public responded enthusiastically to the work, with eighteen performances in the first season alone and a further forty-four in the period up to the First World War,[58] the critics viewed it with suspicion. Once more their comfort zone had been breached. One of the first to report was Julius Korngold, writing for the *Neue Freie Presse* the day after the Vienna premiere. He recognized the ambition and reach of the work, and expounded them interestingly and at length, but his concluding sentences about the possible influence of the work revealed a degree of self-denial amounting to torture:

That the new work of this leading musician even hints at the way
to a new operatic ideal is something we have been unable to bring
ourselves to admit. On the contrary: the path Strauss has taken is one
we would like to warn imitators from taking by erecting a warning
sign.[59]

There was possibly another, unspoken reservation at work here, a more
parochial one. Richard Strauss, unlike Hofmannsthal, was not Viennese; he
did not even live there and, at the time, was working for the rival German
court in Berlin. But the process of becoming a Viennese, as opposed
to a composer who was very popular in Vienna, was already underway.
Librettist and composer were working on another opera set in Vienna,
Ariadne auf Naxos. The management of the court opera certainly sensed an
opportunity to bring Strauss into the Viennese fold. Early in 1914 it began
preparations for a Strauss Week to be held the following autumn, a week
of performances of operas by the composer to coincide with his fiftieth
birthday. As well as *Der Rosenkavalier* it was to include *Guntram*, a new
production of *Elektra* and, following the intervention of Archduchess
Valerie (daughter of Franz Joseph), the first performance at the court
theatre of *Salome*. Until June the plans were still alive. Austria's declaration
of war on Serbia on 28 July 1914 led to the abrupt cancellation of the
Strauss Week.[60]

On 3 October 1914 the first of many charity concerts by the Vienna
Philharmonic Orchestra was given, to raise money for the soldiers in the
field and the widows and orphans of the many who had already fallen. Held
in the new Konzerthaus, the programme included the *Eroica* Symphony.
Beethoven enthusiasts might have been reminded of similar concerts in
Napoleonic Vienna. This time the empire was not to survive, but music in
Vienna, including Richard Strauss, did. Unlike the empire, music proved
indispensable.

Notes

CHAPTER I
Telling Tales of Music in Vienna

1 H. C. Robbins Landon, *Haydn: Chronicle and Works*, 5 vols (London, 1976–80), vol. 4, *Haydn: the Years of 'The Creation' 1796–1800* (London, 1977); vol. 5, *Haydn: the Late Years 1801–1809* (London, 1977). Henry-Louis de La Grange, *Gustav Mahler*, 4 vols (Oxford, 1995–2008), vol. 2, *Vienna: the Years of Challenge (1897–1904)* (Oxford, 1995), vol. 3, *Vienna: Triumph and Disillusion (1904–1907)* (Oxford, 1999).

2 Carl E. Schorske, *Fin-de-siècle Vienna: Politics and Culture* (Cambridge, 1981), pp. 344–58.

3 John A. Rice, *The Temple of Night at Schönau: Architecture, Music, and Theater in a Late Eighteenth-Century Viennese Garden* (Philadelphia, 2006), pp. 19–22.

4 Otto Biba and Ingrid Fuchs, *"Die Emporbringung der Musik": Höhepunkte aus der Geschichte und aus dem Archiv der Gesellschaft der Musikfreunde in Wien* (Vienna, 2012), pp. 14–15.

CHAPTER 2
Music at the Imperial and Royal Court

1 Letter of 14 September 1716, in Robert Halsband, ed., *The Complete Letters of Lady Mary Wortley Montagu*, 3 vols (Oxford, 1965), vol. 1, pp. 262–3.

2 J. H. van der Meer, *Johann Josef Fux als Opernkomponist*, 3 vols (Bilthoven, 1961), vol. 1, pp. 135–57.

3 *Angelica Vincitrice / di Alcina / Festa Teatrale / Da Rappresentarsi / sopra / La Grande Pescheera / Dell'Imperiale Favorita / ... per commando Della Sacra Cesarea e real Cattolica Maesta di Carlo VI. Imperador de' Romani sempre Augusto.* Exemplar: British Library, London, 16.g.59.

4 For authoritative surveys of the history of the Hofkapelle across the centuries, see Elisabeth Hilscher, *Mit Leier und Schwert: Die Habsburger und die Musik* (Graz, 2000); Günter Brosche et al, *Musica Imperialis: 500 Jahre Hofmusikkapelle in Wien 1498–1998* (Tutzing, 1998). For the period 1655–1792 see Frank Huss, *Der Wiener Kaiserhof: Eine Kulturgeschichte von Leopold I. bis Leopold II.* (Gernsbach, 2008).

5 Jeroen Duindam, 'The Archduchy of Austria and the Kingdoms of Bohemia and Hungary: The Court of the Austrian Habsburgs c. 1500–1750', *The Princely Courts of Europe: Ritual, Politics and Culture under the Ancien Régime 1500–1750*, ed. John Adamson (London, 1999), pp. 165–87; Duindam, *Vienna and Versailles: The Courts of Europe's Dynastic Rivals, 1550–1780* (Cambridge,

2003), pp. 69–89. For the very similar structure in the nineteenth century, see Martina Winkelhofer, *The Everyday Life of the Emperor: Francis Joseph and his Imperial Court*, trans. Jeffrey McGabe (Innsbruck, 2012), pp. 53–71.

6 Ludwig Ritter von Köchel, *Die kaiserliche Hof-Musikkapelle in Wien von 1543 bis 1867* (Vienna, 1869). This list of 1513 employees across four centuries was compiled from a variety of court sources that present the information in inconsistent, sometimes contradictory ways; although later scholars have amended, corrected and expanded the material, Köchel's book remains of fundamental utility. On some of the vagaries of the documentation and Köchel's recording of them see Eleanor Selfridge-Field, 'The Viennese court orchestra in the time of Caldara', *Antonio Caldara: Essays on his life and times*, ed. Brian W. Pritchard (Aldershot, 1987), pp. 122–3. The following provides useful supplementary material for the period 1637–1705: Herwig Knaus, *Die Musiker im Archivbestand des kaiserlichen Obersthofmeisteramtes (1637–1705)*, 3 vols (Vienna, 1967–9).

7 Herbert Seifert, *Die Oper am Wiener Kaiserhof im 17. Jahrhundert* (Tutzing, 1985), p. 163.

8 A. Peter Brown, 'The trumpet overture and sinfonia in Vienna (1715–1822): rise, decline and reformulation', *Music in eighteenth-century Austria*, ed. David Wyn Jones (Cambridge, 1996), pp. 14–18; Brown, 'Caldara's trumpet music for the Imperial celebrations of Charles VI and Elisabeth Christine', *Antonio Caldara: Essays on his life and times*, ed. Brian W. Pritchard (Aldershot, 1987), pp. 1–48.

9 For musical relations between the court and the Ursuline convent, see Janet K. Page, *Convent Music and Politics in Eighteenth-Century Vienna* (Cambridge, 2014), pp. 73–110.

10 Knaus, *Die Musiker im Archivbestand*, vol. 3, p. 97. For an account of Matteis's career at court see Andrew D. McCredie, 'Nicola Matteis, the younger: Caldara's collaborator and ballet composer in the service of the Emperor Charles VI', *Antonio Caldara: Essays on his life and times*, ed. Brian W. Pritchard (Aldershot, 1987), pp. 153–82.

11 Quoted in Guido Adler, 'Die Kaiser Ferdinand III., Leopold I., Joseph I., und Karl VI. als Tonsetzer und Forderer der Musik', *Vierteljahrsschrift für Musikwissenschaft*, 8 (1892), p. 268.

12 Guido Adler, *Musikalische Werke der Kaiser Ferdinand III., Leopold I. und Joseph I.*, 2 vols (Vienna, 1893), vol. 1, pp. v–xix. John P. Spielman, *Leopold I of Austria* (London, 1977), pp. 33–6.

13 Quoted in Huss, *Der Wiener Kaiserhof*, p. 18.

14 Ibid., pp. 13–15, 270–1.

15 Theophil Antonicek, 'Die musikalischen Jugendwerke Kaiser Leopolds I.', *Studien zur Musikwissenschaft*, 42 (1993), pp. 97–113.

16 Günter Brosche, 'Die musikalischen Werke Kaiser Leopolds I.: Ein systematisch- thematisches Verzeichnis der erhaltenen Kompositionen', *Beiträge zur Musikdokumentation: Franz Grasberger zum 60. Geburtstag*, ed. Günter Brosche (Tutzing, 1975), pp. 27–82. Brosche's catalogue does not include musical numbers written for the operas and oratorios of other composers; that number is deduced from Herbert Seifert, 'Draghi', *Die Musik in Geschichte und Gegenwart*, 2nd edn, ed. Ludwig Finscher, Personenteil, vol. 5 (Kassel, 2001), cols 1376–9.

17 Josef Gmeiner, 'Die "Schlafkammerbibliothek" Kaiser Leopolds I.', *Biblos: Österreichische Zeitschrift für Buch- und Bibliothekwesen, Dokumentation, Bibliographie, und Bibliophie*, 43/3–4 (1994), pp. 199–213, tables 14–20.

18 John Hawkins, *A General History of the Science and Practice of Music*, 2 vols (New York, 1963; repr. of 1776 edn), vol. 2, p. 850.

19 Adler, 'Die Kaiser Ferdinand III.', p. 268.

20 Frank Huss, 'Die Oper am Wiener Kaiserhof unter den Kaisern Josef I. und Karl VI. Mit einem Spielplan von 1706 bis 1740' (Ph.D. diss., University of Vienna, 2003), p. 53. Huss, *Der Wiener Kaiserhof*, pp. 43–8.

21 Personnel listed in Köchel, *Die kaiserliche Hof-Musikkapelle*, pp. 65–72.

22 Andrea Sommer-Mathis, 'Von Barcelona nach Wien: Die Einrichtung des Musik- und Theaterbetriebes am Wiener Hof durch Kaiser Karl VI.', *Musica conservata: Günter Brosche zu 60. Geburtstag*, eds Josef Gmeiner, Zsigmond Kokits, Thomas Leibnitz and Inge Pechotsch-Feichtinger (Tutzing, 1999), pp. 356–65.

23 Personnel listed in Köchel, *Die kaiserliche Hof-Musikkapelle*, pp. 72–81.

24 Huss, *Der Wiener Kaiserhof*, pp. 81–2.

25 Charles Ingrao, *The Habsburg Monarchy 1618–1815* (Cambridge, 1994), pp. 107–20.

26 Table 2 is extracted from the personnel listed in Köchel, *Die kaiserliche Hof-Musikkapelle*, pp. 72–81.

27 Huss, 'Die Oper am Wiener Kaiserhof', pp. 103–4.

28 Ibid., p. 107.

29 Ibid., pp. 119–20, 170–3.

30 Gerda Mraz, 'Die Kaiserinnen aus dem Welfenhaus und ihr Einfluss auf das geistig-kulturelle Leben in Wien', *Johann Joseph Fux und seine Zeit: Kultur, Kunst und Musik im Spätbarock*, eds Arnfried Edler and Friedrich W. Riedel (Laaber, 1996), pp. 88–9.

31 Letter of 8 September, in Halsband, ed., *The Complete Letters*, vol. 1, pp. 259–60.

32 Günter Düriegl, *Wien 1683: Die zweite Türkenbelagerung* (Vienna, 1981), p. 31.

33 Ibid., p. 57.

34 For an overview see Friedrich Polleroß, 'Monarchen und Minister', *Wien: Geschichte einer Stadt*, eds Peter Csendes and Ferdinand Opll, 3 vols (Vienna, 2000–6), vol. 2, *Die frühneuzeitliche Residenz (16. bis 18. Jahrhundert)*, eds Karl Vocelka and Anita Traninger (Vienna, 2003), pp. 475–88; Sylvia Mattl-Wurm, *Wien vom Barock bis zur Aufklärung* (Vienna, 1999), pp. 11–25.

35 Richard Perger, *Das Palais Esterházy in der Wallnerstraße zu Wien* (Vienna, 1994), pp. 29–30.

36 Jakob Michael Perschy, 'Die Fürsten Esterházy – Zwölf kurzgefasste Lebensbilder', *Die Fürsten Esterházy: Magnaten, Diplomaten & Mäzene*, ed. Jakob Perschy, exhibition catalogue (Eisenstadt, 1995), pp. 47–50.

37 For an overview see Karl Vocelka, 'Die Kirche Wiens in der barocken Entfaltung – Bau-Boom der Orden – Pietas Austriaca – Wiederaufbau und Festigung', *Wien: Geschichte einer Stadt*, vol. 2, *Die frühneuzeitliche Residenz (16. bis 18. Jahrhundert)*, eds Karl Vocelka and Anita Traninger (Vienna, 2003), pp. 333–9.

38 Details on individual churches, particularly as they relate to musical performance, are given in Friedrich W. Riedel, *Kirchenmusik am Hofe Karls VI. (1711–40): Untersuchungen zum Verhältnis von Zeremoniell und musikalischem Stil im Barockzeitalter* (Munich, 1977), pp. 32–57.

39 Mattl-Wurm, *Wien vom Barock bis zur Aufklärung*, pp. 29–38.

40 Nicolaus Buhlmann, 'Zur Geschichte des Stiftes Klosterneuburg und seiner Bewohner', *Wo sich Himmel und Erde Begegnen: Das Stift Klosterneuburg*, ed. Wolfgang Christian Huber (Klosterneuburg, 2014), pp. 41–2, 51–3.

41 Letter to her sister, 17 January 1717, in Halsband, ed., *The Complete Letters*, vol. 1, pp. 294–5.

CHAPTER 3

Catholicism, Ritual and Ceremony

1 Friedrich W. Riedel, *Kirchenmusik am Hofe Karls VI. (1711–40): Untersuchungen zum Verhältnis von Zeremoniell und musikalischem Stil im Barockzeitalter* (Munich, 1977), p. 18.

2 Herwig Knaus, *Die Musiker im Archivbestand des kaiserlichen Obersthofmeisteramtes (1637–1705)*, 3 vols (Vienna, 1967–9), vol. 3, pp. 72–3, 82–3.

3 Riedel, *Kirchenmusik am Hofe Karl VI.*, pp. 17–20. The contents of Reinhardt's volume is transcribed in the appendix to Riedel's volume, richly supplemented by other information: pp. 229–309. The original is available online at the Österreichische Nationalbibliothek website <www.onb.ac.at>, Mus. Hs. 2503.

4 Percy Scholes, ed., *Dr Burney's Musical Tours in Europe*, 2 vols, vol. 2: *An Eighteenth-Century Musical Tour in Central Europe and the Netherlands* (London, 1959), p. 72.

5 Elisabeth Theresia Hilscher, *Mit Leier und Schwert: Die Habsburger und die Musik* (Graz, 2000), pp. 153–4; Riedel, *Kirchenmusik am Hofe Karl VI.*, p. 15.

6 Riedel, *Kirchenmusik am Hofe Karl VI.*, p. 244.

7 Ibid., pp. 33–4.

8 Ibid., p. 284.

9 Ibid., p. 295.

10 Anna Coreth, *Pietas Austriaca*, trans. William D. Bowman and Anna Maria Leitgeb (West Lafayette, 2004), pp. 45–6, 50–5.

11 Riedel, *Kirchenmusik am Hofe Karl VI.*, p. 44.

12 Ibid., pp. 302–3.

13 Ibid., p. 283.

14 Ibid., p. 299.

15 Coreth, *Pietas Austriaca*, pp. 1–12.

16 Ibid., p. 83.

17 Modern edition in Guido Adler, *Musikalische Werke der Kaiser Ferdinand III., Leopold I. und Joseph I.*, 2 vols (Vienna, 1893), vol. 1, pp. 153–66.

18 John P. Spielman, *Leopold I of Austria* (London, 1977), pp. 146–8.

19 Günter Brosche, 'Die musikalischen Werke Kaiser Leopolds I.: Ein systematisch- thematisches Verzeichnis der erhaltenen Kompositionen',

Beiträge zur Musikdokumentation: Franz Grasberger zum 60. Geburtstag, ed.
Günter Brosche (Tutzing, 1975), pp. 45–65.

20 Modern edition in Adler, *Musikalische Werke*, vol. 1, pp. 181–230.

21 Thomas Hochradner, 'Johann Joseph Fux', *Die Musik in Geschichte und
Gegenwart*, 2nd edn, ed. Ludwig Finscher, Personenteil, vol. 7 (Kassel, 2002),
cols 306–13.

22 Modern edition in *Johann Joseph Fux: Sämtliche Werke*, ed. Alfred Mann
(Graz, 1967), vol. 7/1. Partial translation by Alfred Mann, *The Study of
Counterpoint from Johann Joseph Fux's Gradus ad Parnassum*, rev. edn (London,
1965). Translation of final chapters by Susan Wollenberg, 'Johann Joseph Fux:
Gradus ad Parnassum (1725): Concluding Chapters', *Music Analysis*, 11/2–3
(1992), pp. 209–43.

23 Mann, *The Study of Counterpoint*, p. 144.

24 Robert Lindell, 'The Search for the Imperial Chapelmaster in 1567–1568:
Palestrina or De Monte', *Palestrina e l'Europa: Atti del III Convegno
Internazionale di Studi Palestrina, 6–9 Ottobre 1994*, eds Giancarlo Rostirolla,
Stefania Soldati and Elena Zomparelli (Palestrina, 2006), pp. 57–68.

25 Wollenberg, 'Johann Joseph Fux', p. 217.

26 Ibid., p. 218.

27 Ibid., p. 219.

28 Ibid., p. 218.

29 Modern edition in *Denkmäler der Tonkunst in Österreich*, vol. 1, eds Johannes
Evangelist Habert and Gustav Adolf Glossner (Vienna, 1894), pp. 63–88.

30 Wollenberg, 'Johann Joseph Fux', p. 237.

31 Ibid., p. 237–8.

32 Ibid., pp. 240–1.

CHAPTER 4
Italian Opera and the Preservation of the Habsburg Dynasty

1 Herbert Seifert, *Die Oper am Wiener Kaiserhof im 17. Jahrhundert* (Tutzing,
1985), pp. 518–56.

2 Frank Huss, 'Die Oper am Wiener Kaiserhof unter den Kaisern Josef I. und
Karl VI. Mit einem Spielplan von 1706 bis 1740' (Ph.D. diss., University of
Vienna, 2003), pp. 181–225.

3 Herbert Seifert, *Der Sig-prangende Hochzeit-Gott: Hochzeitsfeste am Wiener
Hof der Habsburger und ihre Allegorik 1622–1699* (Vienna, 1998), pp. 67–72.

4 Andrea Sommer-Mathis, *Tu felix Austria nube: Hochzeitsfeste der Habsburger
im 18. Jahrhundert* (Vienna, 1994), pp. 11–30.

5 Seifert, *Die Oper*, pp. 395–7.

6 Huss, 'Die Oper am Wiener Kaiserhof', pp. 191–2.

7 Franz Hadamowsky, *Wien, Theatergeschichte: Von den Anfängen bis zum Ende
des Ersten Weltkriegs* (Vienna, 1988), pp. 143–4; Huss, 'Die Oper am Wiener
Kaiserhof', pp. 83–4.

8 Huss, 'Die Oper am Wiener Kaiserhof', pp. 83–8; Sommer-Mathis, *Tu felix
Austria nube*, pp. 31–5, 53–9.

9   Andrea Sommer-Mathis, 'Opera and Ceremonial at the Imperial Court
    of Vienna', *Italian Opera in Central Europe*, 3 vols (Berlin, 2006–8), vol. 1,
    Institutions and Ceremonies, eds Melania Bucciarelli, Norbert Dubowy and
    Reinhard Strohm (Berlin, 2006), pp. 176–91.

10 John P. Spielman, *Leopold I of Austria* (London, 1977), pp. 99–101.

11 No. 51 in Günter Brosche, 'Die musikalischen Werke Kaiser Leopolds I.:
    Ein systematisch-thematisches Verzeichnis der erhaltenen Kompositionen',
    Beiträge zur Musikdokumentation: Franz Grasberger zum 60. Geburtstag, ed.
    Günter Brosche (Tutzing, 1975), pp. 67–8.

12 Seifert, *Die Oper*, pp. 160, 237, 510.

13 Ibid., p. 95.

14 Seifert sees the work as promoting the dynastic continuity between Leopold
    (= Odysseus) and Joseph (= Telemachus): ibid., p. 277.

15 Ibid., pp. 163–4.

16 Modern edition of aria in Guido Adler, *Musikalische Werke der Kaiser
    Ferdinand III., Leopold I. und Joseph I.*, 2 vols (Vienna, 1893), vol. 2, pp. 154–5.

17 Hadamowsky, *Wien, Theatergeschichte*, p. 155.

18 Friedrich W. Riedel, *Kirchenmusik am Hofe Karls VI. (1711–40):
    Untersuchungen zum Verhältnis von Zeremoniell und musikalischem Stil im
    Barockzeitalter* (Munich, 1977), p. 252. Herbert Seifert, 'Das Sepolcro – ein
    Spezifikum der kaiserlichen Hofkapelle', *Die Wiener Hofmusikkapelle III: Gibt
    es einen Stil der Hofmusikkapelle?*, eds Harmut Krones, Theophil Antonicek
    and Elisabeth Theresia Fritz-Hilscher (Vienna, 2011), pp. 163–73. Howard
    E. Smither, *A History of the Oratorio*, 4 vols (Chapel Hill, 1977–2000), vol. 1,
    The Oratorio in the Baroque Era (Chapel Hill, 1977), pp. 395–7. For similar
    occasions in Viennese churches and convents, often attended by members of
    the imperial family, see Janet K. Page, *Convent Music and Politics in Eighteenth-
    Century Vienna* (Cambridge, 2014), pp. 155–91.

19 Anthony Ford, 'Giovanni Bononcini, 1670–1747', *Musical Times*, 111 (1970),
    pp. 695–9; Lowell Lindgren, 'Giovanni Bononcini', *New Grove Dictionary
    of Music and Musicians*, 2nd edn, ed. Stanley Sadie (London, 2001), vol. 3,
    pp. 872–7.

20 Alexander von Weilen, *Geschichte des Wiener Theaterwesens von den ältesten
    Zeiten bis zu den Anfängen der Hoftheater* (Vienna, 1899), pp. 124–6.

21 Huss, 'Die Oper am Kaiserhof', pp. 194–212; Hermine Weigel Williams,
    Francesco Bartolomeo Conti: His Life and Music (Aldershot, 1999), pp. 39–59,
    126–68.

22 Huss, 'Die Oper am Kaiserhof', pp. 100, 194–5.

23 Modern edition in *Johann Joseph Fux: Sämtliche Werke*, vol. 5/7, ed. Dagmar
    Glüxam (Graz, 2004).

24 Brian W. Pritchard, 'Antonio Caldara', *New Grove*, 2nd edn, vol. 4, pp. 819–26.

25 Huss, 'Die Oper am Kaiserhof', pp. 196–214.

26 Charles Ingrao, *The Habsburg Monarchy 1618–1815* (Cambridge, 1994),
    pp. 128–30, 134, 144–5, 148–9.

27 Huss, 'Die Oper am Kaiserhof', p. 205.

28 Details from contemporary documentation quoted in *Denkmäler der Tonkunst
    in Österreich*, vol. 17/34–5, *Johann Joseph Fux: Costanza e Fortezza*, ed. Egon
    Wellesz (Vienna, 1910), pp. x–xi.

29 *Wienerisches Diarium*, 23 June 1723.

30 Ibid., 30 June 1723.

31 Riedel, *Kirchenmusik am Hofe Karls VI.*, p. 286.

32 *Wienerisches Diarium*, 31 July 1723; Riedel, *Kirchenmusik am Hofe Karls VI.*, p. 288.

33 Anna Coreth, *Pietas Austriaca*, trans. William D. Bowman and Anna Maria Leitgeb (West Lafayette, 2004), p. 84.

34 *Wienerisches Diarium*, 31 July, 16 October and 3 November 1723.

35 The engravings are reproduced in *Denkmäler der Tonkunst in Österreich*, vol. 17/34–5, *passim*.

36 Ulrike Dembski-Riss, 'Bühnenarchitektur und Bühnendekoration in den Wiener Opernaufführungen zur Zeit von Johann Joseph Fux: Anmerkungen zu den Szenenbildern der Opern *Angelica Vincitrice Di Alcina* und *Costanza e Fortezza*', *Johann Joseph Fux und seine Zeit: Kultur, Kunst und Musik im Spätbarock*, eds Arnfried Edler and Friedrich W. Riedel (Laaber, 1996), pp. 189–92, 194–202; Pavel Preiss, 'Baroque Theatre in Bohemia and its Scenic Design', *The Glory of the Baroque in Bohemia: Essays on Art, Culture and Society in the 17th and 18th Centuries*, ed. Vít Vlnas (Prague, 2001), pp. 291–3.

37 Manuscript score: Österreichische Nationalbibliothek, Mus. Hs. 17630.

38 Riedel, *Kirchenmusik am Hofe Karl VI.*, p. 293.

39 *Wienerisches Diarium*, 4 September 1723.

40 Friedrich W. Riedel, 'Krönungszeremoniell und Krönungsmusik im Barockzeitalter', *Mitteleuropäische Kontexte der Barockmusik: Bericht über die Internationale musikwissenschaftliche Konferenz Bratislava, 23. bis 25. März 1994*, ed. Pavol Polák (Bratislava, 1997), pp. 109–32.

41 Modern edition in *Johann Joseph Fux: Sämtliche Werke*, vol. 2/2, eds Ingrid Schubert and Gösta Neuwirth (Graz, 1979).

42 Riedel, *Kirchenmusik am Hofe Karl VI.*, p. 294.

43 Markéta Kabelková, 'Music in Bohemia in the Baroque Era', *The Glory of the Baroque in Bohemia: Essays on Art, Culture and Society in the 17th and 18th Centuries*, ed. Vít Vlnas (Prague, 2001), p. 267.

44 Riedel, *Kirchenmusik am Hofe Karl VI.*, p. 295.

45 *Wienerisches Diarium*, 22 September 1723.

46 Huss, 'Die Oper am Wiener Hof', pp. 119–20.

47 J. H. van der Meer, *Johann Josef Fux als Opernkomponist*, 3 vols, (Bilthoven, 1961), vol. 1, pp. 225–41.

48 Quantz's report was included in Friedrich Wilhelm Marpurg, *Historische-Kritische Beyträge zur Aufnahme der Musik*, 5 vols (Berlin, 1754–78), vol. 1 (Berlin, 1754), pp. 216–20. It is quoted in full in *Denkmäler der Tonkunst in Österreich*, vol. 17/34–5, pp. ix–x.

49 Ibid., p. ix.

50 Manuscript score: Österreichische Nationalbibliothek, Mus. Hs. 18236.

51 Report on coronation service in *Wienerisches Diarium*, 11 September 1723.

52 *Wienerisches Diarium*, 13 October and 23 October 1723.

53 Manuscript score: Österreichische Nationalbibliothek, Mus. Hs. 17222.

54 *Wienerisches Diarium*, 24 November 1723.

55 Manuscript score: Österreichische Nationalbibliothek, Mus. Hs. 17138.

56 *Wienerisches Diarium*, 24 November 1723; Hadamowsky, *Wien,*
Theatergeschichte, pp. 160–1.

57 Percy Scholes, ed., *Dr Burney's Musical Tours in Europe*, 2 vols, vol. 2: *An*
Eighteenth-Century Musical Tour in Central Europe and the Netherlands
(London, 1959), p. 189.

58 Preiss, 'Baroque Theatre in Bohemia and its Scenic Design', p. 293.

59 Letter to her sister, 17 November 1716, in Robert Halsband, ed., *The Complete*
Letters of Lady Mary Wortley Montagu, 3 vols (Oxford, 1965), vol. 1, pp. 280–1.

60 See the illustrated survey by Kabelková, 'Music in Bohemia in the Baroque Era',
pp. 262–80.

CHAPTER 5

Court, Aristocrats and Connoisseurs

1 Charles Ingrao, *The Habsburg Monarchy 1618–1815* (Cambridge, 1994),
pp. 203–12.

2 John A. Rice, *W. A. Mozart: La clemenza di Tito* (Cambridge, 1991), pp. 1–7;
H. C. Robbins Landon, *1791: Mozart's Last Year* (London, 1988), pp. 84–90.

3 Dorothea Link, 'Mozart's appointment to the Viennese court', *Words About*
Mozart: Essays in Honour of Stanley Sadie, ed. Dorothea Link with Judith
Nagley (Woodbridge, 2005), pp. 163–78; David Ian Black, 'Mozart and the
Practice of Sacred Music, 1781–91' (Ph.D. diss., Harvard University, 2007),
p. 180.

4 Frank Huss, 'Die Oper am Wiener Kaiserhof unter den Kaisern Josef I. und
Karl VI. Mit einem Spielplan von 1706 bis 1740' (Ph.D. diss., University of
Vienna, 2003), p. 234.

5 Librettos listed in Claudio Sartori, *I libretti italiani a stampa dalle origini al*
1800, 7 vols (Cuneo, 1990–4), vol. 2 (Cuneo, 1990), pp. 143–50.

6 Adam Wandruszka, 'Die "Clementia Austriaca" und der Aufgeklärte
Absolutismus: Zum politischen und ideellen Hintergrund von "La clemenza di
Tito"', *Österreichische Musikzeitschrift*, 31 (1976), pp. 188–91.

7 Don J. Neville, 'La clemenza di Tito: Metastasio, Mazzolà and Mozart', *Studies*
in Music from the University of Western Ontario, 1 (1976), p. 127.

8 Rice, *La clemenza di Tito*, pp. 62–4; Landon, *Mozart's Last Year*, pp. 115, 118.

9 John A. Rice, 'La clemenza di Tito', *The Cambridge Mozart Encyclopedia*, eds
Cliff Eisen and Simon P. Keefe (Cambridge, 2006), p. 97.

10 Landon, *Mozart's Last Year*, p. 117.

11 Kathleen Lamkin, *Esterházy Musicians 1790 to 1809: Considered from New*
Sources in the Castle Forchtenstein Archives (Tutzing, 2007), p. 39.

12 Otto Biba, ed., *"Eben komme ich von Haydn ...": Georg August Griesingers*
Korrespondenz mit Joseph Haydns Verleger Breitkopf & Härtel 1799–1819
(Zurich, 1987), pp. 105, 151.

13 Marianne Helms, 'Ein Schwesterwerk der "Nelsonmesse"? Zur Edition von
Haydns *Te Deum* Hob. XXIIIc:2', *Haydn-Studien*, 9/1–4 (2006), pp. 173–5.

14 *Te Deum, Johann Joseph Fux: Sämtliche Werke*, vol. 2/1, ed. István Kecskeméti
(Graz, 1963), p. vii. The work was entered as item 558, without the composer's

name, in a catalogue of Haydn's artistic effects prepared after his death. See H. C. Robbins Landon, *Haydn: Chronicle and Works*, 5 vols (London, 1976–80), vol. 5, *Haydn: the Late Years 1801–1809* (London, 1977), p. 402.

15 John A. Rice, *Empress Marie Therese and Music at the Viennese Court, 1792–1807* (Cambridge, 2003), pp. 17–20; Elisabeth Hilscher, *Mit Leier und Schwert: Die Habsburger und die Musik* (Graz, 2000), pp. 186–9.

16 Kurt Dorfmüller, Norbert Gertsch and Julia Ronge, *Ludwig van Beethoven: Thematisch-bibliographisches Werkverzeichnis*, 2 vols (Munich, 2014), vol. 1, p. 127.

17 Susan Kagan, *Archduke Rudolph, Beethoven's Patron, Pupil, and Friend* (Stuyvesant, 1988), pp. 1–37.

18 Letter of 3 March 1819, in Emily Anderson, ed., *The Letters of Beethoven*, 3 vols (London, 1961), vol. 2, pp. 814–15; Sieghard Brandenburg, ed., *Ludwig van Beethoven: Briefwechsel Gesamtausgabe*, 7 vols (Munich, 1996–8), vol. 4 (Munich, 1996), p. 246.

19 Thematic catalogue in Kagan, *Archduke Rudolph*, pp. 313–46.

20 *Alphabetisches Verzeichnis der Musik-Compositoren*, Gesellschaft der Musikfreunde, Vienna, 1268/33.

21 Johann Ferdinand von Schönfeld, *Jahrbuch der Tonkunst von Wien und Prag* (Vienna, 1796, facsimile edn Munich, 1976), pp. 92–4. Schönfeld's numbers reflect payrolls from 1794: see Theodore Albrecht, 'Anton Dreyssig (c 1753/4–1820): Mozart's and Beethoven's Zauberflötist', *Words about Mozart: Essays in Honour of Stanley Sadie*, ed. Dorothea Link with Judith Nagley (Woodbridge, 2005), p. 184.

22 Ludwig Köchel, *Die Kaiserliche Hof-Musikkapelle in Wien von 1543 bis 1867* (Vienna, 1869), p. 89.

23 Leopold M. Kantner, 'Die Zeit der Wiener Klassik', *Musica Imperialis: 500 Jahre Hofmusikkapelle in Wien 1498–1998*, ed. Günter Brosche et al (Tutzing, 1998), pp. 110–14.

24 Schönfeld, *Jahrbuch der Tonkunst von Wien und Prag*, Preface, pp. i–ii.

25 Ibid., p. 77.

26 Otto Biba, 'Beobachtungen zur Österreichischen Musikszene des 18. Jahrhunderts', *Österreichische Musik – Musik in Österreich*, ed. Elisabeth Theresia Hilscher (Tutzing, 1998), pp. 215–17.

27 For an account of this relationship, see Karel Bozenek, 'Beethoven und das Adelsgeschlecht Lichnowsky', *Ludwig van Beethoven im Herzen Europas*, eds Oldřich Pulkert and Hans-Werner Küthen (Prague, 2000), pp. 120–66.

28 Exemplar: British Library, London, Hirsch IV.238.

29 Contract with Artaria in Anderson, *The Letters of Beethoven*, vol. 3, pp. 1417–18; Dorfmüller, Gertsch and Ronge, *Ludwig van Beethoven*, vol. 1, p. 127.

30 Georg Feder, *Joseph Haydn: Die Schöpfung* (Kassel, 1999), pp. 125–6; D. Edward Olleson, 'Gottfried van Swieten, Patron of Haydn and Mozart', *Proceedings of the Royal Musical Association*, 89 (1962–3), pp. 63–74.

31 Schönfeld, *Jahrbuch der Tonkunst von Wien und Prag*, p. 72; translation of Georg August Griesinger, *Biographische Notizen über Joseph Haydn* (Leipzig, 1809) and Albert Christoph Dies, *Biographische Nachrichten von Joseph Haydn* (Berlin, 1810) by Vernon Gotwals as *Haydn: Two Contemporary Portraits* (Madison, 1968), p. 38.

32 Wiebke Thormählen, 'Art, Education and Entertainment: The String Quintet in Late Eighteenth-Century Vienna' (Ph.D. diss., Cornell University, 2008), pp. 26–35; Thormählen, 'Playing with Art: Musical Arrangements as Educational Tools in van Swieten's Vienna', *Journal of Musicology*, 27 (2010), pp. 360–6, 374–6.

33 Otto Biba, 'Nachrichten über Joseph Haydn, Michael Haydn und Wolfgang Amadeus Mozart in der Sammlung handschriftlicher Biographien der Gesellschaft der Musikfreunde in Wien', *Studies in Music History presented to H. C. Robbins Landon on his seventieth birthday*, eds Otto Biba and David Wyn Jones (London, 1996), p. 163.

34 *Allgemeine musikalische Zeitung*, 3 (1801), col. 579.

35 Gerhard Croll, 'Mitteilungen über die "Schöpfung" und die "Jahreszeiten" aus dem Schwarzenberg-Archiv', *Haydn-Studien*, 3/2 (1974), pp. 87–8.

36 Ibid., p. 144; H. C. Robbins Landon, *Haydn: Chronicle and Works, Haydn: the Years of 'The Creation' 1796–1800* (London, 1977), p. 453.

37 Wilhelm Beetz, *Das Wiener Opernhaus 1869–1955* (Zurich, 1955), pp. 48–9.

38 Haydn's manuscript subscription list is transcribed in H. C. Robbins Landon, *Haydn: Chronicle and Works*, 5 vols (London, 1976–80), vol. 4, *Haydn: the Years of 'The Creation' 1796–1800* (London, 1977), pp. 622–32.

39 Otto Biba, 'Beethoven und die "Liebhaber Concerte" in Wien im Winter 1807/08', *Beiträge '76–78: Beethoven Kolloquium 1977: Dokumentation und Aufführungspraxis*, ed. Rudolf Klein (Kassel, 1978), pp. 82–93; David Wyn Jones, *The Symphony in Beethoven's Vienna* (Cambridge, 2006), pp. 123–9; Rita Steblin, *Beethoven in the Diaries of Johann Nepomuk Chotek* (Bonn, 2013), pp. 37–65.

40 Johann Friedrich Reichardt, *Vertraute Briefe: geschrieben auf einer Reise nach Wien und den Österreichischen Staaten zu Ende des Jahres 1808 und zu Anfang 1809*, ed. Gustav Gugitz, 2 vols (Munich, 1915), vol. 1, pp. 234–5, 261–2; vol. 2, p. 154.

41 Franz Hadamowsky, *Wien, Theatergeschichte: Von den Anfängen bis zum Ende des Ersten Weltkriegs* (Vienna, 1988), pp. 304–9.

42 Ibid., pp. 313–17.

43 Elliot Forbes, ed., *Thayer's Life of Beethoven* (Princeton, 1964), p. 452–7.

44 Anderson, *The Letters of Beethoven*, vol. 3, pp. 1420–2.

45 Jaroslav Macek, 'Beethoven und Ferdinand Fürst Kinsky', *Ludwig van Beethoven im Herzen Europas*, eds Oldřich Pulkert and Hans-Werner Küthen (Prague, 2000), pp. 218–32; Steblin, *Diaries of Johann Nepomuk Chotek*, pp. 173–6.

46 Eliška Bastlová, *Collectio operum musicalium quae in Bibliotheca Kinsky adservantur* (Prague, 2013), pp. 24–5.

47 Macek, 'Beethoven und Ferdinand Fürst Kinsky', pp. 232–44.

48 Lamkin, *Esterházy Musicians*, pp. 24–81; Roger Hellyer, 'The Wind Ensembles of the Esterházy Princes, 1761–1813', *Haydn Yearbook*, 15 (1985), pp. 21–77.

49 Lamkin, pp. 46, 48–9.

50 Julia Moore, 'Beethoven and Inflation', *Beethoven Forum*, 1 (1992), pp. 198–204.

51 Jaroslav Macek, 'Die Musik bei den Lobkowicz', *Ludwig van Beethoven im Herzen Europas*, eds Oldřich Pulkert and Hans-Werner Küthen (Prague, 2000), pp. 175–216; Jones, *The Symphony in Beethoven's Vienna*, pp. 43–6.

52 Jones, *The Symphony in Beethoven's Vienna*, pp. 64–75.

53 Walther Brauneis, '"... composta per festiggare il sovvenire di un grand Uomo." Beeethovens "Eroica" als Hommage des Fürsten Franz Joseph Maximilian von Lobkowitz für Louis Ferdinand von Preußen', *Jahrbuch des Vereins für Geschichte der Stadt Wien*, 52–3 (1996–7), pp. 72–3; Tomislav Volek and Jaroslav Macek, 'Beethoven und Fürst Lobkowitz', *Beethoven und Böhmen: Beiträge zu Biographie und Wirkungsgeschichte Beethovens*, eds Sieghard Brandenburg and Martella Gutiérrez-Denhoff (Bonn, 1988), p. 208.

54 Reichardt, *Vertraute Briefe*, vol. 2, pp. 39–40.

55 Schönfeld, *Jahrbuch der Tonkunst von Wien und Prag*, pp. 1–2; translation from '*A Yearbook of the Music of Vienna and Prague, 1796*: Johann Ferdinand Ritter von Schönfeld, Vienna 1796', *Haydn and His World*, ed. Elaine Sisman (Princeton, 1997), p. 291.

56 Schönfeld, *Jahrbuch der Tonkunst von Wien und Prag*, p. 38; translation from '*A Yearbook of the Music of Vienna and Prague*', p. 298.

57 Landon, *Haydn: the Years of 'The Creation' 1796–1800*, p. 627.

58 Schönfeld, *Jahrbuch der Tonkunst von Wien und Prag*, p. 41; translation from '*A Yearbook of the Music of Vienna and Prague*', p. 306.

59 Irving Godt, *Marianna Martines: A Woman Composer in the Vienna of Mozart and Haydn*, ed. John A. Rice (Rochester, 2010), pp. 17–23.

60 Schönfeld, *Jahrbuch der Tonkunst von Wien und Prag*, pp. 41–2; translation (amended) from '*A Yearbook of the Music of Vienna and Prague*', p. 307.

CHAPTER 6

Demand, Aspiration and the Ennobling of the Spirit

1 Hannelore Gericke, *Der Wiener Musikalienhandel von 1700 bis 1778* (Graz, 1960), pp. 16–97.

2 Alexander Weinmann, *Vollständiges Verlagsverzeichnis Artaria & Comp.*, Beiträge zur Geschichte des alt-Wiener Musikverlages, vol. 2/2 (Vienna, 1952); Rosemary Hilmar, *Der Musikverlag Artaria & Comp.: Geschichte und Probleme der Druckproduktion* (Tutzing, 1977); Rupert Ridgewell, 'Music Printing in Mozart's Vienna: the Artaria Press, 1778–1794', *Fontes Artis Musicae*, 48 (2001), pp. 217–36; Friedrich Slezak, *Beethovens Wiener Originalverleger* (Vienna, 1987), pp. 6–22.

3 Alexander Weinmann, *Verlagsverzeichnis Tranquillo Mollo (mit und ohne Co.)*, Beiträge zur Geschichte des alt-Wiener Musikverlages, vol. 2/9 (Vienna, 1964), pp. 6–12, 22–3.

4 Alexander Weinmann, *Verlagsverzeichnis Giovanni Cappi bis A. O. Witzendorf*, Beiträge zur Geschichte des alt-Wiener Musikverlages, vol. 2/11 (Vienna, 1967); Slezak, *Beethovens Wiener Originalverleger*, pp. 29–35.

5 Weinmann, *Verlagsverzeichnis Giovanni Cappi*, pp. III–VI.

6 Ibid., pp. 26–44.

7 Alexander Weinmann, 'Vollständiges Verlagsverzeichnis der Musikalien des Kunst- und Industrie-Comptoirs in Wien, 1801–1819', *Studien zur Musikwissenschaft*, 22 (1955), pp. 217–52; Slezak, *Beethovens Wiener Originalverleger*, pp. 54–60; David Wyn Jones, *The Symphony in Beethoven's Vienna* (Cambridge, 2006), pp. 164–5.

8 Jones, *The Symphony in Beethoven's Vienna*, pp. 164–7.

9 Alexander Weinmann, *Verzeichnis der Musikalien des Verlages Joseph Eder – Jeremias Bermann*, Beiträge zur Geschichte des alt-Wiener Musikverlages, vol. 2/12 (Vienna, 1968); Slezak, *Beethovens Wiener Originalverleger*, pp. 39–41.

10 Weinmann, *Verzeichnis der Musikalien des Verlages Joseph Eder*, pp. V–VIII.

11 Alexander Weinmann, *Verzeichnis der Verlagswerke des Musikalischen Magazins in Wien, 1784–1802: Leopold (und Anton) Kozeluch*, 2nd edn, Beiträge zur Geschichte des alt-Wiener Musikverlages, vol. 2/1a (Vienna, 1979).

12 Rudolf Rasch, 'Basic Concepts', *Music Publishing in Europe 1600–1900: Concepts and Issues. Bibliography*, ed. Rudolf Rasch (Berlin, 2005), pp. 13–14.

13 For intermittent and small-scale music publishing, see Alexander Weinmann, *Wiener Musikverlag 'Am Rande': Ein lückenfüllender Beitrag zur Geschichte des Alt-Wiener Musikverlages*, Beiträge zur Geschichte des alt-Wiener Musikverlages, vol. 2/13 (Vienna, 1970).

14 Alexander Weinmann, *Johann Traeg: Die Musikalienverzeichnisse von 1799 und 1804 (Handschrift und Sortiment)*, Beiträge zur Geschichte des alt-Wiener Musikverlages, vol. 2/17 (Vienna, 1973); Weinmann, *Die Anzeigen des Kopiaturbetriebs Johann Traeg in der Wiener Zeitung zwischen 1782 und 1805*, Wiener Archivstudien, vol. 6 (Vienna, 1981); Weinmann, *Verlagsverzeichnis Johann Traeg (und Sohn)*, 2nd edn, Beiträge zur Geschichte des alt-Wiener Musikverlages, vol. 2/16 (Vienna, 1973); Slezak, *Beethovens Wiener Originalverleger*, pp. 91–4; Dexter Edge, 'Mozart's Viennese Copyists' (Ph.D. diss., University of Southern California, 2001), pp. 749–86; Jones, *The Symphony in Beethoven's Vienna*, pp. 11–27.

15 Weinmann, *Die Anzeigen*, p. 17.

16 Facsimile in Weinmann, *Die Musikalienverzeichnisse*, pp. [iv–x], 1–364.

17 Facsimile in ibid., pp. 366–433.

18 Letter of 2 June 1781 in Wilhelm A. Bauer, Otto Erich Deutsch and Joseph Heinz Eibl (eds), *Mozart: Briefe und Aufzeichnungen, Gesamtausgabe*, 8 vols (Kassel, 1962–2005), vol. 3, 1780–1786 (Kassel, 1962), pp. 124–5.

19 Ludwig von Köchel, *Chronologisch-thematisches Verzeichnis sämtlicher Tonwerke Wolfgang Amadé Mozarts*, 6th edn, eds Franz Giegling, Alexander Weinmann and Gerd Sievers (Wiesbaden, 1964), p. 915–16.

20 Sources for the table: Kurt Dorfmüller, Norbert Gertsch and Julia Ronge, *Ludwig van Beethoven: Thematisch-bibliographisches Werkverzeichnis*, 2 vols (Munich, 2014); Michael Jahn, *Die Wiener Hofoper von 1794 bis 1810: Musik und Tanz im Burg- und Kärnthnerthortheater* (Vienna, 2011); Alexander Weinmann, *Die Wiener Verlagswerke von Franz Anton Hoffmeister*, Beiträge zur Geschichte des alt-Wiener Musikverlages, vol. 2/8 (Vienna, 1964); Weinmann, *Verlagsverzeichnis Giovanni Cappi*; Weinmann, *Verlagsverzeichnis Johann Traeg*; Weinmann, *Verlagsverzeichnis Tranquillo Mollo*; Weinmann, *Verzeichnis der Musikalien des Verlages Joseph Eder*; Weinmann, *Vollständiges Verlagsverzeichnis Artaria & Comp.*

21 Carl van Beethoven's letter to Breitkopf & Härtel, 22 April 1802, in Theodore Albrecht (trans. and ed.), *Letters to Beethoven and Other Correspondence*, 3 vols (Lincoln, Nebraska, 1996), vol. 1, p. 70; Sieghard Brandenburg, ed., *Ludwig van Beethoven: Briefwechsel Gesamtausgabe*, 7 vols (Munich, 1996–8), vol. 1 (Munich, 1996), p. 107.

22 Johann Friedrich Reichardt, *Vertraute Briefe: geschrieben auf einer Reise nach Wien und den Österreichischen Staaten zu Ende des Jahres 1808 und zu Anfang 1809*, ed. Gustav Gugitz, 2 vols (Munich, 1915), vol. 1, p. 168.

23 Johann Ferdinand von Schönfeld, *Jahrbuch der Tonkunst von Wien und Prag* (Vienna, 1796, facsimile edn Munich, 1976), pp. 51–2.

24 Otto Erich Deutsch, 'Leopold von Sonnleithners Erinnerungen an die Musiksalons des Vormärzlichen Wiens', *Österreichische Musikzeitschrift*, 16/3 (1961), pp. 97–101; Marion Fürst, *Maria Theresia Paradis: Mozarts berühmte Zeitgenossin* (Cologne, 2005).

25 Schönfeld, *Jahrbuch der Tonkunst von Wien und Prag*, pp. 46–7.

26 Leopold von Sonnleithner (1797–1873), Joseph's nephew, writing in 1853, in Deutsch, 'Leopold von Sonnleithners Erinnerungen', p. 101.

27 Schönfeld, *Jahrbuch der Tonkunst von Wien und Prag*, pp. 4–5.

28 Ibid., pp. 26–8.

29 Weinmann, *Die Musikalienverzeichnisse*, pp. 190–201.

30 Schönfeld, *Jahrbuch der Tonkunst von Wien und Prag*, pp. 6, 10, 14.

31 Ibid., pp. 16, 35.

32 Ibid., pp. 55–6.

33 Oldřich Pulkert, 'Das Knabenquartett des Fürsten Lichnowsky', *Ludwig van Beethoven im Herzen Europas*, eds Oldřich Pulkert and Hans-Werner Küthen (Prague, 2000), pp. 451–8; Rita Steblin, *Beethoven in the Diaries of Johann Nepomuk Chotek* (Bonn, 2013), pp. 36–44; John Gingerich, 'Ignaz Schuppanzigh and Beethoven's Late Quartets', *The Musical Quarterly*, 93/3–4 (2010), pp. 450–513.

34 Jaroslav Macek, 'Die Musik bei den Lobkowicz', *Ludwig van Beethoven im Herzen Europas*, eds Oldrich Pulkert and Hans-Werner Küthen (Prague, 2000), pp. 184–5.

35 *Allgemeine musikalische Zeitung*, 7 (1805), cols 534–5.

36 Steblin, *Beethoven in the Diaries of Johann Nepomuk Chotek*, pp. 36–7, 39–40, 42, 44.

37 Wayne M. Senner, Robin Wallace and William Meredith, eds, *The Critical Reception of Beethoven's Compositions by His German Contemporaries*, 2 vols (Lincoln, Nebraska, 1999), vol. 2, pp. 52–3.

38 *Allgemeine musikalische Zeitung*, 18 (1816), col. 291.

39 *Allgemeine musikalische Zeitung*, 17 (1815), cols 570–1.

40 Ingrid Fuchs, 'The First Performers and Audiences of Haydn's Chamber Music', *The Land of Opportunity: Joseph Haydn and Britain*, eds Richard Chesser and David Wyn Jones (London, 2013), pp. 158–9.

41 See letter from Count Razumovsky to Prince Subow, quoted in Boris Steinpress, 'Haydns Oratorien in Russland zu Lebzeiten des Komponisten', *Haydn-Studien*, 2/2 (1969), pp. 83–4.

42 Jana Fojtíková and Tomislav Volek, 'Die Beethoveniana der Lobkowitz-Musiksammlung und ihre Kopisten', *Beethoven und Böhmen: Beiträge zu Biographie und Wirkungsgeschichte Beethovens*, eds Sieghard Brandenburg and Martella Gutiérrez-Denhoff (Bonn, 1988), pp. 275, 286.

43 As described in Anthony van Hoboken, *Joseph Haydn: Thematisch-bibliographisches Werkverzeichnis*, 3 vols (Mainz, 1957–78), vol. 3 (Mainz, 1978), p. 43.

44 Köchel, *Chronologisch-thematisches Verzeichnis*, p. 917.

45 Hubert Unverricht, 'Privates Quartettspiel in Schlesien von 1780 bis 1850', *Musica privata: die Rolle der Musik im privaten Leben: Festschrift zum 65. Geburtstag Walter Salmen*, ed. Monika Fink (Innsbruck, 1991), p. 106.

46 Alexander Weinmann, *Vollständiges Verlagsverzeichnis Senefelder, Steiner, Haslinger*, 3 vols (Munich, 1979–83), vol. 1, *A. Senefelder, Chemische Druckerey, S. A. Steiner, S. A. Steiner & Comp. (Wien, 1803–1826)*, Beiträge zur Geschichte des alt-Wiener Musikverlages, vol. 2/19 (Munich, 1979), pp. 51–81.

47 Undated letter (c. 7 October 1816) in English, in Sieghard Brandenburg, ed., *Ludwig van Beethoven: Briefwechsel Gesamtausgabe* (Munich, 1996), vol. 3, p. 306.

48 'Uebersicht des gegenwärtigen Zustandes der Tonkunst in Wien', *Vaterländische Blätter*, 27 May 1808, pp. 39–44; 31 May 1808, pp. 49–54.

49 Hartmut Krones, ' "... Der schönste und wichtigste Zweck von allen ...": Das Conservatorium der "Gesellschaft der Musikfreunde des österreichischen Kaiserstaates" ', *Österreichische Musikzeitschrift*, 43 (1988), p. 66.

50 Jones, *The Symphony in Beethoven's Vienna*, pp. 126–8.

CHAPTER 7

Music, War and Peace

1 Charles Ingrao, *The Habsburg Monarchy 1618–1815* (Cambridge, 1994), pp. 220–3; C. A. Macartney, *The Habsburg Empire 1790–1918* (London, 1969), pp. 134–6.

2 *Deutsches Monument Ludwigs des Unglücklichen von J. Riedinger und im Klavier und Gesang gesetzt von Maria Theresia Paradis*. Exemplar: British Library, London, E.46.a. Marion Fürst, *Maria Theresia Paradis: Mozarts berühmte Zeitgenossin* (Cologne, 2005), pp. 148, 162–4.

3 Printed single sheet. Exemplar: Gesellschaft der Musikfreunde, Vienna, VI. 12809; Fürst, *Maria Theresia Paradis*, pp. 165–6.

4 Paul P. Bernard, *From the Enlightenment to the Police State: The Public Life of Johann Anton Pergen* (Urbana, 1991), pp. 186–95; Franz Hadamowsky, 'Ein Jahrhundert Literatur- und Theaterzensure in Österreich', *Die österreichische Literatur: Ihr Profil an der Wende vom 18. zum 19. Jahrhundert (1750–1830)*, 4 vols (Graz, 1979–89), ed. Herbert Zeman, vol. 1 (Graz, 1979), pp. 289–306.

5 Ernst Wangermann, *From Joseph II to the Jacobin Trials: Government Policy and Public Opinion in the Hapsburg Dominions in the Period of the French Revolution*, 2nd edn (Oxford, 1969), pp. 149–71.

6 Emily Anderson, ed., *The Letters of Beethoven*, 3 vols (London, 1961), vol. 1, p. 18; Sieghard Brandenburg, ed., *Ludwig van Beethoven: Briefwechsel Gesamtausgabe*, 7 vols (Munich, 1996–8), vol. 1 (Munich, 1996), p. 26.

7 Alexander Weinmann, *Verzeichnis der Musikalien des Verlages Joseph Eder – Jeremias Bermann*, Beiträge zur Geschichte des alt-Wiener Musikverlages, vol. 2/12 (Vienna, 1968), p. 2; Alexander Weinmann, *Vollständiges Verlagsverzeichnis Artaria & Comp.*, Beiträge zur Geschichte des Alt-Wiener Musikverlages, vol. 2/2 (Vienna, 1952), p. 45.

8 Exemplar: Gesellschaft der Musikfreunde, Vienna, III. 13461. This copy is from Archduke Rudolph's library, as indicated by the handwritten initial 'R'; my thanks to Ingrid Fuchs for pointing this out.

9 Mary Sue Morrow, *Concert Life in Haydn's Vienna: Aspects of a Developing Musical and Social Institution* (Stuyvesant, 1989), pp. 292–3.

10 *Der Retter in Gefahr; Eine Cantata von Rautenstrauch; In Musik und fürs Clavier gesetzt von F. X. Sussmayer*. Exemplar: Gesellschaft der Musikfreunde, Vienna, III. 9003.

11 Ignaz de Luca, *Topographie von Wien* (Vienna, 1794; facsimile edn, Vienna, 2003), p. 289.

12 Weinmann, *Verzeichnis der Musikalien des Verlages Joseph Eder*, p. 4.

13 Otto Biba, *Gott erhalte! Joseph Haydns Kaiserhymne* (Vienna, 1982), pp. 25–8; H. C. Robbins Landon, *Haydn: Chronicle and Works*, 5 vols (London 1976–80), vol. 4, *Haydn: the Years of 'The Creation' 1796–1800*, (London, 1977), pp. 241–9.

14 Weinmann, *Verzeichnis der Musikalien des Verlages Joseph Eder*, p. 2.

15 Otto Biba, 'Der Piaristenorden in Österreich: Seine Bedeutung für bildene Kunst, Musik und Theater im 17. und 18. Jahrhundert', *Jahrbuch für Österreichische Kulturgeschichte*, 5 (1975), pp. 128–9, 133–4.

16 Georg August Griesinger, *Biographische Notizen über Joseph Haydn* (Leipzig, 1809), p. 117.

17 David Wyn Jones, *The Symphony in Beethoven's Vienna* (Cambridge, 2006), pp. 90–2.

18 David Wyn Jones, 'Haydn, Austria and Britain: Music, Culture and Politics in the 1790s', *The Land of Opportunity: Joseph Haydn and Britain*, eds Richard Chesser and David Wyn Jones (London, 2013), pp. 16–20.

19 *Die große Seeschlacht bei Abukir vom 1ten bis 3ten August [1]798 eine charakterische Sonate fürs Clavier oder Piano Forte*. Exemplar: Gesellschaft der Musikfreunde, Vienna, VII. 73635; Alexander Weinmann, *Themen-Verzeichnis der Kompositionen von Johann Baptiste Wanhal*, 2 vols (Vienna, 1988), vol. 2, pp. 156–9.

20 C. A. Macartney, *The House of Austria: The Later Phase 1790–1918* (Edinburgh, 1978), pp. 29–31.

21 Birgit Lodes, '"Le congrès danse": Set Form and Improvisation in Beethoven's Polonaise for Piano, Op. 89', *The Musical Quarterly*, 93/3–4 (2010), pp. 415–18.

22 Jones, *The Symphony in Beethoven's Vienna*, pp. 92–5.

23 For the wider intellectual background see Mark Ferraguto, 'Beethoven *à la moujik*: Russianness and Learned Style in the "Razumovsky" String Quartets', *Journal of the American Musicological Society*, 67 (2014), pp. 101–12.

24 They are itemized in the list of goods and chattels compiled after Haydn's death: Landon, *Haydn: Chronicle and Works*, vol. 5, *Haydn: The Late Years 1801–1809* (London, 1977), p. 392.

25 Otto Erich Deutsch, *Admiral Nelson und Joseph Haydn: Ein britisch-österreichisches Gipfeltreffen* (Vienna, 1982), pp. 105–16.

26 David Rowland, 'Haydn's Music and Clementi's Publishing Circle', *The Land of Opportunity: Joseph Haydn and Britain*, eds Richard Chesser and David Wyn Jones (London, 2013), pp. 100–7.

27 Barry Cooper, 'The Clementi–Beethoven Contract of 1807: A Reinvestigation', *Muzio Clementi: Studies and Prospects*, eds Roberto Illiano, Luca Sala and Massimiliano Sala (Bologna, 2002), pp. 337–53.

28 John A. Rice, *Antonio Salieri and Viennese Opera* (Chicago, 1998), pp. 562–4.

29 Franz Hadamowsky, *Wien, Theatergeschichte: Von den Anfängen bis zum Ende des Ersten Weltkrieges* (Vienna, 1988), pp. 507–11.

30 Ibid., p. 522; Rice, *Antonio Salieri*, pp. 565–7. Full details of the repertory at the Burgtheater and Kärntnertortheater from 1802–3 onwards are given in Michael Jahn, *Die Wiener Hofoper von 1794 bis 1810: Musik und Tanz im Burg- und Kärnthnerthortheater* (Vienna, 2011), pp. 97–175.

31 Ingrao, *The Habsburg Monarchy*, p. 229.

32 Thomas Sipe, *Beethoven: Eroica Symphony* (Cambridge, 1998), pp. 44–8.

33 Jane Schatkin Hettrick, 'Music in the Celebrations of Franz's 1804 Assumption of the Austrian *Kaiserwürde*, as reported in the *Wiener Zeitung*', *Figaro Là, Figaro Quà: Gedenkschrift Leopold M. Kantner (1932–2004)*, eds Michael Jahn and Angela Pachovsky (Vienna, 2006), pp. 223–35.

34 Jahn, *Die Wiener Hofoper*, p. 119.

35 *Remembering Beethoven: The Biographical Notes of Franz Wegeler and Ferdinand Ries*, trans. of *Biographische Notizen über Ludwig van Beethoven* (Koblenz, 1838, 1845) by Frederick Noonan (London, 1988), p. 68.

36 Walther Brauneis, ' "... composta per festiggare il sovvenire di un grand Uomo." Beethovens "Eroica" als Hommage des Fürsten Franz Joseph Maximilian von Lobkowitz für Louis Ferdinand von Preußen', *Jahrbuch des Vereins für Geschichte der Stadt Wien*, 52–3 (1996–7), pp. 59–66, 69–70.

37 Sipe, *Eroica Symphony*, pp. 30–51.

38 Ingrao, *The Habsburg Monarchy*, p. 229.

39 Landon, *Haydn: the Late Years*, pp. 334–5.

40 Jahn, *Die Wiener Hofoper*, pp. 243–7.

41 Wolfgang Hochstein, 'Cherubini', *Die Musik in Geschichte und Gegenwart*, 2nd edn, ed. Ludwig Finscher, Personenteil, vol. 4 (Kassel, 2000), col. 858.

42 Ingrao, *The Habsburg Monarchy*, pp. 234–6; Macartney, *The Habsburg Empire*, pp. 185–7.

43 Landon, *Haydn: the Late Years*, pp. 360–1.

44 *Lieder mit Melodien für die Oesterreichische Landwehre. Von H. J. v. Collin. Im Musik gesetzt von Joseph Weigl* (Vienna, 1809); preface dated 28 September 1808. Exemplar: Österreichische Nationalbibliothek, 27516-B; digital version via online catalogue at <www.onb.ac.at>.

45 *Wiener Zeitung*, 8 March 1809.

46 Johann Friedrich Reichardt, *Vertraute Briefe: geschrieben auf einer Reise nach Wien und den Österreichischen Staaten zu Ende des Jahres 1808 und zu Anfang 1809*, ed. Gustav Gugitz, 2 vols (Munich, 1915), vol. 2, pp. 58–9.

47 A facsimilie of Beethoven's autograph draft is given in Wilfried Seipel, ed., *Die Botschaft der Musik: 1000 Jahre Musik in Österreich*, exhibition catalogue (Vienna, 1996), pp. 22–3.

48 Hugo Schmidt, 'The Origins of the Austrian National Anthem and Austria's Literary War Effort', *Austria in the Age of the French Revolution 1789–1815*, eds Kinley Brauer and William E. Wright (Minneapolis, 1990), pp. 176, 178–9.

49 Morrow, *Concert Life*, pp. 354–5.

50 Jahn, *Die Wiener Hofoper*, p. 160.

51 Alexander Weinmann, *Verlagsverzeichnis Giovanni Cappi bis A. O. Witzendorf*, Beiträge zur Geschichte des alt-Wiener Musikverlages, vol. 2/11 (Vienna, 1967), p. 39.

52 Else Radant, ed., 'The Diaries of Joseph Carl Rosenbaum 1770–1829', *Haydn Yearbook*, 5 (1968), p. 151; Landon, *Haydn: the Late Years*, pp. 385–6, 388–9.

53 Jahn, *Die Wiener Hofoper*, pp. 469–75.

54 Morrow, *Concert Life*, pp. 357–8.

55 Elliot Forbes, ed., *Thayer's Life of Beethoven* (Princeton, 1964), pp. 470–1.

56 Ingrao, *The Habsburg Monarchy*, pp. 236–9; Macartney, *The Habsburg Empire*, p. 189; Walter Kleindel, *Österreich: Zahlen, Daten, Fakten*, 5th edn (Salzburg, 2004), p. 223.

57 L. Poundie Burstein, ' " Lebe wohl tönt überall!" and a "Reunion after So Much Sorrow": Beethoven's Op. 81a and the Journeys of 1809', *The Musical Quarterly*, 93/3–4 (2010), pp. 382–5, 392–9.

58 *Die Feyer der Rückkehr unsers allgeliebten Monarchen Franz I. am 29ten November 1809 für das Forte Piano in Musik gesetzt und allen Patrioten gewidmet von Johann Wanhal*. Exemplar: Gesellschaft der Musikfreunde, Vienna. VII. 16575.

59 Jahn, *Die Wiener Hofoper*, pp. 166, 362.

60 Vanhal, *Fantasie: Glückwunsch zur Vermählung und Abreise Ihrer Kais. Königl. Majestät Maria Kaiserin von Frankreich* (published by Weigl); Preindl, *Hymne zur Vermählungs-Feyer Ihrer Kais. Hoheit der Erzherzogin Lousie M. S. Maj. Napoleon* (published by Mollo); Gyrowetz, *Die Wonne der Nationen* (published by Chemische Druckerey).

61 Julia Moore, 'Beethoven and Inflation', *Beethoven Forum*, 1 (1992), pp. 199–204; Macartney, *The Habsburg Empire*, pp. 194–8.

62 Hadamowsky, *Wien, Theater Geschichte*, pp. 313–21.

63 Alexander Weinmann, 'Vollständiges Verlagsverzeichnis der Musikalien des Kunst- und Industrie-Comptoirs in Wien, 1801–1819', *Studien zur Musikwissenschaft*, 22 (1955), pp. 242–3; Alexander Weinmann, *Verlagsverzeichnis Tranquillo Mollo (mit und ohne Co.)*, Beiträge zur Geschichte des alt-Wiener Musikverlages, vol. 2/9 (Vienna, 1964), pp. 61–4; Weinmann, *Verzeichnis der Musikalien des Verlages Joseph Eder*, pp. VIII, 28–31.

64 Ingrao, *The Habsburg Monarchy*, pp. 238–41.

65 Morrow, *Concert Life*, pp. 356–97; Forbes, ed., *Thayer's Life of Beethoven*, pp. 559–60.

66 Forbes, ed., *Thayer's Life of Beethoven*, pp. 564–7.

67 Michael Ladenburger, 'Der Wiener Kongreß im Spiegel der Musik', *Beethoven: Zwischen Revolution und Restauration*, eds Helga Lühning and Sieghard Brandenburg (Bonn, 1989), pp. 293, 298–9; Nicholas Mathew, *Political Beethoven* (Cambridge, 2013), pp. 184–5, 169–70.

68 Ladenburger, 'Der Wiener Kongreß', pp. 282–5.

69 See list of events in Elisabeth Fritz-Hilscher, 'Musik und Musikleben rund um den Wiener Kongress (1814/15) aus der Sicht einiger Zeitzeugen', *Studien zur Musikwissenschaft*, 57 (2013), pp. 236–9.

70 Mathew, *Political Beethoven*, pp. 71–81.

71 Ignaz von Mosel, 'Skizze einer musikalischen Bildungsanstalt für die Haupt- und Residenzstadt des österreichischen Kaiserstaats', *Vaterländische Blätter*, 2 February 1811, pp. 57–9; 6 February 1811, pp. 64–6.

72 Eduard Hanslick, *Geschichte des Concertwesens in Wien* (Vienna, 1869), pp. 179–80; Max Vancza, 'Ein Alt-Wiener Konzertsaal. (Der Sitzung des n.ö. Landhauses.) Ein Beitrag zur Geschichte des Konzertwesens im Wien des Vormärz', *Musikbuch aus Österreich: Ein Jahrbuch der Musikpflege in Österreich und den bedeutendsten Musikstädten des Auslandes*, 1 (1904), p. 39.

73 Richard von Perger, *Geschichte der K. K. Gesellschaft der Musikfreunde in Wien. I. Abteilung: 1812–1870* (Vienna, 1912), pp. 5–6.

74 *Allgemeine musikalische Zeitung*, 14 (1812), cols 226–7.

75 Peter Csendes, ed., *Oesterreich 1790–1848: Das Tagebuch einer Epoche* (Vienna, 1987), p. 113.

76 *Allgemeine musikalische Zeitung*, 14 (1812), col. 772.

77 Ibid., cols 851–4.

78 Sonja Gerlach, 'Johann Tost, Geiger und Grosshandlungsgremialist', *Haydn-Studien*, 7/3–4 (1998), pp. 353–5.

79 Perger, *Geschichte der K. K. Gesellschaft der Musikfreunde*, pp. 7–8.

80 Given in full in Eusebius Mandyczewski, *Zusatz-Band zur Geschichte der K. K. Gesellschaft der Musikfreunde in Wien: Sammlungen und Statuten* (Vienna, 1912), pp. 189–96.

81 Ibid., pp. 197–215.

82 Perger, *Geschichte der K. K. Gesellschaft der Musikfreunde*, pp. 323–8.

83 Hanslick, *Geschichte des Concertwesens in Wien*, pp. 139–63; Jones, *The Symphony in Beethoven's Vienna*, pp. 184–5.

84 Otto Biba and Ingrid Fuchs, *"Die Emporbringung der Musik": Höhepunkte aus der Geschichte und aus dem Archiv der Gesellschaft der Musikfreunde in Wien* (Vienna, 2012), pp. 22–3.

CHAPTER 8

Vienna, City of Music

1 *Fromme's Musikalische Welt: Notiz-Kalender für das Jahr [1876–1901]*, 26 vols, ed. Theodor Helm (Vienna, 1875–1900).

2 *Musikbuch aus Österreich: Ein Jahrbuch der Musikpflege in Österreich und den bedeutendsten Musikstädten des Auslandes*, 10 vols, eds Richard Heuberger

(vols 1–3), Hugo Botstiber (vols 4–8) and Josef Reitler (vols 9–10) (Leipzig, 1904–1913).

3 La Mara, 'Briefe alter Wiener Hofmusiker', *Musikbuch*, 6 (1909), pp. 3–25; *Musikbuch*, 7 (1910), pp. 3–24; Eusebius Mandyczewski, 'Die Bibliothek Brahms', *Musikbuch*, 1 (1904), pp. 7–17; Ludwig Karpath, 'Richard Wagners Wohnhäuser in Wien', *Musikbuch*, 6 (1909), pp. 45–54.

4 Sandra McColl, *Music Criticism in Vienna 1896–1897: Critically Moving Forms* (Oxford, 1996), pp. 20–4.

5 On the history of the term see Lutz Musner, *Der Geschmack von Wien: Kultur und Habitus einer Stadt* (Frankfurt, 2009), pp. 143–53.

6 Peter Csendes and Ferdinand Opll (eds), *Wien: Geschichte einer Stadt*, 3 vols (Vienna, 2000–6), vol. 3, *Von 1790 bis zur Gegenwart* (Vienna, 2006), pp. 16–18, 177–8.

7 Ibid., pp. 66–8, 178–80; Michaela Pfunder, ed., *Wien wird Weltstadt: Die Ringstrasse und ihre Zeit* (Vienna, 2015); Carl E. Schorske, *Fin-de-Siècle Vienna: Politics and Culture* (Cambridge, 1981), pp. 24–115.

8 Karl Baedeker, *Austria-Hungary with Excursions to Cetinje, Belgrade, and Bucharest: Handbook for Travellers*, 11th edn (Leipzig, 1911).

9 Csendes and Opll, eds, *Wien*, vol. 3, pp. 872–4.

10 Ibid., p. 178.

11 See the summary lists in Wilhelm Beetz, *Das Wiener Opernhaus 1869 bis 1955*, 2nd edn (Zurich, 1955), pp. 209–13.

12 John Tyrrell, *Janáček: Years of a Life*, 2 vols (London, 2006–7), vol. 2, *1914–28: Tsar of the Forests* (London, 2007), pp. 61, 148, 150–2, 162–3, 179, 208–26.

13 Walter Kleindel, *Österreich: Zahlen, Daten, Fakten*, 5th edn (Salzburg, 2004), p. 279; Paula Sutter Fichtner, *The Habsburgs: Dynasty, Culture and Politics* (London, 2014), pp. 191–5.

14 Steven Beller, *Vienna and the Jews 1867–1938: A Cultural History* (Cambridge, 1989), pp. 37–40; Leon Botstein, 'Einführung: Tragödie und Ironie des Erfolgs: Juden in Wiener Musikleben' and 'Sozialgeschichte und die Politik des Ästhetischen: Juden und Musik in Wien 1870–1938', *quasi una fantasia: Juden und die Musikstadt Wien*, eds Leon Botstein and Werner Hanak (Vienna, 2003), pp. 11–20, 43–63; Csendes and Opll, eds, *Wien*, vol. 3, pp. 273–87.

15 *Musikbuch*, 4 (1907), p. 121; Michael Jahn, 'Klassische Traditionen im 19. Jahrhundert', *Die Wiener Hofmusikkapelle III: Gibt es einen Stil der Hofmusikkapelle?*, eds Hartmut Krones, Theophil Antonicek and Elisabeth Theresia Fritz-Hilscher (Vienna, 2011), pp. 287–95.

16 Richard Steurer, *Das Repertoire der Wiener Hofmusikkapelle im neunzehnten Jahrhundert* (Tutzing, 1998), pp. 161–71, 508–639.

17 Erich Wolfgang Partsch, 'Die Hofmusikkapelle in der zweiten Hälfte des 19. Jahrhunderts', *Musica Imperialis: 500 Jahre Hofmusikkapelle in Wien 1498–1998*, ed. Günter Brosche et al, exhibition catalogue (Tutzing, 1998), pp. 151–70; Theophil Antonicek and Karlheinz Schenk, '1900–1918: Die Wiener Hofmusikkapelle im Abendrot der untergehenden Monarchie', ibid., pp. 175–84.

18 Maria Winkelhofer, *The Everyday Life of the Emperor: Francis Joseph and his Imperial Court* (Innsbruck, 2012), pp. 102–13.

19 Franz Hadamowsky, *Wien, Theatergeschichte: Von den Anfängen bis zum Ende des Ersten Weltkrieges* (Vienna, 1988), pp. 430–2; Beetz, *Das Wiener Opernhaus*, pp. 21–38, 47–54.

20 Beetz, *Das Wiener Opernhaus*, pp. 168–83; *Fromme's Musikalische Welt 1895*, p. 85.

21 *Fromme's Musikalische Welt 1895*, p. 169.

22 Beetz, *Das Wiener Opernhaus*, p. 57.

23 Henry-Louis de La Grange, *Gustav Mahler*, 4 vols (Oxford 1995–), vol. 2, *Vienna: the Years of Challenge (1897–1904)* (Oxford, 1995), pp. 20–2, 24–6, 41–7, 50–4.

24 *Fromme's Musikalische Welt 1900*, p. 55; *Fromme's Musikalische Welt 1899*, pp. 59–60.

25 La Grange, *Gustav Mahler*, vol. 3, *Vienna: Triumph and Disillusion (1904–1907)* (Oxford, 1999), pp. 247–53.

26 Otto Biba and Ingrid Fuchs, *"Die Emporbringung der Musik": Höhepunkte aus der Geschichte und aus dem Archiv der Gesellschaft der Musikfreunde in Wien* (Vienna, 2012), pp. 66–7.

27 *Fromme's Musikalische Welt 1895*, p. 68; *Musikbuch*, 4 (1907), p. 115.

28 *Fromme's Musikalische Welt 1895*, pp. 165, 159.

29 Edward R. Reilly, *Gustav Mahler and Guido Adler: Records of a Friendship* (Cambridge, 1982), pp. 100–3.

30 Hartmut Krones, ' "... Der schönste und wichtigste Zweck von Allen ...": Das Conservatorium der "Gesellschaft der Musikfreunde des österreichischen Kaiserstaates" ', *Österreichische Musikzeitschrift*, 43 (1988), pp. 80–1.

31 *Fromme's Musikalische Welt 1895*, p. 165.

32 *Fromme's Musikalische Welt 1898*, p. 112; *Fromme's Musikalische Welt 1900*, p. 89; *Musikbuch*, 5 (1908), p. 91; *Musikbuch*, 7 (1910), pp. 76–7.

33 *Musikbuch*, 4 (1907), p. 71; *Musikbuch*, 6 (1909), p. 90.

34 Clemens Hellsberg, *Demokratie der Könige: Die Geschichte der Wiener Philharmoniker* (Zurich, 1992), pp. 9–34, 117–28, 205–92.

35 Ibid., pp. 368–70.

36 *Musikbuch*, 4 (1907), pp. 115–16; Baedeker, *Austria-Hungary*, preliminary page.

37 Hellsberg, *Demokratie der Könige*, pp. 305–9.

38 See the catalogue of completed works in La Grange, *Gustav Mahler*, vol. 4, *A New Life Cut Short (1907–11)*, (Oxford, 2008), pp. 1280–5.

39 *Musikbuch*, 5 (1908), p. 88.

40 *Musikbuch*, 9 (1912), p. 99.

41 La Grange, *Gustav Mahler*, vol. 2, pp. 133, 188.

42 *Fromme's Musikalische Welt 1901*, pp. 92–3.

43 *Musikbuch*, 2 (1905), p. 68; *Musikbuch*, 4 (1907), p. 69; *Musikbuch*, 10 (1913), p. 100.

44 *Musikbuch*, 1 (1904), p. 93; *Musikbuch*, 2 (1905), p. 68; *Musikbuch*, 4 (1907), p. 69; *Musikbuch*, 6 (1909), pp. 74, 86–7; *Musikbuch*, 9 (1912), p. 99; *Musikbuch*, 10 (1913), p. 100.

45 *Musikbuch*, 5 (1908), p. 143.

46 *Musikbuch*, 9 (1912), pp. 97–9.

47 *Fromme's Musikalische Welt 1899*, pp. 104–5.

48 Hadamowsky, *Wien, Theatergeschichte*, pp. 618–22; Camille Crittenden, *Johann Strauss and Vienna: Operetta and the Politics of Popular Culture* (Cambridge, 2000), pp. 63–5.

49 *Fromme's Musikalische Welt 1895*, p. 169.

50 *Fromme's Musikalische Welt 1895*, p. 168; *Musikbuch*, 4 (1907), p. 118.

51 Hadamowsky, *Wien, Theatergeschichte*, pp. 599–615; Crittenden, *Johann Strauss and Vienna*, pp. 66–7; *Fromme's Musikalische Welt 1895*, p. 169.

52 Hadamowsky, *Wien, Theatergeschichte*, pp. 529, 542–3; Crittenden, *Johann Strauss and Vienna*, pp. 67–9.

53 Hadamowsky, *Wien, Theatergeschichte*, pp. 642–4; *Fromme's Musikalische Welt 1895*, p. 169.

54 Hadamowsky, *Wien, Theatergeschichte*, pp. 751–8.

55 Ibid., pp. 759–61.

56 Antony Beaumont, *Zemlinsky* (Ithaca, 2000), pp. 135–6.

57 Richard Kurdiovsky, 'Architektur für die "moderne" Großstadt zwischen Sport, Kunst und Geselligkeit: Zur Entstehung des Wiener Konzerthauses', *Österreichische Musikzeitschrift*, 68/5 (2013), pp. 6–15.

CHAPTER 9

'Seid umschlungen, Millionen'

1 *Fromme's Musikalische Welt: Notiz-Kalender für das Jahr 1901*, ed. Theodor Helm (Vienna, 1900), p. 92.

2 Henry-Louis de La Grange, *Gustav Mahler*, 4 vols (Oxford 1995–), vol. 2, *Vienna: the Years of Challenge (1897–1904)* (Oxford, 1995), pp. 232–7.

3 *Fromme's Musikalische Welt 1900*, pp. 84–5.

4 *Fromme's Musikalische Welt 1901*, pp. 91–2.

5 La Grange, *Gustav Mahler*, vol. 2, p. 315.

6 La Grange, *Gustav Mahler*, vol. 3, *Vienna: Triumph and Disillusion (1904–1907)* (Oxford, 1999), pp. 1–14.

7 *Fromme's Musikalische Welt 1899*, p. 63.

8 *Fromme's Musikalische Welt 1898*, p. 148.

9 H. H. Stuckenschmidt, *Schönberg: Leben, Umwelt, Werk* (Zurich, 1974), pp. 30, 32.

10 Leonard Stein, ed., *Style and Idea: Selected Writings of Arnold Schoenberg*, trans. Leo Black (London, 1975), p. 329.

11 *Fromme's Musikalische Welt 1898*, p. 105.

12 Hannes Heer, 'All rotten, treacherous – and so crude: Richard Wagner's view of Vienna', *Euphorie und Unbehagen: Das jüdische Wien und Richard Wagner*, ed. Andrea Winklbauer (Vienna, 2013), pp. 37–42.

13 Wilhelm Beetz, *Das Wiener Opernhaus 1869 bis 1955*, 2nd edn (Zurich, 1955), pp. 180–2.

14 Stuckenschmidt, *Schönberg*, p. 32.

15 *Fromme's Musikalische Welt 1895*, pp. 229–30.

16 Monika Sommer and Alexandra Steiner-Strauss, 'Richard Wagner's traces in Vienna', *Euphorie und Unbehagen: Das jüdische Wien und Richard Wagner*, ed. Andrea Winklbauer (Vienna, 2013), pp. 159–60.

17 Beetz, *Das Wiener Opernhaus*, pp. 176, 178; Liselotte Regler, 'Hans Gregor – Die Ära des letzten Hofoperndirektors in Wien' (Ph.D. diss., University of Vienna, 2010), pp. 113, 274.

18 *Fromme's Musikalische Welt 1900*, p. 84; *Fromme's Musikalische Welt 1901*, p. 99.

19 *Musikbuch aus Österreich: Ein Jahrbuch der Musikpflege in Österreich und den bedeutendsten Musikstädten des Auslandes*, 1 (1904), p. 93; *Musikbuch*, 3 (1906), p. 86; *Musikbuch*, 5 (1908), p. 89.

20 *Musikbuch*, 8 (1911), p. 88.

21 *Fromme's Musikalische Welt 1893*, pp. 116, 96, 145.

22 *Fromme's Musikalische Welt 1893*, p. 119; *Musikbuch*, 4 (1907), p. 68.

23 *Fromme's Musikalische Welt 1900*, p. 89; *Musikbuch*, 8 (1911), p. 91. For performances of Mozart's Requiem in the Hofkapelle, including commemorative performances for several emperors and empresses, see Richard Steurer, *Das Repertoire der Wiener Hofmusikkapelle im neunzehnten Jahrhundert* (Tutzing, 1998), pp. 95–7.

24 Listed in *Musikbuch*, 5 (1908), p. 140.

25 Otto Biba, *Gott erhalte! Joseph Haydns Kaiserhymne* (Vienna, 1982), pp. 21–3.

26 *Fromme's Musikalische Welt 1900*, p. 84.

27 *Fromme's Musikalische Welt 1898*, p. 105; *Musikbuch*, 4 (1907), p. 69; *Musikbuch*, 6 (1909), p. 86; *Musikbuch*, 9 (1912), p. 99.

28 *Musikbuch*, 7 (1910), pp. 70–2.

29 Ibid., pp. 69–70.

30 *Neue Freie Presse*, 22 May 1809.

31 Otto Biba and Ingrid Fuchs, *"Die Emporbringung der Musik": Höhepunkte aus der Geschichte und aus dem Archiv der Gesellschaft der Musikfreunde in Wien* (Vienna, 2012), pp. 74–5.

32 Richard von Perger, 'Brahms's letzte Tage', *Musikbuch*, 5 (1908), pp. 41–5.

33 Stefan Zweig, *The World of Yesterday* (Nebraska, Lincoln, 1964), pp. 16–17. Zweig's account is faulty in one respect. Since the hall was opened in 1872, twenty-three years after Chopin's death, he could not have played there; his piano music, however, was a constant presence. Date and programme of concert from *Fremden Blatt*, 3 May 1913.

34 Biba and Fuchs, *"Die Emporbringung der Musik"*, pp. 90–1.

35 Eusebius Mandyczewski, 'Die Bibliothek Brahms', *Musikbuch*, 1 (1904), pp. 7–17.

36 Karl Baedecker, *Austria-Hungary with Excursions to Cetinje, Belgrade, and Bucharest: Handbook for Travellers*, 11th edn (Leipzig, 1911), p. 52.

37 Zweig, *The World of Yesterday*, pp. 161–2.

38 See survey in Sandra McColl, *Music Criticism in Vienna 1896–1897: Critically Moving Forms* (Oxford, 1996), pp. 11–32.

39 Clemens Hellsberg, *Demokratie der Könige: Die Geschichte der Wiener Philharmoniker* (Zurich, 1992), p. 258.

40 Stein, ed., *Style and Idea*, p. 196.

41 Edward R. Reilly, *Gustav Mahler and Guido Adler: Records of a Friendship* (Cambridge, 1982), pp. 80–1.

42 Carl Ferdinand Pohl, *Joseph Haydn*, vol. 1 (Berlin, 1875), vol. 2 (Leipzig, 1882), vol. 3, completed by Hugo Botstiber (Leipzig, 1927); Eduard Hanslick, *Geschichte des Concertwesens in Wien* (Vienna, 1869); Carl Ferdinand Pohl, *Die Gesellschaft der Musikfreunde des österreichischen Kaiserstaates und ihr Conservatorium* (Vienna, 1871).

43 Elisabeth Th. Hilscher, *Denkmalpflege und Musikwissenschaft: Einhundert Jahre Gesellschaft zur Herausgabe der Tonkunst in Österreich (1893–1993)* (Tutzing, 1995), pp. 45–55.

44 Given ibid, pp. 221–3.

45 Ibid., p. 273.

46 Ibid. pp. 56–78, 247–56.

47 Reilly, *Gustav Mahler and Guido Adler*, pp. 93, 98.

48 *Denkmäler der Tonkunst in Österreich*, vol. 1/1 (Vienna, 1894), p. V.

49 Theophil Antonicek, 'Musikwissenschaft in Wien zur Zeit Guido Adlers', *Studien zur Musikwissenschaft*, 37 (1986), pp. 171–81.

50 Guido Adler, 'Umfang, Methode und Ziel der Musikwissenschaft', *Vierteljahrsschrift für Musikwissenschaft*, 1 (1885), pp. 5–20.

51 For this and similar patriotic publications, see Paula Sutter Fichtner, *The Habsburgs: Dynasty, Culture and Politics* (London, 2014), pp. 210–19.

52 *Musikbuch*, 9 (1911), pp. 140–3.

53 John Tyrrell, *Janáček: Years of a Life*, 2 vols (London, 2006–7), vol. 1, *1854–1914: The Lonely Blackbird* (London, 2006), pp. 627–8, 642, 655–8, 673, 725–6, 743, 757–8, 785–6, 815.

54 Franz Mailer, ed., *Johann Strauss (Sohn): Leben und Werk in Briefen und Dokumenten*, 10 vols (Tutzing, 1983–2007), vol. 5, *1890–91* (Tutzing, 1996), pp. 369–70.

55 Mailer, ed., *Johann Strauss (Sohn)*, vol. 6, *1892–93* (Tutzing, 1996), pp. 82–3.

56 Ibid., vol. 6, pp. 62–3.

57 Ibid., vol. 6, pp. 160–2.

From Johann Strauss to Richard Strauss

1 Franz Mailer, ed., *Johann Strauss (Sohn): Leben und Werk in Briefen und Dokumenten*, 10 vols (Tutzing, 1983–2007), vol. 9, *1898–99* (Tutzing, 2002), pp. 256–62, 328.

2 Helmut Kretschmer, 'Strauß-Stätten', *Johann Strauss: Unter Donner und Blitz*, ed. Otto Brusatti, exhibition catalogue (Vienna, 1999), pp. 203–5.

3 For a complementary set of differences, see Camille Crittenden, *Johann Strauss and Vienna: Operetta and the Politics of Popular Culture* (Cambridge, 2000), p. 10.

4 *Fromme's Musikalische Welt: Notiz-Kalender für das Jahr 1896*, ed. Theodor Helm (Vienna, 1895), pp. 74–5. *Fromme's Musikalische Welt 1895* had contained an article on Johann Strauss, marking the fiftieth anniversary of his

debut as the director of his own orchestra: Theodor Helm, 'Johann Strauss: Zum 50. jährigen Künstlerjubiläum des "Walzerkönigs"', pp. 39–45.

5 Henry-Louis de La Grange, *Gustav Mahler*, 4 vols (Oxford 1995–), vol. 2, *Vienna: the Years of Challenge (1897–1904)* (Oxford, 1995), pp. 83–4.

6 Ibid., p. 473.

7 From 'Brahms the Progressive', in Leonard Stein, ed., *Style and Idea: Selected Writings of Arnold Schoenberg*, trans. Leo Black (London, 1975), p. 415.

8 Mailer, ed., *Briefen und Dokumenten*, vol. 9, *1898–99* (Tutzing, 2002), pp. 332–3.

9 Marion Linhardt, *Residenzstadt und Metropole: Zu einer kulturellen Topographie des Wiener Unterhaltungstheaters (1858–1918)* (Tübingen, 2006), pp. 277, 288.

10 Franz Hadamowsky, *Wien, Theatergeschichte: Von den Anfängen bis zum Ende des Ersten Weltkriegs* (Vienna, 1988), pp. 770–2.

11 Linhardt, *Residenzstadt und Metropole*, pp. 277, 281–2.

12 Anton Mayer, *Franz Lehár – Die lustige Witwe: Der Ernst der leichten Muse* (Vienna, 2005), pp. 59–60.

13 Linhardt, *Residenzstadt und Metropole*, tables on pp. 276–82, 267–9.

14 Ibid., p. 277.

15 William M. Johnston, *The Austrian Mind: An Intellectual and Social History 1848–1938* (Berkeley, 1972), pp. 19–23.

16 Otto Erich Deutsch, 'Leopold von Sonnleithners Erinnerungen an die Musiksalons des Vormärzlichen Wiens', *Österreichische Musikzeitschrift*, 16/3 (1961), p. 50.

17 See the collection of essays in Wolfgang Kos and Christian Rapp, eds, *Alt-Wien: Die Stadt die niemals war*, exhibition catalogue (Vienna, 2004).

18 Renata Kassal-Mikula, 'Alt-Wien unter dem Demolierungskrampen: Wiens Innenstadt nach 1858', *Alt-Wien*, eds Kos and Rapp, pp. 46–61.

19 Christian Glanz, 'Himmelblaue Zeit: Alt-Wien in der Operette', *Alt-Wien*, eds Kos and Rapp, pp. 228–34; Linhardt, *Residenzstadt und Metropole*, pp. 276, 280.

20 Ursula Storch, 'Alt-Wien dreidimensional: Die Altstadt als Themenpark', *Alt-Wien*, eds Kos and Rapp, pp. 160–2.

21 Péter Hanák, *The Garden and the Workshop: Essays on the Cultural History of Vienna and Budapest* (Princeton, 1998), pp. 137–40.

22 Moritz Csáky, *Ideologie der Operette und Wiener Moderne: Ein kulturhistorischer Essay*, 2nd rev. edn (Vienna, 1998), pp. 74–5, 79–81.

23 Karl Kraus, *Pro domo et mundo* (Munich, 1912), p. 116.

24 *Franz Lehár, Die lustige Witwe*, ed. Norbert Rubey (Vienna, 2005), p. ix.

25 Karl Baedecker, *Austria-Hungary with Excursions to Cetinje, Belgrade, and Bucharest: Handbook for Travellers*, 11th edn (Leipzig, 1911), pp. 411–14.

26 Csáky, *Ideologie der Operette*, pp. 89–100; Micaela Baranello, '*Die lustige Witwe* and the Creation of the Silver Age of Viennese Operetta', *Cambridge Opera Journal*, 26/2 (2014), p. 187.

27 Csáky, *Ideologie der Operette*, pp. 129–31.

28 Stefan Zweig, *The World of Yesterday* (Lincoln, Nebraska, 1964), pp. 85–6.

29 Csáky, *Ideologie der Operette*, pp. 125–34.

30 *Musikbuch aus Österreich: Ein Jahrbuch der Musikpflege in Österreich und den bedeutendsten Musikstädten des Auslandes*, 8 (1911), pp. 86–8.

31 Carl E. Schorske, *Fin-de-Siècle Vienna: Politics and Culture* (Cambridge, 1981), pp. 212–14.

32 Ibid., pp. 214–25; Christian Brandstätter, ed., *Wien 1900: Kunst und Kultur, Fokus der europäischen Moderne* (Vienna 2005), pp. 19–119. La Grange, *Gustav Mahler*, vol. 2, pp. 502–8.

33 La Grange, *Gustav Mahler*, vol. 2, p. 512.

34 Ibid., vol. 2, pp. 512–14.

35 Antony Beaumont, *Zemlinsky* (Ithaca, 2000), pp. 130–4.

36 Details of the programmes are given in *Musikbuch*, 3 (1906), p. 101; see also La Grange, *Gustav Mahler*, vol. 3, *Vienna: Triumph and Disillusion (1904–1907)* (Oxford, 1999), pp. 124–5.

37 *Musikbuch*, 7 (1910), p. 84.

38 *Neue Freie Presse*, 22 December 1908, translation from Ursula von Rauchhaupt, *Schoenberg, Berg, Webern: The String Quartets, A Documentary Study* (Hamburg, 1971), p. 142; Darla M. Crispin, 'Arnold Schoenberg's Wounded Work: "Litanei" from The String Quartet in F sharp minor, Op. 10', *Austrian Studies*, 17 (2009), pp. 62–6.

39 Otto Biba and Ingrid Fuchs, *"Die Emporbringung der Musik": Höhepunkte aus der Geschichte und aus dem Archiv der Gesellschaft der Musikfreunde in Wien* (Vienna, 2012), pp. 92–3; Beaumont, *Zemlinsky*, pp. 225–6.

40 *Fromme's Musikalische Welt 1896*, pp. 108–9.

41 Performed on 19 November 1899: *Fromme's Musikalische Welt 1901*, p. 92.

42 Clemens Hellsberg, *Demokratie der Könige: Die Geschichte der Wiener Philharmoniker* (Zurich, 1992), p. 342.

43 *Musikbuch*, 5 (1908), p. 88.

44 *Musikbuch*, 6 (1909), p. 87.

45 Wilhelm Beetz, *Das Wiener Opernhaus 1869–1955*, 2nd edn (Zurich, 1955), p. 170; <www.gustavmahler.org/mahler/hofoper> (accessed 28 March 2015).

46 La Grange, *Gustav Mahler*, vol. 3, p. 656.

47 Beaumont, *Zemlinsky*, p. 186.

48 Ibid., p. 187.

49 Fredrik Lindström, *Empire and Identity: Biographies of the Austrian State Problem in the Late Habsburg Empire* (West Lafayette, 2008), pp. 105–35.

50 Arnold Klaffenböck, 'Literarische Positionen zu Alt-Wien: Alt-Wien 1880–1930', *Alt-Wien*, eds Kos and Rapp, pp. 219–24; Schorske, *Fin-de-Siècle Vienna*, pp. 15–22.

51 Selma Krasa-Florian, 'Maria Theresia in Denkmalskult', *Maria Theresia und ihre Zeit: Eine Darstellung der Epoche von 1740–1780 aus Anlaß der 200. Wiederkehr des Todestages der Kaiserin*, ed. Walter Koschatzky (Salzburg, 1979), pp. 450–3.

52 Linhardt, *Residenzstadt und Metropole*, p. 280.

53 Letter of 24 April 1909, in *A Working Friendship: The Correspondence between Richard Strauss and Hugo von Hofmannsthal*, trans. Hanns Hammelmann and Ewald Osers, introduction by Edward Sackville-West (London, 1961), p. 30.

54 Günter Brosche, 'Musical Quotations and Allusions in the Work of Richard Strauss', *Cambridge Companion to Richard Strauss*, ed. Charles Youmans (Cambridge, 2010), pp. 217–18.

55 Letter of 12 May 1909, in *A Working Friendship*, p. 31.

56 Letter of 1 January 1910, on display in exhibition '"Trägt die Sprache schon Gesang in sich …": Richard Strauss und die Oper', Theatermuseum, Vienna, 12 June 2014 – 9 February 2015.

57 Letters of 10 October 1910 and 12 October 1910, in *A Working Friendship*, pp. 66–8.

58 *Musikbuch*, 9 (1912), pp. 95–6; Beetz, *Das Wiener Opernhaus*, p. 178.

59 *Neue Freie Presse*, 9 April 1911; trans. from Leon Botstein, 'Richard Strauss and the Viennese Critics (1896–1924): Reviews by Gustav Schoenaich, Robert Hirschfeld, Guido Adler, Max Kalbeck, Julius Korngold and Karl Kraus', *Richard Strauss and his World*, ed. Bryan Gilliam (Princeton, 1992), p. 358.

60 Liselotte Regler, 'Hans Gregor – Die Ära des letzten Hofoperndirektors in Wien' (Ph.D. diss., University of Vienna, 2010), pp. 120–5.

Bibliography

On-line resources

Allgemeine musikalische Zeitung: <www.archive.org>, <www.google.de>

Mahler at the Vienna Court Opera (1897–1907): <www.gustavmahler.org/mahler/hofoper>

The Vienna Singakademie: <www.wienersingakademie.at>

The Vienna Singverein: <www.singverein.at>

Viennese newspapers including the *Fremden Blatt, Neue Freie Presse, Vaterländische Blätter, Wienerisches Diarium* and *Wiener Zeitung*: <www.anno.onb.ac.at>

Printed material

Adler, Guido, 'Die Kaiser Ferdinand III., Leopold I., Joseph I., und Karl VI. als Tonsetzer und Forderer der Musik', *Vierteljahrsschrift für Musikwissenschaft*, 8 (1892), pp. 252–74

—— *Musikalische Werke der Kaiser Ferdinand III., Leopold I. und Joseph I.*, 2 vols (Vienna, 1893)

—— 'Umfang, Methode und Ziel der Musikwissenschaft', *Vierteljahrsschrift für Musikwissenschaft*, 1 (1885), pp. 5–20

Albrecht, Theodore, 'Anton Dreyssig (*c.* 1753/4–1820): Mozart's and Beethoven's Zauberflötist', *Words about Mozart: Essays in honour of Stanley Sadie*, ed. Dorothea Link with Judith Nagley (Woodbridge, 2005), pp. 179–92

—— (trans. and ed.), *Letters to Beethoven and Other Correspondence*, 3 vols (Lincoln, Nebraska, 1996)

Anderson, Emily, ed., *The Letters of Beethoven*, 3 vols (London, 1961)

Antonicek, Theophil, 'Die musikalischen Jugendwerke Kaiser Leopolds I.', *Studien zur Musikwissenschaft*, 42 (1993), pp. 97–113

—— *Musik im Festsaal der Österreichischen Akademie der Wissenschaften* (Vienna, 1972)

—— 'Musikwissenschaft in Wien zur Zeit Guido Adlers', *Studien zur Musikwissenschaft*, 37 (1986), pp. 165–93

Antonicek, Theophil, and Karlheinz Schenk, '1900–1918: Die Wiener Hofmusikkapelle im Abendrot der untergehenden Monarchie', *Musica Imperialis. 500 Jahre Hofmusikkapelle in Wien 1498–1998*, ed. Günter Brosche et al, exhibition catalogue (Tutzing, 1998), pp. 175–84

Baedeker, Karl, *Austria-Hungary with Excursions to Cetinje, Belgrade, and Bucharest: Handbook for Travellers*, 11th edn (Leipzig, 1911)

Banks, Paul, 'Mahler and Music Publishing in Vienna, 1878–1903', *Music and the Book Trade from the Sixteenth to the Twentieth Century*, eds Robin Myers, Michael Harris and Giles Mandelbrote (London, 2008), pp. 179–98

Baranello, Micaela, '*Die lustige Witwe* and the Creation of the Silver Age of Viennese Operetta', *Cambridge Opera Journal*, 26/2 (2014), pp. 175–202

Bastlová, Eliška, *Collectio operum musicalium quae in Bibliotheca Kinsky adservantur* (Prague, 2013)

Bauer, Wilhelm A., Otto Erich Deutsch and Joseph Heinz Eibl, eds, *Mozart: Briefe und Aufzeichnungen, Gesamtausgabe*, 8 vols (Kassel, 1962–2005)

Beaumont, Antony, *Zemlinsky* (Ithaca, 2000)

Beetz, Wilhelm, *Das Wiener Opernhaus 1869 bis 1955*, 2nd edn (Zurich, 1955)

Beller, Steven, *A Concise History of Austria* (Cambridge, 2006)

—— 'Kraus's Firework: State Consciousness Raising in the 1908 Jubilee Parade in Vienna and the Problem of Austrian Identity', *Staging the Past: The Politics of Commemoration in Habsburg Central Europe, 1848 to the Present*, eds Maria Bucur and Nancy M. Wingfield (West Lafayette, 2001), pp. 46–71

—— *Vienna and the Jews 1867–1938: A Cultural History* (Cambridge, 1989)

Bennett, Lawrence, *The Italian Cantata in Vienna: Entertainment in the Age of Absolutism* (Indiana, 2013)

Bernard, Paul P., *From the Enlightenment to the Police State: The Public Life of Johann Anton Pergen* (Urbana, 1991)

Berry, Mark 'Power and Patronage in Mozart's *La clemenza di Tito* and *Die Zauberflöte*', *Cultures of Power in Europe during the Long Eighteenth Century*, eds Hamish Scott and Brendan Simms (Cambridge, 2007), pp. 325–47

Biba, Otto, 'Beethoven und die "Liebhaber Concerte" in Wien im Winter 1807/08', *Beiträge '76–78: Beethoven Kolloquium 1977: Dokumentation und Aufführungspraxis*, ed. Rudolf Klein (Kassel, 1978), pp. 82–93

—— 'Beobachtungen zur Österreichischen Musikszene des 18. Jahrhunderts', *Österreichische Musik – Musik in Österreich*, ed. Elisabeth Theresia Hilscher (Tutzing, 1998), pp. 213–30

—— 'Der Piaristenorden in Österreich: Seine Bedeutung für bildene Kunst, Musik und Theater im 17. und 18. Jahrhundert', *Jahrbuch für Österreichishe Kulturgeschichte*, 5 (1975), whole issue

—— *"Eben komme ich von Haydn ...": Georg August Griesingers Korrepondenz mit Joseph Haydns Verleger Breitkopf & Härtel 1799–1819* (Zurich, 1987)

—— *Gott erhalte! Joseph Haydns Kaiserhymne* (Vienna, 1982)

—— ' "Grundsäulen der Tonkunst" – Von der Entstehung des Bildes der klassischen Trias', *Wiener Klassik: Ein musikalischer Begriff in Diskussion*, ed. Gernot Gruber (Vienna, 2002), pp. 53–63

—— 'Nachrichten über Joseph Haydn, Michael Haydn und Wolfgang Amadeus Mozart in der Sammlung handschriftlicher Biographien der Gesellschaft der Musikfreunde in Wien', *Studies in Music History Presented to H. C. Robbins Landon on his Seventieth Birthday*, eds Otto Biba and David Wyn Jones (London, 1996), pp. 152–64

Biba, Otto, and Ingrid Fuchs, *"Die Emporbringung der Musik": Höhepunkte aus der Geschichte und aus dem Archiv der Gesellschaft der Musikfreunde in Wien* (Vienna, 2012)

Black, David Ian, 'Mozart and the Practice of Sacred Music, 1781–91' (Ph.D. diss., Harvard University, 2007)

Blanning, T. C. W., *The Culture of Power and the Power of Culture: Old Regime Europe 1660–1789* (Oxford, 2002)

Blaukopf, Kurt, and Herta Blaukopf, eds, *Mahler: His Life, Work and World* (London, 1991)

Botstein, Leon, 'Einführung: Tragödie und Ironie des Erfolgs: Juden im Wiener Musikleben', *quasi una fantasia: Juden und die Musikstadt Wien*, eds Leon Botstein and Werner Hanak (Vienna, 2003), pp. 11–20

—— 'Gustav Mahler's Vienna', *The Mahler Companion*, ed. Donald Mitchell and Andrew Nicholson (Oxford, 1999), pp. 6–38

—— 'Richard Strauss and the Viennese Critics (1896–1924): Reviews by Gustav Schoenaich, Robert Hirschfeld, Guido Adler, Max Kalbeck, Julius Korngold and Karl Kraus', *Richard Strauss and his World*, ed. Bryan Gilliam (Princeton, 1992), pp. 311–71

—— 'Sozialgeschichte und die Politik des Ästhetischen: Juden und Musik in Wien 1870–1938', *quasi una fantasia: Juden und die Musikstadt Wien*, eds Leon Botstein and Werner Hanak (Vienna, 2003), pp. 43–63

Bozenek, Karel, 'Beethoven und das Adelsgeschlecht Lichnowsky', *Ludwig van Beethoven im Herzen Europas*, eds Oldřich Pulkert and Hans-Werner Küthen (Prague, 2000), pp. 119–70

Brandenburg, Sieghard, ed., *Ludwig van Beethoven: Briefwechsel Gesamtausgabe*, 7 vols (Munich, 1996–8)

Brandstätter, Christian, ed., *Wien 1900: Kunst und Kultur, Fokus der europäischen Moderne* (Vienna, 2005)

Branscombe, Peter, 'The Land of the Piano: Music, Theatre and Performance in Vienna around 1800', *Theatre and Performance in Austria: From Mozart to Jelinek*, eds Ritchie Robertson and Edward Timms (Edinburgh, 1993), pp. 3–19

Brauneis, Walther, ' "… composta per festiggiare il sovvenire di un grand Uomo." Beethovens "Eroica" als Hommage des Fürsten Franz Joseph Maximilian von Lobkowitz für Louis Ferdinand von Preußen', *Jahrbuch des Vereins für Geschichte der Stadt Wien*, 52–3 (1996–7), pp. 53–88

Brodbeck, David, *Defining Deutschtum: Political Ideology, German Identity, and Music-Critical Discourse in Liberal Vienna* (New York, 2014)

Brosche, Günter, 'Die musikalischen Werke Kaiser Leopolds I.: Ein systematisch-thematisches Verzeichnis der erhaltenen Kompositionen', *Beiträge zur Musikdokumentation: Franz Grasberger zum 60. Geburtstag*, ed. Günter Brosche (Tutzing, 1975), pp. 27–82

—— 'Musical Quotations and Allusions in the Work of Richard Strauss', *Cambridge Companion to Richard Strauss*, ed. Charles Youmans (Cambridge, 2010), pp. 213–25

Brosche, Günter, et al., *Musica Imperialis: 500 Jahre Hofmusikkapelle in Wien 1498–1998*, exhibition catalogue (Tutzing, 1998)

Brown, A. Peter, 'Caldara's trumpet music for the Imperial celebrations of Charles VI and Elisabeth Christine', *Antonio Caldara: Essays on his life and times*, ed. Brian W. Pritchard (Aldershot, 1987), pp. 1–48

—— 'The trumpet overture and sinfonia in Vienna (1715–1822): rise, decline and reformulation', *Music in eighteenth-century Austria*, ed. David Wyn Jones (Cambridge, 1996), pp. 13–69

Brusatti, Otto, Günter Düriegl and Regina Karner, eds, *Johann Strauss: Unter Donner und Blitz*, exhibition catalogue (Vienna, 1999)

Buhlmann, Nicolaus, 'Zur Geschichte des Stiftes Klosterneuburg und seiner Bewohner', *Wo sich Himmel und Erde Begegnen: Das Stift Klosterneuburg*, ed. Wolfgang Christian Huber (Klosterneuburg, 2014), pp. 8–73

Burstein, L. Poundie, '"Lebe wohl tönt überall!" and a "Reunion after So Much Sorrow": Beethoven's Op. 81a and the Journeys of 1809', *The Musical Quarterly*, 93/3–4 (2010), pp. 366–413

Cooper, Barry, 'The Clementi–Beethoven Contract of 1807: A Reinvestigation', *Muzio Clementi: Studies and Prospects*, eds Roberto Illiano, Luca Sala and Massimiliano Sala (Bologna, 2002), pp. 337–53

Coreth, Anna, *Pietas Austriaca*, trans. William D. Bowman and Anna Maria Leitgeb (West Lafayette, 2004)

Crispin, Darla M., 'Arnold Schoenberg's Wounded Work: "Litanei" from The String Quartet in F sharp minor, Op. 10', *Austrian Studies*, 17 (2009), pp. 62–74

Crittenden, Camille, *Johann Strauss and Vienna: Operetta and the Politics of Popular Culture* (Cambridge, 2000)

Croll, Gerhard, 'Mitteilungen über die "Schöpfung" und die "Jahreszeiten" aus dem Schwarzenberg-Archiv', *Haydn-Studien*, 3/2 (1974), pp. 85–92

Csáky, Moritz, *Ideologie der Operette und Wiener Moderne: Ein kulturhistorischer Essay*, 2nd rev. edn (Vienna, 1998)

Csendes, Peter, ed., *Österreich 1790–1848: Das Tagebuch einer Epoche* (Vienna, 1987)

Csendes, Peter, and Ferdinand Opll, eds, *Wien. Geschichte einer Stadt*, 3 vols (Vienna, 2000–6), vol. 2, *Die frühneuzeitliche Residenz (16. bis 18. Jahrhundert)*, eds Karl Vocelka and Anita Traniger (Vienna, 2003); vol. 3: *Von 1790 bis zur Gegenwart* (Vienna, 2006), eds Peter Csendes and Ferdinand Opll

Dembski-Riss, Ulrike, 'Bühnenarchitektur und Bühnendekoration in den Wiener Opernaufführungen zur Zeit von Johann Joseph Fux: Anmerkungen zu den Szenenbildern der Opern *Angelica Vincitrice di Alcina* und *Costanza e Fortezza*', *Johann Joseph Fux und seine Zeit: Kultur, Kunst und Musik im Spätbarock*, eds Arnfried Edler and Friedrich W. Riedel (Laaber, 1996), pp. 187–202

DeNora, Tia, *Beethoven and the Construction of Genius: Musical Politics in Vienna 1792–1803* (Berkeley, 1995)

Deutsch, Otto Erich, *Admiral Nelson und Joseph Haydn. Ein britisch-österreichisches Gipfeltreffen* (Vienna, 1982)

—— 'Leopold von Sonnleithners Erinnerungen an die Musiksalons des Vormärzlichen Wiens', *Österreichische Musikzeitschrift*, 16/2–4 (1961), pp. 49–62, 97–110, 145–57

Dorfmüller, Kurt, Norbert Gertsch and Julia Ronge, *Ludwig van Beethoven: Thematisch-bibliographisches Werkverzeichnis*, 2 vols (Munich, 2014)

Duindam, Jeroen, 'The Archduchy of Austria and the Kingdoms of Bohemia and Hungary: The Court of the Austrian Habsburgs c. 1500–1750', *The Princely Courts of Europe: Ritual, Politics and Culture under the Ancien Régime 1500–1750*, ed. John Adamson (London, 1999), pp. 165–87

Duindam, Jeroen, *Vienna and Versailles: The Courts of Europe's Dynastic Rivals, 1550–1780* (Cambridge, 2003)

Düriegl, Günter, *Wien 1683: Die zweite Türkenbelagerung* (Vienna, 1981)

Edge, Dexter, 'Mozart's Viennese Copyists' (Ph.D diss., University of Southern California, 2001)

Edler, Arnfried, and Friedrich W. Riedel, eds, *Johann Joseph Fux und seine Zeit: Kultur, Kunst und Musik im Spätbarock* (Laaber, 1996)

Erickson, Raymond, ed., *Schubert's Vienna* (New Haven, 1997)

Feder, Georg, *Joseph Haydn: Die Schöpfung* (Kassel, 1999)

Ferraguto, Mark, 'Beethoven *à la moujik*: Russianness and Learned Style in the "Razumovsky" String Quartets', *Journal of the American Musicological Society*, 67 (2014), pp. 77–123

Fichtner, Paula Sutter, *The Habsburgs: Dynasty, Culture and Politics* (London, 2014)

Flotzinger, Rudolf, *Geschichte der Musik in Österreich: Zum Lesen und Nachschlagen* (Graz, 1988)

——'Herkunft und Bedeutung des Ausdrucks "(Wiener) Klassik"', *Wiener Klassik: Ein musikgeschichtlicher Begriff in Diskussion*, ed. Gernot Gruber (Vienna, 2002)

Forbes, Elliot, ed., *Thayer's Life of Beethoven* (Princeton, 1964)

Ford, Anthony, 'Giovanni Bononcini, 1670–1747', *Musical Times*, 111 (1970), pp. 695–9

Fojtíková, Jana, and Tomislav Volek, 'Die Beethoveniana der Lobkowitz-Musiksammlung und ihre Kopisten', *Beethoven und Böhmen: Beiträge zu Biographie und Wirkungsgeschichte Beethovens*, eds Sieghard Brandenburg and Martella Gutiérrez-Denhoff (Bonn, 1988), pp. 219–58

Fritz-Hilscher, Elisabeth, 'Musik und Musikleben rund um den Wiener Kongress (1814/15) aus der Sicht einiger Zeitzeugen', *Studien zur Musikwissenschaft*, 57 (2013), pp. 215–39

Fritz-Hilscher, Elisabeth, and Helmut Kretschmer, eds, *Wien Musikgeschichte: Von der Prähistorie bis zur Gegenwart* (Vienna, 2011)

Fromme's Musikalische Welt: Notiz-Kalender für das Jahr [1876–1901], 26 vols, ed. Theodor Helm (Vienna, 1875–1900)

Fuchs, Ingrid, 'The First Performers and Audiences of Haydn's Chamber Music', *The Land of Opportunity: Joseph Haydn and Britain*, eds Richard Chesser and David Wyn Jones (London, 2013), pp. 147–62

Fürst, Marion, *Maria Theresia Paradis: Mozarts berühmte Zeitgenossin* (Cologne, 2005)

Fux, Johann Joseph, *Gradus ad Parnassum*, facsimile edn in *Johann Joseph Fux: Sämtliche Werke*, vol. 7/1 (Graz, 1967)

Gericke, Hannelore, *Der Wiener Musikalienhandel von 1700 bis 1778* (Graz, 1960)

Gerlach, Sonja, 'Johann Tost, Geiger und Grosshandlungsgremialist', *Haydn-Studien*, 7/3–4 (1998), pp. 344–65

Gingerich, John, 'Ignaz Schuppanzigh and Beethoven's Late Quartets', *The Musical Quarterly*, 93/3–4 (2010), pp. 450–513

Glanz, Christian, 'Himmelblaue Zeit: Alt-Wien in der Operette', *Alt-Wien: Die Stadt die niemals war*, eds Wolfgang Kos and Christian Rapp, exhibition catalogue (Vienna, 2004), pp. 228–34

Gmeiner, Josef, 'Die "Schlafkammerbibliothek" Kaiser Leopolds I.', *Biblos: Österreichische Zeitschrift für Buch- und Bibliothekwesen, Dokumentation, Bibliographie, und Bibliophilie*, 43/3–4 (1994), pp. 199–213, tables 14–20

Godt, Irving, *Marianna Martines: A Woman Composer in the Vienna of Mozart and Haydn*, ed. John A. Rice (Rochester, 2010)

Gotwals, Vernon, *Haydn: Two Contemporary Portraits* (Madison, 1968), translation of Georg August Griesinger, *Biographische Notizen über Joseph Haydn* (Leipzig,1809) and Albert Christoph Dies, *Biographische Nachrichten von Joseph Haydn* (Berlin, 1810)

Haas, Michael, *Forbidden Music: The Jewish Composers banned by the Nazis* (London, 2013)

Hadamowsky, Franz, 'Ein Jahrhundert Literatur- und Theaterzensure in Österreich', *Die österreichische Literatur: Ihr Profil an der Wende vom 18. zum 19. Jahrhundert (1750–1830)*, 4 vols (Graz, 1979–89), ed. Herbert Zeman, vol. 1 (Graz, 1979), pp. 289–306

—— *Wien, Theatergeschichte: Von den Anfängen bis zum Ende des Ersten Weltkriegs* (Vienna, 1988)

Halsband, Robert, ed., *The Complete Letters of Lady Mary Wortley Montagu*, 3 vols (Oxford, 1965)

Hammelmann, Hanns, and Ewald Osers (trans.), *A Working Friendship: The Correspondence between Richard Strauss and Hugo von Hofmannsthal*, introduction by Edward Sackville-West (London, 1961)

Hanák, Péter, *The Garden and the Workshop: Essays on the Cultural History of Vienna and Budapest* (Princeton, 1998)

Hanslick, Eduard, *Geschichte des Concertwesens in Wien* (Vienna, 1869)

Hawkins, John, *A General History of the Science and Practice of Music*, 2 vols (New York, 1963; repr. of 1776 edn)

Heer, Hannes, 'All rotten, treacherous – and so crude: Richard Wagner's view of Vienna', *Euphorie und Unbehagen: Das jüdische Wien und Richard Wagner*, ed. Andrea Winklbauer (Vienna, 2013), pp. 36–65

Hellsberg, Clemens, *Demokratie der Könige: Die Geschichte der Wiener Philharmoniker* (Zürich, 1992)

Hellyer, Roger, 'The Wind Ensembles of the Esterházy Princes, 1761–1813', *Haydn Yearbook*, 15 (1985), pp. 5–92

Helms, Marianne, 'Ein Schwesterwerk der "Nelsonmesse"? Zur Edition von Haydns *Te Deum* Hob. XXIIIc:2', *Haydn-Studien*, 9/1–4 (2006), pp. 157–75

Hettrick, Jane Schatkin, 'Music in the Celebrations of Franz's 1804 Assumption of the Austian *Kaiserwürde*, as reported in the *Wiener Zeitung*', *Figaro Là, Figaro Quà: Gedenkschrift Leopold M. Kantner (1932–2004)*, eds Michael Jahn and Angela Pachovsky (Vienna, 2006), pp. 223–35

Hilmar, Rosemary, *Der Musikverlag Artaria & Comp.: Geschichte und Probleme der Druckproduktion* (Tutzing, 1977)

Hilscher, Elisabeth, *Mit Leier und Schwert: Die Habsburger und die Musik* (Graz, 2000)

—— *Denkmalpflege und Musikwissenschaft: Einhundert Jahre Gesellschaft zur Herausgabe der Tonkunst in Österreich (1893–1993)* (Tutzing, 1995)

Hochradner, Thomas, 'Johann Joseph Fux', *Die Musik in Geschichte und Gegenwart*, 2nd edn, ed. Ludwig Finscher, Personenteil, vol. 7 (Kassel, 2002), cols 303–19

Hochstein, Wolfgang, 'Cherubini', *Die Musik in Geschichte und Gegenwart*, 2nd edn, ed. Ludwig Finscher, Personenteil, vol. 4 (Kassel, 2000), cols 853–911

Höslinger, Clemens, 'Kulturelles Leben des Wiener Kleinadels: Das Tagebuch des Mathias Perth', *Haydn Yearbook*, 10 (1978), pp. 56–71

Huss, Frank, *Der Wiener Kaiserhof: Eine Kulturgeschichte von Leopold I. bis Leopold II.* (Gernsbach, 2008)

—— 'Die Oper am Wiener Kaiserhof unter den Kaisern Josef I. und Karl VI. Mit einem Spielplan von 1706 bis 1740' (Ph.D. diss., University of Vienna, 2003)

Ingrao, Charles, *The Habsburg Monarchy 1618–1815* (Cambridge, 1994)

—— *Josef I: Der 'vergessene' Kaiser* (Graz, 1982)

Jahn, Michael, *Die Wiener Hofoper von 1794 bis 1810: Musik und Tanz im Burg- und Kärnthnerthortheater* (Vienna, 2011)

—— 'Klassische Traditionen im 19. Jahrhundert', *Die Wiener Hofmusikkapelle III: Gibt es einen Stil der Hofmusikkapelle?*, eds Hartmut Krones, Theophil Antonicek and Elisabeth Theresia Fritz-Hilscher (Vienna, 2011), pp. 287–95

Janik, Allan, and Stephen Toulmin, *Wittgenstein's Vienna* (Chicago, 1996)

Johnston, William M., *The Austrian Mind: An Intellectual and Social History 1848–1938* (Berkeley, 1972)

Jones, David Wyn, 'Haydn, Austria and Britain: Music, Culture and Politics in the 1790s', *The Land of Opportunity: Joseph Haydn and Britain*, eds Richard Chesser and David Wyn Jones (London, 2013), pp. 1–21

—— *The Life of Beethoven* (Cambridge, 1995)

—— *The Life of Haydn* (Cambridge, 2009)

—— *The Symphony in Beethoven's Vienna* (Cambridge, 2006)

Kabelková, Markéta, 'Music in Bohemia in the Baroque Era', *The Glory of the Baroque in Bohemia: Essays on Art, Culture and Society in the 17th and 18th Centuries*, ed. Vít Vlnas (Prague, 2001), pp. 262–80

Kagan, Susan, *Archduke Rudolph, Beethoven's Patron, Pupil, and Friend* (Stuyvesant, 1988)

Kantner, Leopold M., 'Die Zeit der Wiener Klassik', *Musica Imperialis. 500 Jahre Hofmusikkapelle in Wien 1498–1998*, ed. Günter Brosche et al (Tutzing, 1998), pp. 107–16

Karnes, Kevin C., *A Kingdom Not of This World: Wagner, the Arts, and Utopian Visions in Fin-de-Siècle Vienna* (New York, 2013)

Kassal-Mikula, Renata, 'Alt-Wien unter dem Demolierungskrampen: Wiens Innenstadt nach 1858', *Alt-Wien: Die Stadt die niemals war*, eds Wolfgang Kos and Christian Rapp, exhibition catalogue (Vienna, 2004), pp. 46–61

Kauffmann, Kai, *'Es ist nur ein Wien!': Stadtbeschreibungen von Wien 1700 bis 1873* (Vienna, 1994)

Kennedy, Michael, *Richard Strauss: Man, Musician, Enigma* (Cambridge, 1999)

Klaffenböck, Arnold, 'Literarische Positionen zu Alt-Wien: Alt-Wien 1880–1930', *Alt-Wien: Die Stadt die niemals war*, eds Wolfgang Kos and Christian Rapp, exhibition catalogue (Vienna, 2004), pp. 217–27

Kleindel, Walter, *Österreich: Zahlen, Daten, Fakten*, 5th edn (Salzburg, 2004)

Knaus, Herwig, *Die Musiker im Archivbestand des kaiserlichen Obersthofmeisteramtes (1637–1705)*, 3 vols (Vienna, 1967–9)

Köchel, Ludwig von, *Chronologisch-thematisches Verzeichnis sämtlicher Tonwerke Wolfgang Amadé Mozarts*, 6th edn, eds Franz Giegling, Alexander Weinmann and Gerd Sievers (Wiesbaden, 1964)

—— *Die kaiserliche Hof-Musikkapelle in Wien von 1543 bis 1867* (Vienna, 1869)

Komlós, Katalin, 'The Viennese Keyboard Trio in the 1780s: Sociological Background and Contemporary Reception', *Music and Letters*, 68 (1987), pp. 222–34

Kos, Wolfgang, and Christian Rapp, eds, *Alt-Wien: Die Stadt die niemals war*, exhibition catalogue (Vienna, 2004)

Krasa-Florian, Selma, 'Maria Theresia im Denkmalskult', *Maria Theresia und ihre Zeit: Eine Darstellung der Epoche von 1740–1780 aus Anlaß der 200. Wiederkehr des Todestages der Kaiserin*, ed. Walter Koschatzky (Salzburg, 1979), pp. 447–55

Krones, Helmut, '"… Der schönste und wichtigste Zweck von Allen …": Das Conservatorium der "Gesellschaft der Musikfreunde des österreichischen Kaiserstaates"', *Österreichische Musikzeitschrift*, 43 (1988), pp. 66–83

Kurdiovsky, Richard, 'Architektur für die "moderne" Großstadt zwischen Sport, Kunst und Geselligkeit: Zur Entstehung des Wiener Konzerthauses', *Österreichische Musikzeitschrift*, 68/5 (2013), pp. 6–15

Ladenburger, Michael, 'Der Wiener Kongreß im Spiegel der Musik', *Beethoven: Zwischen Revolution und Restauration*, eds Helga Lühning and Sieghard Brandenburg (Bonn, 1989), pp. 275–306

La Grange, Henry-Louis de, *Gustav Mahler*, 4 vols (Oxford 1995–2008), vol. 2, *Vienna: the Years of Challenge (1897–1904)* (Oxford, 1995); vol. 3, *Vienna: Triumph and Disillusion (1904–1907)* (Oxford, 1999); vol. 4, *A New Life Cut Short (1907–11)* (Oxford, 2008)

Lamkin, Kathleen, *Esterházy Musicians 1790 to 1809: Considered from New Sources in the Castle Forchtenstein Archives* (Tutzing, 2007)

Landon, H. C. Robbins, *Haydn: Chronicle and Works*, 5 vols (London, 1976–80), vol. 4, *Haydn: the Years of 'The Creation' 1796–1800* (London, 1977); vol. 5, *Haydn: the Late Years 1801–1809* (London, 1977)

—— *1791: Mozart's Last Year* (London, 1988)

Leibnitz, Thomas, '"… mit wienerischer Grazie und Leichtigkeit …": Wien als atmosphärischer und dramaturgischer Faktor in den Opern von Richard Strauss', *"Trägt die Sprache schon Gesang in sich …": Richard Strauss und die Oper*, eds Christiane Mühlegger-Henhapel and Alexandra Steiner-Strauss (Vienna, 2014), pp. 49–61

Lindell, Robert, 'The Search for the Imperial Chapelmaster in 1567–1568: Palestrina or De Monte', *Palestrina e l'Europa: Atti del III Convegno Internazionale di Studi Palestrina, 6–9 Ottobre 1994*, eds Giancarlo Rostirolla, Stefania Soldati and Elena Zomparelli (Palestrina, 2006), pp. 57–68

Lindgren, Lowell, 'Giovanni Bononcini', *New Grove Dictionary of Music and Musicians*, 2nd edn, ed. Stanley Sadie (London, 2001), vol. 3, pp. 827–7

Lindström, Fredrik, *Empire and Identity: Biographies of the Austrian State Problem in the Late Habsburg Empire* (West Lafayette, 2008)

Linhardt, Marion, *Residenzstadt und Metropole: Zu einer kulturellen Topographie des Wiener Unterhaltungstheaters (1858–1918)* (Tübingen, 2006)

Link, Dorothea, 'Mozart's appointment to the Viennese court', *Words About Mozart: Essays in Honour of Stanley Sadie*, ed. Dorothea Link with Judith Nagley (Woodbridge, 2005), pp. 163–78

Linke, Norbert, *Franz Lehár* (Hamburg, 2001)

Lodes, Birgit, ' "Le congrès danse": Set Form and Improvisation in Beethoven's Polonaise for Piano, Op. 89', *The Musical Quarterly*, 93/3–4 (2010), pp. 414–49

Luca, Ignaz de, *Topographie von Wien* (Vienna, 1794; facsimile edn, Vienna, 2003)

Macartney, C. A., *The Habsburg Empire 1790–1918* (London, 1969)

—— *The House of Austria: The Later Phase 1790–1918* (Edinburgh, 1978)

Macek, Jaroslav, 'Beethoven und Ferdinand Fürst Kinsky', *Ludwig van Beethoven im Herzen Europas*, eds Oldřich Pulkert and Hans-Werner Küthen (Prague, 2000), pp. 217–44

—— 'Die Musik bei den Lobkowicz', *Ludwig van Beethoven im Herzen Europas*, eds Oldřich Pulkert and Hans-Werner Küthen (Prague, 2000), pp. 171–216

Mailer, Franz, ed., *Johann Strauss (Sohn): Leben und Werk in Briefen und Dokumentation*, 10 vols (Tutzing, 1983–2007)

Mandyczewski, Eusebius, 'Die Bibliothek Brahms', *Musikbuch aus Österreich: Ein Jahrbuch der Musikpflege in Österreich und den bedeutendsten Musikstädten des Auslandes*, 1 (1904), pp. 7–17

—— *Zusatz-Band zur Geschichte der K. K. Gesellschaft der Musikfreunde in Wien: Sammlungen und Statuten* (Vienna, 1912)

Mann, Alfred, *The Study of Counterpoint from Joseph Fux's Gradus ad Parnassum*, rev. edn (London, 1965)

Mathew, Nicholas, *Political Beethoven* (Cambridge, 2013)

Mattl-Wurm, Sylvia, *Wien vom Barock bis zur Aufklärung* (Vienna, 1999)

Mayer, Anton, *Franz Lehár – Die lustige Witwe: Der Ernst der leichten Muse* (Vienna, 2005)

McColl, Sandra, *Music Criticism in Vienna 1896–1897: Critically Moving Forms* (Oxford, 1996)

McCredie, Andrew D., 'Nicola Matteis, the younger: Caldara's collaborator and ballet composer in the service of the Emperor Charles VI', *Antonio Caldara: Essays on his life and time*, ed. Brian W. Pritchard (Aldershot, 1987), pp. 153–82

Meer, J. H. van der, *Johann Josef Fux als Opernkomponist*, 3 vols (Bilthoven, 1961)

Moore, Julia, 'Beethoven and Inflation', *Beethoven Forum*, 1 (1992), pp. 191–223

Morrow, Mary Sue, *Concert Life in Haydn's Vienna: Aspects of a Developing Musical and Social Institution* (Stuyvesant, 1989)

—— 'Of Unity and Passion: The Aesthetics of Concert Criticism in Early Nineteenth-Century Vienna', *19th-Century Music*, 13/3 (1990), pp. 193–206

Mraz, Gerda, 'Die Kaiserinnen aus dem Welfenhaus und ihr Einfluss auf das geistig-kulturelle Leben in Wien', *Johann Joseph Fux und seine Zeit: Kultur, Kunst und Musik im Spätbarock*, eds Arnfried Edler and Friedrich W. Riedel (Laaber, 1996), pp. 75–92

Musikbuch aus Österreich: Ein Jahrbuch der Musikpflege in Österreich und den bedeutendsten Musikstädten des Auslandes, 10 vols, eds Richard Heuberger (vols 1–3), Hugo Botstiber (vols 4–8) and Josef Reitler (vols 9–10) (Leipzig, 1904–1913)

Musner, Lutz, *Der Geschmack von Wien: Kultur und Habitus einer Stadt* (Frankfurt, 2009)

Neville, Don J., 'La clemenza di Tito: Metastasio, Mazzolà and Mozart', *Studies in Music from the University of Western Ontario*, 1 (1976), pp. 124–48

Okey, Robin, *The Habsburg Monarchy c. 1765–1918: From Enlightenment to Eclipse* (London, 2001)

Olleson, D. Edward, 'Gottfried van Swieten, Patron of Haydn and Mozart', *Proceedings of the Royal Musical Association*, 89 (1962–3), pp. 63–74

Page, Janet K., *Convent Music and Politics in Eighteenth-Century Vienna* (Cambridge, 2014)

Partsch, Erich Wolfgang, 'Die Hofmusikkapelle in der zweiten Hälfte des 19. Jahrhunderts', *Musica Imperialis. 500 Jahre Hofmusikkapelle in Wien 1498–1998*, ed. Günter Brosche et al, exhibition catalogue (Tutzing, 1998), pp. 151–70

Perger, Richard, *Das Palais Esterházy in der Wallnerstraße zu Wien* (Vienna, 1994)

Perger, Richard von, 'Brahms's letzte Tage', *Musikbuch aus Österreich: Ein Jahrbuch der Musikpflege in Österreich und den bedeutendsten Musikstädten des Auslandes*, 5 (1908), pp. 41–5

—— *Geschichte der K. K. Gesellschaft der Musikfreunde in Wien. I. Abteilung: 1812–1870* (Vienna, 1912)

Perschy, Jakob Michael, 'Die Fürsten Esterházy – Zwölf kurzgefasste Lebensbilder', *Die Fürsten Esterházy: Magnaten, Diplomaten & Mäzene*, ed. Jakob Michael Perschy, exhibition catalogue (Eisenstadt, 1995), pp. 47–59

Pfunder, Michaela, ed., *Wien wird Weltstadt: Die Ringstrasse und ihre Zeit* (Vienna, 2015)

Praschl-Bichler, Gabriele, *Das blieb vom Wien Maria Theresias* (Graz, 2001)

Preis, Pavel, 'Baroque Theatre in Bohemia and its Scenic Design', *The Glory of the Baroque in Bohemia: Essays on Art, Culture and Society in the 17th and 18th Centuries*, ed. Vít Vlnas (Prague, 2001), pp. 282–311

Pritchard, Brian W., 'Antonio Caldara', *New Grove Dictionary of Music and Musicians*, 2nd edn, ed. Stanley Sadie (London, 2001), vol. 4, pp. 819–26

Pulkert, Oldřich, 'Das Knabenquartett des Fürsten Lichnowsky', *Ludwig van Beethoven im Herzen Europas*, eds Oldřich Pulkert and Hans-Werner Küthen (Prague, 2000), pp. 451–8

Radant, Else, ed., 'The Diaries of Joseph Carl Rosenbaum 1770–1829', *Haydn Yearbook*, 5 (1968), whole issue

Rasch, Rudolf, 'Basic Concepts', *Music Publishing in Europe 1600–1900: Concepts and Issues, Bibliography*, ed. Rudolf Rasch (Berlin, 2005), pp. 13–46

Rauchhaupt, Ursula von, *Schoenberg, Berg, Webern: The String Quartets, A Documentary Study* (Hamburg, 1971)

Regler, Liselotte, 'Hans Gregor – Die Ära des letzten Hofoperndirektors in Wien' (Ph.D. diss., University of Vienna, 2010)

Reichardt, Johann Friedrich, *Vertraute Briefe: geschrieben auf einer Reise nach Wien und den Österreichischen Staaten zu Ende des Jahres 1808 und zu Anfang 1809*, ed. Gustav Gugitz, 2 vols (Munich, 1915)

Reilly, Edward R., *Gustav Mahler and Guido Adler: Records of a Friendship* (Cambridge, 1982)

Rice, John A., *Antonio Salieri and Viennese Opera* (Chicago, 1998)

—— *Empress Marie Therese and Music at the Viennese Court, 1792–1807* (Cambridge, 2003)

—— *The Temple of Night at Schönau: Architecture, Music, and Theater in a Late Eighteenth-Century Viennese Garden* (Philadelphia, 2006)

—— *W. A. Mozart: La clemenza di Tito* (Cambridge, 1991)

Ridgewell, Rupert, 'Music Printing in Mozart's Vienna: the Artaria Press, 1778–1794', *Fontes Artis Musicae*, 48 (2001), pp. 217–36

Riedel, Friedrich W., 'Kaiserliche Musik', *Die Wiener Hofmusikkapelle III: Gibt es einen Stil der Hofmusikkapelle?*, eds Hartmut Krones, Theophil Antonicek and Elisabeth Theresia Fritz-Hilscher (Vienna, 2011), pp. 211–31

—— *Kirchenmusik am Hofe Karls VI. (1711–40): Untersuchungen zum Verhältnis von Zeremoniell und musikalischem Stil im Barockzeitalter* (Munich, 1977)

—— 'Krönungszeremoniell und Krönungsmusik im Barockzeitalter', *Mitteleuropäische Kontexte der Barockmusik: Bericht über die Internationale musikwissenschaftliche Konferenz Bratislava, 23. bis 25. März 1994*, ed. Pavol Polák (Bratislava, 1997), pp. 109–32

Rowland, David, 'Haydn's Music and Clementi's Publishing Circle', *The Land of Opportunity: Joseph Haydn and Britain*, eds Richard Chesser and David Wyn Jones (London, 2013), pp. 92–111

Sartori, Claudio, *I libretti italiani a stampa dalle origini al 1800*, 7 vols (Cuneo, 1990–4)

Schmidt, Hugo, 'The Origins of the Austrian National Anthem and Austria's Literary War Effort', *Austria in the Age of The French Revolution 1789–1815*, eds Kinley Brauer and William E. Wright (Minneapolis, 1990), pp. 163–83

Scholes, Percy, ed., *Dr Burney's Musical Tours in Europe*, 2 vols, vol. 2: *An Eighteenth-Century Musical Tour in Central Europe and the Netherlands* (London, 1959)

Schönfeld, Johann Ferdinand von, *Jahrbuch der Tonkunst von Wien und Prag* (Vienna, 1796, facsimile edn Munich 1976); partially translated as '*A Yearbook of the Music of Vienna and Prague, 1796*: Johann Ferdinand Ritter von Schönfeld, Vienna 1796', *Haydn and His World*, ed. Elaine Sisman (Princeton, 1997), pp. 289–320

Schorske, Carl E., *Fin-de-Siècle Vienna: Politics and Culture* (Cambridge, 1981)

Seifert, Herbert, 'Das Sepolcro – ein Spezifikum der kaiserlichen Hofkapelle', *Die Wiener Hofmusikkapelle III: Gibt es einen Stil der Hofmusikkapelle?*, eds Hartmut Krones, Theophil Antonicek and Elisabeth Theresia Fritz-Hilscher (Vienna, 2011), pp. 163–73; reprinted in Herbert Seifert, *Texte zur Musikdramatik im 17. und 18. Jahrhundert: Aufsätze und Vorträge*, ed. Matthias J. Pernerstorfer (Vienna, 2014), pp. 783–90

—— *Der Sig-prangende Hochzeit-Gott: Hochzeitsfeste am Wiener Hof der Habsburger und ihre Allegorik 1622–1699* (Vienna, 1998)

—— 'Die kaiserliche Hofkapelle im 17.–18. Jahrhundert', *Österreichische Musikzeitschrift*, 53/2 (1998), pp. 17–26

—— *Die Oper am Wiener Kaiserhof im 17. Jahrhundert* (Tutzing, 1985)

—— 'Draghi', *Die Musik in Geschichte und Gegenwart*, 2nd edn, ed. Ludwig Finscher, Personenteil, vol. 5 (Kassel, 2001), cols 1374–82

—— *Texte zur Musikdramatik im 17. und 18. Jahrhundert: Aufsätze und Vorträge*, ed. Matthias J. Pernerstorfer (Vienna, 2014)

Seipel, Wilfried, ed., *Die Botschaft der Musik: 1000 Jahre Musik in Österreich*, exhibition catalogue (Vienna, 1996)

Selfridge-Field, Eleanor, 'The Viennese court orchestra in the time of Caldara', *Antonio Caldara: Essays on his life and times*, ed. Brian W. Pritchard (Aldershot, 1987), pp. 115–51

Senner, Wayne M., Robin Wallace and William Meredith, eds, *The Critical Reception of Beethoven's Compositions by His German Contemporaries*, 2 vols (Lincoln, Nebraska, 1999)

Sipe, Thomas, *Beethoven: Eroica Symphony* (Cambridge, 1998)

Slezak, Friedrich, *Beethovens Wiener Originalverleger* (Vienna, 1987)

Smither, Howard E., *A History of the Oratorio*, 4 vols (Chapel Hill, 1977–2000), vol. 1, *The Oratorio in the Baroque Era* (Chapel Hill, 1977)

Sommer, Monika, and Alexandra Steiner-Strauss, 'Richard Wagner's traces in Vienna', *Euphorie und Unbehagen: Das jüdische Wien und Richard Wagner*, ed. Andrea Winklbauer (Vienna, 2013), pp. 154–63

Sommer-Mathis, Andrea, 'Opera and Ceremonial at the Imperial Court of Vienna', *Italian Opera in Central Europe*, 3 vols (Berlin, 2006–8), vol. 1, *Institutions and Ceremonies*, eds Melania Bucciarelli, Norbert Dubowy and Reinhard Strohm (Berlin, 2006), pp. 176–91

—— *Tu felix Austria nube: Hochzeitsfeste der Habsburger im 18. Jahrhundert* (Vienna, 1994)

—— 'Von Barcelona nach Wien: Die Einrichtung des Musik- und Theaterbetriebes am Wiener Hof durch Kaiser Karl VI.', *Music conservata: Günter Brosche zu 60. Geburtstag*, eds Josef Gmeiner, Zsigmond Kokits, Thomas Leibnitz and Inge Pechotsch-Feichtinger (Tutzing, 1999), pp. 355–80

Spielmann, John P., *Leopold I of Austria* (London, 1977)

Steblin, Rita, *Beethoven in the Diaries of Johann Nepomuk Chotek* (Bonn, 2013)

Stein, Leonard, ed., *Style and Idea: Selected Writings of Arnold Schoenberg*, trans. Leo Black (London, 1975)

Steinpress, Boris, 'Haydns Oratorien in Russland zu Lebzeiten des Komponisten', *Haydn-Studien*, 2/2 (1969), pp. 77–112

Steurer, Richard, *Das Repertoire der Wiener Hofmusikkapelle im neunzehnten Jahrhundert* (Tutzing, 1998)

Storch, Ursula, 'Alt-Wien dreidimensional: Die Altstadt als Themenpark', *Alt-Wien: Die Stadt die niemals war*, eds Wolfgang Kos and Christian Rapp, exhibition catalogue (Vienna, 2004), pp. 159–64

Stuckenschmidt, H. H., *Schönberg: Leben, Umwelt, Werk* (Zurich, 1974)

Telesko, Werner, Richard Kurdiovsky and Dagmar Sachsenhofer, 'The Vienna Hofburg between 1835 and 1918 – A Residence in the Conflicting Fields of Art, Politics, and Representation', *Austrian History Yearbook*, 44 (2013), pp. 37–61

Thormählen, Wiebke, 'Art, Education and Entertainment: The String Quintet in Late Eighteenth-Century Vienna' (Ph.D. diss., Cornell University, 2008)

Thormählen, Wiebke, 'Playing with Art: Musical Arrangements as Educational Tools in van Swieten's Vienna', *Journal of Musicology*, 27 (2010), pp. 342–76

Toman, Rolf, ed., *Vienna: Art and Architecture* (Königswinter, 2010)

Tyrrell, John, *Janáček: Years of a Life*, 2 vols (London, 2006–7), vol. 1, *1854–1914: The Lonely Blackbird* (London, 2006); vol. 2, *1914–28: Tsar of the Forests* (London, 2007)

Ulrich, Hermann, 'Aus vormärzlichen Konzertsälen Wiens', *Jahrbuch des Vereins für Geschichte der Stadt Wien*, 28 (1972), pp. 106–30

Unverricht, Hubert, 'Privates Quartettspiel in Schlesien von 1780 bis 1850', *Musica privata: die Rolle der Musik im privaten Leben: Festschrift zum 65. Geburtstag Walter Salmen*, ed. Monika Fink (Innsbruck, 1991), pp. 105–12

Vancza, Max, 'Ein Alt-Wiener Konzertsaal. (Der Sitzung des n.ö. Landhauses.) Ein Beitrag zur Geschichte des Konzertwesens im Wien des Vormärz', *Musikbuch aus Österreich: Ein Jahrbuch der Musikpflege in Österreich und den bedeutendsten Musikstädten des Auslandes*, 1 (1904), pp. 38–50

Volek, Tomislav, and Jaroslav Macek, 'Beethoven und Fürst Lobkowitz', *Beethoven und Böhmen: Beiträge zu Biographie und Wirkungsgeschichte Beethovens*, eds Sieghard Brandenburg and Martella Gutiérrez-Denhoff (Bonn, 1988), pp. 203–17

Wandruska, Adam, 'Die "Clementia Austriaca" und der Aufgeklärte Absolutismus: Zum politischen und ideellen Hintergrund von "La clemenza di Tito"', *Österreichische Musikzeitschrift*, 31 (1976), pp. 186–93

Wangermann, Ernst, *From Joseph II to the Jacobin Trials: Government Policy and Public Opinion in the Habsburg Dominions in the Period of the French Revolution*, 2nd edn (Oxford, 1969)

Weilen, Alexander von, *Geschichte des Wiener Theaterwesens von den ältesten Zeiten bis zu den Anfängen der Hoftheater* (Vienna, 1899)

Weinmann, Alexander, *Die Anzeigen des Kopiaturbetriebes Johann Traeg in der Wiener Zeitung zwischen 1782 und 1805*, Wiener Archivstudien, 6 (Vienna, 1981)

—— *Die Wiener Verlagswerke von Franz Anton Hoffmeister*, Beiträge zur Geschichte des alt-Wiener Musikverlages, vol. 2/8 (Vienna, 1964)

—— *Johann Traeg: Die Musikalienverzeichnisse von 1799 und 1804 (Handschrift und Sortiment)*, Beiträge zur Geschichte des alt-Wiener Musikverlages, vol. 2/17 (Vienna, 1973)

—— *Themen-Verzeichnis der Kompositionen von Johann Baptiste Wanhal*, 2 vols (Vienna, 1988)

—— *Verlagsverzeichnis Giovanni Cappi bis A. O. Witzendorf*, Beiträge zur Geschichte des alt-Wiener Musikverlages, vol. 2/11 (Vienna, 1967)

—— *Verlagsverzeichnis Johann Traeg (und Sohn)*, 2nd edn, Beiträge zur Geschichte des alt-Wiener Musikverlages, vol. 2/16 (Vienna, 1973)

—— *Verlagsverzeichnis Tranquillo Mollo (mit und ohne Co.)*, Beiträge zur Geschichte des alt-Wiener Musikverlages, vol. 2/9 (Vienna, 1964)

—— *Verzeichnis der Musikalien des Verlages Joseph Eder – Jeremias Bermann*, Beiträge zur Geschichte des alt-Wiener Musikverlages, vol. 2/12 (Vienna, 1968)

—— *Verzeichnis der Verlagswerke des Musikalischen Magazins in Wien, 1784–1802: Leopold (und Anton) Kozeluch*, 2nd edn, Beiträge zur Geschichte des alt-Wiener Musikverlages, vol. 2/1a (Vienna, 1979)

—— *Vollständiges Verlagsverzeichnis Artaria & Comp.*, Beiträge zur Geschichte des alt-Wiener Musikverlages, vol. 2/2 (Vienna, 1952)

—— 'Vollständiges Verlagsverzeichnis der Musikalien des Kunst- und Industrie-Comptoirs in Wien, 1801–1819', *Studien zur Musikwissenschaft*, 22 (1955), pp. 217–52

—— *Vollständiges Verlagsverzeichnis Senefelder, Steiner, Haslinger*, 3 vols (Munich, 1979–83), vol. 1, *A. Senefelder, Chemische Druckerey, S. A. Steiner, S. A. Steiner & Comp. (Wien, 1803–1826)*, Beiträge zur Geschichte des alt-Wiener Musikverlages, vol. 2/19 (Munich, 1979)

—— *Wiener Musikverlag 'Am Rande': Ein lückenfüllender Beitrag zur Geschichte des Alt-Wiener Musikverlages*, Beiträge zur Geschichte des alt-Wiener Musikverlages, vol. 2/13 (Vienna, 1970)

Wessely, Othmar, 'Kaiser Leopolds I. "Vermeinte Bruder- und Schwesterliebe": Ein Beitrag zur Geschichte des Wiener Hoftheaters in Wien', *Studien zur Musikwissenschaft*, 25 (1962), pp. 586–608

White, Harry, ed., *Johann Joseph Fux and the Music of the Austro-Italian Baroque* (Aldershot, 1992)

Williams, Hermine Weigel, *Francesco Bartolomeo Conti: His Life and Music* (Aldershot, 1999)

Winkelhofer, Martina, *The Everyday Life of the Emperor: Francis Joseph and his Imperial Court* (Innsbruck, 2012)

Winklbauer, Andrea, ed., *Euphorie und Unbehagen: Das jüdische Wien und Richard Wagner* (Vienna, 2013)

Wollenberg, Susan, 'Johann Joseph Fux: *Gradus ad Parnassum* (1725): Concluding Chapters', *Music Analysis*, 11/2–3 (1992), pp. 209–43

Zweig, Stefan, *The World of Yesterday* (Lincoln, Nebraska, 1964)

Index